RELIGIOUS DRAMA
AND THE
HUMANIST TRADITION

# STUDIES IN THE HISTORY
## OF
# CHRISTIAN THOUGHT

EDITED BY

HEIKO A. OBERMAN, Tucson, Arizona

IN COOPERATION WITH

HENRY CHADWICK, Cambridge
JAROSLAV PELIKAN, New Haven, Connecticut
BRIAN TIERNEY, Ithaca, New York
E. DAVID WILLIS, Princeton, New Jersey

VOLUME XXXIX

JAMES A. PARENTE, Jr.

RELIGIOUS DRAMA
AND THE
HUMANIST TRADITION

# RELIGIOUS DRAMA
# AND THE
# HUMANIST TRADITION

## CHRISTIAN THEATER IN GERMANY
## AND IN THE NETHERLANDS
## 1500-1680

BY

JAMES A. PARENTE, Jr.

E.J. BRILL
LEIDEN • NEW YORK • KØBENHAVN • KÖLN
1987

**Library of Congress Cataloging-in-Publication Data**

Parente, James A.
  Religious drama and the humanist tradition.

  (Studies in the history of Christian thought,
ISSN 0081-8607; v. 39)
  Bibliography: p.
  Includes indexes.
  1. German drama—Early modern, 1500-1700—History and
criticism.   2. Christian drama, German—History and
criticism.   3. Dutch drama—Early modern, 1500-1700—
History and criticism.   4. Christian drama, Dutch—
History and criticism.   5. Christian drama, Latin
(Medieval and modern)—History and criticism.
6. Humanists—Europe, Northern.   I. Title.   II. Series.
PT633.P37   1987      832'.4'09      87-24242
ISBN 90-04-08094-5

ISSN 0081-8607
ISBN 90 04 08094 5

PRINTED IN THE NETHERLANDS BY E. J. BRILL

For Meredith

## CONTENTS

# ACKNOWLEDGEMENTS

My research in the complex field of German and Netherlandic Renaissance and Baroque theater could not have been carried out successfully without the assistance of several scholars and institutions. I should first like to thank Professor Heiko A. Oberman for his careful reading of the entire manuscript and his decision to publish it in his series *Studies in the History of Christian Thought*. I should also like to thank Professor George C. Schoolfield, my former teacher during my graduate school years at Yale, for awakening my interest in early modern German, Dutch and Neo-Latin drama through his elegant and witty lectures and for serving as an inspiring model of rigorous scholarship which few critics ever attain. Through the years I have profited greatly from his encyclopedic knowledge of Renaissance and Baroque literature in both central Europe and Scandinavia—an invaluable gift when dealing with the polymaths of the early modern *respublica litteraria*—his close, incisive interpretation of texts and especially his promulgation of an urbane and lively literary-critical style. Special thanks are also due to Professor Jozef IJsewijn (Leuven) for his learned advice on Netherlandic Neo-Latin theater and his continued encouragement of a Germanist in a Latin world and Professor Leonard Forster (Cambridge) for his critical comments on my interpretation of Andreas Gryphius' *Leo Armenius* when it appeared in *Daphnis*, 13 (1984). I should like to thank Professor Hans-Gert Roloff (Berlin) and Mr. Fred van der Zee of Editions Rodopi for their permission to reprint sections of that article, "Andreas Gryphius and Jesuit Theater," in the fourth chapter. I am also grateful to Professor Robert V. Schnucker (Northeast Missouri State) for granting permission to reprint parts of my article "The Development of Religious Tragedy: The Humanist Reception of the *Christos Paschon* in the Renaissance," which first appeared in *The Sixteenth Century Journal*, 16 (1985), in the discussion of Christian tragedy in the first chapter. Finally, I should like to extend warm thanks to my Princeton colleagues in Renaissance studies, Anthony Grafton, Thomas DaCosta Kaufmann and David Quint, who provided many hours of stimulating discussion and debate about the Holy Roman Empire and the Netherlands which helped me to formulate my own ideas on theater more clearly.

The research for the present study was completed with the assistance of the Princeton University Research Fund for the Humanities and Social Sciences and the Princeton University Department of Germanic Languages and Literatures. Several libraries provided access to rare printings and manuscripts of Renaissance Latin drama: The British Library, Staatsbibliothek München, Universitätsbibliothek München, Herzog August Bibliothek Wolfenbüttel, Stadtbibliothek Trier, Stadtbibliothek Köln, Universitätsbibliothek Düsseldorf, Staatsarchiv Koblenz and the Beinecke Library of Yale University. I am deeply grateful to the gracious staffs of all these institutions and their willingness to supply me with microfilms and photocopies of numerous plays. I owe a special debt of gratitude to the indefatigable staff of the Inter-Library Loan department at Princeton who expeditiously obtained most of the secondary literature on Vondel for my use. Finally, I should like to thank Mrs. Geraldine DiCicco for her careful and skillful typing of the manuscript and her inestimable editorial advice about the final preparation of the text.

James A. Parente, Jr.
University of Illinois at Chicago

# LIST OF ABBREVIATIONS

| | |
|---|---|
| ACNL | Actus Conventus Neo-Latini Lovaniensis |
| BLVS | Bibliothek des litterarischen Vereins in Stuttgart |
| CR | *Philippi Melanthonis Opera quae supersunt omnia.* Ed. Carolus Gottlieb Bretschneider. 28 vols. Halle (Saale), 1834-1860. |
| DLE | Deutsche Literatur in Entwicklungsreihen |
| DNB | Dictionary of National Biography |
| DVLG | Deutsche Vierteljahrsschrift für Literaturwissenschaft und Geistesgeschichte |
| EG | Études Germaniques |
| GLL | German Life & Letters |
| GRM | Germanisch-Romanische Monatsschrift |
| HumLov | Humanistica Lovaniensia |
| HZM | Handelingen van de Koninklijke Zuidnederlandse Maatschappij voor Taal- en Letterkunde en Geschiedenis |
| JEGP | Journal of English and Germanic Philology |
| JMRS | Journal of Medieval and Renaissance Studies |
| LJGG | Literaturwissenschaftliches Jahrbuch im Auftrage der Görres Gesellschaft |
| MLN | Modern Language Notes |
| MLR | Modern Language Review |
| NTg | De Nieuwe Taalgids |
| OL | Orbis Litterarum |
| PL | Patrologiae cursus completus. Series latina |
| PMLA | Publications of the Modern Language Association of America |
| RQ | Renaissance Quarterly |
| SCJ | Sixteenth Century Journal |
| SpL | Spiegel der Letteren |
| TNTL | Tijdschrift voor Nederlandse Taal- en Letterkunde |
| WA | *D. Martin Luthers Werke. Kritische Gesamtausgabe.* 61 vols. Weimar, 1883-1983. |
| WATR | *D. Martin Luthers Werke: Tischreden.* 6 vols. Weimar, 1912-1921. |
| WB | Joost van den Vondel. *De Werken.* Ed. J. F. M. Sterck, et al. 10 vols. Amsterdam: Wereldbibliotheek, 1927-1937. |
| ZDA | Zeitschrift für deutsches Altertum und deutsche Literatur |
| ZDP | Zeitschrift für deutsche Philologie |

# INTRODUCTION

The sixteenth and seventeenth centuries in Germany and the Netherlands were periods of intense activity in religious drama. Given the pious fervor which accompanied the religious renewal of the Reformation and Counter-Reformation, this enormous production was not surprising. What was astonishing, however, was the manner in which biblical and hagiographical subjects were presented by the Christian humanists of the sixteenth century and the significance which their plays had for the development of Baroque sacred theater over the next hundred years.

Since the late middle ages, dramatic performances of episodes from the Bible and hagiography contributed to the entertainment and education of the general public about the virtues of a Christian existence and the mystery of salvation. The expansive Passion plays of the late fifteenth and early sixteenth centuries provided their viewers with a popular interpretation of Old and New Testament events as they represented the course of man's salvation history from his tragic Fall until his reunion with Christ at the Last Judgment. Miracle plays extolling the charitable actions of the saints and the fortitude of the martyrs similarly instructed the audience about their moral obligations towards God and their fellow men. But when around 1520 the humanists of the Northern Renaissance adapted these same topics for their own dramatic works, religious theater mirrored the conflict between two philosophically distinct traditions: Christianity and the ancient civilization of Greece and Rome. The purpose of the following study is to examine the nature of this humanist religious drama in the Renaissance and Baroque and to analyze the complex, if not contradictory, aesthetic, moral and theological concerns of its practitioners.

At first glance, the religious theater of the sixteenth and seventeenth centuries seems to have deserved the neglect which it has traditionally received. The playwrights' moralistic bias and their uninspired representation of the same few sacred subjects have little immediate appeal to contemporary readers whose post-romantic tastes demand that a literary work possess an intrinsic aesthetic value. The ever decreasing familiarity of late twentieth-century audiences with the Judaeo-Christian tradition has contributed further to the aura of obscurity which surrounds these works; even the greatest religious dramatist of the Baroque, Joost van den Vondel (1587-1679), is gravely in danger of becoming a cultural

artifact.[1] Such observations are not meant to imply that all the plays
which will be discussed here have been unjustly overlooked; as with any
large body of literature, the quality varies greatly. Rather, it is hoped
that the present study will provide an interpretive methodology whereby
the seemingly undistinguished religious theater of the Renaissance and
Baroque will be seen as an important reflection of early modern thought
on literature, education and theology.

There are currently two critical approaches for the interpretation of
religious drama: the one formalistic, and the other contextual. Both
methods developed in reaction to earlier critical practice. The formalists
rejected the tendency of the late nineteenth-century literary positivists to
compile ancillary historical data about specific religious plays. They
deemed the studies of scholars such as Hugo Holstein on Protestant
theater (1886),[2] Alexander von Weilen on Joseph dramas (1887)[3] and
August Wick on Tobias plays (1899)[4] inadequate because these critics
failed to consider the literary (i.e. ahistorical) aspects of the texts. In contrast, the contextual writers disapproved of the use of philosophical
models about the development of early modern culture as a basis for
literary interpretations. Though interesting as documents of intellectual
history, the sociological presuppositions of Hennig Brinkmann on
sixteenth-century drama (1933)[5] and the epistemological theories of
Walter Benjamin (1927)[6] about the Baroque did not provide an accurate
framework for the analysis of sacred drama in the context of early
modern history and society.

In present-day criticism, the formalistic interpretation of religious
drama is based on the commentators' perception of the author's
adherence to a set of normative aesthetic principles. The standards are
in turn derived partly from the interpreter's own aesthetic values and
partly from his understanding of Renaissance rules governing the composition of a good play. In investigating the form of religious dramas,

---

[1] Peter King remarked in his review (*Times Literary Supplement,* 7 August 1981, p. 905)
of the scholarly anthologies published in commemoration of the 300th anniversary of
Vondel's death that contemporary disinterest in the works of this writer have reduced
him to a literary curiosity.

[2] Hugo Holstein, *Die Reformation im Spiegelbilde der dramatischen Literatur des sechzehnten
Jahrhunderts,* Schriften des Vereins für Reformationsgeschichte, 14-15 (Halle, 1886).

[3] Alexander von Weilen, *Das ägyptische Joseph im Drama des XVI. Jahrhunderts. Ein Beitrag
zur vergleichenden Literaturgeschichte* (Vienna, 1887).

[4] August Wick, "Tobias in der dramatischen Literatur Deutschlands," Diss.
Heidelberg 1899.

[5] Hennig Brinkmann, *Anfänge des modernen Dramas in Deutschland* (Jena: Walter Biedermann, 1933).

[6] Walter Benjamin, *Ursprung des deutschen Trauerspiels* (1927; rpt. Frankfurt a.M.:
Suhrkamp, 1963).

these writers assess the artistic unity of its parts and the purity of its style. Neo-classical assumptions about structure, plot, characterization and language, often more pertinent to eighteenth-century rather than Renaissance praxis, are employed in an attempt to determine the aesthetic value, if any, of the text. Formalistic critics, such as Derek van Abbé on sixteenth-century theater (1961)[7] and W. A. P. Smit on Vondel (1956),[8] generally pose the following questions about religious drama: has the playwright arranged the plot over the requisite three (comedy) or five (tragedy) acts so as to please the audience and to make evident the central theme or lesson of the play; does the subplot cohere with the main action or serve as an effective contrast to it; do the characters appear to be more than the stock figures of the playwright's Graeco-Roman model; do the biblical and hagiographical characters possess any individual traits or complexities which distinguish them from their prototypes in the historical sources; has the playwright retained a style consistent with his understanding of the classical tradition, or do any of the inconsistencies, such as the author's introduction of medieval dramatic figures or the use of ecclesiastical Latin, disrupt the unity of the playwright's intentions. If the dramatist has successfully handled these formalistic matters, so it is argued, his sacred dramas deserve a place in the canon of early modern theater. Thus, Nicholas Grimald's tragedy (1548) on St. John the Baptist deserves attention for its lively characterization of Herod and Herodias,[9] but Johann Krüginger's presentation (1545) of the same material in a less inventive manner does not;[10] Vondel's *Joseph in Egypten* (1640) is a splendid tragedy because of its tightly-organized structure and unified theme, but his *Maeghden* (1639) with its unnecessary subplot is not.[11] In the formalistic approach, literary interpretation thus serves not only to explicate the structure of a given text, but also to induce the commentator to formulate an aesthetic judgment about its quality.

In contrast, the contextual critics concentrate on the reconstruction of the cultural environment in which a particular sacred drama was written. The recreation of this context occurs in a variety of ways each dictated by the critic's perception of a given work's major theme. Two techniques

---

[7] Derek van Abbé, *Drama in Renaissance Germany and Switzerland* (Melbourne: University Press, 1961).

[8] W. A. P. Smit, *Van Pascha tot Noah. Een verkenning van Vondels drama's naar continuïteit en ontwikkeling in hun grondmotief en structuur,* 3 vols. (Zwolle: W. E. J. Tjeenk Willink, 1956-62).

[9] H. B. Norland, "Grimald's *Archipropheta.* A Saint's Tragedy," *JMRS,* 14 (1984), 63-76.

[10] See Wilhelm Scherer's article on Johann Krüginger in *Allgemeine Deutsche Biographie,* vol. 17.

[11] Smit, p. 385; p. 258.

have generally been used by contextual writers for their interpretations of religious dramas. First, some commentators have supplied the historical tradition of a particular theme or aspect of the playwright's work by tracing its development from earliest times until the Renaissance. Jean Lebeau (1977),[12] for example, sketched the theological interpretation of the Old Testament Joseph figure from its biblical origins through patristic and medieval versions until its moralistic and political transformation on the sixteenth-century stage; A. Schöne (1964)[13] detected parallels between the language and structure of Baroque tragedy and the visual images and didactic function of Renaissance emblem books; and H.-J. Schings (1966)[14] explicated the debt of the German Baroque tragedian Andreas Gryphius to Stoic and patristic thought, described his reception of these ideas and illustrated his adaptation of them in his tragedies. Other commentators have analyzed the content of a religious play in light of its relevance to contemporary social and political conditions. These writers connect a dramatist's choice of a particular topic to a special set of historical circumstances: Jean Lebeau (1980)[15] demonstrated that the Apocryphal figure of Judith in Sixt Birck's tragedy (1539) echoed the early humanists' call for a crusade against the Turks; and E. M. Szarota[16] argued that Gryphius' *Catharina von Georgien* (1657) reflected the perilous geopolitical situation of the playwright's native Silesia in the mid-seventeenth century. In adopting the contextual method, critics have thus focused on a distinctive idea or theme within a specific work or group of plays in order to establish a valid historical basis for their interpretation.

Although the formalistic and contextual approaches are useful for illuminating the significance of individual plays, they do not provide the best framework for the study of religious drama as a genre. The utility of both methods lies in their emphasis on the unique characteristics of a single work in terms of its form or its historical role. In the present generic study on humanist religious drama, however, I have thought it more important to delineate the common aspirations of its practitioners

---

[12] Jean Lebeau, *Salvator Mundi: l'"exemple" de Joseph dans le théâtre allemand au XVIe siècle*, 2 vols., Bibliotheca Humanistica et Reformatorica, 20.1/2 (Nieuwkoop: B. de Graaf, 1977).

[13] Albrecht Schöne, *Emblematik und Drama im Zeitalter des Barock* (1964; 2nd. ed. Munich: Beck, 1968).

[14] Hans-Jürgen Schings, *Die patristische und stoische Tradition bei Andreas Gryphius*, Kölner Germanistische Studien, 2 (Cologne and Graz: Böhlau, 1966).

[15] Jean Lebeau, "Sixt Bircks *Judith* (1539), Erasmus und der Türkenkrieg," *Daphnis*, 9 (1980), 679-98.

[16] E. M. Szarota, *Künstler, Grübler und Rebellen. Studien zum europäischen Märtyrerdrama des 17. Jahrhunderts* (Munich and Bern: Francke, 1967), pp. 206-07.

rather than those elements which distinguish their works from each other. Instead of regarding the structure and style of religious plays in a particular historical setting, I shall examine the literary, theological and pedagogical goals which all sacred dramatists shared. Only in this way can the nature of humanist religious drama be determined, its development described and its importance assessed for Renaissance and Baroque theater history.

The present work is intended to be a literary-historical investigation of the relationship between Renaissance and Baroque sacred theater. The need for such a study seems especially pressing, for despite the increasing number of editions and monographs on individual playwrights, no attempt has been made to reassess outdated views about Renaissance and Baroque dramatic praxis. Even today a demarcation line continues to be drawn between Renaissance and Baroque drama by literary historians such as J. P. Aikin (1982)[17] and R. J. Alexander (1984),[18] a division which is in fact based on the antiquated aesthetic prejudices of German and Netherlandic scholars of the early twentieth century. Where seventeenth-century drama has been variously described as worldly, heroic and artistic, sixteenth-century theater is considered pedagogical, prosaic and naive.[19] Since Northern piety is believed to have been first allied with Renaissance aesthetics in the tragedies of Vondel and Gryphius, sixteenth-century religious drama has been assigned an insignificant place in literary history. The fact that the majority of sixteenth-century dramas which were similar in style and intention to the major plays of Vondel and Gryphius were written in Latin has contributed further to their exclusion from national literary histories. As a consequence, the tragedies of Vondel and Gryphius seldom have been viewed in light of sixteenth-century praxis except as an occasion to demonstrate their superiority to early writers. In Erik Lunding's seminal interpretation of seventeenth-century German theater[20]—now long in need of a revision—the sixteenth-century is completely overlooked and doubtful parallels are drawn between medieval religious drama and Gryphius' tragedies. The situation is only slightly better in Dutch literature. Although the sixteenth-century allegorical plays of the Dutch chambers of rhetoric (Rederijkers) have been accorded a small place in

---

[17] Judith P. Aikin, *German Baroque Drama* (Boston: Twayne, 1982).

[18] Robert J. Alexander, *Das deutsche Barockdrama* (Stuttgart: Metzler, 1984).

[19] Johannes Maassen, *Drama und Theater der Humanistenschulen in Deutschland* (Augsburg: Benno Filser, 1929), pp. 88-9.

[20] Erik Lunding, *Das schlesische Kunstdrama: eine Darstellung und Deutung* (Copenhagen: P. Haase, 1940), especially pp. 13-69.

Vondel's development,[21] the humanist tradition of religious drama has been either ignored or dismissed as didactic and uninspired.

The present study has been written as a corrective to this prejudicial view of sixteenth- and seventeenth-century religious drama. As will be seen, Renaissance and Baroque playwrights did not compose their sacred dramas in historical isolation, but as active participants in the Christian humanist culture of the late Renaissance. As writers in both centuries attempted to bridge the gulf between the classical and modern world, they shared the same literary, theological and moral goals, and they represented this common inheritance in their religious plays.

In order to establish a basis for investigating the relationship between Renaissance and Baroque drama, the present study focuses exclusively on religious theater written in the humanist style. The reason for this limitation lies primarily in the nature of sixteenth- and seventeenth-century dramatic praxis in Germany and the Netherlands. During this 200-year period, religious dramas were written in a variety of forms. Passion and mystery plays, farcial Shrovetide dramas and the allegorical works of the Rederijkers appeared alongside humanist plays on biblical and hagiographical topics. Of these four styles, humanist religious drama was the youngest. The liturgical, Shrovetide and Rederijker plays had their origins in earlier medieval dramatic practice and reached their high point in the first half of the sixteenth century. In contrast, humanist religious drama began in the 1520s and remained the predominant form for sacred theater until the middle of the eighteenth century. The humanist dramatic style did not, of course, remain uninfluenced by the other forms of religious theater. As in the case of any period of stylistic transition, elements from both the late medieval and humanist traditions were interchanged. Cunning devils, allegorical figures and heroic saints familiar from the medieval stage reappeared in humanist drama while the plots of the latter were frequently transposed into Shrovetide plays. But with the codification of the humanist style in the late Renaissance poetics of Julius Caesar Scaliger (1561) and Gerardus Vossius (1647), such symbiotic exchanges were discouraged, and the neo-classical style of the humanists became the chief form for the dramatic presentation of a religious subject.

Given the confusion which has traditionally surrounded the concept of Renaissance humanism, my use of the term "humanist dramatic style"

---

[21] Kåre Langvik-Johannessen, *Zwischen Himmel und Erde. Eine Studie über Joost van den Vondels biblische Tragödie in gattungsgeschichtlicher Perspektive* (Oslo: Universitetsforlaget, 1963). Langvik-Johannessen devotes the first third of his book to the Rederijker background of Vondel's plays and only begins his investigation of the humanist tradition with Grotius in the early seventeenth century.

must be clarified. In literary history, humanist drama has generally referred to plays written by Renaissance schoolteachers for performance by their pupils so that the latter might sharpen their command of Latin (and later the vernacular) and gain useful instruction in Christian ethics. For this reason, humanist drama was accorded a major place in the Renaissance curriculum of *studia humanitatis* in which Latin and later Greek writers were read, interpreted and, most importantly, imitated so that schoolboys could acquire a competency in grammar, rhetoric and moral philosophy. In a strictly formal sense, the humanist dramatic style can thus be said to connote a playwright's purposeful effort to emulate the language, structure and, in some cases, the plots of Graeco-Roman theater. However, the composition of religious plays in the humanist style transformed this simple pedagogical exercise into an attempt to assimilate Christianity into the pagan classical tradition. As Christian writers, the humanists frequently tempered their enthusiasm for the ancients by replacing the suspiciously immoral content of Graeco-Roman theater with biblical and hagiographical subjects. Moreover, with the introduction of religious themes, the customary ethical teachings of humanist theater were supplemented by theological lessons. Man's relationship to his Creator and the prerequisites for his eternal salvation were attributed an equal if not greater importance than the moral guidelines which judicious humanists had derived from ancient literature and imitated in their own works. In contrast to the usual didactic aspirations of secular humanist drama, the religious theater of the humanists was distinguished by its explicitly critical approach towards classical literature and its dual concern with both theological and moral issues.

Humanist religious drama will consequently be examined here in the context of its two chief characteristics: its relationship to Graeco-Roman theater and its theological content. The present study has been restricted to the years 1500-1680, for they roughly correspond to the period in which humanist religious drama predominated, from its inception in the early 1500s until the death of Vondel (1679). In the first two chapters, humanist religious drama will be shown to be more than a didactic text, but rather a sophisticated literary genre which reflected the leading currents of sixteenth-century thought on classical literary imitation, education and religion. Having established the literary and theological foundation of humanist religious theater, I shall then suggest that Vondel and Gryphius represented the dramatic culmination of this tradition. In their Christian tragedies, they achieved the ideal balance between the aesthetic, moral and theological goals of the earlier humanists and thereby transformed their dramas into sacred texts about man's Fall and Redemption.

A final word must be added about my use of specific terms such as "humanist religious drama," "Christian sacred theater" and "allegory." Humanist religious drama refers to plays based on biblical or hagiographical sources which have been adapted to the form and language of Graeco-Roman theater; this designation includes Latin and vernacular dramas which strictly adhere to the five-act structure attributed to the ancients by the Renaissance. I have purposely excluded the inventive polemical dramas (the so-called *Kampfdramen*) of humanist writers like Thomas Naogeorgus and Andreas Fabricius from the present discussion, for their concern with religious issues was confined to critiques of the social institution of religion rather than its theological significance. "Christian or sacred theater" is here understood to mean secular as well as biblical and hagiographical plays whose primary function was the depiction of Christian salvation; similarly, besides the specific meanings attributed to allegory in the historical discussion in chapter two, allegory is used here in the christological (or soteriological) sense to signify the representation of Christian salvation through a biblical, hagiographical or secular plot. For this reason, it is possible to speak of Vondel's *Hierusalem verwoest* and Gryphius' historical dramas as Christian plays even though their subjects were drawn from secular history.

# CHAPTER ONE

# THE NATURE OF HUMANIST RELIGIOUS DRAMA: CLASSICAL IMITATION AND REFORM

During the sixteenth century and the first half of the seventeenth century, the majority of religious dramas published in the Holy Roman Empire and the Netherlands were composed by Christian humanists. These biblical, hagiographical and allegorical plays, written first in Latin and then in both Latin and the vernacular, were the newest and perhaps most innovative of all Renaissance styles. Despite the obscurity of many of its practitioners, the Renaissance schoolteachers, Protestant pastors and Jesuit scholars who devised these original plays for the delight and edification of their audiences were generally familiar with recent developments in Renaissance literature theory and contemporary theology. The dramatists took pains to provide a cautious if not an occasionally adroit imitation of Graeco-Roman theater as they wrestled with the presentation of complex religious issues in a clear and correct manner.

The humanist style assumed different forms during its 150-year domination of the religious stage, and before proceeding any further, it is necessary to clarify what types of plays were encompassed by this generic heading. In the following discussion, humanist drama will be generally understood to signify plays, both comedies and tragedies, whose structure and language were based on the Renaissance concept of Graeco-Roman theater. The dramatists themselves betrayed their humanist ties through their imitation of the form and language of the ancients. Between 1500 and 1630, three main styles of humanist religious drama developed, each based on a different classical precedent: Roman comedy, Senecan tragedy and the hybrid neo-classical tragic form in which the structure of Seneca was adapted to sixteenth- and seventeenth-century interpretations of Aristotle's *Poetics*. Occasionally other styles appeared such as the imitation of Euripides by the Silesian humanist Georg Calaminus (1547-1595), but such deviations failed to establish a new dramatic form, especially in Germany and in the Netherlands.

Humanist religious dramas were not only distinguished by style, but also by the audiences for whom they were intended. The majority of these plays were written by humanist pedagogues for performances in their schools. In this way, they hoped not only to contribute to the spiritual and moral education of the pupil who watched or acted in the work, but also to broaden his command of Latin and later the vernacular in order to prepare him for a life of public service to the city or the state. Because of the financial support which schools received from their city or local court, humanist religious plays were also often presented before a varied audience of princes, magistrates, burghers and even illiterate citizens. Gryphius' tragedies, for example, were staged at both the St. Elisabeth gymnasium in Breslau and at the courts of the dukes of Brieg and Wohlau. The popular success of the Jesuit theater lay in a single work's appeal to viewers of several social classes; the fathers prudently had program sheets printed with plot summaries in both Latin and the vernacular to help the audiences through the Latin plays.

Humanist religious drama, especially at the beginning of the seventeenth century, was also practiced by an elite circle of classical scholars eager to create a Christian tragic style to rival the ancients. These dramas were rarely intended for public performances but rather for the unabashed approbation of a private circle of friends, all practitioners of *bonae literae*, whose laudatory poems and epigrams prefaced the published text. Where the dramatic style of the school playwrights had been clear, direct and even simplistic, the elite writers such as the Netherlandic humanists Hugo Grotius (1583-1645), Rochus Honerdus (1572-1638) and Jacob Cornelius Lummenaeus à Marca (1570-1629) preferred the convoluted and disjointed language of Senecan and Sophoclean tragedy whose manneristic flourishes were not so much intended to inform as to impress. Finally, in the biblical tragedies of Joost van den Vondel, humanist religious drama attained, for a brief time, the favor of a vast urban audience in the Amsterdam public theater. Without eschewing the moralistic goals of the school writers or the stylistic elegance of the elite academic dramatists, Vondel entertained the viewers with his complex neo-classical dramas in the 1630s and 1640s before popular interest waned and his conversion to Catholicism isolated him from Calvinist and Dutch society.

Despite these distinctions between style and audience, humanist dramatists in both centuries were beset with similar problems arising from their attempt to combine Christian doctrine with their enthusiasm for the ancients. The adaptation of certain plots to the form and theory of ancient drama, the selection of a classical dramatic style suited to the sacred material and an accurate representation of man's relationship to God forced Renaissance and Baroque writers to devise a delicate balance between theological, moral and literary concerns. But the coalescence of humanist ideals with Christian goals did not always occur as smoothly as the dramatists wished or even recognized. Their resolution or avoidance of the conflicts which followed from the clash between two traditionally opposing philosophies, the ancient pagan world and Christianity, created a tension within the works themselves which, in the hands of accomplished playwrights like Vondel and Gryphius, transformed didactic religious plays into sophisticated portraits of man's complex relationship to his Creator. This chapter will focus on the dramas written between 1500 and 1620 and specifically on the paradoxical solutions which the playwrights devised to reconcile their Christian goals with their secular aspirations.

Humanist religious drama in Germany and the Netherlands evolved through the unceasing efforts of Renaissance schoolmen to join the literary form and the language of antiquity to the precepts of Christianity. Inspired by the stylistic elegance and verbal virtuosity of Graeco-Roman dramatists, the humanists were eager to preserve this tradition without allowing the questionable morality of the pagan writers to distract the pupils in their charge. To this end Christian pedagogues in northern schools in the late fifteenth century quickly formulated a canon of Graeco-Roman authors whose language was deemed worthy of constant study and imitation. Most of the ancient dramatists were approved for instruction. Euripides, Menander, Terence and, to a lesser extent, Sophocles, Aristophanes, Plautus and Seneca were all regarded as suitable texts for the exercise of a student's written command of the classics and, in the case of Terence, an oral facility in colloquial Latin.[1]

But to many Christian teachers, the purity of the classical dramatists' style was seldom matched by the purity of the morals represented. Both characters and plots contained possible temptations for young minds who, so the humanists believed, were too impressionable to control their proclivity for evil. Wily servants, impassioned youths and lusty whores populated the Roman comic stage while incest, revenge and tyranny awaited the readers of classical tragedy. For this reason, Christian schoolmasters developed a cautious approach to the ancients, lest they be accused by critics skeptical of the new curriculum of fostering impiety among their students. To obviate these charges, the Christian humanists devised two methods for dealing with pagan drama. First, they defended the moral and stylistic utility of studying unexpurgated texts of the classical writers. Drawing on antique, patristic and contemporary

---

[1] Only Terence, Plautus and, to a lesser degree, Seneca have been investigated as school performance texts: Otto Francke, *Terenz und die lateinische Schulcomoedie in Deutschland* (Weimar, 1877); Otto Günther, *Plautuserneuerungen in der deutschen Litteratur des XV.-XVII. Jahrhunderts* (Leipzig, 1886); Paul Dittrich, *Plautus und Terenz in Pädagogik und Schulwesen der deutschen Humanisten* (Leipzig: Böhme und Lehmann, 1915): Paul Stachel, *Seneca und das deutsche Renaissancedrama* (Berlin: Mayer & Müller, 1907).

sources, Christian humanists such as Philip Melanchthon (1497-1560) and Joannes Sturm (1507-1589) zealously argued that the frank immorality of the pagan writers could nonetheless serve to deter young men from evil. At the same time, however, another group of schoolmen, disturbed by the religious controversies of the 1520s, drew on the same patristic and contemporary sources to argue the opposite point, namely, the banishment of all forms of pagan drama from the school stage. As a substitute for the pagan texts they offered their own original plays with plots based on biblical, hagiographical and medieval allegorical topics in the language of classical theater so as to uphold the stylistic ideal of the ancients without spiritual peril to the students. The christianization of classical theater was thus carried out from two opposing perspectives: the imputation of ethical lessons compatible with Christianity to pagan drama and, conversely, the replacement of the allegedly immoral plots of these same pagan dramas with Christian material.

The assimilation of Christian ethics to the form and language of classical drama was not, however, as smooth or consistent a process as its practitioners would have liked. Despite the distinctions between the critics and the defenders of classical theater, both groups desired to preserve the dramatic form and language of Graeco-Roman theater. Where the apologists for classical drama argued for the moral and stylistic utility of the pagan texts, the new religious playwrights sought to achieve the same goal except through the introduction of Christian topics to the stage.

Humanist religious drama was consequently characterized by two contradictory tendencies which the writers variously balanced according to their own moral and literary intentions. On the one hand, they distinguished themselves sharply from the ancients by arguing for the superiority of their religious plots to the mythological or fictional material of classical theater. At the same time, they betrayed their admiration for the ancients through their aesthetic concern that their new sacred subjects be presented in a style equal, if not more elegant, to the classical writers. To this end, they retained many of the immoral characters and episodes in the plays to which they so fervently objected elsewhere and devised clever arguments to justify this practice. Additionally, a few ambitious writers, such as the academic dramatists Hugo Grotius and Daniel Heinsius (1580-1655), primarily used the religious material not so much for moral ends as for innovative variations of the Graeco-Roman tragic style. Humanist religious drama thus existed as a hybrid literary form in which the writer's practical interest in the aesthetic presentation of a Christian topic betrayed his implicit fondness for the ancients whose dramas he explicitly wished to revise and replace.

*The Christian Reception of Classical Drama*

Before discussing the religious dramatists' revisions of classical drama, it is useful to examine the rationale which Christian humanists employed to justify their enthusiasm for Graeco-Roman theater. As in the case of other literary genres, such as historical narrative and the ode, the humanists were less interested in the content than in the form and style of the classical text. With the establishment of the classical educational ideal of the orator, the morally good and eloquent man ("vir bonus dicendi peritus") as outlined by Cicero and Quintilian, Renaissance schoolmen voraciously studied and annotated the numerous Graeco-Roman texts edited and printed in the late fifteenth century in an effort to acquire, master and finally surpass the verbal mannerisms of the ancients.[2]

The classical dramatists, especially Euripides (in Latin translation), Terence, Plautus and Seneca, played a major role in the humanists' quest for eloquence. Indeed, by 1500 several editions of individual plays as well as the complete works of the Roman dramatists were being printed and read in the leading humanists centers from Deventer to Strasbourg in the west to Wittenberg and Vienna in the east.[3] By 1550 all the dramas of Euripides, Sophocles and Aristophanes had appeared in both Greek and Latin translation in Basel and Frankfurt, and single works by the same authors had been made available to Netherlandic writers through presses in Louvain and Antwerp.[4] The colloquial style of Terence and Plautus was, moreover, especially well suited to the humanists' interest in developing the oral Latin competence of their students. Since Cicero and Quintilian had both underlined the importance of enunciation ("pronuntiatio") and memory ("memoria") in the rhetorical training of the orator, the schoolmen were easily moved to pro-

---

[2] The literature on Renaissance education is immense; for a general overview of the subject, see E. Garin, *L'Éducation de l'homme moderne. La pédagogie de la Renaissance (1400-1600),* trans. J. Humbert (Paris: Fayard, 1968); for historical accounts of education in Germany and the Netherlands, see Friedrich Paulsen, *Geschichte des gelehrten Unterrichts auf den deutschen Schulen und Universitäten vom Ausgang des Mittelalters bis zur Gegenwart,* 2 vols. (Leipzig, 1896) and P. N. M. Bot, *Humanisme en onderwijs in Nederland* (Utrecht: Spectrum, 1955).

[3] The first complete German printing of Terence was published in Strasbourg ca. 1470. Both Plautus and Terence were staged in Vienna ca. 1500 under Celtes' direction and performed in Erfurt in the humanist circle around Eobanus Hessus. Celtes first suggested the study of Seneca in 1487; all the tragedies later appeared ca. 1500 in the Leipzig edition of Martinus Herbipolensis. Dittrich, pp. 14-38; Stachel, pp. 30-9. For Netherlandic performances of the Roman dramatists, see J. A. Worp, *Geschiedenis van het drama en van het tooneel in Nederland* (Groningen:J. B. Wolters, 1904), pp. 193-202.

[4] Rudolf Hirsch, "The Printing Tradition of Aeschylus, Euripides, Sophocles and Aristophanes," *Gutenberg-Jahrbuch,* 1963, pp. 138-46.

mote school performances of the classical plays.[5] In this way, the students not only gained a verbal proficiency through the memorization and oral declamation of the classical text, but they also reaped the moral benefits of the learned proverbs ("sententiae") which, so the humanists argued, were found in the speeches of the plays.

In accordance with the humanists' enthusiasm for classical drama, performances of Plautus, Terence and Seneca became familiar occurrences in their schools at least once and sometimes several times a year in the early sixteenth century. The German arch-humanist, Conrad Celtes (1459-1508), not only edited Seneca's *Hercules furens* and *Thyestes* for his Leipzig students in 1487, but during his professorship in Vienna (1497-1508) he arranged for the public recitation of Plautus' *Aulularia* and Terence's *Eunuchus*.[6] Between 1500 and 1530, other dramas of Plautus, especially *Miles gloriosus*, and the remaining five plays of Terence were staged by humanists in Louvain, Ghent and Haarlem and in Saxony, at Erfurt, Leipzig and Wittenberg.[7] Seneca, whose dramas were more often read than performed, also appeared briefly on the stage: in 1525-1526 Melanchthon offered *Thyestes* in his "schola privata" in Wittenberg and in 1544, the Deventer Hieronymites presented *Hercules furens*.[8] Sophocles' notoriety had been delayed in Germany by the relatively late publication of his works, but in the 1580s and 1590s he became a school-performance text in Strasbourg where the humanists supplemented his dramas with vernacular interludes.[9]

In light of the appearance of humanist religious drama in the 1520s and 1530s to counteract the popularity of Graeco-Roman theater in the schools, it is important to remember that the new plays did not necessarily replace the works of the ancient playwrights. Rather, the classical dramas existed alongside the religious plays throughout the sixteenth century. Despite the 1538 production of Joannes Sapidus' *Lazarus redivivus* (on the raising of Lazarus, John 11) in Strasbourg, for example,

---

[5] For an investigation of the relationship between classical rhetoric and the Renaissance reception of Roman comedy, see Marvin T. Herrick, *Comic Theory in the Sixteenth Century*, Illinois Studies in Language and Literature, 34, nos. 1 & 2 (Urbana: University of Illinois Press, 1950).

[6] On Celtes and Seneca, see Raimund Kemper, "Zur Seneca Ausgabe des Conrad Celtes, mit Beiträgen zur Geschichte seines Freundeskreises," *Leuvense Bijdragen*, 66 (1977), 257-310.

[7] See note 3 above. For an account of the Wittenberg performances staged by Philip Melanchthon, see Ludwig Koch, *Philipp Melanchthon's Schola Privata* (Gotha, 1859), pp. 56-93.

[8] Koch, pp. 79-80; Worp, p. 200.

[9] Consider, for example, the 1587 and 1608 performance of Sophocles' *Aiax lorarius*: August Jundt, *Die dramatischen Aufführungen im Gymnasium zu Straßburg* (Strasbourg, 1888), pp. 51-2.

the repertoire was subsequently confined to frequent performances of Greek and Latin drama until 1562. Between 1562 and 1583, only one religious play was staged, Rudolf Gwalther's *Nabal* (based on 1 Samuel 25), and when the enlarged Strasbourg Academy theater opened in 1583, religious drama by contemporary Catholics and Protestants returned, but along with classical comedy and tragedy.[10] Many religious dramatists, moreover, composed secular plays as well. Whereas some writers such as Macropedius turned away from worldly topics as they grew older,[11] others remained equally prolific in both types of drama throughout their careers. Indeed, the author of the popular *Terentius Christianus* (1592; 1599; 1602-3) collection, the Haarlem school rector, Cornelius Schonaeus (1540-1611), included three peasant farces in this anthology of chiefly biblical plays in which he intended to christianize Terence with his sacred topics.[12] Similarly, Michael Virdung (1575-1637), a *poeta laureatus* of Jena, who composed tragedies in the Senecan mode on Saul and Brutus, perceived no distinction between the topics and regarded both works merely as two different exempla of the evil consequences of political ambition.[13]

The reason for the coexistence of secular and religious drama lay primarily in the way the humanists had interpreted classical theater and incorporated it into the literary canon of approved writers for Christian readers. The late medieval critics of the New Learning had questioned

---

[10] For a detailed summary of the Strasbourg repertoire, see Günter Skopnik, *Das Straßburger Schultheater* (Frankfurt a.M.: Selbstverlag des Elsaß-Lothringen Instituts, 1935), pp. 15-171.

[11] Macropedius may well have been so troubled by the controversies of the Reformation that he confined himself solely to religious topics in his last plays: *Lazarus* (1541); *Josephus* (1544); *Adamus* (1552); *Hypomone* (1554); and *Jesus scholasticus* (1556). *Hypomone* ("Patience") presented several examples of Christian constancy—Job, Elijah, blind Tobit, the beggar Lazarus—as if to urge the audience to adhere to Scripture during such an uncertain age. The title recalled the opening chapter of the Epistle of James (on ὑπομονή or patience), a favorite text for Catholic writers who advocated the active practice of faith in contrast, so they believed, to the Pauline-Lutheran emphasis on salvation by faith alone. This distinction had lately landed Macropedius in difficulty. In the 1552 edition of his Everyman play, *Hecastus* (1539), Macropedius took pains to reassure his readers that the last-minute, deathbed conversion and salvation of the protagonist by no means implied that the author denied the efficacy of good works for gaining eternal life. On the contrary, Macropedius suggested that Hecastus was not saved so much by faith as by the hatred which he bore his former sins; such contrition served as a visible sign ("paenitentiae opera") of his fear of God and hope for salvation. For the complete text of this revised prose prologue, see Georgius Macropedius, *Hecastus*, ed. Johannes Bolte, BLVS, 269-270 (Leipzig: W. Hiersemann, 1927), pp. 151-2.

[12] For a discussion of the Christian Terence tradition, see Marvin Herrick, *Tragicomedy. Its Origins and Development in Italy, France and England* (1955; rpt. Urbana: University of Illinois Press, 1962), pp. 16-62.

[13] Michael Virdungus, *Iuvenalia ... Tragoedias: Saul et Brutum* (Nuremberg: Paulus Kaufmann, 1598), pp. 38-40.

the value of classical literature and rhetoric over their emphasis on speculative grammar and logic and had consequently forced the humanists to defend their educational program. Indeed, to judge by the vehement response of the humanists, the scholastics not only challenged the new curriculum, but also implied that the reading of classical literature would lead to rampant immorality.[14] To refute these charges, the humanists borrowed the arguments of the Greek and Latin Church fathers who had likewise once attempted to reconcile the pagan inheritance with Christianity. The patristic writers provided these Renaissance schoolmen with precedents for the moral utility of classical literature and the necessity for understanding and interpreting the literary style of the ancients. St. Basil in his *Address to the Young* and St. Augustine in *De doctrina christiana,* for example, had both admitted that moral benefit could be gained through a prudent reading of the ancients.[15] Christians were consequently advised to collect precepts from pagan learning as selectively as a bee gathered nourishment from flowers, lest they imbibe any teachings inconsistent with their faith. Similarly, in his famous letter to Paulinus of Nola, St. Jerome had argued that a command of classical grammar and rhetoric could assist the Christian scholar in the interpretation of Holy Scripture.[16] Since the Bible contained complex philosophical ideas, such as St. John's remarks on the Logos (John 1:1) as well as several philological difficulties arising from the translation of Scripture from Hebrew and Greek into Latin, Christian scholars would be well advised to have a thorough knowledge of antiquity.

The humanist apologists of classical drama used the moral and philological arguments of the Church fathers to support the study, translation and performance of Graeco-Roman theater in the schools. Of the two approaches, however, the humanists' appeal to the ethical value of the ancients generally made a more persuasive case, for the defense of *eloquentia* did not actually respond to the scholastics' criticism of the immorality of classical literature. Indeed, the weaknesses inherent in the exclusive use of the philological argument were made most apparent by Erasmus in his dedicatory letters to William Warham, Archbishop of

---

[14] For an overview of the humanist polemicists, see James D. Tracy, "Against the 'Barbarians': The Young Erasmus and His Humanist Contemporaries," *SCJ*, 11 (1980), 1-22.

[15] Saint Basil, "Address to Young Men on Reading Greek Literature," in his *Letters*, vol. 4, trans. R. J. Deferrari and M. R. P. McGuire (Cambridge: Harvard University Press, 1934), pp. 378-435; Augustine, *De doctrina christiana* 2.18.

[16] As cited in Ernst Robert Curtius, *European Literature and the Latin Middle Ages,* trans. Willard R. Trask (New York: Harper & Row, 1953), p. 447.

Canterbury, for his 1506 edition of Euripides' *Hecuba* and *Iphigenia at Aulis*.[17] Here Erasmus boldly suggested that the medieval churchmens' neglect of the classics had resulted in the perversion of Christianity; his translation thus reflected his own effort to expand his knowledge of Greek, lest he too commit the same error: "cum in animo statuissem ... vertendis Graecis autoribus rem theologicam, Deum immortalem quam indigne sophisticis nugis depravatam, pro virili mea vel restituere vel adiuuare...."[18] Erasmus' brief remarks were in fact part of a much larger argument he had first formulated in the *Antibarbari* (written ca. 1501-1502; printed 1520), his scathing critique of the scholastics ("barbari"). Since medieval schoolmen did not possess a firm command of classical rhetoric and, more importantly, correct philological interpretation of the biblical languages, including the Latin of the Vulgate, they were no longer competent to explicate the Bible as God had intended. Instead of accusing the humanists of fostering immorality, the scholastics were now advised to reflect on the state of their own souls which, so Erasmus implied, had been corrupted through their neglect of Graeco-Roman learning. Classical grammar and rhetoric were consequently essential for the contemporary theologian, for without this knowledge he would be unable to understand God's Word.[19] Erasmus' motive for his translation of Euripides thus originated from his belief in the interdependence of philology and theology.

Given the theological justification for Erasmus' translation exercise and the indispensability of rhetoric, it is not surprising that he would regard the Greek tragedian as eminently suitable for the Christian scholar. His initial attraction to Euripides was probably aroused, as it doubtless may have been for Euripides' Quattrocento admirers in Italy,[20] by Quintilian's praise of the tragedian's practical rhetorical skills over Sophocles' mannered, noble style.[21] Erasmus' remarks on the natural-

---

[17] Desiderius Erasmus, *Euripidis Hecuba et Iphigenia. Latinae factae Erasmo interprete*, ed. Jan Hendrik Waszink, in *Opera omnia Des. Erasmi Roterodami*, vol. I.1 (Amsterdam: North Holland, 1969).

[18] Erasmus, *Euripidis*, p. 216.

[19] Majorie O'Rourke Boyle, *Christening Pagan Mysteries* (Toronto: University of Toronto, 1981), pp. 3-25

[20] For a brief discussion of Euripides reception in Italy in the Latin translations of Leonizio Pilato (ca. late fourteenth century) and Francesco Filelfo (ca. 1490), see the introduction by Waszink in Erasmus, *Euripidis*, pp. 203-05.

[21] "namque is et sermone (quod ipsum reprehendunt quibus gravitas et cothurnus et sonus Sophocli videtur esse sublimior) magis accedit oratorio generi et sententiis densus et illis, quae a sapientibus tradita sunt, paene ipsis par, et dicendo ac respondendo cuilibet eorum, qui fuerunt in foro diserti, comparandus, in adfectibus vero cum omnibus mirus, tum in his, qui in miseratione constant, facile praecipuus." Quintilian, *Institutionis oratoriae* 10.1.68.

ness ("'plusculum candoris'") of Euripides' language in *Iphigenia at Aulis* were essentially a paraphrase of Quintilian's comments.[22] But Erasmus' careful defense of his Euripides translation did not actually respond to the scholastics' misgivings about the classics. Eloquence did not exclusively serve theology, for in these translations, Erasmus appeared more interested in developing his own Latin style than he was in interpreting Scripture. Despite his remark to Warham that his Greek exercise was merely propaedeutic to his Bible translation, Erasmus dispensed with verbal accuracy in *Iphigenia at Aulis* and allowed himself to render the text more freely ("'fusior'") without neglecting the sense of the original.[23] Erasmus' argument for the subordination of classical learning to theology was consequently weakened by his clear enthusiasm for the pursuit of stylistic elegance for its own sake.

When the humanists used moral arguments to defend the study of classical drama, they were able to construct a stronger case against their critics than Erasmus. From a Christian perspective, the frank immorality of classical literature, from the amatory verse of the Roman elegists to the whores of comedy and the pagan gods of tragedy and epic, had to be either justified or discarded. Accordingly, the humanists reacted to these lascivious episodes in various ways: the Florentine scholar Leonardo Bruni felt that such infelicities were acceptable, for the Bible too contained equally pernicious events;[24] the Tübingen humanist Heinrich Bebel, perhaps the most cautious receiver of the New Learning, believed that the ancients should be censored.[25] Still others, such as the Leipzig professor Hermann von dem Busche and Erasmus' Jacobus Batt character in *Antibarbari*, held that their narrow-minded clerical opponents were guilty of the same sins.[26] For the apologists of classical drama, however, the fortuitous 1433 discovery by Giovanni Aurispa of the commentary on the comedies of Terence by the fourth-century grammarian Aelius

---

[22] Cf. Erasmus comments with Quintilian in note 21: "Quo quidem nomine Sophoclea videri queat; at rursus argumentorum densitate quasique declamatoria quadam suadendi ac dissuadendi facultate parentem Euripidem magis refert." Erasmus, *Euripidis,* pp. 271-2.

[23] Erasmus, *Euripidis,* p. 272.

[24] Leonardo Bruni, *De studiis et litteris,* in Leonardo Bruni Aretino, *Humanistisch-philosophische Schriften,* ed. Hans Baron (Leipzig: Teubner, 1928), pp. 17-8. Martin Luther used this same argument to defend performances of Terence in the 1530s: "Nec impedit eas agere, quod amatoria et interdum etiam obscoena continent, alioqui eadem ratione biblia christiano non essent legenda, quod passim contineant amatoria, etc." D. Martin Luther, *Tischreden,* vol. 1 (Weimar: H. Böhlaus Nachfolger, 1912), pp. 430-1.

[25] Heinrich Bebel, *Opusculum de institutione puerorum* (Strasbourg: Schürer, 1513), sig. Aiv[v]; Avii[v].

[26] Hermann von dem Busche, *Vallum humanitatis* (Cologne: Nic. Caesar, 1518), sig. Kiii[v]. Erasmus, *Antibarbarorum liber,* ed. Kazimierz Kumaniecki, in *Opera omnia Des. Erasmi Roterodami,* vol. I.1 (Amsterdam: North Holland, 1969), pp. 74-6.

Donatus,[27] the teacher of St. Jerome, provided them with their strongest evidence for their moral interpretation and ultimately for their christianization of classical theater. As readers of Horace, the humanists were of course aware of the familiar dictum that poetry fulfilled both a utilitarian and aesthetic function ("aut prodesse volunt aut delectare poetae").[28] But, in contrast to Horace's vague injunction, Donatus specifically suggested what the moral benefits were. In the preface ("de tragoedia et comoedia") to his commentary, Donatus ascribed an ethical function to all drama: "in Tragoedia, fugienda vita; in Comoedia, capessenda exprimitur."[29] Shortly thereafter he contradicted himself and attributed both ethical tasks to comedy: "Comoedia est fabula diversa instituta continens, affectuumque civilium ac privatorum: quibus discitur, quid sit in vita utile, quid contra evitandum."[30] Where tragedies clearly only presented negative models for behavior, comedies instructed through the juxtaposition of both positive and negative exempla.

The humanist commentators on Graeco-Roman theater borrowed both Donatian definitions to explain the inconsistencies between antique drama and their Christian beliefs. Because of Donatus' own confusing distribution of the moral function of theater between two genres, it is not surprising that tragedy and comedy were subsequently believed to contain both useful and dangerous advice for the audience. In his *Ars versificandi* (1486), for example, Conrad Celtes promoted public performances of drama, for both comedy and tragedy were thought "sublimi persuasione remotisque invencionibus poete spectantium animos ad virtutes inflammabant et pubescentum iam indolem a viciis deterrebant."[31] Additionally, Celtes applied Donatus' observations on the decorous characterizations of ancient comedy ("personarum leges circa habitum, aetatem, officium, partes agendi")[32] to drama in general; all classical theater, he stated, advised the spectators about their duties toward their country, parents and friends.[33] Donatus' remarks on comedy likewise

---

[27] Aelius Donatus, *Commentum Terenti*, 3 vols., ed. Paulus Wessner (Stuttgart: Teubner, 1962).

[28] Horace, *Ars poetica* 333.

[29] Donatus, vol. 1, p. 21. The essay, *De tragoedia et comoedia*, which is now attributed to the post-classical grammarian Evanthius, was considered the work of Donatus in the sixteenth century. For this reason, the text will be ascribed to Donatus in the following discussion.

[30] Donatus, vol. 1, p. 22.

[31] As quoted in D. George, *Deutsche Tragödientheorien vom Mittelalter bis zu Lessing* (Munich: Beck, 1972), p. 47.

[32] Donatus, vol. 1, p. 19.

[33] "ut quid patrie: quid amicis: parentibus: hospitibusque deberent: vivis exemplis acciperent." As quoted in George, p. 47.

reappeared in contemporary interpretations of tragedy. Gellius Bernardinus wrote in his preface to the 1514 Paris edition of Seneca—the first in Northern Europe—that through the terrifying portrayal of the hero's demise, Seneca's tragedies inspired men to embrace virtue and yearn for eternal life.[34] The exemplum of the "vita fugienda" had thus served to remind the Christian reader of the qualities and advantages of the "vita capessenda."

The applicability of Donatus' rules to all Graeco-Roman drama was best demonstrated by Philip Melanchthon in his commentaries, prefaces and verse prologues to specific plays. In his 1516 *Enarratio comoediarum Terentii*, Melanchthon expanded Donatus' brief definitions into a methodology for the assimilation of the pagan drama into the teachings of Christianity.[35] Doubtlessly troubled by the ambiguity of Donatus' ascription of a positive and negative moral lesson to comedy, Melanchthon argued that ethical lessons ("consilia") could only be derived from a play, regardless of its genre, if the viewers were confronted with a choice between virtuous and evil behavior.[36] As a student of classical rhetoric, Melanchthon associated drama with the "genus deliberativum," the orator's art of persuasion or dissuasion of the audience to adopt a certain course of action.[37] Since Cicero and Quintilian had held that successful orators explicated all aspects of a problem so as to demonstrate the advantage of their opinion,[38] Melanchthon likewise believed that dramatists used the same method to educate their viewers. With one stroke Melanchthon not only eliminated Donatus' confusing distinction between the specific lessons of tragedy and comedy, but he also successfully disarmed any critics who might object to the immorality of classical drama. By arguing for the necessity of immoral exempla for an effective Christian education, Melanchthon cleverly justified the reading and performance of Graeco-Roman plays in the schools. The raucous misadventures of comic heroes and the passion and adultery of tragic protagonists were no longer thought to induce the viewers to practice

---

[34] "Ex tragoediis utilitas multifariam habetur: carminis nitor elegans, et venusta dicendi copia: cognitio rerum varia, ut si homines intelligant fortunam esse mutabilem: et illius levitati non esse fidendum: solamque virtutem esse colendam et ad beatam vitam properandum." In *L. Annei Senecae Tragoediae pristinae integritati restitutae per exactissimi iudicii viros* (Paris: Badius, 1514), sig. Aa iiii.

[35] *CR*, XIX, cols. 681-696.

[36] *CR*, XIX, col. 695.

[37] In his 1531 *Elementa rhetorices*, Melanchthon defined the "genus deliberativum" as follows: "Genus deliberativum versatur in suadendo ac dissuadendo, adhortando et dehortando, petendo, precando, consolando, et similibus negociis, ubi finis est non cognitio, sed praeter cognitionem actio aliqua." *CR*, XIII, col. 445.

[38] Cicero, *De oratore* 2.82; Quintilian, *Inst. orat.* 3.8.1-6.

similar vices but rather to remind them of the rewards of virtue and their need for God.

Melanchthon's remarks on individual dramas did not, however, so much accord with the play as with his eagerness to eliminate any doubts about the moral utility of Graeco-Roman theater. Like his fellow humanists, Melanchthon strongly supported the study of classical theater, especially Terence, for the rhetorical training of his students. In his "schola privata" in Wittenberg where he staged dramas by Plautus, Terence, Seneca and Euripides (ca. 1525-1526), Melanchthon responded sharply to critics of the humanist curriculum by likening them to the conceited braggarts in Plautus' (*Miles gloriosus*) and Terence's (*Eunuchus*) plays.[39] It is not surprising therefore that Melanchthon's enthusiasm for the New Learning would have resulted in tenuous claims about the moral utility of classical theater. Since an ethical function was attributed to immoral episodes, Melanchthon was often at pains to explain how some positive moral counsel could be derived from certain plots. In the case of Terence's *Andria,* for example, Melanchthon disregarded the adolescent ravings of the enamored Pamphilus and characterized him cooly as "mediocri ingenio, satis cordatus, pius et in patrem et in mulierculam."[40] In his cursory evaluation, Melanchthon conveniently overlooked the fact that Pamphilus' willingness to agree to his father's choice of a bride did not arise from Pamphilus' rejection of his mistress Glycerium but rather from his erroneous belief that his father's demand was merely a ruse to test his obedience. As for the youth's treatment of women, Melanchthon disregarded Pamphilus' earlier seduction of Glycerium, who now carried his child, and judged the play solely on the basis of the ending where the revelation of Glycerium's true identity eased Pamphilus' request for her hand. Finally, Melanchthon's suggestion that the other romantic youth, Charinus, was intended as a negative

---

[39] In the verse prologue to his production of the *Miles gloriosus,* Melanchthon remarked:

> Nec lac enim lacti, nec ovo est ovum magis
> Simile, huic inepto militi quam sunt modo
> Qui cum meliores literas fastidiunt,
> Rerum omnium tamen scientiam sibi
> Audacter arrogant, et inter pocula
> In compitisque venditant suum σοφός, (Koch, pp. 68-9)

Similarly, in reference to the braggart Thraso in *Eunuchus,* Melanchthon noted:

> Proventus huius generis est uberrimus
> Hoc saeculo, cum se titulo sapientiae,
> Musarum ubique venditant, hostes feri
> Prophana divinaque miscent omnia. (Koch, p. 73)

[40] *CR,* XIX, col. 696.

counterpart (''furiosum et amentem adolescentem'')[41] to Pamphilus was not evidenced by the text, for Charinus was just as desirous of marrying his girl friend as Pamphilus. Pamphilus' actions may have actually been more reprehensible, for Charinus at least had not yet seduced his beloved. Despite Melanchthon's attempts to reconcile the amorous escapades of the *Andria* with Christian ethics, his arguments were in fact weakened by the play itself.

Similar problems beset Melanchthon in his interpretation of tragedy. Until the mid-1540s, Melanchthon essentially adhered to Donatus' moralistic reading of tragedy as the exemplum of the life to be avoided. The additional remarks of the Senecan commentators of the 1514 edition also influenced his ideas. Two of the Senecan scholars, Danielis Gaietanus and Benedictus Philologus, had harmonized the medieval commonplace about tragedy as the bloody history of the downfall of kings with Donatus' views.[42] But Gellius Bernardinus suggested a possible positive response. The catastrophes in Seneca did not necessarily evoke a pessimistic reaction; rather, Christian readers were induced to reaffirm their faith by reflecting anew on the eternal life which awaited them beyond the grave.[43] Melanchthon likewise believed in the moral advantages of tragedy; he presented Seneca's *Thyestes* and Euripides' *Hecuba* (the Erasmus translation) in Wittenberg as reminders to the audience of the mutability of the world and the dangers of sin. He expressly chose *Thyestes* for student recitation in 1525-1526 as a warning against the folly of political ambition, a particularly timely counsel in light of the Wittenberg religious riots of 1521-1522 and the recent bloody defeat of the peasants in Thuringia (1525).[44]

In 1545, however, Melanchthon expanded his ideas on the moral benefits of tragedy to accord with recent developments in the interpretation of Greek drama. Since the 1520s, Melanchthon had read broadly in the works of Euripides and Sophocles. His close friend, the accomplished Hellenist and editor of Sophocles, Joachim Camerarius (1500-1574), a

---

[41] *Ibid.*

[42] *Senecae Tragoediae* (1514), sig. Aa v^v. Benedictus Philologus (sig. Aa vi) paraphrased Donatus: ''in tragoedia tristes exitus et funesti habentur ... in tragoedia tranquilla sunt prima, et turbulenta ultima ... fugienda vita in tragoedia exprimitur.'' Cf., Donatus, p. 21.

[43] *Senecae Tragoediae* (1514), sig. Aa iiii (as quoted in note 34 above).

[44] In the verse prologue, Melanchthon warned:
Nil esse peius ambitione, quae omnia
Divina, humana, iusque et fas vertere solet,
Quae florentissimis quibusque fere fuit
Exitio civitatibus, quae denique
Tum plurimum nocet, cum in templa irruperit,
Ubi hoc tempore saevam exercet tyrannidem. (Koch, p. 79)

professor in Leipzig since 1541, not only encouraged him in this pursuit, but he also introduced him to Aristotle's concept of tragedy from the *Poetics*. To please his fellow humanist, Melanchthon summarized his views on classical drama in a brief essay "De legendis Tragoediis et Comoediis," which was then printed as the preface to Camerarius' 1545 edition of Terence. Here, on the basis of new examples from Greek theater, Melanchthon restated the medieval commonplaces about the instability of the tragic world and elaborated further on Bernardinus' suggestion that the lessons of tragedy were compatible with the Christian faith. To support this argument, Melanchthon offered two examples from Greek tragedy: Jocasta's suicide from Euripides' *Phoenissae* and a general reference to the vengeful Erinyes. In the former instance, Melanchthon first equated Aristotelian catharsis with temperance ("moderatio") and self-control ("gubernatio vitae") and then concluded that the arousal of pity and fear served a moral function: "eventus isti commonefaciebant homines de causis humanarum calamitatum, quas accersi et cumulari pravis cupiditatibus, in his exemplis cernebant."[45] By referring to the Erinyes, moreover, Melanchthon hoped to illustrate that tragedy, like comedy in the Donatian sense, contained positive and negative moral exempla. The ultimate victory of divine justice which the Erinyes guaranteed not only terrified the audience with the punishment of crimes ("atrocia scelera"), but also reassured them that God would always triumph: "haec sententia multos ad moderationem flectebat, quae nos quidem magis movere debet, qui scimus eam et Ecclesiae clara Dei voce saepe traditam esse."[46] The Donatian inheritance was evidenced even further by Melanchthon's ascription of the social decorum of comic characterizations to tragedy. Except for the obvious differences in style, plot and the social station of the protagonists, Melanchthon's defense of tragedy hardly deviated from his remarks on comedy; tragedy too was useful "cum ad commonefaciendos animos de multis vitae officiis et de frenandis immoderatis cupiditatibus, tum vero etiam ad eloquentiam."[47] Social deportment, moral restraint and the development of style were the primary elements of his apology for classical drama.

But, as in the case of Roman comedy, Melanchthon's theories about the utility of tragedy were not reinforced by his examples. Instead of strengthening his case for "moderatio" and divine justice, his description of Jocasta's suicide and the Erinyes betrayed inconsistencies in his

---

[45] *CR*, V, col. 568.
[46] *Ibid.*
[47] *Ibid.*

argument. Although Melanchthon stated that the reading of tragedy could teach temperance and self-control, he contradicted this conclusion with his unabashedly morbid account of Jocasta's death. He not only enthusiastically recorded his terrified reaction to this lugubrious scene in which Jocasta slew herself over the bodies of her sons, but he also embellished the episode by adding more bloody details to the original version.[48]

Melanchthon's reference to the Erinyes likewise revealed another weakness in his utilitarian defense of tragedy. For many sixteenth-century commentators, divine justice was evident in several Greek plays: Jason was punished for his infidelity to Medea with the death of his children, and Phaedra perished because of her incestuous designs on her stepson Hippolytus. But in a few instances, such as Euripides' *Phoenissae* where the innocent Jocasta was driven to suicide by grief, the Greek denouement could not easily be reconciled with the Christian concept of justice as punishment for sin. Melanchthon was not troubled by, nor was he probably aware of, the subtleties in the original characterizations, but he was disturbed by those many instances when justice was not immediately apparent. Since some misfortunes could never adequately be explained, Melanchthon introduced the Erinyes so that readers might be reminded that every truly serious crime would be avenged. In attempting to demonstrate the centrality of divine justice in ancient tragedy, Melanchthon had paradoxically been constrained to admit that injustices frequently occurred: "*et quanquam hos etiam interdum fortuiti casus opprimunt, sunt enim multae arcanae causae,* tamen illa manifesta regula non propterea aboletur, videlicet semper Erinnyas et saevas calamitates comites esse atrocium delictorum."[49] Despite Melanchthon's efforts, divine justice remained a problematic aspect of classical tragedy for all Christian readers.

Though flawed by a few inconsistent arguments, Melanchthon's justification for the study of Graeco-Roman drama remained the chief method for the interpretation and legitimization of the ancients until the beginning of the seventeenth century. His remarks in the 1545 essay provided the basis for several sixteenth-century commentaries on both tragic and comic writers assembled by schoolmen throughout the Holy Roman

---

[48] "Nec vero quisquam tam ferreus est, qui sine animi consternatione legat fratrum *Thebanorum* certamen, et matris *Iocastae* exitum, quae diremptura praelium, cum tardius venisset, ex alterius filii vulnere ensem extrahit, ex hoc ipse ense, qui filii cruore madebat, miserrima mater sese transfigit. Postea se mediam inter filios abiicit, brachia spargens, quasi in utriusque complexu moritura. Quid hac imagine lugubrius cogitari potest?" *CR,* V, cols. 567-568.

[49] *Ibid.,* italics mine.

Empire. And, as in the case of Melanchthon, these readings often owed more to the biased language of an apology than to an accurate reading of the text. Gulielmus Xylander, for example, the editor of Melanchthon's translations of Euripides (published in Basel, 1553) abstracted theological lessons from the Greek tragedian which were completely foreign to the ancient world. Following Quintilian, Xylander regarded Euripides' works as a cornucopia of maxims ("sententiae"), many of which were eminently useful for Christian readers.[50] As was customary, these sentences were set off from the text by quotation marks so they might be appreciated, copied and most likely memorized regardless of their relationship to the plot. But the generality of some "sententiae" required Xylander's inventive explication before their Christian relevance could be apparent. Having cited a passage from *Orestes* on man's helplessness before an angry God, Xylander resourcefully noted: "Quod si Christiani interdum secum reputarent, magis de placenda numinis ira, quam novis ea peccatis exasperanda cogitarent."[51] As Melanchthon had done in his 1545 letter, Xylander did not hesitate to attribute new meanings to the classical text in order to defend the ancients from censure.

In keeping with Melanchthon's approach, Xylander had further suggested that tragedy spurred the reader on to virtue through the depiction of a sinner's downfall. Similar opinions appeared in the 1566 Sophocles commentary of Joachim Camerarius, the essay on Seneca, *De tragoediarum usu* (1566) by Georg Fabricius, a former student of Melanchthon in Wittenberg, and in the dedicatory prefaces of Thomas Naogeorgus, the famed polemical Protestant dramatist, to his 1552 Latin translations of Sophocles' *Ajax* and *Philoctetes*. In all three cases, arguments were introduced which accorded with the pedagogical idea, propounded by Melanchthon in his reading of Donatus, that moral lessons were imparted through the juxtaposition of good and evil. Camerarius suggested that the instability of the tragic world induced the reader to seek refuge with God;[52] Fabricius asserted that tragic punishments not only deterred man from evil but also assured him of

---

[50] "quot capita sunt philosophiae moralis, quot res ad vitam communem dirigendam utiles, tot in uno Euripide thesauri latent, hoc est, innumeri." *CR*, XVIII, cols. 283-284. Cf. Quintilian, *Inst. orat.* 10.1.68.

[51] *CR*, XVIII, col. 283-284.

[52] "quum plurima eveniant contra spem et expectationem hominum, esse aliquam vim maiorem quàm humana esse possit, moderatricem et gubernatricem rerum omnium in hoc mundo: quod numen divinum necesse est intelligi et perhiberi ...." Joachim Camerarius, ed. and trans., *Sophoclis Tragoediae septem unà cum omnibus Graecis scholiis* (Geneva: H. Stephanus, 1568), p. 4.

divine justice;[53] and Naogeorgus paraphrased Donatus for his theory that tragedy persuaded man to scorn impiety and embrace virtue.[54]

Melanchthon's moral justification of classical drama was further strengthened by the establishment of a biblical precedent for the genre itself. In his preface to the Apocryphal book of Tobias (1534), Martin Luther introduced a common patristic argument that the wisdom of the Greeks, including drama, had been derived from the Jews. The great encyclopedic scholar Isidore of Seville had systematized this belief in his seventh-century compendium of world history, the *Etymologiae,* by drawing temporal correspondences between events in biblical and pagan history.[55] In his account of literature, Isidore took pains to demonstrate that the forms of Greek poetry had originated in the Bible: Moses had invented the hexameter; Solomon had composed the first epithalamium and Jeremiah, the first threnody. In Isidore's fifth chronological period, between the Babylonian Captivity and the Incarnation, Greek tragedy developed contemporaneously with the Apocrypha, a fact which had probably caused Luther to associate two Apocryphal books with drama: "denn Judith gibt eine gute/ernste/dapffere Tragedien/so gibt Tobias eine feine, liebliche/gottselige Comedien."[56]

The discovery of this biblical precedent for drama further reinforced Luther's own promotion of classical theater as a pedagogical tool for Latin language training and social deportment. Under the influence of Melanchthon he was known to have encouraged classical dramatic performances by local students in his home, the former Augustinian cloister, at Shrovetide in 1525.[57] In a 1533 conversation with Johann Cellarius, a pastor from Bautzen in Upper Lusatia, Luther voiced his disapproval of the critics of Terence's *Andria* and responded to their charges of immorality ("'multi offensi sunt ex tali actione'")[58] by directing their attention to similar romantic, if not obscene, episodes from the Bible. Doubtlessly following Melanchthon's counsel, Luther freely acknowledged the frank immorality of Terentian comedy, but nonetheless held that its exemplary style and decorous characterizations far outweighed

---

[53] "Itaque voluerunt veteres illi sapientes, scelerum poenas extare, et sceleratorum exitus miserabiles,..." as quoted in George, p. 71.

[54] "docere pietatem verumque Dei cultum, et vitam Deo placentem bonaque opera tradere, atque è regione reprehendere impietatem, falsosque cultus vitamque pravam ...." Thomas Naogeorgus, *Iudas Iscariotes. Tragoedia nova et sacra. Adiunctae sunt quoque duae Sophoclis Tragoediae, Aiax flagellifer et Philoctetes* (n.p., 1552), sig. A 3.

[55] Curtius, pp. 450-57.

[56] D. Martin Luther, trans., *Die gantze Heilige Schrifft Deudsch. Wittenberg 1545,* eds. Hans Volz and Heinz Blanke, vol. 2 (Munich: Rogner & Bernhard, 1972), p. 1731.

[57] Koch, pp. 57-8.

[58] *WATR,* I, p. 430, n. 12.

the potential dangers of its plot: "Ego Terencium ideo amo, quod video id esse rhetoricam, das man ein comoediam daraus macht, das einer hat ein magd beschlaffen; deinde fingit, was der vatter dazu sag, quid servus, quid die freundtschafft."[59]

But Luther's new case for the priority of the Jews to the ancients significantly shifted the emphasis of previous defenses of classical drama. With this remark Luther had explicitly stated the implicit assumption of humanists like Erasmus, Melanchthon and Camerarius that classical literature was compatible with Christianity, for like the Bible, its wisdom was derived from God. Sixteenth-century readers simply needed to view Graeco-Roman drama from the perspective of their faith before its divine origins could be discerned.

Luther's biblical precedent also had profound consequences for the subsequent development of religious theater. If the Jews had composed sacred dramas, then contemporary Christians could do likewise without fear that their literary pursuits conflicted with their faith. The biblical precedent for drama not only confirmed the humanists' moralistic defense of the ancients but also justified the creation of a new religious theater. As a consequence, several sixteenth-century writers safely supported the performances of classical drama as they wrote their own religious plays. Joachim Greff (1510-1552), for example, a schoolteacher in Magdeburg, followed Luther's interpretation of the book of Judith as a tragedy and composed a German drama on that topic in 1536 in the form of classical theater.[60] Two years earlier, Greff had translated Plautus' *Aulularia* into German and had published it with the *Andria* translation of his fellow student Henricus Ham. Since Greff and Ham had both studied in Wittenberg in the 1520s, it was not surprising that Melanchthon's concept of comedy as a mirror of positive and negative morality would reappear in Greff's understanding of classical comedy. Following Luther, Greff believed that his biblical play provided a useful contrast between Judith's exemplary heroism, the despair of the beleaguered Jews and the *superbia* of the tyrant Holofernes.[61]

Other writers familiar with Donatus' interpretation of Terence had ascribed the same moral function to their religious plays independently of Luther's remarks. The Basel schoolteacher Sixt Birck (1501-1554), who had been trained in the humanist centers of Tübingen, Erfurt and Basel, noted in his 1532 German *Susanna* play:

---

[59] *WATR,* I, p. 204.
[60] Joachim Greff, *Tragedia des Buchs Judith* (Wittenberg: Georg Rhaw, 1536). On Greff see Reinhard Buchwald, *Joachim Greff. Untersuchungen über die Anfänge des Renaissancedramas in Sachsen,* Probefahrten, 11 (Leipzig: R. Voigtländer, 1907).
[61] Greff, sig. A ii[v].

Das ist der aller gröste gwin
Dann so ein mensch zů Gott würt kert
Die tugent allenthalb gemert
Die laster khumend inn ein hass[62]

Georg Binder (d. 1545), the first German translator of Gulielmus Gnapheus' (1493-1568) *Acolastus* (1529), the most popular Latin play of the century, had also paraphrased the Terentian commentator.[63] Birck had composed only religious works, but Binder, a Zürich humanist, used the Donatian argument to justify performances of classical drama (Terence and a Greek version of Aristophanes' *Plutus*) and religious theater on the same stage. Similarly, Thomas Naogeorgus had his translations of Sophocles' *Ajax* and *Philoctetes* printed along with his biblical tragedy, *Judas* (1552), for he did not perceive any moral distinctions between the three texts. On the contrary, following the medieval practice of equating classical heroes with Christian virtues, Naogeorgus regarded Sophocles' characters as pagan versions of biblical figures. Ajax was seen as the model of a great man ruined by emotions whose tragic demise recalled the fate of Samson and Ahab. Philoctetes was likened to Job, and his oppressor Odysseus with the cruel mockers of Job's suffering. Since Sophocles' protagonists displayed biblical virtues, Naogeorgus concluded, they were just as appropriate for the school stage as religious subjects.[64]

The dramatists' elimination of the moral distinctions between classical and Christian drama also served to defend the performances of school plays regardless of the topic. The Ingolstadt schoolteacher, Hieronymus Ziegler (1514-1562), the most prolific Catholic dramatist in the sixteenth century, justified the utility of Terence since the Roman comedian had presented so many examples both positive and negative of the ideal parent. In Terence's *Adelphi*, for example, Ziegler argued that the strict Demea had driven his son Ctesipho to defiance while the mild but firm Micio had guided his nephew Aeschinus to virtue. With the fervor of an apologist, Ziegler conveniently overlooked the lustful ravings of both

---

[62] Sixt Birck, *Sämtliche Dramen,* vol. 2, ed. Manfred Brauneck (Berlin and New York: Walter de Gruyter, 1976), p. 4.
[63] Daruß man lart in kurtzer yl
Der menschen sitten manigfalt;
Wie es umb yeden hett ein gstalt,
Ward jm darinn schön für gebildt,
Zů allen zyten daruff gspilt,
Das man der Dugend hangte an,
Die laster welte faren lan,
Georg Binder, *Acolastus (1535),* in *Schweizerische Schauspiele des sechzehnten Jahrhunderts,* vol. 1, ed. Jakob Bächtold (Zürich, 1890), p. 185.
[64] Naogeorgus, *Iudas,* sig. A 5-A 5ᵛ.

Ctesipho and Aeschinus, which had culminated in the abduction of a slave girl, in order to direct his readers to the varied behavior of their parents. In adapting Terence's contrastive technique for his religious tragedy *Abel iustus* (1559), Ziegler hoped to provide the same advice through his juxtaposition of Adam and Eve. Where Adam had instructed Cain and Abel in temperance and piety, Eve encouraged the same impetuosity which had, according to the misogynistic Ziegler, earlier resulted in man's Fall.[65]

The moral interpretation of Graeco-Roman drama thus reflected the humanist tendency to preserve the literary achievements of the ancients by reading their works in accordance with Christian truth. In their enthusiasm for the classics, these commentators, translators and playwrights did not detect any historical break between the Jewish, classical and Christian world and consequently argued for the pedagogical utility of the Graeco-Roman inheritance. It is true that these Christian humanists perceived the obvious moral and religious differences between classical and modern civilization, but they also felt equally strongly that the distinction did not warrant the complete condemnation of the ancients. The discovery of Donatus' commentary enabled them to interpret the ancients from a Christian perspective, justify the imitation of classical theater and to import the technique of contrastive moral instruction into their own works.

But the assimilation of classical drama to the precepts of Christianity which had been so carefully argued on moral grounds was paradoxically susceptible to moral censure. Since the apologists had deemed the immoral characterizations and episodes of classical theater useful for the education of the contemporary Christian, their ethical defense of the ancients seemed to rest on a tenuous foundation indeed. As we have seen in the case of Melanchthon and Xylander, the alleged utility of classical theater arose more often from the apologetic ambition of the commentators than from the texts themselves. Nonetheless, the justification of immoral content, so firmly established by the humanist reading of Graeco-Roman theater remained an essential element of Christian drama throughout the sixteenth and seventeenth centuries. The opposition detected by humanist commentators between Demea and Micio in Terence's *Adelphi*; Philoctetes and Odysseus in Sophocles; and Medea and Jason in Euripides reappeared in sixteenth-century confrontations

---

[65] It was no accident that Eve took a natural liking to Cain:
    Thesaurus est Cain noster, nihil valet
    Abelus, homo simplex, vivens solo sibi. (Act I; scene 3)
Hieronymus Ziegler, *Abel iustus. Tragoedia* (Ingolstadt: Alexander & Samuel Weissenhornius, 1559), sig. C 3.

between Judith and Holofernes, Susanna and the elders and between pagan tyrants and Christian martyrs. Small wonder then that dramatists like Greff, Naogeorgus and Ziegler could defend Graeco-Roman plays and their own secular and religious plays with such facility. The humanists' emphasis on the pedagogical utility of contrastive moral and immoral choices thus not only legitimized the study of the ancients, but also established the basic rhetorical structure for the creation of Christian drama in the sixteenth century.

The accepted pedagogical practice of moral instruction by contrast did raise new problems for the large number of religious playwrights who were eager to condemn pagan drama and replace it with their own biblical works. Since these writers objected strongly to the retention of any immoral elements from classical drama in their religious plays, they were consequently forced to reconcile their conservative moralistic stance with the contrastive pedagogical method. Because of their eagerness to provide the best ethical instruction, however, they often retained and amplified many of the immoral episodes of the ancients which they otherwise vehemently rejected. Like the humanist apology for ancient theater, the christianization of Graeco-Roman drama, i.e., the substitution of religious plots for those of pagan theater, was based on the paradoxical assumption that immorality played an essential role in a Christian education.

### The Imitation and Reform of the Ancients

To the modern reader, most sixteenth-century religious playwrights appeared to maintain an uncertain, if not contradictory, relationship to Graeco-Roman drama. As ardent supporters of the humanist educational curriculum, these writers, many of whom had studied and performed in classical dramas in the early humanist centers in the North, admired the language and style of the ancients and realized the utility of these texts for the development of the "vir bonus dicendi peritus." As former students of the initial defenders of classical theater, they had been trained to recognize the moral indiscretions in the classical texts and were directed nonetheless to derive some benefit from the frankly pagan episodes. As we have already seen, moral lessons could be gained either through the exemplary behavior of a pagan character, as in Melanchthon's interpretations of Terence's Pamphilus (*Andria*), or in tragedy through the downfall of a villain whose sins the youths were then advised to avoid. But for many sixteenth-century humanist dramatists this prudent reading of the ancients was considered an inadequate justification for such potentially dangerous texts. By their own declarations—and they were the most vehement critics of antique theater—they proposed to replace these dramas in the school repertoire with their own religious works written in the style of the ancients. In this way, the schoolboys could be guarded from danger since all the objectionable elements of classical theater had been removed.

A brief glance at many of the humanist religious plays, however, reveals that the characters and episodes which the playwrights had ostensibly rejected often reappeared in their new works. The parasites, pimps, whores and lusty youths of Roman comedy and the vengeful tyrants of Senecan tragedy populated the religious school stage with such frequency that the moral reformation which the playwrights propounded hardly seemed to have occurred at all. In his *Acolastus*, Gulielmus Gnapheus expanded the sparse biblical account of the Prodigal Son (Luke 15:11-32) by devoting the middle acts to the prodigal's adventures with an array of Terentian figures; Petrus Papeus introduced a similar group of thieves, parasites and lovers into his drama on the simple biblical version of the Good Samaritan (Luke 10:29-37); and Cornelius Crocus and Thiebolt Gart embellished their two Joseph plays by introducing amatory language from Ovid and Terence into their characterization of the seductive wife of Potiphar. The retention of these classical episodes did not mean that the dramatists themselves were wanting in piety. On the contrary, though immoral characters might temporarily triumph, the dramatists clearly demonstrated the ultimate victory of the Christian hero and exhorted their readers to imitate his virtues. Since religious dramatists ascribed the same moral utility to both classical and religious drama, the contradictions between the pious goals of some religious writers and their actual practice does not seem too surprising. But this discrepancy between theory and execution provided an important clue about the motivation for the humanist critique of his antique model. Humanist religious drama did not develop solely out of the playwright's moralistic efforts to expurgate the ancients, nor did it serve exclusively as a didactic text for the Christian schoolboys. Rather, humanist religious drama arose from a unique combination of aesthetic and moral elements which were varied by individual playwrights according to their concept of the function of theater and their own artistic ambitions. By virtue of the moralistic content and in some cases the linguistic virtuosity and aesthetic disposition of the plot, humanist religious dramatists attempted to create a new Christian theater which equalled and hopefully surpassed its Graeco-Roman model.

The christianization of antique theater was based on a variety of moralistic and aesthetic arguments which betrayed the religious playwright's attempt to establish an ideal balance between these two tendencies. Whereas their admiration for the stylistic elegance of the ancients had induced them to avoid the monotonous presentation of moral lessons, their fear of sacrilege and charges of paganism forced them to temper their aesthetic imitation. To guide them in their transformation of classical drama, the religious playwrights derived aesthetic inspiration from patristic and Renaissance writings on the imitation of the ancients and received moral direction from medieval dramatic practice.

The creation of humanist religious drama in the sixteenth century would not have been possible without the patristic fathers' promulgation of the study of classical literature. As noted previously,[66] the Greek and Roman Church fathers, particularly St. Basil and Jerome, had justified the selective reading of classical literature so that Christians could safely acquire the learning of the pagan world without endangering their faith. More importantly for Renaissance writers, however, the fathers had also supported the composition of a new Christian literature through the adaptation of the Bible and other religious topics, such as hagiography and the cult of the Virgin, to the poetic forms of the ancients. The gospel epics of Juvencus (ca. 330) and Sedulius (ca. early fifth century), the allegorical and hagiographical poetry of Prudentius, the hymns of St. Ambrose and Gregorius Nazianzenus were frequently referred to by Renaissance writers of Christian poetry in defense of their adaptation of antique forms. Similarly, during the sixteenth and seventeenth centuries, humanist dramatists turned to patristic and late antique examples to justify the composition of Christian comedy and tragedy. In the dedicatory preface to his comedy *Joseph* (1536), the Amsterdam school rector, Cornelius Crocus (ca. 1500-1550), an accomplished patristic scholar, referred to the fathers' support of Christian poetry and their own compositions of it in his argument for the potential moral utility of literature. In adapting this argument, however, Crocus had to proceed cautiously. In contrast to the large corpus of surviving Christian Latin poetry, there was no extant evidence of early Christian drama for him to use as a precedent for his religious play. The first printing of the Greek drama, ΧΡΙΣΤΟΣ ΠΑΣΧΩΝ, attributed by many sixteenth-century writers to Gregorius Nazianzenus, did not occur until 1542.[67] As a consequence, Crocus prudently appended the few references to Christian dramatists he had gathered from encyclopedia handbooks such as the

---

[66] See above p. 16.

[67] For a brief survey of sixteenth-century translations of this work, see Sister Agnes Clare Way, "S. Gregorius Nazianzenus," in *Catalogus translationum et commentariorum: Medieval and Renaissance Latin Translations and Commentaries,* vol. 2, ed. Paul Oskar Kristeller (Washington: Catholic University, 1971), pp. 106-11.

Suidas to his list of Christian Greek and Latin poets so as to suggest his continuation of that tradition. His references to the lost adaptations of Menander and Euripides by the mid-fifth-century poet Sozomenus and to Stephanus of Byzantium's sixth-century tragedy on Christ's passion were subsequently cited by several religious playwrights including Joost van den Vondel, as part of their claims for the acceptability of christianized classical drama.[68]

But the value of these late antique citations was not limited to their use as historical precedents. Crocus' adaptation of the patristic apologies for Christian literature also helped him justify the retention of the immoral characters and language of classical drama in his biblical play. To argue this point, Crocus followed the implicit assumption of the patristic defenders of Christian literature that poetic forms and language, when adapted to Christian ends, could exert a more powerful influence on young minds than other means of religious instruction. He cited the famous passage from Lucretius (*De rerum natura* 1.936-38), which had been popularized by Quintilian (*Inst. orat.* 3.1.4), that the poetic form of didactic literature adorned its dry moral content as sweetly as the honey with which doctors lined a goblet of bitter medicine so that their patients might more readily drink it. Similarly, Crocus intended that his poetic presentation of Joseph's adventures at Pharaoh's court would pleasingly lead his audience to God.[69]

This same confidence in the positive effect of poetry, however, was matched by an awareness of its dangers. Having extolled the aesthetic ability of poetic language, Crocus launched into a diatribe against the moral threats it posed. His earlier references to the benefits of literature, reinforced by examples from early Christian literature, were now contradicted by warnings from the same sources: St. Jerome complained of the immorality of the ancients and Lactantius criticized the depravity of pagan theater.[70] Crocus, however, resolved this incongruity by emphasizing the moral purpose which underlay his imitation of pagan language and characters. To his mind, the objectionable figures of the ancients were just as much a part of the formal classical inheritance as the structure of the play. The appearance of a pagan figure in a Christian drama—such as Crocus' casting of Potiphar's wife as a courtesan—did not so much distort as embellish the religious message. Since the characters themselves were morally neutral, they could thus be applied to a virtuous or immoral argument as the playwright deemed appropriate.

---

[68] Cornelius Crocus, *Joseph* (Antwerp: Ioan. Steelsius, 1538), sig. A 7-A 7ᵛ. See also the preface to Vondel's *Lucifer* (1654): Vondel, *WB*, V, pp. 611-12.

[69] Crocus, sig. A 6ᵛ.

[70] Crocus, sig. A 7ᵛ-A 8.

The reduction of a classical character to a formal element helped
Crocus to resolve another problem which subsequently confronted
several sixteenth-century dramatists. A religious playwright was often
constrained by his biblical or hagiographical source to introduce an
otherwise objectionable pagan characterization into his play. In Crocus'
portrait of the unrequited passion of Potiphar's wife, for example, the
tormented woman voiced her frustation in language reminiscent of Pamphilus' desperation in *Andria*:

> Nequeo durare. tantum mihi in pectore amor facit incendium
> Qui amarore et moerore me implet nimio ...
> .......................................................................
> Quid igitur faciam? quid restat miserae mihi? eheu nequeo
> Quin lacrumem. quanto minus spei est, tanto magis amo.
> Nulla est me miserior, domi quae quod amem assidue videam,
> Neque potiri liceat, nec qua via sententia eius
> Flecti possit scio.[71]

Despite his announcement of a "castam comoediam," free of the
"ludicras ac lubricas" of Plautus and Terence, Crocus had in fact re-
created a whore from Roman comedy. Similar difficulties arose in the
depiction of lust in works by other religious dramatists. The amorous
discourse of classical comedy reappeared in the tempestuous speeches of
Herodias in Jacob Schoepper's *Ectrachelistis sive decollatus Ioannes* (1546)
and in the heated impatience of Susanna's admirers in the comedies
about that chaste heroine of Joannes Placentius (d. 1548) and Paul
Rebhun (1505-1546).[72] In all these cases, however, the patristic argument provided the most sensible defense. Since the seduction scenes
served a moral purpose, viz. the unassailable virtue of the protagonist,
the dramatists were content to incorporate these otherwise offensive
episodes into their plays.

---

[71] Crocus, sig. B 4-B 4$^v$.

[72] Jacob Schoepper, *Ectrachelistis sive decollatus Ioannes* (Cologne: Maternus Cholinus,
1562), sig. C 6; Joannes Placentius, *Susanna* (Antwerp: Willem Vorstermann, 1536), sig.
Avii. The most expansive *confessio amoris* was offered by the Judge, Ichaboth, in Rebhun's
*Susanna*:
> Ich sitz, odr steh, ich schlaff, odr wache
> Ich eß, odr trinck, odr was ich mache
> Ich sitz zu gricht, odr geh von dannen
> So denck ich an die fraw Susannen.
> Von yhrer lieb kein rhue nicht habe
> Zu tisch, zu bett, bey nacht, noch tage
> Al meine synn seind mir verrucket
> Vnd jn yhren zarten leib verzucket
> Mein hertz das schmilzt mir itzt zusammen
> Als leg es mitten in der flammen
Paul Rebhun, *Dramen,* ed. Hermann Paul, BLVS, 49 (Stuttgart, 1859), p. 10.

Despite the dramatists' fondness for the patristic distinction between poetic language and moral intention, the argument did not protect religious playwrights from moral censure. The reason lay with the patristic writers themselves, for in promoting the moral neutrality of the literary form, the Church fathers had not explicitly established any limits on the degree to which a writer could safely christianize pagan literature. Many sixteenth-century playwrights such as Crocus and Schoepper who had freely allowed the objectionable characters of the ancients to reappear in biblical guise consequently exposed themselves to critics who might judge their imitation of the ancients to have exceeded the bounds of propriety. Several sixteenth- and seventeenth-century playwrights revised and expurgated early humanist religious dramas because they detected an imbalance between the writer's moral argument and his literary imitation of the ancients. The conservative Haarlem school rector Cornelius Schonaeus adapted Crocus' *Joseph* and Schoepper's *Ectrachelistis* for his *Terentius Christianus* collection (1602-03) by severely reducing the romantic language of Potiphar's wife and Herodias. In the *Ratio studiorum* of 1598, the Jesuits, ever watchful of threats to Christian souls, attempted to enforce the elimination of female roles from the school stage, except for virtuous heroines such as virgin martyrs and chaste widows, so as to remove temptation completely.[73] Similarly, Antonius Schottus, the seventeenth-century editor of Crocus' *Opera omnia* radically pruned *Joseph* by suppressing the attempted seduction of Joseph (I.4) before recommending the play for school performance.[74]

The disharmony between a religious playwright's rejection of the ancients on the one hand and his retention of pagan language and characterizations on the other was thus perceived as a serious threat to Christian morality by many dramatic writers. Although the dramatists' concept of the ideal balance between aesthetic license and moral intentions often differed radically, the conservatives' attack on humanist dramatic praxis revealed the weaknesses inherent in the patristic defense of Christian literature. The playwrights' contradictory praxis of reforming pagan theater through the retention of its immorality thus required a stronger apologetic argument before the moral qualms of more conservative writers could be allayed.

A curious correspondence between classical and religious methods for moral education provided a better argument for the use of pagan

---

[73] G. M. Pachtler, *Ratio studiorum et institutiones scholasticae Societatis Jesu per Germaniam olim vigentes,* vol. 2 (Berlin, 1887), pp. 234 ff. in which "Regula 13 rectoris" stated "nec persona ulla muliebris vel habitus introducatur." Despite this proscription, female characters were often portrayed on the Jesuit stage.

[74] *Bibliotheca Belgica,* vol. 6 (Brussels: Culture et Civilisation, 1970), p. 189.

language on the stage. As noted previously,[75] many religious playwrights such as Ziegler and Naogeorgus were unperturbed by the ethical distinctions between classical and Christian theater, for both forms were believed to possess a useful, albeit different, moral lesson for the contemporary audiences. Their conclusions had in turn been based on the humanists' reading of Donatus' commentary that drama, like the deliberative oration of Cicero and Quintilian, imparted its moral argument through the juxtaposition of its positive and negative aspects. This rhetorical structure was also fundamental to the moral lessons which could profitably be derived from Holy Scripture. Several parables of Jesus, the Prodigal Son, the Good Samaritan, the wise and foolish virgins, Lazarus and the rich man—all popular subjects on the humanist stage—provided contrastive examples for Christian behavior. Through the juxtaposition of good and evil on the stage, humanist religious dramatists could thus both satisfy the prescriptions of Donatus and retain the biblical mode of instruction.

The moral utility of immorality was initially used as a justification for pagan characters in religious drama by the tenth-century Saxon nun, Hrotsvitha of Gandersheim. Hrotsvitha was the first Christian imitator of Terence and her works were published as a nationalistic gesture by Conrad Celtes in 1501.[76] She possessed only an elementary understanding of Terentian theater, and in contrast to ancient practice, she composed her plays in prose. Despite her limited knowledge, Hrotsvitha admired Terence's elegant syle—she freely admitted her fondness for pagan writers in general—but was offended by his plots in which lascivious rather than virtuous women had been portrayed. To amend the immorality of Terence she derived her arguments from contemporary legends and hagiography. Four of her dramas, *Dulcitius, Calimachus, Sapientia* and, to a lesser degree, *Gallicanus* displayed the triumph of chaste women over their lustful admirers. In *Dulcitus* and *Sapientia,* the refusal of Christian women to submit to pagan advances resulted in their martyrdom; in *Calimachus* the vision of the deceased virgin, Drusiana, reformed the enraptured Calimachus whose unrequited passion for her had induced him to desecrate her grave. In *Gallicanus*, the princess Constantia effected the conversion of her smitten admirer, Gallicanus, and thereby preserved her chastity. In contrast, *Abraham* and *Pafnutius* depicted the atonement of two fallen women ("meretrices") through the intercession of the hermits Abraham and Pafnutius who, having

---

[75] See above, pp. 28-9.
[76] Conradus Celtes, *Opera Hrosvite illustris virginis et monialis Germane gente Saxonica orte nuper a Conrade Celte inventa* (n.p., 1501).

disguised themselves as lovers, were able to visit the women and persuade them to repent.

As is immediately evident from this brief overview, Hrotsvitha had been obliged to keep the "turpia lascivarum incesta feminarum" she had originally criticized to bring about her moral reform of Terence.[77] She herself was embarrassingly aware of her retention of Terentian language and claimed that her characterizations of the immoral figures had made her blush. But at the same time, Hrotsvitha argued that the moral utility of her dramas as well as her literary intention to imbue Terence with sacred material would have been severely impaired had she dispensed with the offensive characters:

> Sed (si) haec erubescendo neglegerem, nec proposito satisfacerem nec innocentium laudem adeo plene iuxta meum posse exponerem, quia, quanto blanditiae amentium ad illiciendum promptiores, tanto et superni adiutoris gloria sublimior et triumphantium victoria probatur gloriosior, praesertim cum feminea fragilitas vinceret et virilis robur confusioni subiaceret.[78]

Through her retention of Terentian courtesans and lovers, Hrotsvitha hoped that readers who like herself had delighted in the Roman's graceful language ("facundia sermonis")[79] would also be able to derive both aesthetic pleasure and moral instruction from her works. Having enjoyed the ravings of the lovesick Calimachus and the foolishness of the lustful Dulcitius, the readers would be reminded of the immorality of such sentiments through the contrastive characterization of the Christian heroine. Hrotsvitha's rhetorical juxtaposition of Christian and pagan figures thus mirrored her own critical reception of Terentian comedy.

In contrast to later writers like Crocus and Schoepper who defended the purity of their plays despite their pagan characterizations, Hrotsvitha had openly admitted her introduction of immoral Terentian figures. She was eager in fact to direct the reader's attention to the moralistic opposition between Terentian and Christian heroes and thereby avoid any possible censure. Hrotsvitha's frank discussion of the utility of immoral characters and language adumbrated later Renaissance views on the ideal imitation of the ancients. Whereas the patristic boundaries between christianized poetry and paganized Christianity varied considerably for many sixteenth-century writers—even Luther had deemed Sedulius "Christianissimus poeta"[80] despite the bombastic flourishes of his

---

[77] Hrotsvitha von Gandersheim, *Opera,* ed. Helene Homeyer (Paderborn: Ferdinand Schöningh, 1970), p. 233.

[78] Hrotsvitha, pp. 233-4.

[79] Hrotsvitha, p. 233.

[80] Curtius, p. 462, n. 44.

religious lyric—Hrotsvitha's self-consciousness about her writing, its few offensive characters and her distinctively Christian stance toward paganism suggested where the balance between moral and aesthetic concerns might lie. Many religious dramatists proclaimned the sanctity of their works over the immorality of their classical models. But in light of their silence about their retention of pagan characterizations and language, their remarks may have arisen more from classical and humanist secular drama than from a systematic program of reform. Like the humanist apologists for classical theater, sixteenth-century playwrights justified their admiration for the ancients with a moral argument whose validity was undermined by the texts themselves. The dramatists' own uncertainty about their works further implied their possible disinterest in literary crusades. Ziegler's opinions, for example, varied according to his audience: he favored sacred dramas over secular plays in the preface to his *Ophiletes* (1549), but a few years later in his *Regales nuptiae* (1553) and *Abel iustus* (1559) he defended the utility of all types of theater.[81] The Ulm school dramatist Martin Balticus (ca. 1532-1600), a former student of Melanchthon, also extolled the virtues of sacred drama over pagan literature to justify his *Adelphopolae sive Josephus* (1556) but, within the same discursive preface, he strongly advocated the study of ancient theater.[82] In many dedicatory prefaces and verse prologues, the boundaries between Christian and pagan drama were too strictly drawn by playwrights like Crocus and Schoepper to provide an accurate description of the complex relationship between humanist religious drama and its model. As Hrotsvitha had anticipated, a writer's self-consciousness about the propriety of his ambiguous tie to the ancients would subsequently become the foundation for the sixteenth-century moral and aesthetic reform of the pagan drama.

During the sixteenth century, a Christian humanist's awareness of the historical and philosophical differences between his work and his classical model (and the extent to which he portrayed this distinction in his text) became the standard by which a decorous imitation of the ancients could be determined. Humanists such as Melanchthon and Erasmus who were equally concerned about literary and theological matters were especially desirous that the imitation of the classical writer in no way interfer with the imitator's religious beliefs. Consequently, they developed the notion

---

[81] H. Ziegler, *Ophiletes* (1549; Basel: Ioan. Oporinus, 1551), pp. 48-50; H. Ziegler, *Regales nuptiae* (Augsburg: Philippus Ulhardus, 1553), sig. A 2: H. Ziegler, *Abel*, sig. A 3-A 3ᵛ.

[82] Martin Balticus, *Adelphopolae sive Josephus* (1556; Ulm: Ioan. Anton. Ulhardus, 1579), sig. A 3ᵛ-A 5.

of historical decorum in order to establish a limit to the contemporary writer's imitation of his model.

In Erasmus' *Ciceronianus* (1528) and Melanchthon's *Elementorum rhetorices libri duo* (1531), historical decorum was understood as a Christian writer's awareness of the distinction between the modern era and antiquity. In reaction to the excessive imitations of Cicero by Italian and French humanists, Erasmus and Melanchthon argued that such a practice was not only stylistically reprehensible (after Quintilian *Inst. orat.* 10.2.7) but also religiously unsound. Slavish imitators of Cicero, such as the fictional character of Nosoponus, the butt of Erasmus' satire in *Ciceronianus*, were so obsessed with the stylistic perfection of their model— Nosoponus even had pictures of Cicero hanging throughout his house— that they avoided the use of any word which had not appeared in the Roman's writings. This habit was not only deemed unimaginative but also perilous for a Christian orator dealing with religious subjects. An unrestrained adherence to Cicero in a Christian speech could endanger the faith of a believer in two ways. First, through the omission of any religious terms, the Christian subject would effectively be paganized; as an example, Erasmus referred to the avid Ciceronian Fedra Inghirami whose use of pagan vocabulary in his 1509 Good Friday sermon had transformed Christ from the Redeemer into a classical self-sacrificial hero.[83] Secondly, the description of religious concepts such as faith ("fides") and church ("ecclesia") in exclusively classical terms could well confuse rather than enlighten a Christian listener. Melanchthon, who himself disapproved of the usage of any words which had not appeared in Cicero and Quintilian, made an exception for religious subjects by promoting orthodoxy and clarity as the Christian orator's stylistic ideal.[84] For Erasmus and Melanchthon, the inventive, selective manner in which Vergil had imitated Homer, or Cicero had followed Demosthenes, was no longer merely the mark of an inspired poet or orator, but an absolute necessity. Christian writers were thus not only advised, but also obliged to imitate the ancients with caution lest they misrepresent or, even worse, distract their audiences from religious truth.

In the *Ciceronianus*, however, Erasmus expanded the concept of historical decorum beyond the stylistic level and used it as a basis for establishing a competitive relationship between a contemporary writer

---

[83] Des. Erasmus, *Dialogus cui titulus Ciceronianus sive de optimo dicendi genere,* in *Erasmus von Rotterdam Ausgewählte Schriften,* vol. 7, ed. Werner Welzig (Darmstadt: Wissenschaftliche Buchgesellschaft, 1972), pp. 138-44.

[84] *CR*, XIII, cols. 462; 497. See also Karl Hartfelder, *Philipp Melanchthon als Praeceptor Germaniae,* Monumenta Germaniae Paedagogica, 7 (Berlin, 1889), pp. 343-8.

and his model. In contrast to Melanchthon, Erasmus had not been content to provide a list of proscriptive rules for humanist imitators. He had
not only argued persuasively for a congruity between the sixteenth century and a contemporary author's style, but he had also stated that if
Cicero were alive in the present era he would doubtlessly write as a
Christian.[85] Such an assumption safely settled the controversy about
using pagan epithets for God instead of the usual biblical terms—a problem which later vexed many religious dramatists—by implying that a
sixteenth-century Cicero would in fact be a Christian. But this resolution
went even a step further: by transferring Cicero into a sixteenth-century
context, Erasmus believed that contemporary imitators who tempered
their Ciceronianism with Christianity could in fact equal if not surpass
him.

Erasmus' remarks on historical decorum were thus closely related to
his concept of competitive imitation with the ancients. Because of the
philosophical differences between paganism and Christianity, Erasmus
regarded classical concepts of imitation (''imitatio'') as both dangerous
and indecorous. Building on Quintilian's discussion of imitation (*Inst.
orat.* 10.2), Erasmus distinguished sharply between the classical *imitatio*
tradition and his own concept of historical competition. Like Quintilian,
Erasmus scorned slavish imitators and, invoking the famous simile of
Seneca (*Epistolae morales* 84), he suggested that an inspired author
carefully selected and transformed (or digested) the style of his model so
that his new product appeared to have originated from his own mind.
Erasmus went even further: he introduced the idea of competitive imitation (''aemulatio'') in which the author underscored the distinctiveness
of his own text and, most importantly, demonstrated its superiority to the
model.[86]

The concept of competitive imitation had not originated with
Erasmus; Quintilian for example had concluded his section on imitation
in the *Institutiones oratoriae* (10.2.27-8) with praise for writers who at least
attempted to equal their model. But Erasmus' arguments for the
superiority of the Renaissance text were not so much based on stylistic
as on religious reasons. By directing the reader's attention to the gap
between the ancient and modern worlds, the contemporary writer could
outstrip the pagan model because of the religious superiority of Christianity to paganism. In this way Erasmus implied that piety rather than

---

[85] Erasmus, *Ciceronianus*, p. 346.
[86] Erasmus, *Ciceronianus*, pp. 346; 348. For an excellent overview of the distinctions
between *imitatio* and *aemulatio* in the Renaissance, see G. W. Pigman, III, ''Versions of
Imitation in the Renaissance,'' *RQ*, 33 (1980), 1-32.

*elegantia* sufficed to raise a contemporary work above any Graeco-Roman achievement. Indeed, recalling his earlier argument in *Antibarbari,* Erasmus reiterated his belief that the goal of acquiring antique learning was ultimately religious: "Huc discuntur disciplinae, huc philosophia, huc eloquentia, ut Christum intelligamus, ut Christi gloriam celebremus. Hic est totius eruditionis et eloquentiae scopus."[87] The function of all humanist Christian literature, therefore, was not merely the author's skillful and learned imitation of antiquity, but rather the demonstration, preferably within the text itself, of the superiority of Christianity to the pagan model.

To humanist religious dramatists, wrestling on the one hand with critics of any religious literature and on the other with exacting adherents to classical style and form, Erasmus' concept of historical decorum provided them with a convenient and versatile defense of their praxis. By referring to Erasmus' principle, the playwrights could justify both stylistic and poetological deviations from humanist dramatic theory (i.e., Donatus) as well as conservative charges about the sacrilegious combination of literature and religion. Erasmus' ideas on classical imitation did in fact reappear in several dedicatory letters and verse prologues between 1525 and 1560, the most intense period of humanist dramatic composition, as the main apologetic argument for religious theater.

The applicability of historical decorum to moral, religious and aesthetic aspects of sacred drama was best illustrated by Joannes Sapidus' introductory remarks to his *Lazarus redivivus* (1538; printed in 1539). As a schoolteacher and later rector in Selestat, Sapidus had maintained close ties to the leading representatives of humanism in Alsace and southwest Germany, Jacob Wimpheling, Joannes Sturm and Erasmus, whom Sapidus had met during the latter's first sojourn in Basel (1514-1516). Sapidus greatly admired the Dutchman's writings—Erasmus had dedicated the first edition (1520) of *Antibarbari* to him—and he incorporated the idea of historical decorum into his defense of sacred drama in the verse prologue to his only play.

*Lazarus redivivus* had been presented in 1538 to celebrate the opening of the new humanist gymnasium in Strasbourg under the rectorship of Joannes Sturm and was published the following year. The play itself also inaugurated a new type of school drama, humanist religious theater, in Protestant Strasbourg, whose three former humanist schools had hitherto exclusively presented Plautus and Terence. For this reason Sapidus felt obliged to defend the novelty of his work from conservatives skeptical of his literary treatment of the Bible, as well as the admirers of secular

---

[87] Erasmus, *Ciceronianus,* pp. 352; 354.

theater who deemed religious dramas too serious. In the former instance, Sapidus purposely overlooked the conservatives' charges of sacrilege and hoped to appease them by underlining the sanctity of his plot. To the promoters of secular theater, however, Sapidus, echoing Erasmus' accusations of the Ciceronians, sternly warned that he intended to christianize ("christianizare") rather than paganize ("ethnicissare") classical drama.[88] Any deviations from the Donatian rules of comedy which these literary scholars might perceive could thus be justified on the basis of historical decorum; Sapidus implied that, given the distance between the Christian and pagan eras, changes would be inevitable:

> At nos nec potuimus, nec voluimus sequi
> Artem atque morem, quem tenuit antiquitas.
> Nam aetate nostra, prisco ab isto tempore,
> Rerum alia facies, ordo et institutio,
> Alius modus vitae, alius est cultus Dei,
> Alia hominum communicatio invicèm,
> Non publicè solum, sed et domesticè:
> Undè et alia ratione scribendi est opus.[89]

Having established the necessity of change, Sapidus was further able to defend his use of a biblical-historical plot in comedy which, after Donatus, had hitherto been dominated by fictional events. Conversely, he used the same argument to respond to possible criticism from conservative critics about his amplification of the sparse biblical plot into a five-act play through the invention of fictional episodes. Referring to Horace's favorable remarks on verisimilar events in a poetic work (*Ars poetica* 338), Sapidus asserted that the verity of the new Christian drama had in no way been impaired through his fictional verisimilar additions.[90] In the new Christian literature, all fiction had been subordinated to truth or discarded in order to underscore the superiority of piety to aesthetic concerns. Historical decorum thus provided Sapidus with a religious rather than a literary standard for the composition of his work and thereby excused any alterations of classical praxis and, at the same time, any charges of secularization.

The use of historical decorum as a justification for the transformation of the classical tradition, or to some dramatists, for the purported originality of their plays, appeared in the works of several other writers, especially Netherlandic playwrights between 1525 and 1560. The first

---

[88] Joannes Sapidus, *Anabion sive Lazarus redivivus. Comoedia nova et sacra* (1539; Cologne: Ioan. Gymnicus, 1541), sig. A 5ᵛ.

[89] Sapidus, sig. A 7.

[90] Sapidus, sig. A 6.

published humanist religious dramatist, Gulielmus Gnapheus, whose
*Acolastus,* a Prodigal Son play, appeared the year after (1529) *Ciceronianus,*
had been inspired to compose his work by the absence of any contemporary Christian humanist playwrights. In the age of the Christian
Cicero and Livy, it seemed only just that dramatists catch up with the
achievements in the other humanist disciplines:

> Laudata est comoedia Tullio ut humanae vitae speculum, celebrata est doc-
> torum virorum calculis sed indigne, si ipsa indigne sit, quam multi conen-
> tur vel imitari vel ad vivum exprimere. Habet haec aetas nostra suos
> Tullios et Livios, habet suos Vergilios et Demosthenes, ut Solones, Hip-
> pocrates et Chrysostomos taceam; Menandros et Terentios nullos habet.[91]

Having distinguished himself from antiquity, Gnapheus then excused his
indecorous mixture of tragic and comic styles in the play. After the entertaining misadventures of the prodigal son Acolastus at the hands of
whores and thieves—the stuff of Roman comedy—the speeches of the
title hero sharply assumed an ominous tone, more akin to the lamentations in classical tragedy, as the protagonist bemoaned the consequences
of his wasteful life. Notably, Gnapheus was not content to uphold the
propriety of the tragic-comic style with a reference to Horace's favorable
assessment of such practice (*Ars poetica* 94-98); rather, in keeping with
Erasmus' views on Christian literature, Gnapheus maintained the
significance of piety over style: "Malui enim pietatis respectui quam lit-
teraturae decoro alicubi servire."[92]

The piety of contemporary Christian writing was similarly used by the
Liège humanist Gregorius Holonius (1531-1594) to defend the stylistic
deficiencies in his 1556 tragedy, *Lambertias,* on the martyrdom of St.
Lambert (ca. seventh century). In the dedicatory preface to that work,
Holonius introduced Erasmus' notion of historical decorum to explicate
his omissions of pagan epithets for the Christian God—a major point in
the *Ciceronianus*—and, in a curious reversal of Gnapheus' tragic-comic
argument, to justify the low social class of his tragic hero.[93] Holonius
knew from his study of Seneca, whose style he imitated in all his dramas,
that his model had presented a domestic subject in his tragedy *Octavia*
rather than the customary downfall of kings. Holonius likewise founded

---

[91] Gulielmus Gnapheus, *Acolastus (1529),* ed. P. Minderaa, Zwolse Drucken en Herdrucken, 15 (Zwolle: W. E. J. Tjeenk Willink, 1956), p. 48.

[92] Gnapheus, p. 50.

[93] Gregorius Holonius, *Lambertias. Tragoedia de oppressione B. Lamberti* (Antwerp: Ioan.
Bellerus, 1556), sig. Av$^v$-Avi. Cf. Erasmus, *Ciceronianus,* p. 164. On Holonius'
tragedies, see J. A. Parente, Jr., "Counter-Reformation Polemic and Senecan Tragedy:
The Dramas of Gregorius Holonius (1531?-1594)," *HumLov,* 30 (1981), 156-80.

his *Lambertias* plot on a domestic rather than a political issue—namely, Pippin of Herstal's destructive relationship to the courtesan Alpais—but he suggested this formal change not so much by citing *Octavia* but by historical decorum. Regal and political plots may have been suited for the general public for whom classical drama was written; for a schoolboy audience, however, simple, moralistic domestic dramas were sufficient.[94] Since the lessons of pagan subjects were no longer valid, Holonius concluded, a new religious theater was consequently needed to instill the uniquely Christian virtues of reverence, piety and charity.

In the hands of Sapidus, Gnapheus and Holonius, historical decorum thus proved to be a useful device for defending their transformation of classical dramatic praxis. But in the works of the last two writers, the distinctions between the Christian and pagan eras were not merely confined to apologetic prefaces; following Erasmus' dictum of competitive imitation with the ancients, the plays themselves actually represented the superiority of Christianity to the ancient world.

The triumph of Christianity over paganism, of virtue over evil and of God over the devil had been the basic structure implicit in all humanist religious drama. For humanist playwrights eager to outstrip the ancients, however, this opposition provided a rare opportunity to expose the flaws of the pagan world and by extension of the classical model itself. Joseph's rejection of the advances of the classical "meretrix," Potiphar's wife, represented a Christian victory over pagan values. But this confrontation, already predetermined by the biblical source, was primarily based on moral rather than historical or literary distinctions. In contrast, in *Acolastus,* Gnapheus illustrated his historical concept of a new Christian age, as outlined in his preface, within the play itself by juxtaposing figures from the pagan and Christian worlds.

Because of the brief account of the prodigal son parable in the Bible (Luke 15:11-32), Gnapheus was obliged to devise many fictional characters and episodes to expand the limited material into a five-act comedy. To this end he added a counselor, Eubulus, for the troubled father of the prodigal, Pelargus, as well as a devilish adviser with the revealing name Philautia (Self-love) to seduce the protagonist, Acolastus, from his home. As a contrast to the virtuous figures, Gnapheus introduced two pairs of characters from Roman comedy: the parasites Pamphagus and Pantolobus and the innkeeper-pimp Sannio and his prostitute Lais. In this way Gnapheus not only imbued the work with an artistic unity by constructing his plot around the conflicts between the four character groups,

---

[94] Holonius, sig. Avii.

but he also distinguished the world of Roman comedy from his new religious theater.[95]

In the middle acts of his play, Gnapheus re-created the atmosphere of Roman comedy by depicting the parasites' schemes to unburden the foolish prodigal of his money by showering him with inflated praise. As the glutton Gnatho deceived the conceited Thraso in Terence's *Eunuchus*, Pantolabus and Pamphagus convinced Acolastus of his unlimited appeal and romantic prowess. Having noted his great wealth as well as his naiveté, they attached themselves to his service so as to benefit from his propensity for luxury. Similarly, just as Gnatho misled his master Thraso into thinking that the courtesan Thais actually adored him, so did Gnapheus' parasites convince Acolastus of the undying love of the courtesan Lais. In both plays the lusty ambitions of the egotistical Thraso and Acolastus blinded them to the women's schemes, and they were rejected once the parasites and ''meretrices'' had secured their goals. At this point, however, Gnapheus made a significant alteration in the Terentian denouement. Instead of allowing the misguided lover to lead an unreformed existence, he portrayed Acolastus' gradual discovery of the falsity of the world. The prodigal's perception of his former foolishness and the immorality of his former companions paralleled Gnapheus' aesthetic transformation of Terentian theater. As Erasmus had advised in the *Ciceronianus*, through the retention of classical characters and language, Gnapheus directed the viewer's attention to his model only to expose its inferiority in the light of Christianity. Having subordinated the classical inheritance to his religious ideals, Gnapheus was thus able to create a new type of drama which accorded with the ethics of the contemporary Christian era.

Gregorius Holonius likewise criticized his model, Seneca, in his 1556 tragedy *Catharina* on the martyrdom of St. Catherine of Alexandria. As in the hagiographical plays of Hrotsvitha, a pagan's love for a Christian virgin provided a good occasion for the juxtaposition of chastity to lust. Such a configuration reappeared in *Catharina* where the audacious heroine refused both to honor the pagan gods and to accept the marriage proposal of the tyrannical Roman emperor Maxentius. But Holonius' selection of St. Catherine, a learned Christian scholar, as topic for his tragedy enabled him to use her as a mouthpiece for his own literary critique of his model. Though he admired Seneca's style, Holonius objected

---

[95] For a thorough study of the parallel characterizations, see the introduction of W. E. D. Atkinson to his edition: Gulielmus Gnapheus, *Acolastus,* ed. and trans. W. E. D. Atkinson (London, Ontario: Humanities Departments of the University of Western Ontario, 1963), pp. 8-20. The following parallels to the *Eunuchus* are indebted to his remarks, pp. 33-4.

strongly to the fictionality of his terrifying tragic plots (*Thyestes, Medea, Hercules furens*) in which such violent emotions were aroused; he consequently was eager to replace the immoral mythological tales of Seneca with a pantheon of historical Christian heroes.[96] Such sentiments were similarly voiced by St. Catherine in her disputation with Alexandrian philosophers about the nature of the pagan gods. Just as Holonius had disapproved of the fictionality of Seneca, so did Catherine rail against the artificiality and sinfulness of the pagan deities:

> Nullum deorum numen esse in fictili,
> Nec magis in auro muscido, quàm stipite
> Dignum supremo qui Deus colitur locum
> .................................................................................
> Turbam deorum et inde vestrorum nego,
> Numinaque ficta mille, tercentum Ioves:
> Patres, sorores, coniuges et pellices,
> Natos, parentes, et procul ab atavis genus,
> Infame stupris unde coelum fluctuet.[97]

In portraying St. Catherine's glorious death and triumphant entrance into heaven, Holonius thus suggested the superiority of his Christian adaptation to the immorality of his model.

Gnapheus, Sapidus and Holonius, then, established Erasmus' ideas on imitation and historical decorum in Christian oratory as a theoretical basis for the composition of religious drama. Although explicit references to the Erasmian tradition in religious drama disappeared after Holonius, his ideas had already been subsumed into the apologetic literature for Christian poetry and continued to influence religious playwrights into the early seventeenth century. By 1550, generic classifications such as "comoedia sacra" (Cornelius Crocus, *Joseph*) or "tragoedia nova et sacra" (Levin Brechtus, *Euripus,* 1549) reminiscent of Erasmus' call for a new style, not only designated a work's sacred content, but almost always implied formal changes as well. Variations of this same Erasmian argument also appeared in prefaces to secular works such as Macropedius' *Rebelles* and *Aluta* (1535), where in a brash paraphrase of Gnapheus' introduction to *Acolastus* (1529), Macropedius proclaimed himself the first Netherlander to adapt a modern subject to the form and language of Roman comedy. Since Macropedius had allegedly written his works around 1510, he had full claim to priority. But Macropedius, fearful that his unacknowledged debt to Erasmus and Gnapheus might

---

[96] Holonius, *Lambertias,* sig. Aiiiv-Aiiii.

[97] Gregorius Holonius, *Catharina. Tragoedia de fortissimo S. Catharinae virginis ... certamine* (Antwerp: Ioan. Bellerus, 1556), sig. Ciiv-Ciii.

be discovered, overlooked the latter and cast himself as the first published humanist dramatist since the 1490s.[98] Erasmus' promotion of a new Christian style thus served not only as an approach to the ancients, but as a means to draw artistic distinctions between contemporaries.

Whereas Erasmus' remarks on historical decorum could be easily assimilated to the patristic fathers' selective imitation of the ancients, his concept of *aemulatio,* emulating and surpassing the ancients, rarely reappeared. This waning of interest in competitive imitation was hardly surprising. In the early years of humanist religious drama (1525-1560), Erasmus' *aemulatio* played a crucial role in attributing an aesthetic value, equal to the ancients, to the new religious texts. Once the religious plays became a familiar practice in the humanist schools, their status as literary works no longer required justification. But in the early seventeenth century, competitive imitation was revived by religious playwrights in order to solve two major problems in the christianization of classical drama: the use of pagan language and characters on the religious stage and the composition of Christian tragedy. In the former instance, German Jesuit school dramatists, troubled by their students' fascination with pagan literature, attempted to set new and more conservative restrictions on the study of classical texts. In the latter case, Netherlandic humanists, eager to conjure up the horror and pessimism of Senecan tragedy, were forced by their choice of religious subject to expose the philosophical flaws of their model.

Among seventeenth-century Jesuit playwrights, the Bavarian writer Jacob Bidermann adopted the most cautious attitude toward the imitation of the ancients. In his first play *Cenodoxus* (written 1602), Bidermann exposed the dangers which beset many humanists through their adherence to pagan values.[99] The learned medieval scholar Cenodoxus,

---

[98] Cf. Gnapheus, p. 48 with Macropedius' introductory remarks: "Miratur quidam (et ipse profecto doleo) inter tot saeculi nostri viros doctissimos nullos Menandros, nullos Terentios reperiri." Later Macropedius acknowledged his debt to the dramas of Joannes Reuchlin [*Scaenica Progymnasmata* (1498) and *Sergius* (1507)] and proclaimed his own originality: "Is [Reuchlin] mihi primus, ut verum fatear, ansam scribendi dedit, is me primus excitavit. Si praeter eum alii ante me scripserint, nescio; hoc scio, quod alios non viderim." In light of his earlier paraphrase of Gnapheus, such claims were clearly untrue. Georgius Macropedius, "*Rebelles*" und "*Aluta,*" ed. Johannes Bolte, Lateinische Litteraturdenkmäler des XV. und XVI. Jahrhunderts, 13 (Berlin, 1897), pp. 3-4.

[99] Max Wehrli, "Bidermann-*Cenodoxus,*" in *Das deutsche Drama,* vol. 1, ed. Benno von Wiese (Düsseldorf: August Bagel, 1958), p. 24; Jacob Bidermann, *Cenodoxus,* ed. and trans. D. G. Dyer, Edinburgh Bilingual Library, 9 (Austin: University of Texas, 1974), p. 13. There is no evidence in the text that the character of Cenodoxus foreshadowed the late-humanist polyhistors of the Baroque (cf. Wehrli, p. 24); rather, Cenodoxus was a parody of Erasmus, whose feigned, ironic humility doubtless troubled the earnest pedagogical sensibilities of Bidermann.

whose revealing name (Κενοδοξία = vain-glory) signified his excessive pride, was portrayed as a contemporary humanist whose confidence about his intelligence and reason had led him to ignore God. The suspicion that the humanist pursuit of *eloquentia* and secular wisdom might distract Christian man from his faith had long troubled many Renaissance scholars such as Ludovicus Vives and Erasmus:[100] But the perilous consequences of an all-too-worldly humanism, namely, eternal damnation, had hitherto never been depicted with such terrifying realism. Bidermann presented Cenodoxus as a parody of the urbane humanist who sought inspiration and comfort in his garden (*locus amoenus*) where he discussed philosophy with his friends. Cenodoxus' apparently sincere works of charity and Stoic forbearance of death had further convinced his followers of his wisdom and sanctity. But this pursuit of learning and virtue was subsequently revealed as vain and hypocritical, for Cenodoxus had not been inspired by piety. In a grisly scene typical of the Jesuits' belief in the pedagogical utility of visual images, the soul of Cenodoxus was dragged into hell as his corpse announced the punishment to the terrified mourners. Through the example of Cenodoxus, humanist ideals were consequently exposed as valueless unless they were directed toward a religious end.

The subordination of the classical inheritance to piety also informed Bidermann's imitation of ancient drama. In *Cenodoxus*, Bidermann, following Gnapheus' practice in *Acolastus,* used comic figures to indicate the weaknesses of his protagonist. In the opening scene, for example, the insatiable hunger of the parasite Mariscus foreshadowed Cenodoxus' constant hunger for praise while Mariscus' gullibility similarly anticipated the protagonist's obstinate blindness to the state of his soul.[101] Bidermann also included such figures in the early scenes as a dramatic equivalent to the *captatio benevolentiae* in order to gain the audience's attention for the earnest lesson which followed. The opening debate between Mariscus and Cenodoxus' servant Darus doubtlessly appealed to Jesuit schoolboys who had studied Plautus and Terence in school. By establishing parallels between the comic figures and Cenodoxus, however, Bidermann subsequently exposed the immorality of these entertaining characters as he warned his viewers to adopt a more cautious attitude toward the ancients.

Bidermann developed his ideas on classical imitation still further in his most explicit critique of antiquity, *Philemon Martyr*. This comedy on the

---

[100] P. N. M. Bot, *Humanisme en onderwijs in Nederland* (Utrecht: Spectrum, 1955), pp. 93-7.

[101] Wehrli, p. 16; Dyer, p. 22.

martyrdom of the converted pagan mime Philemon (performed 1618 in Constance) may have been the most elaborate parody of Roman comedy on the humanist religious stage. In this work, Bidermann did not merely rely on the commonplace juxtaposition of pagan and Christian characters—a structure already inherent in his hagiographical plot—but on the conversion of the pagan hero into a martyr to demonstrate Christianity's superiority to antiquity.

The choice of a converted actor as a martyr immediately suggested an implicit criticism of classical drama. This dissatisfaction was made even more apparent through Bidermann's juxtaposition of the foolishness of Philemon's actions before the conversion and the earnestness with which Philemon the Christian approached his death. In the first act, Philemon displayed the characteristics of three comic characters whose immorality had frequently been criticized by Renaissance religious dramatists: the rogue ("scurra"), the parasite and the imposter. From his first appearance on stage, Philemon lamented his inability to satiate his enormous appetite. Shortly thereafter he and his drinking companions convinced a guileless messenger that he had arrived in the wrong town. In the next scene, Philemon persuaded a neighbor's servant to change clothes with him so he could attend a banquet. In this manner Philemon succeeded not only in gaining access to large quantities of food, but also in cleverly escaping the punishment of the irate messenger when he returned. This first exchange of clothing in fact prefigured the more important disguise Philemon donned in the third act. Instead of scheming for food, Philemon now agreed to impersonate the cowardly Christian leader Apollonius at the public sacrifices to Jupiter. While on his way to this ceremony, however, Philemon was miraculously converted by an angelic chorus. The comic roles which Philemon played earlier were now transferred into a Christian context where they assumed a graver significance. His parasitical hunger was henceforth equated with his spiritual yearning for Christ; the flute ("tibia") used to amuse his friends during his pantomimes was shattered by a lightning bolt, and he renounced all disguises by openly proclaiming his faith in Christ. The entertaining but roguish charades of Philemon the mime were now replaced by the fervent oration of Philemon the Christian attempting to convince the Roman persecutors of their errors. When Philemon's warnings fell on death ears, the former pagan mime became a Christian mime, an *imitator Christi*, whose courageous endurance of Christ-like torments earned him an eternal reward. In light of this ending, the Plautine and Terentian episodes of the early acts now appeared as a foil for Bidermann's later christianization of these same classical motifs. The conversion of Philemon was therefore intended to be an aesthetic reflection of Bidermann's own transformation of Roman comedy into a showplace for Christian ethics.

Bidermann's revision of antique theater was further demonstrated by his choice of topic. There were several ecclesiastical legends about pagan actors at Bidermann's disposal. The most popular version concerned St. Genesius, whose conversion and death were in fact variously portrayed by Lope de Vega, Jean Rotrou, Nicolas-Marc Desfontaines and several anonymous seventeenth-century Jesuit playwrights.[102] Genesius' renown as a theatrical subject was so broad that the dramatization of his conversion was reduced to a few scenes and used to embellish the sparse plots of other plays about early Church martyrs such as the *Vitus* of the English Jesuit Joseph Simons.[103] But Bidermann's work remained an exception, for he alone turned to the history of St. Philemon. Essentially, the legends of both saints resembled each other in every respect save for geographical and historical details. Genesius, a distinguished actor, was executed in Rome at Diocletian's behest; Philemon, a comic mime, died in Egypt at Antinoë under the prefect Arrianus who subsequently converted to Christianity. Bidermann was not, however, solely interested in providing a hagiographical model for his audience; he chose St. Philemon, for he was also eager to illustrate the historical gap between Christianity and paganism.

Although the Philemon material was derived from the usual Renaissance hagiographical sources, especially Laurentius Surius,[104] the similarity between the martyr's name and that of the famous Greek comic dramatist, Philemon, could hardly have escaped the attention of learned viewers. Philemon, along with Menander, had been the leading representative of Greek New Comedy. Fragments of his plays survived, but he was primarily known as the author of *Thesauros* (The Treasure), a drama which Plautus subsequently translated and retitled *Trinummus*. *Trinummus* was much admired by Christian humanists for its overtly moral tone: the opening scene in which the allegorical figures of Luxury

---

[102] Lope de Vega, *Lo fingido verdadero* (ca. 1618); Jean Rotrou, *Le Véritable Saint-Genest* (1647); Nicolas-Marc Desfontaines, *L'Illustre Comédien* (1645). For a discussion of each of these plays in light of the St. Genesius legend, see E. M. Szarota, *Künstler, Grübler und Rebellen. Studien zum europäischen Märtyrerdrama des 17. Jahrhunderts* (Munich and Bern: Francke, 1967), pp. 7-71. On the legend itself, see Bertha von der Lage, *Studien zur Genesiuslegende* (Berlin, 1898-99). A list of Jesuit Genesius plays can be found in Johannes Müller, *Das Jesuitendrama in den Ländern deutscher Zunge vom Anfang (1555) bis zum Hochbarock (1665)*, vol. 2 (Augsburg: Benno Filser, 1930), p. 108.

[103] Joseph Simons, *Vitus sive Christiana fortitudo* in his *Tragoediae quinque* (Liège: Ioan. Mathias Hovius, 1656), pp. 409-16; *S. Quirinus*, ms. Bayerische Staatsbibliothek, clm. 24674, fol. 31 ff. (Act IV. scenes 5 and 6).

[104] Laurentius Surius, *Historiae seu vitae sanctorum iuxta optimam Coloniensem editionem*, vol. 3 (1570-81; Turin, 1879), pp. 204-5.

and Poverty recount the perils of wealth was perfectly compatible with the moralizing tendencies of religious dramatists. Melanchthon and Sturm considered the *Trinummus* one of the few Plautine works suited for Christian youths, and South German Jesuits, in whose schools young Bidermann had been trained, recommended it to their students as entertaining reading during hot summer days.[105] Yet, despite its didacticism, Plautus' comedy dealt with the misadventures of a profligate youth. For this reason alone, Bidermann may have wished to suggest an ethical revision. His criticism was, however, primarily directed elsewhere. Instead of objecting to Plautine immorality, he attacked the method and motivation of the comic intrigue.

The relationship between *Trinummus* and *Philemon Martyr* extended beyond the nominal resemblances between St. Philemon and Philemon the dramatist. The similarity between the central event in both plays—a rogue's impersonation of another character—strengthened Bidermann's disapproval of Plautine plot complications. The title of Plautus' comedy (*Trinummus*, i.e., "tres nummi" or three silver coins) referred to the wages paid a *sycophanta* or rogue for assuming the role of a pivotal character in the drama. The sycophant had been instructed to act as a messenger from Charmides, a wealthy Athenian, who during his temporary absence from home had entrusted his household and children to the care of his friend, Callicles. Charmides' son, Lesbonicus, proceeded to squander the paternal wealth at his disposal and in a short time completely impoverished himself and his sister. When Lesbonicus was compelled by creditors to sell the family house, Callicles secretly arranged to purchase it back and thereby managed to secure the treasure hidden in it for his absent friend. Meanwhile a new problem arose: Charmides' daughter needed a dowry in order to marry her beloved Lysiteles. Instead of causing her unhappiness, Callicles, without anyone's knowledge, removed some of the money from the hidden treasure and hired the sycophant to deliver it to her as a gift from Charmides. The sycophant, however, encountered Charmides, who had just returned from abroad, and the whole innocent plot was revealed. The sycophant was dismissed, Callicles explained how he preserved the hidden treasure from the prodigal Lesbonicus, and the young couple were married.

---

[105] *Trinummus* was one of the five Plautine comedies approved by most sixteenth-century schoolmen (the others were: *Aulularia; Menaechmi; Captivi* and *Miles gloriosus*); they appeared together with the less popular *Amphitruo* in Joannes Sturm's 1566 edition of Plautus for school performance use: Jundt, p. 18. In the 1604 *Ratio studiorum* for Jesuit schools, *Trinummus* and *Captivi* were recommended. See ms. Bayerische Staatsbibliothek, clm. 1550, fol. 53ᵛ; and Fidel Rädle, "Das Jesuitentheater in der Pflicht der Gegenreformation," *Daphnis,* 8 (1979), 178.

The lightheartedness of the Plautine play, so appropriate to its romantic temper, was absent from Bidermann's christianization of the sycophant. Initially Philemon resembled this deceitful and parasitical rogue. He not only devoted most of his time and artistic skill to the acquisition of food and drink, but he also deceived other men, such as the messenger, for his own amusement. The sycophant's greed was likewise shared by Bidermann's hero: only the love of money could induce Philemon to disguise himself as the fearful Christian leader Apollonius. Here Bidermann drew the closest connection to Plautus. Like the sycophant, Philemon was engaged for "tres nummi" (*Trinummus*) to impersonate Apollonius. The crafty Philemon subsequently exacted a promise of four "nummi" instead of three, but later references to the fair and proper wage were sufficient to remind learned spectators of the Plautine parallel.[106] In this manner Bidermann was able to contrast the Plautine imposter with his own protagonist. The Plautine Philemon of the opening acts had, like the sycophant, impersonated a servant in order to satiate his ravenous appetite. As Apollonius, however, Philemon was directed to Christ. Whereas Plautus had employed the sycophant to advance the romantic intrigue and delight his viewers, Bidermann used the same device to effect the conversion of his hero so he could exemplify Christian virtue.

Through the dramatization of the Philemon legend Bidermann offered the most radical criticism of Roman comedy on the humanist stage. He did not merely use the classical figures to embody his objections to the immoral content of classical drama, nor was he content to extol the virtues of his Christian hero over his pagan opposites. In contrast to earlier humanist practice, the pagan character had actually become a Christian. To underscore this transformation, Bidermann altered his style in the course of the play from the pre-conversion colloquial speech of Plautus to the moralistic tone of ecclesiastical and hagiographical Latin. Moreover, in christianizing Plautus, Bidermann resolved the vexing problem of retaining classical language and characters on the religious stage. In the new Christian age, Bidermann intimated, such characters were no longer required; a new pantheon of Christian heroes, like Philemon, would be formed to instill schoolboys with the requisite virtue for salvation. In converting a Plautine character into a martyr, Bidermann in effect implied the valuelessness of classical literature. Where earlier religious dramatists had followed Erasmus in subordinating the study of

---

[106] Jacob Bidermann, *Philemon Martyr*, ed. Max Wehrli (Cologne: Jakob Hegner), p. 164.

the ancients to piety, Bidermann suggested that obedience and piety alone sufficed to guide Christian man to his Creator.

According to Bidermann's concept of *aemulatio* in *Philemon Martyr*, the imitation of the ancients was a vain pursuit which Christian writers could safely avoid. During the same period (1600-1620) in Netherlandic humanist circles, however, a competitive imitation with classical drama was encouraged in order to create a Christian tragic style. For the most part, sixteenth-century humanist playwrights had confined their critical remarks about the ancients to Roman comedy. Since Donatus had emphasized the pedagogical value of comedy, it was not surprising that most humanists favored this dramatic form. As we have seen, tragedy could be similarly adopted for didactic purposes: Senecan commentators such as Melanchthon and Georg Fabricius had noted the utility of his warnings about the dangers of political ambition; and Gregorius Holonius had likewise adopted the Senecan style to exhort his schoolboys to imitate the fortitude of his martyr heroes.[107]

But sixteenth-century Senecan commentators did not solely emphasize the moral value of the tragedian; they also praised the "gravitas" and "sublimitas" of his magniloquent style. As students of Quintilian, moreover, they were well aware of the grand emotions (πάθος) which such language aroused. Antonio Minturno, an early Cinquecento theorist, explicated this effect further by attributing the three functions of the Ciceronian orator to the tragedian: to delight, to teach and to move ("delectare, docere, movere"); he especially emphasized the last reaction and defined it as the arousal of terror or pity to accord with his recent study of Aristotle.[108] As a reader of Minturno and other Cinquecento commentators on Aristotle, such as Franciscus Robortellus and Vincentius Madius, Julius Caesar Scaliger shared their belief in the emotional effect of tragedy and joined Aristotle's "φόβος" to the reactions traditionally ascribed to Seneca's dramas by his editors. For Scaliger, tragedy was formally defined as "oratio gravis, culta, a vulgi dictione aversa, tota facies anxia, metus, minae, exilia, mortes."[109] Notably, Scaliger discarded Aristotle's idea of catharsis and focused exclusively on the pathetic effect of tragic texts with their bloody and terrifying plots; his favorite dramatist, Seneca, excelled in the representation of such

---

[107] Koch, pp. 79-80 (Melanchthon's prologue to *Thyestes*); Georg Fabricius as quoted in George, pp. 71-2; Gregorius Holonius, *Laurentias. Tragoedia de martyrio constantissimi Levitae D. Laurentii* (Antwerp: Ioan. Bellerus, 1556), sig. Aii-Aii$^{v}$.

[108] Antonio Sebastiano Minturno, *De poeta (1559),* ed. Bernhard Fabian (Munich: Fink, 1970), p. 179.

[109] Julius Caesar Scaliger, *Poetics libri septem,* ed. August Buck, Faksimile-Neudruck der Ausgabe von Lyon 1561 (Stuttgart and Bad Cannstatt: Frommann, 1964), p. 11. Cf. *Senecae Tragoediae* (1514), sig. Aa v$^{v}$.

violence.[110] Despite the gradual incorporation of Aristotelian ideas into dramatic theory among a few sixteenth-century scholars—Melanchthon, Joachim Camerarius, J. C. Scaliger—tragedy was still primarily written by Christian humanists in the early seventeenth century in order to evoke the strong emotions (πάθος) prescribed by Senecan commentators.

As long as the humanists adopted Seneca as their tragic model, the dramatization of terrifying and violent subjects remained the leading method to arouse an appropriate response in the audience. This emphasis caused a particular problem for religious dramatists, for the pessimism implicit in Seneca's tragic vision did not correspond to the Christian world view where divine justice and the grace of the Redemption prevailed. The evocation of a lugubrious response to a biblical or hagiographical tragedy might well induce the viewer to doubt rather than to discern the working of divine providence behind the horrible events. To avert this sinful reaction, the Senecan imitators, Hugo Grotius and Daniel Heinsius, adopted Erasmus' concept of *aemulatio* for their religious plays.[111] Whereas the pathos of their tragic language evoked a mournful reaction, their frequent references to the Redemption exposed the folly of this typically Senecan response and saved the reader from despair.

The spiritual dangers implicit in an exceedingly faithful imitation of Senecan tragedy had been exemplified almost a century earlier in the closet play *Theoandrothanatos* (1508) by the Italian humanist, Quintianus Stoa (b. 1484). Since Grotius and Heinsius were both voracious readers, they may well have known this tragedy on Christ's passion. In the preface to his *Christus patiens* (1608), Grotius at least intimated that he had studied all prior humanist dramas on Christ so that he could avoid their errors.[112] Stoa, who spent his poetic career at the French court of Louis XII, had dedicated himself to the difficult task of representing various

---

[110] Scaliger, p. 12; on Seneca, Scaliger commented: "Seneca ... quem nullo Graecorum maiestate inferiorem existimo: culto verò ac nitore etiam Euripide maiorem." Scaliger, p. 323. For a brief overview of Scaliger on tragedy, see Eduard Brinkschulte, *Julius Caesar Scaligers kunsttheoretische Anschauungen und deren Hauptquellen* (Bonn: Peter Hanstein, 1914), pp. 61-73.

[111] Grotius wrote three tragedies on sacred subjects: *Adamus exul* (1601); *Christus patiens* (1608); and *Sophompaneas* (1635). Heinsius composed only one religious play: *Herodes infanticida* (written 1611; published 1632).

[112] "Argumentum hoc, religionis non dubie caput, iam olim Gregorius Nazianzenus in morem Tragoediae digerere ausus similes aliorum conatus a morosis iudiciis exempli sui auctoritate absolvit: post quem Latino sermone alii idem aggressi sunt, ita tamen plerique ut post se venturis eandem materiam accuratius tractandi spem non praeciderent. Ad eorum numerum nos postremi accessimus ...." Hugo Grotius, *Christus patiens* in *De dichtwerken van Hugo Grotius. Oorspronkelijke dichtwerken,* Tweede deel, Pars 5A & B, ed. B. L. Meulenbroek (Assen: Van Gorcum, 1978), p. 59.

stages of Christ's life in separate classical genres. For his interpretation of the Passion, Stoa chose Senecan drama as his model. The Roman tragedian was a natural choice for Stoa, for the humanist later argued in his *Epographia* (1511) in language reminiscent of contemporary Senecan commentaries that tragedy consisted solely of violent, mournful action.[113] Stoa consequently conceived of a five-act tragedy on Christ's death in which the bloody tortures of the hero were vividly described. Although Stoa's emphasis on Christ's Stoic forbearance of his persecution was eminently suited to the divine tragic hero, his establishment of the same dispassionate fortitude as a moral ideal undermined the work's religious significance. This shortcoming was especially apparent in Stoa's characterization of the blessed Virgin. As was customary, the Virgin was overwhelmed by an uncontrollable grief because of Jesus' death. Stoa intended that Mary exemplify the instability of human existence:

> Ante sint nostros oculos querelae
> Virginis divae: horribilesque luctus:
> Ut recordemur tumidum quot horis
> Ponere fastum.[114]

But instead of consoling the Virgin, Magdalene and the apostle John resorted to Stoic exhortations:

> Magdalene:   Quidquid superno trinitas semel polo
> Statuit: necesse est fiat: exitii genus
> Crudele magnum competit primum scelus[115]

> Joannes:    Est nulla firma temporis felicitas:
> Quandoque rebus se malum immiscet bonis[116]

Grotius and Heinsius hoped to avoid the excesses of Stoa's paganization of a Christian topic by following Erasmus' counsel and directing their readers' attention to the philosophical differences between a Christian and pagan response to religious tragedy. Confident of the superiority of their faith, both men held that sorrow was merely a temporary state of mind which would ultimately be alleviated by Christ's promise of justice and salvation. In incorporating these ideas into their plays, they adhered to the imitative practice of Gregorius Nazianzenus to whom the

---

[113] "Tragoedia est heroicae conditionis in adverso statu comprehensio; cujus subjectum et materia sunt dolores, lachrymae, odium, caedes, venena, incendia, amaritudines, aerumnae, cordolia, singultus, suspiria ...," as quoted in Raymond Lebègue, *La Tragédie religieuse en France. Les débuts (1514-1573)* (Paris: Honoré Champion, 1929), p. 137. Cf. Danielis Gaietanus' definition of tragedy printed in the 1514 Badius edition of Seneca: "tragici poematis subiectum et materia dolor: lachrymae, odium: insanae caedes, propterea iambica rabie fervescit carmen tragicum," *Senecae Tragoediae*, sig. Aa v.

[114] Quintianus Stoa, *Theoandrothanatos* in his *Christiana opera* (Paris, n.d.), fol. 37.

[115] Stoa, fol. 13.

[116] Stoa, fol. 14.

Byzantine drama ΧΡΙΣΤΟΣ ΠΑΣΧΩΝ (first printed 1542; Latin translation by Franciscus Fabricius of Roermond, 1550) had been ascribed.[117] This tragedy was in fact an unusual mix of classical language and Christian content. It was for the most part a Euripidean cento in which the lamentations of the Virgin and other mourners at the foot of the cross were recorded. But the anonymous dramatist was no slavish transcriber of Euripides; rather, he arranged the quotations from his model so as to expose the vanity and error of Euripidean sentiments in light of Christian truth. Whenever the Virgin indulged in the excessive grief of a Phaedra (*Hippolytus*) or in Medea's unquenchable desire for vengeance, she was quickly reprimanded by the dying Christ or by St. John (called here "the theologian") for her temporary distrust in God's justice:

Christus:    Te vero adhortor hinc odisse neminem,
                Ne istos quidem, qui jure nullo me necant.[118]

Theologus:   Regina, tandem siste planctum et lachrymas
                Volens enim mortem subivit ac lubens
                Ut hoste prostrato qui cuncta devorat,
                Rex victor et vindex et autor omnium
                Redeat triumphans. Ipse nam mystis suis
                Die reversurum se ad auras tertia
                Praedixit, allaturum et illis gaudium.[119]

Admittedly, since the Greek play was a cento, there were many passages which the writer could adapt without undermining the virtue of his protagonist. But in contrast to Stoa, the Byzantine author exploited every stylistic opportunity to incite the appropriate Christian reponse to the Passion.

In his first tragedy, *Adamus exul* (1601), Hugo Grotius similarly uncovered the philosophical flaws of his model Seneca by contrasting the Roman's pessimistic tragic style with the Christian world view. The Fall of man had been a common topic on the humanist school stage: Hieronymus Ziegler adapted the scenes on the Creation and the Fall from medieval passion plays to the language of Terentian comedy in his *Protoplastus* (1542), and Macropedius began his episodic play on the Old Testament, *Adamus* (1556), with the lamentations of Adam and Eve as they were banished from Paradise. But where Ziegler and Macropedius

---

[117] On the Byzantine drama, see J. A. Parente, Jr., "The Development of Religious Tragedy: The Humanist Reception of the *Christos Paschon* in the Renaissance," *SCJ*, 16 (1985), 351-68.

[118] Franciscus Fabricius, trans. *Divi Gregorii Nazianzeni theologi, tragoedia Christus patiens* (Antwerp: Ioan. Steelsius, 1550), fol. 21ᵛ.

[119] Fabricius, fol. 23ᵛ.

had strictly adhered to the biblical sequence of events, Grotius cast the fateful encounter between the serpent and man in the form of Senecan drama and thereby criticized the Roman's concept of tragedy.

Grotius' revision of Seneca was based on his juxtaposition of the fatalism of his model with Christian optimism. As a student of Seneca, Grotius well knew that the violent and horrible outcomes of the tragedies were precipitated by the characters' inability or unwillingness to control their passions ("furor"). Hercules destroyed his wife and children because of his madness (*Hercules furens*); Medea was driven to kill her children by jealousy; Hippolytus was dismembered because of a misunderstanding arising from the unrequited lust of his stepmother Phaedra, and Atreus slaughtered Thyestes' children to avenge the wrongs of their father against him. In *Adamus exul* Grotius focused on the dangers of three passions in particular, vengeance, lust and jealousy in order to provide a Christian response to Seneca. In the course of the play he demonstrated that the tragedy which these emotions provoked could be converted into comedy by the grace of God. Where Seneca, with the exception of *Hercules Oetaeus,* had portrayed the inescapable cycle of crime and retribution, Grotius avoided this pessimistic pagan view by referring to God's just liberation of all good men from evil.

To establish this Christian victory over paganism, Grotius attributed Senecan characteristics to the three main characters, Satan, Adam and Eve. Grotius' temptor bore only a faint resemblance to his devilish counterparts on the late medieval and humanist stage; rather, Satan was depicted here as a bloodthirsty Senecan avenger. Jealous of man's earthly paradise as he had earlier envied God's rule in heaven, Satan vowed to avenge the loss of his angelic status by inducing man to sin. Envy had traditionally been regarded as the primary motive for Satan's temptation of man, and it often recurred in medieval and Renaissance accounts of the Fall. But Grotius' Satan was clearly intended as a Senecan figure. He not only opened the play in Senecan fashion with a soliloquy from the depths of hell and the summoning of the Furies, but he also used Stoic arguments from Seneca's moral essays to induce Eve to sin. Like the Neo-Stoic scholar, Justus Lipsius, whose influential treatise *De constantia* had appeared in 1584, Grotius had been disturbed by incongruities between the Stoic philosophy of Seneca and Christianity.[120] Accordingly, he voiced his criticisms of the Stoics by attributing their ideas to the devil. In his seduction of Eve, Satan echoed Seneca's belief in the flawlessness

---

[120] For a brief overview of the Neo-Stoic movement in the late sixteenth century in the North, see the afterword to Justus Lipsius, *De constantia. Von der Bestendigheit,* ed. Leonard Forster (Stuttgart: Metzler, 1965), pp. 19*-31*.

of human reason, the insignificance of death and man's ability, if not his right, to disentangle himself from the workings of Fate and Providence. All three points had been particularly troublesome for Christian readers since they suggested man's independence from God. But Grotius immediately exposed the folly of Satan's remarks in his portrait of Eve. Instead of being moved by the devil's praise of man's rationality, Eve ultimately ate the forbidden fruit because its appearance delighted her senses. Despite Seneca's claims about man's rationality, Grotius implied that man's senses and passions could not be checked by reason but only by God.

The destructiveness of man's emotions and his consequent need for God were further evidenced by Grotius' portrait of Adam. Having been endowed with wisdom and eternal happiness, Adam freely worshipped his Creator and sought to please him through his obedience. Adam did, however, betray a weakness, a yearning for human companionship, and his excessive delight with Eve's presence would ultimately lead to his own downfall. Adam's passionate nature had in fact already misled him into believing his imperviousness to Satan's temptations—he had repulsed the Temptor's first attempt to seduce him (Act III)—and this same brashness subsequently blinded him to the consequences of sin. Eve, jealous of Adam's close relationship to God, forced him to choose between their marriage and their Creator by demanding that he taste the fruit. Since Adam's fascination with Eve precluded his renunciation of their union, he succumbed to his lust and acceded to her request. As in Senecan tragedy, the unfortunate Fall of man was brought about by vengeance, jealousy and lust. But in contrast to the Senecan denouement, Grotius, paraphrasing Genesis 3:15, alleviated the sorrow with God's promise of a Redeemer:

> IPSE veniet, ipse carnem sumet humanam Deus,
> Non viro genitus, sed uno feminino ex semine,
> Virginali natus alvo, generis humani Salus,
> Qui Triumphator superbum conteret tibi verticem,
> Et feri victor veneni tempus utrunque opprimet.[121]

In christianizing Seneca, Grotius had thus preserved Erasmus' concept of *aemulatio* as competition between the ancient and modern world by demonstrating the superiority of Christianity to paganism.

The aesthetic competition between pagan model and an original Christian text remained the foundation of a religious playwright's imitation of

---

[121] Hugo Grotius, *Sacra in quibus Adamus exul (1601)*, in *De dichtwerken van Hugo Grotius. Oorspronkelijke dichtwerken*, Eerste deel, A en B, ed. B. L. Meulenbroek (Assen: Van Gorcum 1970-1971), p. 175.

the ancients in many seventeenth-century works. As long as dramatists continued to measure the success of their imitations in terms of their moral and hence their aesthetic superiority to the ancients, Christian writers continued to use the religious stage to criticize and parody Graeco-Roman theater. The fact that their disapproval of their model's immorality was often coupled with an aesthetic admiration for its structure and language was frequently overlooked in their eagerness to equate moral improvements with an aesthetic victory. In Grotius' *Christus patiens* (1608), Daniel Heinsius' *Herodes infanticida* (written 1611 and published 1632) and Joost van den Vondel's *Hierusalem verwoest* (1620), the christianization of Seneca continued through the juxtaposition of the glorious Christian era of grace and Redemption to the hopelessness of the antique world. The Virgin Mary overcame her grief in Grotius' tragedy through her vision of the resurrection; respite from the tyranny of Heinsius' Herod was afforded by the birth of the Redeemer in Bethlehem,[122] and in Vondel's early play, the witnesses of the destruction of Jerusalem were consoled by angelic reminders of Christ's mercy and justice. Occasionally a Senecan imitator such as Jacob Cornelius Lummenaeus à Marca would give vent to his enthusiasm for the violence of his model and, as in *Amnon* (1617) on Amnon's rape of Thamar (2 Samuel 13), select a biblical topic for its similarities to Seneca. But, for the most part, the humanist writers of biblical tragedy maintained a decorous distance from their classical model as befitted their sacred content. Rochus Honerdus, a close friend of Grotius and Heinsius, for example, composed his tragedy on the rape of Thamar (*Thamara,* 1611) not to revel in Amnon's lust, but to analyze the sorrow of his father, King David, for his unwitting complicity in the affair.[123]

This competitive imitation with the ancients, however, was soon discarded in favor of a new aesthetic ideal: Aristotle's *Poetics.* The uneasy equation of the aesthetic value of Christian drama to its moral content, though never resolved, was gradually replaced by a poetic system free

---

[122] Heinsius had been sharply criticized by the French literary scholar, Jean-Louis Guez de Balzac, for his mixture of Christian and pagan (e.g., the Furies) elements in his play. He replied in his *Epistola, qua dissertationi D. Balsaci ad Heroden infanticidam respondetur* (written 1635; published 1636) that Herod was characterized as a victim of the Furies since he represented a decadent pagan world which was now being replaced by Christianity. For an account of this controversy, see Gustave Cohen, *Écrivains Français en Hollande dans le première moitié du XVIIᵉ siècle* (Paris: Édouard Champion, 1920), pp. 275-91, and Zobeidah Youssef, *Polémique et littérature chez Guez de Balzac* (Paris: Nizet, 1972), pp. 117-64.

[123] Instead of portraying the familiar victorious figure of David as the slayer of Goliath or as the psalmist, Honerdus intentionally focused on David and his restless family, "quorum flagitiis et contumelia in poenam illius (Davidem intelligo) usus est Deus." Rochus Honerdus, *Thamara tragoedia* (Leiden: Ioan. Patius, 1611), sig. ∗*ᵛ∗.

from the immorality which had marred so many pagan works in Christian eyes. Instead of acquiring the purpose, structure and language of classical drama from texts whose content was considered offensive, Aristotle provided a set of rules derived from a variety of authors which could then be applied to moral and theological ends. As the biblical dramas of Vondel would shortly demonstrate, with the establishment of Aristotle as a model the moral rivalry between classical and Christian writers ended, and an aesthetic rivalry began in which the tragedy of Christian man was presented in the style of the Greeks.

# CHAPTER TWO

# THEOLOGY AND MORALITY ON THE HUMANIST STAGE

The development of humanist religious drama was closely associated with the religious controversies of the Reformation and Counter-Reformation. As Protestants and Catholics engaged in bitter doctrinal disputes about the historical hegemony of Rome and the nature of salvation, partisan educators familiar with the utility of drama in schools quickly adapted this medium to disseminate their respective religious doctrines and train cadres of youth to defend them. In the hands of sixteenth-century pastors and priests burning with missionary zeal, biblical, hagiographical and even historical dramas were explicitly designed to instill piety and extol the virtues of a specific church.

The main objective of humanist religious drama in the sixteenth-century was the dissemination of moral guidelines for the attainment of salvation. Since Protestant and Catholic schoolmen were engaged in establishing and strengthening their churches, their dramas did not dwell on complex theological topics such as the nature of the Eucharist and the concept of a sacrament, but rather on the more immediate matter of man's relationship to his Creator. The problem of eternal salvation about which Protestants and Catholics so vehemently disagreed was especially emphasized, for this point alone defined man's need for God. Humanist religious dramatists consequently sought to demonstrate a theological and moral point in each of their religious plays: the nature of God's salvation of man and, conversely, the ethical qualities which Christian man had to possess in order to be saved.

In sixteenth-century dramatic praxis, divine salvation was represented in four ways. First, playwrights demonstrated the efficacy of God's justice, for His righteousness was a Christian's surety that the promised salvation would occur. Secondly, religious dramatists interpreted their biblical plays, especially those which dealt with Old Testament topics, according to the medieval typological method in order to impute a soteriological significance to their works. Several dramas, moreover, not only illustrated the act of salvation but also suggested a practical method for its attainment. Finally, most playwrights agreed that a moral education helped a Christian gain eternal life. The dramatists did not always emphasize all of these goals equally in a single work, and, in many cases, the typological interpretation was omitted, but the fundamental soteriological message of every religious play remained.

Catholic and Protestant writers, of course, differed sharply about the bestowal and winning of salvation, but their joint admission of its possibility guaranteed their works a place on all religious stages regardless of the producer's faith. The Protestant Strasbourg academy, for example, presented several dramas by Catholic writers in the late sixteenth century—indeed, some works with a decidedly Counter-Reformation bias[1]—while the otherwise vigilant Jesuits freely allowed Protestant plays in their schools.[2]

Because of the varied audiences for whom their works were intended, religious playwrights presented theological and moral ideas in an elementary fashion so they could be immediately comprehended. Though eminently practical , this adaptation of complex theological concepts about salvation, free will and divine grace to pedagogical ends ultimately reduced these ideas to a set of moral precepts for the edification of the Christian man. The fundamental incongruity between the humanist pedagogue's confidence in man's rational abilities and the theologians' insistence on the significance of God's role in salvation was generally overlooked by the school dramatist. Whereas salvation for both Catholic

---

[1] Obvious Catholic elements appeared in printed versions of two plays performed in late sixteenth-century Strasbourg: Gregorius Holonius' *Laurentias* (printed 1556; performed 1584) and Cornelius Laurimannus' *Esthera* (printed 1563; performed 1596). In the dedicatory letter to the former, Holonius hoped that the example of St. Laurence would serve to inspire Catholic youths to defend the Church: "(ut) ... mundum Christo corrigant, reforment, vendicent," Gregorius Holonius, *Laurentias. Tragoedia de martyrio constantissimi Levitae D. Laurentii* (Antwerp: Ioan. Bellerus, 1556), sig. Aii[v]. Laurimannus, a schoolmaster in Catholic Utrecht in the 1560s, likened Esther to the Virgin Mary ("Deipara Virgo") since both women exemplified modesty and humility: Cornelius Laurimannus, *Esthera regina. Comoedia sacra* (Louvain: Antonius Bergagne, 1562), sig. Avi[v]. Clearly Holonius' hero could just as easily be adapted as a model for future Protestant martyrs; similarly, with a few changes, Esther could be transformed into an ideal Protestant wife. There are no records of any special Strasbourg adaptations of these works. For a brief description of the plays, see Günter Skopnik, *Das Straßburger Schultheater* (Frankfurt a.M.: Selbstverlag des Elsaß-Lothringen Instituts, 1935), pp. 36-8; 57-9.

[2] Consider, for example, the popularity of the *Acolastus* (1529) of Gulielmus Gnapheus who had been forced by the Inquisition to emigrate to Protestant lands from his home in The Hague. *Acolastus* was performed in Vienna in 1560 and in the late 1580s in Munich; the manuscript of the Munich performance supplemented the Gnapheus text with a verse prologue. The success of the *Acolastus* on the Counter-Reformation stage casts doubts on W. E. D. Atkinson's reading of the comedy as a Lutheran statement on salvation *sola fide*: Gulielmus Gnapheus, *Acolastus*, ed. W. E. D. Atkinson (London, Ontario: Humanities Departments of the University of Western Ontario, 1963), pp. 54-60. If Gnapheus did incorporate any Protestant ideas into his play, they were not sufficiently apparent to trouble Catholic readers; their value as polemic was consequently weakened. On *Acolastus* on the Jesuit stage, see Johannes Müller, *Das Jesuitendrama in den Ländern deutscher Zunge vom Anfang (1555) bis zum Hochbarock (1665),* vol. 2 (Augsburg: Benno Filser, 1930), p. 97. The 1587 Munich performance is preserved in ms. Bayerische Staatsbibliothek, clm. 2202, fol. 674 ff.

and Protestant theologians depended on God's merciful granting of grace, the playwright's representation of this mystery frequently suggested that man's adherence to virtue alone would preserve him from evil and earn him an eternal reward. Salvation in sixteenth-century school drama, then, was not so much a theological concept as a moral goal which could be won through man's exemplary conduct.

## The Justice of God

Of all theological ideas, divine justice was the simplest to demonstrate and the most effective means to induce the audience to embrace piety. Religious playwrights essentially derived their concept of justice from the Psalms where God had been praised for his righteous preservation of his faithful from their enemies. Indeed, these writers were especially fond of the psalms not only for their religious message but also for their utility as choral songs in their plays.[3] Following the psalmist, the dramatists adopted a distributive notion of justice according to which men were duly punished or rewarded on the basis of their deeds.[4] This dualistic idea had been apparent in most psalms, especially those in which the singer prayed to God for deliverance (e.g., Psalms 26-28, 37, 63, 73, 76). In these hortatory verses, the psalmist's lamentations about the invincibility of his enemies were eventually stilled by his joyful realization that God would ultimately vanquish his oppressors and honor his perseverance.

This same combination of sorrow and rejoicing was incorporated by religious playwrights into their sacred dramas. In these works, justice was presented either through God's deliverance of his faithful or through his punishment of their oppressors. In the former instance, justice was best revealed through the endangerment of the protagonist and his eventual salvation by God. In Crocus' *Joseph* (1536), for example, the title hero's virtuous rejection of Potiphar's wife and his subsequent imprisonment merely served to create a crisis so that God's final liberation of him from prison would gloriously illustrate His righteousness.[5] Similar pat-

---

[3] Sixt Birck, for example, frequently used psalms in this manner. In his 1537 Latin *Susanna,* the first act ended with Psalm 30, spoken by the heroine, in which she voiced her confidence that God would free her from "omnibus technis, laqueis, dolisque." In his Latin *Judith* (ca. late 1530s), the Jewish citizens of besieged Bethulia called out to God with Psalm 59 so that He might preserve them from misery and tyranny. Sixt Birck, *Sämtliche Dramen,* vol. 2, ed. Manfred Brauneck (Berlin and New York: Walter de Gruyter, 1976), pp. 197; 313.

[4] For the sake of convenience, I follow here Aquinas' definition of Divine Justice: *Summa theologica,* Part I, Question 21. Aquinas in turn borrowed the term "distributive justice" from Aristotle, *Nicomachean Ethics* 5.4 ($1131^b25$-30).

[5] In the final lines, the jailor Gulussa reminded the audience that they could experience the same progression "e paedore ... ad benigniorem sortem" if they continued to adhere to virtue: Cornelius Crocus, *Joseph* (1536; Antwerp: Ioan. Steelsius, 1538), sig. D 7$^v$.

terns reappeared in martyr plays, a favorite genre in this era of religious turmoil, so that audiences might be encouraged to forbear more suffering and thereby gain an eternal reward. In his *Susanna* (1536) Paul Rebhun (1500?-1546), a schoolmaster in Kahla (Thuringia), concluded the third act with an expansion of Psalm 46—the inspiration for Martin Luther's famous hymn "Ein fest' Burg"— to reaffirm the presence of God's justice in a deceitful world.[6]

Additionally, religious dramatists followed the psalmist in his detailed depiction of the enemies of the faithful. The more pernicious the oppressor, the greater God's vengeance would be as He protected his people from persecution. Psalm 58:10-11, which was cited by the Leipzig playwright Balthasar Crusius (ca. 1550-1630) as an epigraph to his *Exodus* (1605) on the destruction of Pharaoh and the flight of the Jews,[7] aptly described the effect dramatists ascribed to their tragic portraits of a tyrant's or sinner's demise:

> The righteous will rejoice when he sees the vengeance;
> he will bathe his feet in the blood of the wicked.
> Men will say, "Surely there is a reward for the righteous;
> surely there is a God who judges on earth."[8]

The benefits to be gained through the witnessing of such violent punishments were especially apprized for their ability to instill the Christian viewer with piety. The Strasbourg dramatist Andreas Saurius (ca. early 1600s), whose *Conflagratio Sodomae* (1607) ended with a spectacular fire storm onstage, believed that the audience would be so terrified by the final tableau that they would immediately be impelled to reform their lives.[9] The Jesuits, ever eager that their Latin plays would impress the largest number of viewers, especially those who had little command of Latin,[10] also favored extensive punishment scenes. Drawing on depictions of hell and devils as they appeared, for example, on the medieval stage and in religious handbooks such as Dionysius Carthusianus' *De*

---

[6] Paul Rebhun, *Dramen,* ed. Hermann Palm, BLVS, 49 (Stuttgart, 1859), pp. 44-5.

[7] Balthasar Crusius, *Exodus. Tragoedia sacra et nova* (Leipzig: Bartholomaeus Voigtus, 1605), sig. A 4ᵛ.

[8] Translation from *The New Oxford Annotated Bible with Apocrypha,* eds. Herbert G. May and Bruce M. Metzger (New York: Oxford, 1977), p. 699. Unless otherwise noted, all subsequent biblical references will be to this edition.

[9] Andreas Saurius, *Conflagratio Sodomae. Drama novum tragicum* (Strasbourg: Conradus Scher, 1607), p. 3.

[10] For this reason, the Jesuits also distributed program sheets to the viewers so that they might better understand the plays. On the Jesuits' concern with the propaganda effect of their works, see E. M. Szarota, "Das Jesuitendrama als Vorläufer der modernen Massenmedien," *Daphnis,* 4 (1975), 129-43.

*quatuor hominis novissimis*,[11] the fathers introduced the "Deus Judex" of the Last Judgement who sternly consigned the sinner to eternal damnation. Such vivid punishments had already been adapted for the humanist stage by the Franciscan Levin Brechtus (ca. 1502-1560) in his 1549 *Euripus* on the subject of a weak man's adherence to Venus—a favorite play of the Jesuits[12]—and was often repeated in Jesuit works such as Jacob Gretser's *Dialogus de Udone episcopo* (1587) on the impiety of Bishop Udo of Magdeburg and with the greatest success in Jacob Bidermann's *Cenodoxus* where, after the Munich performance of 1609, several viewers were alleged to have immediately pledged themselves to the order.[13]

As the psalmist had described, divine justice was thus evidenced through God's deliverance of the faithful from evil or through the condemnation of their oppressors. In many cases both aspects were portrayed in the same work: tyrants lost their sanity or their lives as the victims they persecuted triumphed. Pharaoh drowned while the Jews were saved in Crusius' *Exodus*,[14] and in Jacob Schoepper's *Ectrachelistis* (1546), the guilty Herod went insane after his execution of John the Baptist.[15] Even plays in which the corruption of a sinner was emphasized, dramatists took care to provide a positive alternative to evil. Saurius

---

[11] Dionysius Carthusianus, *De quatuor hominis novissimis, morte videlicet, futuro iudicio, poenis infernis et gaudiis coeli, quibus ... ad meliorem vitam pertrahere conatur omnes, tractatus plane pius ac eruditus* (Cologne, 1532). The significance of this work for Jesuit descriptions of hell was first noted by E. M. Szarota, *Das Jesuitendrama im deutschen Sprachgebiet. Eine Periochen-Edition*, vol. 1 (Munich: Fink, 1979), pp. 118-9.

[12] On the use of *Euripus* in Counter-Reformation polemic, see Jean-Marie Valentin, "Aux origines du théâtre néo-latin de la réforme catholique: l'*Euripus* (1549) de Livinus Brechtus," *HumLov*, 21 (1972), 136-54; Fidel Rädle, "Aus der Frühzeit des Jesuitentheaters," *Daphnis*, 7 (1978), 403-47.

[13] The *Cenodoxus* performance was first described in the preface to the collected dramas: Jacob Bidermann, *Ludi theatrales*, vol. 1, ed. Rolf Tarot, Deutsche Neudrucke: Reihe Barock, 6 (Tübingen: Niemeyer, 1967), sig. †8ᵛ. On the propaganda value to be gained by the Jesuits' invention of this reaction, see Günter Hess, "Spektator-Lector-Actor. Zum Publikum von Jacob Bidermanns *Cenodoxus*," *Internationales Archiv für Sozialgeschichte der deutschen Literatur*, 1 (1976), 30-106.

[14] Crusius, *Exodus*, pp. 38-39. Crusius narrated this event in the epilogue lest his dramatic action exceed the twenty-four hour limit imposed by Julius Caesar Scaliger and other Renaissance commentators on Aristotle's *Poetics*. Crusius was so obsessed by this prescription that he wrote two other plays to demonstrate it: *Tobias* (1605); *Paulus naufragus* (1609). The most visually dramatic drowning of Pharaoh and his armies was depicted in the final scene of the second act of Casparus Brulovius, *Moses sive exitus Israelitarum ex Aegypto. Tragico-comoedia sacra* (Strasbourg: Paul Ledertz, 1621), pp. 76-9. On that occasion, Moses commented on the efficacy of Divine Justice:
Haec sunt futurae signa cladis et ominis.
Pereunt aquis, qui nuper infantes aquis
Misere necarunt, sic sequitur ultor Deus. (Brulovius, p. 78)

[15] Jacob Schoepper, *Ectrachelistis sive decollatus Ioannes* (1546; Cologne: Maternus Cholinus, 1562), sig. F 5ᵛ.

extolled the piety of Lot as he obediently fled from the burning Sodom,[16] and in Wolfhart Spangenberg's *Saul* (1606) the chorus exhorted the viewer to renounce ambition and obey God.[17]

The moral guidance which the viewers could gain through the dramatists' portrayal of divine justice was not, however, the most important lesson to be acquired. Although the playwrights took pains to explicate the ethical utility of their plots, this emphasis often obscured the theological assumption upon which it was based. From a theological perspective, the knowledge of divine justice consoled the Christian audience and reinforced their piety, for its very existence guaranteed them eternal salvation. To underscore this lesson, some religious playwrights suggested parallels between God's preservation of their protagonists and Christ's redemption of man. As God had freed Joseph from prison (Crocus) and acquitted Susanna from the false charges of adultery (Rebhun), so too would Christ redeem the viewer from sin.[18] With the demonstration of divine justice, religious plays established the foundation for the soteriological function of humanist sacred theater.

*Religious Drama and Biblical Exegesis*

The humanist dramatists' emphasis on salvation was evidenced further by their second theological practice, the attribution of biblical exegetical interpretations to their religious plays. Through their presentation of biblical events which, as in the case of Old Testament heroes and New Testament parables, prefigured the Redemption, the dramatists anticipated the salvation of the viewers.

Humanist religious playwrights derived their prefigurative approach to sacred subjects from medieval dramatic praxis. The soteriological intention of their dramas had likewise orginated in late medieval passion and Corpus Christi plays where man's salvation history from the Fall to the Redemption had been narrated. More notably, however, the humanists based a large part of their repertoire on the Old Testament scenes which medieval writers had used in works such as the Eger Corpus Christi Play (MS. ca. 1480), the Künzelsau Corpus Christi Play (MS. 1479) and the Heidelberg Passion Play (MS. 1514), to prefigure events in the New Testament. In these expansive works, which were performed over a three-day period, Old Testament episodes were carefully shown

---

[16] *Teutsche Argumenta oder Inhalt der Tragedien genandt Conflagratio Sodomae* (Strasbourg: Conradus Scher, 1607), sig. ):( 7ᵛ. This German summary was bound with the Latin play in 1607 (see note 9 above).

[17] Wolfhart Spangenberg, *Saul (1606)*, in *Sämtliche Werke*, vol. 2, ed. András Vizkelety (Berlin and New York: Walter de Gruyter, 1975), pp. 334-5.

[18] Crocus, sig. D 7ᵛ. On Rebhun, see the argument below, pp. 80-1.

to have foreshadowed specific occurrences in Jesus' life. Accordingly, Cain and Abel, Abraham and Isaac, Joseph, Moses, David and Goliath and Solomon—all common topics for separate humanist plays—were each connected to specific New Testament events. In the Künzelsau drama, a "rector processionis" served as a commentator for the audience so they might perceive correspondences between Old and New Testament scenes.[19] To the same end, several New Testament episodes were directly preceded by their Old Testament prefiguration in the Heidelberg Passion Play: Judas' betrayal of Christ was thus anticipated by the sale of Joseph, the scourging of Christ by the story of Job and the bearing of the cross by Isaac's carrying of the sacrificial wood for Abraham.[20]

The prefigurative significance of many Old Testament events remained in humanist dramatizations of these subjects. The Schlettstadt playwright Thiebolt Gart (ca. early sixteenth century), for example, followed the practice of the Künzelsau writer in his *Joseph* (1540) by drawing immediate parallels between Joseph's career and the Passion and Resurrection of Jesus. As the "rector processionis" had explicated the prefiguration for the Künzelsau audience, so did Gart introduce St. Peter and Christ to comment on the action.[21] Although typological correspondences were mentioned in other humanist plays, Gart's simultaneous exposition of Old and New Testament events was a rarity. In contrast to medieval playwrights, humanist writers preferred to

---

[19] The "rector processionis," for example, interpreted the encounter between David and Goliath as follows:

Hy merckent, wy konig Davidt vor zeitten
Mit dem risen Goliat must streitten.
Do er jm den sig an gewan
Des ward er ain werder man,
Christus von seinem geslecht ist geborn,
Der versunt vns des vatters zorn.
Ein iglich mensch noch alsüs
Mit dem dewffel streitten muß
der vns dag vnd nacht vichtet an.

Peter K. Liebenow, ed., *Das Künzelsauer Fronleichnamsspiel* (Berlin: Walter de Gruyter, 1969), p. 31.

[20] Gustav Milchsack, ed., *Heidelberger Passionsspiel,* BLVS, 150 (Tübingen, 1880), pp. 127-35; 182-98; 221-5.

[21] Gart presented St. Peter and Christ in the opening scene so the audience would be alerted to the prefigurative significance of the plot. In the later scenes, Christ conversed with the prophets about the meaning of the Old Testament event. For example, after the brothers imprisoned Joseph in the well (I.3), Christ, Jonas (Jonah) and Daniel established the following connections—Joseph in well—Daniel in the lions' den—Jonah in the whale—Christ in the tomb. Thiebolt Gart, *Joseph,* in *Die Schaubühne der Reformation,* vol. 2, ed. Arnold Berger, DLE, Reihe Reformation, 6 (1936; Darmstadt: Wissenschaftliche Buchgesellschaft, 1967), p. 59.

distinguish sharply between their dramatic plots and their theological interpretation of the events. In the *Dialogus de Isaaci immolatione* (1544) of the Louvain humanist Petrus Philicinus, the christological significance of Abraham's sacrifice of Isaac—a familiar prefigurative topic in medieval drama—was explained at length in the epilogue. Drawing on the typological readings of Josephus, Origen, Philo and Chrysostom, Philicinus, who had unimaginatively arranged his plot in strict adherence to the biblical source (Genesis 22:1-19), described Abraham's offering of Isaac as a parallel to God's sacrifice of Jesus.[22] The Dortmund humanist, Jacob Schoepper, who had been trained in Louvain, improved on Philicinus' drama in his *Tentatus Abrahamus* (1552) by elaborating on Abraham's anguished reaction to God's command, but he still restricted the typological commentary to the epilogue.[23]

In other humanist dramas, the typological interpretation of the biblical event was complemented and often complicated by the application of the fourfold method of scriptural exegesis to the play. The introduction of this hermeneutic system, by which a literal, allegorical, tropological (or moral) and anagogical (or mystical) reading was ascribed to a given passage,[24] might at first seem surprising in light of the biting criticism which humanist and Protestant reformers had leveled against it. Erasmus and Melanchthon, for example, had considered such speculative allegorical exegesis of the Scripture especially offensive, for it was not based on a literal, i.e., grammatical understanding of the text.[25] Such unfounded interpretations not only perverted the Bible but also, as Melanchthon argued,[26] exposed Christians to possible censure that their faith was based on the fanciful imaginings of allegorists rather than truth. But this disapproval of the allegorical method arose more from the humanists' desire to separate themselves from the scholastics who practiced it rather than from their own opinions. Both Erasmus and Melan-

---

[22] Petrus Philicinus, *Dialogus de Isaaci immolatione ad puerilem captum accomodatus* (1544; Antwerp: Ioan. Steelsius, 1546), sig. A 3.

[23] Jacob Schoepper, *Tentatus Abrahamus. Actio sacra, comice recens descripta* (1552; Cologne: Petrus Horst, 1564), sig. E-E3.

[24] The fourfold exegetical levels were traditionally defined as follows:
Littera gesta docet, quid credas allegoria,
moralis quid agas, quo tendas anagogia.
as quoted in Winfried Theiss, *Exemplarische Allegorik. Untersuchungen zu einem literaturhistorischen Phänomen bei Hans Sachs* (Munich: Fink, 1968), p. 12, n. 10..

[25] Erasmus, *Ecclesiastes sive concionator evangelicus* in his *Opera omnia*, ed. Jean Le Clerc, vol. 5 (Leiden, 1704), col. 1029, and Melanchthon, *Elementa rhetorices* in *CR*, XIII, col. 469. For a brief survey of Erasmus' opinions on allegory, see Jerry H. Bentley, *Humanists and Holy Writ. New Testament Scholarship in the Renaissance* (Princeton: Princeton University, 1983), pp. 187-91.

[26] *CR*, XIII, col. 469.

chthon held that an allegorical interpretation was acceptable, indeed eminently useful, when it accorded with the literal meaning of the text.[27] After all, both men acknowledged that Scripture itself contained several allegories, such as Christ's parables about salvation as well as his reference to Jonah in the whale (Matthew 12:39-40) as prefigurations of the Redemption.[28] Consequently, Melanchthon and Erasmus encouraged exegetes and preachers to employ allegory in a similar manner to explicate the meaning of the Bible for a general audience. As Erasmus remarked in his rhetorical handbook for Christian orators, *Ecclesiastes sive concionator evangelicus* (1535), although allegory might not be used to prove religious principles such as faith and grace, it could embellish them: "ad excitandum languentes, ad consolandum animo dejectos, ad confirmandum vacillantes, ad oblectandum fastidiosos."[29] Similarly, humanist religious playwrights hoped that their allegorical interpretation of their biblical dramas—which they often described as visual sermons[30]—might amplify the literal meaning of their work, so that its moral and soteriological relevance for the reader might become apparent.

The dramatists' application of the fourfold exegetical method was, however, hampered by the humanists' varied comprehension of the function and importance of the allegorical, tropological and anagogical levels. Erasmus, who advocated an ethical harmony between a Christian man's belief and his actions in the *Enchiridion militis christiani* (1503)[31] and later writings, emphasized the moral lessons which Scripture provided, especially when he could apply them to contemporary clerical and papal abuses.[32] Having noted the patristic fathers' confusion about the distinction between allegorical and anagogical readings in his *Ecclesiastes*,

---

[27] See note 25 above.

[28] Erasmus, *Ecclesiastes,* col. 1045-1048; *CR,* XIII, col. 470.

[29] Erasmus, *Ecclesiastes,* col. 1046.

[30] Several dramatists defended sacred theater by repeating Horace's observation (*Ars poetica* 179) that visual images were pedagogically more effective than lessons conveyed orally. Sixt Birck, for example, noted in the preface to his *Judith* (ca. late 1530s): "sunt huiusmodi actiones, veluti vivae vitae humanae imagines, quae non auditum modo, sed etiam visum, potissimos in homine sensus ita nonnunquam movent, ut nihil aliud aeque," Sixt Birck, *Judith. Drama comicotragicum,* in his *Sämtliche Dramen,* vol. 2, ed. Manfred Brauneck (Berlin and New York: Walter de Gruyter, 1976), p. 277. Similarly, Melchior Neukirch ironically regarded his tedious six-act tragedy on the protomartyr St. Stephen as an attempt to overcome the frequently monotonous effect ("müde und uberdrüssig") of most sermons: Melchior Neukirch, *Stephanus. Ein schöne geistliche Tragedia von dem ersten Merterer* (Magdeburg: Johan Francken, 1592), sig. Aiii.

[31] "Si nivea tunica velatur homo exterior, sint et interioris hominis vestimenta candida sicut nix." Erasmus von Rotterdam, *Enchiridion militis christiani,* in *Ausgewählte Schriften,* ed. Werner Welzig, vol. 1 (Darmstadt: Wissenschaftliche Buchgesellschaft, 1968), p. 232.

[32] Bentley, pp. 187-8.

Erasmus limited his own remarks to the tropological and allegorical levels. The latter he understood alternately in either a typological (i.e., prefigurative) or soteriological (e.g., prodigal son as "symbola" of God's salvation of man) sense.[33] In contrast, Melanchthon rejected fourfold exegesis in his *Elementa rhetorices* (1531) and based his allegorical reading on a grammatical approach to the text. Once the exegete had construed the literal meaning of the passage, he was then advised to construct a logical argument ("ratiocinatio") based on other biblical references to the same ideas in order to gain a complete sense of the original citation.[34] Melanchthon demonstrated this method through an analysis of Genesis 3:15 where, in conjunction with other biblical references, he was able to associate the seed which would ultimately defeat the serpent with Christ.[35]

Despite the disagreement among Catholic and Protestant thinkers about the method and utility of fourfold exegesis, humanist religious playwrights of both faiths did not hesitate to elicit these traditional readings from their works. The dramatists had little difficulty with the historical and tropological levels. Whereas the former established the basis for their plots, the exemplary or, in the case of sinners, reprehensible behavior of the title figure suggested a moral lesson for their plays: Joseph exemplified chastity; Isaac, obedience; the Good Samaritan, charity; and Susanna, constancy; while Saul and Absalom warned against political ambition. The problems began, as they had for Erasmus and Melanchthon, with the allegorical and anagogical readings. The allegorical level had traditionally been applied to the Church, or more appropriately to Christ;[36] for the humanist dramatists, the allegorical sense referred to Christ alone. It was essentially equated with the prefigurative significance of Old Testament events: Martin Balticus (ca. 1532-1601) noted the typological reading of Joseph as the Redeemer of the World ("Salvator Mundi") in his *Adelphopolae* (1556);[37] similarly, in the epilogue to his Prodigal Son drama (1556), Hans Sachs regarded the Father's slaughter of the calf in thanksgiving for his son's return (Luke 15:23) as a prefiguration of the Redemption.[38] Because of its foundation

---

[33] Erasmus, *Ecclesiastes,* col. 1028-1029.

[34] *CR*, XIII, col. 472.

[35] *CR*, XIII, col. 471.

[36] "Tertio loco allegoria sequebatur, quae pertinebat ad Ecclesiam, aut si quis dexterius tractabat ad Christum." *CR*, XIII, col. 467.

[37] Martin Balticus, *Adelphopolae sive Josephus* (1556; Ulm: Ioan. Antonius Ulhardus, 1579), sig. A 6. For a historical account on the "Salvator Mundi" tradition, see Jean Lebeau, *Salvator Mundi: l' "exemple" de Joseph dans le théâtre allemand au XVIe siècle,* vol. 1 (Nieuwkoop: B. de Graaf, 1977), pp. 11-37.

[38] Hans Sachs, *Werke,* ed. Adalbert von Keller, vol. 11, BLVS, 136 (Tübingen, 1878), p. 240.

in medieval dramatic praxis, the allegorical christological interpretations were almost always present in humanist biblical plays, even when the other senses were not made explicit.

The anagogical level which had customarily been used to derive lessons which pertained to heaven and eternal life became the scene of Reformation controversy between Catholic and Protestant dramatists. For both parties, the anagogical reading (or *sensus mysticus*) referred to the Church (*ecclesia*) both in the spiritual sense of the Mystical Body of Christ, and more notably, as the visible Church of Rome or Wittenberg. Martin Balticus, a Lutheran convert forced to leave his teaching post in Munich for Protestant Ulm, regarded the enmity between Joseph and his brothers as a reflection of the contemporary controversy between Catholic and Protestant. Where the brothers signified the fallen members of the true Church—a neutral state which could refer either to corrupt Roman clerics or lax Protestants—Joseph represented the victorious Church of Luther which had recently survived Catholic persecution.[39] In the opposite camp, Cornelius Laurimannus (1520-1573), the school-master at the Hieronymus school in Catholic Utrecht of the turbulent 1560s (the Catholic school became a municipal Protestant school in 1579), likewise attributed an anagogical-ecclesiastical reading to his *Esthera* (1563). In this case, however, Esther was construed as the one true Roman Church which God had created for man's salvation and Ahasuerus, her husband, as Christ who had called man to feast with him at his heavenly table.[40] In contrast to these ecclesiastical readings, the anagogical level could also be used to a soteriological purpose. Basing his interpretation on Christianity alone, Hans Sachs held that dramas such as his *Der Verlorn Sohn* (1556) and *Der Richter Simson* (1556) reflected the salvation which awaited all men through the power of the Redemption.[41]

---

[39] "ecclesia Dei ... adversus peccatum, infernum, et diabolum, à quo etsi variis crucibus et aerumnis affligatur, mirabiliter tamen et praeter hominum opinionem divinitus conservatur, triumphat ...." Balticus, sig. A 6ᵛ.

[40] Laurimannus, p. 45.

[41] Concerning the return of the prodigal, Hans Sachs remarked:
Als denn im Gott entgegen geht,
Mit gnad umbfecht in an der stedt,
Wann Gott wil nicht des sünders todt,
Sonder sich beker und lob Gott
Durch Jesum Christum, seinen son,
Der gnug hat für sein sünd gethon. (Sachs, vol. 11, p. 240)
Similarly, Sachs noted the christological significance of Samson in the epilogue to that tragedy:
Simson ist ein figur Christi,
Welches menschwerdung und geburt
Auch vom engel verkündet wurdt,
Das er auch sein volck solt erlösen

The most noteworthy aspect of these allegorical interpretations, however, was their peripheral relationship to the plays. In most biblical
dramas, the allegorical reading was confined to the prologue and
epilogue and not referred to in the course of the play's action. The writers
themselves were well aware of this separation. In the prologue to his
*Acolastus* (1529), Gnapheus hinted that the Prodigal Son parable might
have a significance beyond the literal:

> Nunc exprimemus ludicra actiuncula
> Cuius sub involucro habes mysterion.[42]

But he withheld the message until the epilogue; the "ludicra fabula" was
kept distinct from the "mysterion." Macropedius also suggested that his
Prodigal Son drama *Asotus* (printed 1537) contained a hidden allegorical
lesson, but having noted the parallel between the father's forgiveness of
the prodigal and God's remission of sins, the drama reverted to an entertaining play about the misadventures of a profligate but ultimately contrite youth.[43] The most glaring disharmony between the literal and
allegorical levels was contained in Petrus Papeus' *Samarites* (1539) on the
Good Samaritan parable (Luke 10:30-37). The first four acts were
devoted exclusively to the activities of the victim Aegio who, having been
attacked by thieves, was attended by the Samaritan in the final act.
Papeus had actually borrowed his characterization of Aegio from
Gnapheus' *Acolastus,* and the parasites and whores who deceived
Gnapheus' hero reappeared as the robbers who deprived Aegio of his
clothing and wealth. In the epilogue to his drama, however, Papeus, a
school rector from Menen (Flanders), offered a decidedly Catholic

---

Von sunden und von allem bösen,

..........................................

Darfür verkündet uns zu letz
Christus, der himelisch Simson,
Das tröstlich evangelion,
Hönig-süß, dem sünder wolgschmach.
Hans Sachs, *Werke,* ed. Adalbert von Keller, vol. 10, BLVS, 131 (Tübingen, 1876), p.
212.
[42] Gulielmus Gnapheus, *Acolastus (1529),* ed. P. Minderaa (Zwolle: W. E. J. Tjeenk
Willink, 1956), p. 58.
[43] Georgius Macropedius, *Asotus* in *Omnes Georgii Macropedii fabulae comicae* (Utrecht:
Harmannus Borculous, 1552), sig. A 3ᵛ. In light of Macropedius' competitive relation-
ship to Gnapheus and his *Acolastus* (see chapter 1, note 98), one wonders whether the
spiritual *mysterium* was added to the *Asotus,* regardless of its separation from the play, so
that Macropedius might challenge the popularity of Gnapheus' work. In any event,
Macropedius seemed more intent on adapting scenes from Plautus's *Mostellaria* and *Cap-
tivi* to a moral end than on offering any religious message. On the connection between
*Asotus* and Plautus, see Franz Spengler, *Der verlorene Sohn im Drama des 16. Jahrhunderts*
(Innsbruck, 1888), pp. 37-50 and, more recently, Thomas W. Best, *Macropedius* (New
York: Twayne, 1972), pp. 40-41.

reading of the parable which had in no way been anticipated by the preceding events. The Samaritan was not only equated with Christ—the allegorical reading suggested by Jesus himself (Luke 10:37)—whose charity and self-sacrifice saved man from sin, but also with the Church. The Samaritan's entrustment of Aegio to the care of the innkeeper was thus interpreted by Papeus as Christ's transmission of his Church to the rule of St. Peter and his successors.[44] In this way, Papeus doubtless hoped to provide a Catholic replique to Gnapheus' *Acolastus,* whose characterizations he had so unabashedly copied, so that his biblical drama would not merely serve to mirror the act of salvation but also to justify and glorify the power of the Church.

Although the reasons for the playwrights' sharp separation between the "fabula" and the "mysterion" were nowhere explicitly stated, some conclusions about this custom may be drawn. Humanist writers eager to revivify the characters and language of the ancients for a moral end may have felt that the inclusion of the allegorical interpretation would interfere with their careful imitation of the ancients. Obvious typological juxtapositions such as those in medieval drama, though present in a few plays such as Gart's *Joseph,* were part of the medieval dramatic inheritance which ambitious humanists wanted to avoid or at least disguise (e.g., characterizing medieval devils as pagan gods),[45] so that its historical roots would be obscured. Secondly, with the humanist emphasis on moral education, the tropological sense of the plot assumed the greatest significance. In the Prodigal Son plays of Gnapheus and Macropedius, the dramatists went to great lengths to insure that the school audience would immediately perceive the ethical importance of the events. In the former, the pious Eubulus counseled the prodigal's troubled father about the joy of forgiveness while the prodigal himself reflected on the vanity of the world and the consequent need for vigilance.[46] The chorus in Macropedius' *Asotus* similarly warned the

---

[44] Petrus Papeus, *Samarites. Comoedia de Samaritano evangelico* (Antwerp: G. Montanus, 1539), sig. B 7-B 7ᵛ.

[45] In Chilianus Eques' comedy on St. Dorothea, for example, the figures of Pluto and Alecto emerged from hell in order to incite the hatred of the pagan prefect, Fabricius, for the Christian virgin: *Chiliani Equitis ... Comoedia gloriosae parthenices et martyris Dorotheae agoniam passionemque depingens* (Leipzig: Wolfgang Monacen, 1507), sig. Bᵛ.

[46] Atkinson proposed the intriguing argument that the friendschip between Eubulus and the father, Pelargus, mirrored the relationship between Luther and Erasmus; as Luther had upbraided Erasmus for his weak theology in *De libero arbitrio,* so did Eubulus counsel Pelargus about the truth. Atkinson, pp. 54-60. But the obscurity of the connection between Gnapheus' characters and these two major figures weakened Atkinson's point; moreover, the gentleness which he ascribed to Eubulus (p. 54) in no way resembled the irascible tone of Luther's *De servo arbitrio.* Rather, I should like to suggest that Gnapheus may have well had Erasmus' sermon *De magnitudine misericordiarum Domini* in mind when he created the conflict between Eubulus-Pelargus and Pelargus-Acolastus.

viewers about the deceitful world as they praised the unceasing and merciful love of a parent for its offspring.[47] When the soteriological lesson of the allegory was appended to the play, the dramatists were then able to suggest that the audience's adherence to their moral precepts would ultimately lead to eternal life. In the humanist drama of the sixteenth century, allegory served the fundamental purpose of reminding the audience of the presence of salvation which they then implied could best be attained through upright moral behavior. In contrast, as we shall see, when the ability of fallen man to attain moral perfection was doubted in the seventeenth century, the allegorical inheritance remained and, in Gryphius' historical tragedies, consoled the viewers with the promise of redemption.

## Catholic and Protestant Paradigms of Salvation

Given the humanists' emphasis on man's moral preparations for accepting the grace of the Redemption, it is not surprising that Protestant and Catholic writers were eager to incorporate their respective theological views about salvation into their plays. Doctrinal differences between Catholics and Protestants had, in fact, first inspired the composition of humanist biblical drama. Burkard Waldis (1490-1556), a Franciscan monk who converted to Lutheranism after being disgusted by the decadence of Rome in the early 1520s, conceived of his 1527 Low German drama *De parabell vam verlorn Szohn* as a Protestant response to the Catholic emphasis on the significance of good works for salvation.[48] Waldis, like most polemical writers, reduced the complex relationship between God's grace, charitable acts and man's free will, which Catholic theologians such as Aquinas and, more recently, Erasmus had designed,[49] to a simple moral conflict between good and evil. As a former

---

As Erasmus stated at the outset of that work, the purpose of his sermon was to expose the foolishness of despair (Eubulus' advice to Pelargus, Act III, scene 3) and the immense mercy of God (Pelargus-Acolastus): "sed tamen hic sermo non solum eo conducit, ut declaremus quantum malum sit, desperatio veniae, verum etiam quam immensa sit Dei misericordia." In Erasmus, *Opera omnia*, vol. 5, col. 559.

[47] Macropedius, *Asotus*, sig. B 2-B 2ᵛ; Cᵛ.

[48] Waldis not only provided a reformed theology but also a reformed dramatic style. Despite his division of the plot into only two acts, he wrote in the humanist tradition with an eye to reforming the secular theater of the ancients and his contemporaries (e.g., Shrovetide plays). Classical characters reappeared in the figure of "Huren werdt" and "Spitzbove" whose resemblances to Gnapheus' whores and parasites suggested a common source. On the social context and structure of Waldis' play, see Barbara Könneker, *Die deutsche Literatur der Reformationszeit. Kommentar zu einer Epoche* (Munich: Winkler, 1975), pp. 157-65.

[49] Aquinas, *Summa theologica*, Part I, Questions 109-114. Erasmus discussed theology in a less systematic fashion since, as he claimed in *De libero arbitrio,* "sunt quaedam, quae

monk, Waldis was most sensitive to the social consequences of Church teachings on the importance of indulgences and almsgiving. Such views had merely resulted in complacent clerics who, like Waldis' inventive characterization of the prodigal's older brother, were unable to comprehend the true nature of a just and merciful God. Angered by his father's loving reception of the prodigal, the older son adhered to his belief in the efficacy of good works and, with a touch of personal irony for Waldis, joined a strict monastic order which specialized in such deeds, possibly even the Franciscans.[50]

Such overt criticism of the Roman Church was most likely welcomed by the newly reformed populace in Waldis' native Riga. But many Protestant writers shunned the use of the Bible for polemical drama and created their own plots to satirize their opponents. Thomas Naogeorgus savagely exposed the decadence of the Papacy in his account of Church history under the corrupt vicar Pammachius (*Pammachius,* 1538) and Martin Rinckhart in *Der eislebisch christliche Ritter* (1613) praised Luther's triumphs over Catholicism and other Protestant sects in his historical drama of the Reformation.[51] Similarly, on the Catholic side, only a few dramatists constructed parallels between the Reformation and biblical events: the Counter-Reformation polemicist, Andreas Fabricius (ca. 1520-1581) likened the Lutheran schism to the revolt of Jeroboam against the house of David (*Jeroboam rebellans,* 1585, based on 1 Kings

---

Deus omnino voluit nobis esse ignota." Erasmus, *Ausgewählte Schriften,* vol. 4, p. 12. Erasmus did, however, attempt later to clarify the complex relationship between free will and grace (section IIa 9-13) in the same work:*Ausgewählte Schriften,* vol. 4, pp. 48-58.

[50] Disgusted with the celebrations for his returned brother, the older son remarked:

Antonius, Franciscus, Dominicus,
De hebbens nicht all gedaen umb sust;
Hadden se nicht gades willn gewüst,
Des ungelückes hadde ße nicht gelüst.
...................................................
Ick will myn vader dar tho bringhenn,
Mit geystlick leven ohn doen dwinghenn,
Will he my anders nicht unrecht doen,
Moet he my geven den himmel tho lohn.
Den hardesten orden ick weet up erdenn.
Dar ynn will ick eyn broder werdenn.

Burkard Waldis, *De parabell vam verlorn Szohn,* in *Die Schaubühne im Dienste der Reformation,* DLE, Reihe Reformation, 5, vol. 1 (1936; rpt. Darmstadt: Wissenschaftliche Buchgesellschaft, 1967), pp. 191-2.

[51] In his dedicatory letter to the Mansfeld nobility, Rinckhart expressly attacked the theatrical practices of the Jesuits, especially those "Teufelsgetichte" in which Luther was condemned: Martin Rinckhart, *Der eislebische christliche Ritter,* ed. Carl Müller, Neudrucke deutscher Litteraturwerke des XVI. und XVII. Jahrhunderts, 53 & 54 (Halle: Max Niemeyer, 1883), p. 9.

12-14);[52] and in his *Redemptio nostra* (1579) the Brussels (Anderlecht) schoolmaster, Jacob Vivarius, compared the Jews who failed to heed Christ's teachings to the Protestants who refused to acknowledge the legitimacy of Rome.[53] Instead of serving partisan ends, biblical topics were generally adapted by writers of both churches to impart the general Christian message of salvation and to exhort their audiences to maintain their faith. Both Catholic and Protestant playwrights, in fact, enjoyed the dramatic works of their confessional opponents. The anthologies of biblical plays printed in Basel by the commercially minded houses of Nicolaus Brylinger (1541) and Joannes Oporinus (1547)[54] included texts by authors of both religions. Similarly, Gulielmus Gnapheus' play *Acolastus* enjoyed equal success in Protestant (e.g., Zurich, 1535; Georg Binder) and Catholic (Vienna, 1545; Wolfgang Schmeltzl) schools despite the fact that as a Protestant reformer he was forced by the Catholic Inquisition to flee his home in The Hague for the safety of Protestant Elbing.[55] The Jesuits were especially fond of Gnapheus' drama and presented it several times as part of their Counter-Reformation program.[56] Three popular Protestant topics, Susanna, Judith and Tobias, were also common themes for Catholic writers. The first humanist Susanna play had been composed in 1532 by Joannes Placentius, the chronicler of the bishopric of Liège,[57] and the Jesuits produced several plays on each of these figures through the mid-eighteenth century.[58] To be sure, Protestant and Catholic writers stressed different moral aspects of the same topic—Susanna was a model Protestant mother and wife for Paul Rebhun and a symbol of chastity for Placentius—but the theological message, viz., God's preservation of his faithful and the consolation of salvation, appealed to both Christian parties.

Overt polemical distinctions between Catholic and Protestant dramatists were thus primarily confined to moral issues (the utility of

---

[52] The Counter-Reformation tendency of the work was already apparent on the title page where, having mentioned Jeroboam, Fabricius added: "successus et miserandos fructus earum defectionum et Schismatum, quae nostris temporibus in Religione emerserunt." Andreas Fabricius, *Jeroboam rebellans. Tragoedia* (Ingolstadt: Wolfgang Eder, 1585), sig. *1.

[53] Jacob Vivarius, *Redemptio nostra. Comoedia nova* (Antwerp: Antonius Tilenius Brechtanus, 1579), sig. A 3v; A 4v.

[54] On Joannes Oporinus' daring publications which even included the first Latin edition of the Koran (1542), see: Hans R. Guggisberg, *Basel in the Sixteenth Century* (St Louis: Center for Reformation Research, 1982), pp. 43-5.

[55] For an account of Gnapheus as a victim of religious persecution, see Hendrik Roodhuyzen, *Het leven van Gulielmus Gnapheus* (Amsterdam, 1858).

[56] See note 2 above.

[57] On Placentius see Hugo Holstein, "Zur Litteratur des lateinischen Schauspiels des 16. Jahrhunderts," *ZDP,* 23 (1891), 436-51.

[58] Müller, pp. 115; 126; 127.

charitable works) or, more often, to matters concerning the legitimacy of their respective institutions whether Rome or Wittenberg. There were, however, implicit theological presuppositions in their preferences for certain religious topics which in turn influenced the characterizations of their biblical and hagiographical heroes. To demonstrate this point, let us first consider the motives which underlay Luther's preference for the three Apocryphal figures Susanna, Tobias, and Judith, who subsequently dominated the sixteenth-century stage. In this regard, it is important to remember that Luther himself did not openly speak in favor of dramas on these subjects.[59] Rather, Saxon playwrights, like Joachim Greff and Paul Rebhun, eager to justify their new plays, gave the impression that Luther supported their efforts by citing the Reformer's 1533 comparison of Judith to tragedy and Tobias to comedy.[60] Luther's suggestion that Judith and Tobias had previously been dramatic subjects was sufficient to inspire Protestant schoolmasters searching for pious subjects to restore the prose Apocryphal narratives to their original form.

Luther's attraction to these plots cannot be reduced to a single reason. Literary, moral and, more importantly, theological aspects of the three stories contributed to his favorable opinion. In the first instance, the probable fictionality of the three tales (''ein geticht'') as well as of the Apocryphal book of Bel and the Dragon, was welcomed as evidence of a sacred Jewish literature, which, so Luther believed, antedated the literature of the Greeks.[61] The historical priority of Jewish poetry was especially important for Christian writers such as Luther the hymnist, for it justified their own literary activities. Secondly, Luther was clearly impressed by the piety which such figures displayed, especially in times of adversity. The courageous Judith preserved the Jewish nation from tyranny; Susanna's virtuous rebuke of her lustful admirers exemplified marital fidelity and constancy, and the elder Tobias' forbearance of his accidental blindness and the unshakable resistance of his kinswoman Sara to the curse of the demon Asmodeus (Tobias 3:10-15) instilled the

---

[59] Luther's pronouncements on drama were generally confined to a defense of Terence and to the prohibition of Passion Plays. For Luther's opinions on drama, see: Hugo Holstein, *Die Reformation im Spiegelbilde der dramatischen Literatur des sechzehnten Jahrhunderts,* Schriften des Vereins für Reformationsgeschichte, 14-15 (Halle, 1886), pp. 18-25; Thomas I. Bacon, *Martin Luther and the Drama* (Amsterdam: Rodopi, 1976), pp. 42-77; and Wolfgang Michael, ''Luther and Religious Drama,'' *Daphnis,* 7 (1978), 365-7.

[60] In Luther's ''Vorrede auffs Buch Tobie.'' Rebhun justified his composition of ''ein geistlich spiel'' in his dedicatory letter to Steffanus Reich of Kahla for his *Susanna* (1535): ''So ist auch one das solcher spiel nutz vor mir/von andern/und sonderlich von D. Martin Luther/in der vorrede Judit und Tobie zum mehrern theil angezeigt ...'' as quoted in Paul Rebhun, *Susanna,* ed. Hans-Gert Roloff (Stuttgart: Reclam, 1967), p. 7.

[61] See the discussion above, p. 26.

reader with fortitude.[62] From a theological perspective, however, Luther probably admired these Apocryphal characters because God's preservation of them from death exemplified the Reformer's concept of salvation *sola fide* and the triumph of the Gospel of Christ over the Law of Moses.

Luther had written on several occasions about the distinction between Law (i.e., Old Testament Jewish law) and Gospel (i.e., New Testament), especially in his commentary on St. Paul's epistle to the Galatians.[63] His description of active and passive righteousness in that work can, in fact, shed some light on his preference for these Apocryphal heroes. In his commentary, Luther contrasted the behavior of a man who abided solely by the Law with the attitude of a Christian enlightened by the Gospel. The former was continually troubled by his conscience and consequently fearful of incurring God's wrath for the sins he had committed and of dying before he had the opportunity to amend his life.[64] For this reason, he sought comfort in strict adherence to the Law by acting righteously. Luther argued, however, that if man were governed by his conscience, he would become overconfident in his ability to alleviate his anguish and attempt to attain salvation through works

---

[62] Sara's constancy in such adversity was apparent in her prayer: "Why should I live? But if it not be pleasing to thee to take my life, command that respect be shown to me and pity taken upon me, and that I hear reproach no more" (Tobias 3:15).

[63] Despite the philological problems of dealing with the commentary on Galatians as a Lutheran text—the commentary was based on the lecture notes of the Reformer's students—no other single work so aptly summarized Luther's teachings on faith, salvation and justification. In the following discussion, Law is most often used to denote Old Testament Jewish (or Mosaic) law (including the Decalogue). On Luther's tripartite concept of law as (1) the law of nature; (2) the Law of Moses; and (3) the law which Christ reveals, see B. A. Gerrish, *Grace and Reason. A study of the Theology of Luther* (Oxford: Clarendon Press, 1962), pp. 107-13. On the application of Luther's concept of Law and Gospel to other Protestant plays (Gnapheus, *Acolastus*; Sapidus, *Lazarus redivivus* and Gart, *Joseph*) see Jean Lebeau, "De la comédie des humanistes à la divine comédie: aux origines du théâtre biblique Luthérien," in *L'Humanisme allemand*, eds. Joël Lefebvre and Jean-Claude Margolin (Paris: Vrin, 1979), pp. 477-91. Of Lebeau's three examples only Sapidus' drama clearly represented the contrast between the skeptical Pharisees (Law) and the Gospel of Christ. As noted above (n. 2 and n. 46), *Acolastus* cannot be regarded as an explicit Protestant polemic. Lebeau's suggestion that the allegorical-christological significance of Gart's drama represented the triumph of the Gospel could easily have been ascribed to a Catholic play as well; Gart's model had in part been the *Joseph* of the devout Catholic polemicist Cornelius Crocus, who was also well aware of the customary christological reading of the story. Distinctions between Law and Gospel alone are not sufficient to determine a definite Protestant influence; rather, as we shall see, the contrast between the active and passive righteousness of the protagonist is a more effective point of comparison between Catholic and Protestant praxis.

[64] "Sed eiusmodi est humana imbecillitas et miseria, quod in pavoribus conscientiae et in periculo mortis nihil aliud spectamus quam nostra opera, nostram dignitatem et legem. Quae cum ostendit nobis peccatum nostrum, legem dei quae est longe infra iusticiam christianam. Nobis hoc malum affixum in tentatione, ut nihil spectemus quam hoc: Ach, were ich nur from." *WA*, vol. 40, part 1, pp. 41-2.

alone.[65] He therefore urged Christians to recognize the limitations of this active righteousness and to acknowledge that his spiritual fate depended on his passive reception of God's grace.[66]

The three Apocryphal figures exemplified this victory of the Gospel over the Law, and their conduct served to exhort the Protestant reader to make the transition from active to passive righteousness. Luther's ideas on Law and salvation were evident in two ways: the inability of the Law alone to preserve man from evil, and the success of those men who submit passively to God's will. In the book of Judith, the Jewish leaders, having learned of Assyria's plans for conquest, prepared to resist them by fasting and public prayer as the high priest, Joakim, the representative of the Law, had prescribed. When the armies of Holofernes entrapped them in the city of Bethulia, however, they were immediately seized with the fear that they had offended God through disobedience, and they despaired that God would ever save them. Judith upbraided her fellow Jews for their lack of faith (Judith 8:11-17) and subsequently demonstrated the validity of her exhortations by her successful penetration of the Assyrian camp and the murder of Holofernes. Whereas her reproaches of the citizens reflected Luther's criticism of those men whose desperation under the Law was so great that they doubted divine assistance, her humble submission to God's will (Judith 9:7-14; 16:6-7) and final victory mirrored God's salvation of those Christians who acknowledged the valuelessness of their own actions and the unlimited power of faith.

The Tobias and Susanna stories provided similar paradigms of Lutheran salvation. In the former, the elder Tobias was a strict follower of the Law. Despite the objections of his Assyrian captors, he obeyed Jewish dietary rules, supported his impoverished countrymen with alms and buried Jewish prisoners who had been executed by the Assyrians. When the elder Tobias was accidentally stricken blind, he did not despair; on the contrary, his faith was strengthened as he submitted to his fate. Tobias responded to his friends who mocked his predicament,

---

[65] "Nec potest ratio humana ... ex hoc spectro iustitiae activae seu propriae evolvere et attollere sese ad conspectum iustitiae passivae seu christianae, sed simpliciter haeret in activa. Atque istas cogitationes abutens naturae infirmitate auget et urget Satan. Tum aliter fieri potest, quin magis trepidet, confundatur et perterrefiat conscientia." *WA,* vol. 40, part 1, p. 42.

[66] "Quare nullum remedium habet afflicta conscientia contra desperationem et mortem aeternam, nisi apprehendat promissionem gratiae oblatae in Christo, hoc est hanc fidei, passivam seu christianam iustitiam, quae cum fiducia dicat: Ego non quaero iustitiam activam, deberem quidem habere et facere eam, et posito, quod eam haberem et facerem, tamen in eam non possum gratiae, remissionem peccatorum misericordiae, spiritus sancti et Christi quam ipse dat, quam recipimus et patimur." *WA,* vol. 40, part 1, pp. 42-3.

especially after he had been such a loyal follower of the Law, with a characteristically Lutheran reminder: "Saget nicht also/Denn wir sind kinder der Heiligen/vnd wartten auf ein Leben/welchs Gott geben wird/denen so im glauben starck vnd feste bleiben fur jm."[67] Just as God had sent the angel Raphael to cure the old man (Tobias 11:10-15), so too would Christians ultimately be saved because of their faith.

Susanna likewise gained salvation through faith. Her loyalty to the Law, in this case, her fidelity to her husband, was insufficient to protect her from evil; rather, her obedience to the Law only served to inflame the passions of the lustful admirers who, having been rejected, accused her of adultery. The fact that her accusers were also Jewish judges only heightened the contrast between the Law and faith. These representatives of Mosaic Law not only scorned its precepts, but also used it as a weapon to punish Susanna for her refusal to accede to their demands. Her innocence was, however, upheld by the intervention of the young prophet Daniel who revealed the calumny. Because of her spiritual reliance on God's justice, she was freed from the death sentence imposed on her by the Jewish judges, and her slanderers were condemned in her place. Where Mosaic Law had failed, God rewarded faith with salvation.

Sixteenth-century Protestant dramatists, especially in Lutheran Saxony, were well aware of the similarities between the fate of their protagonists and Protestant theology. Joachim Greff in his *Judith* (1536) emphasized the contrast between the disheartened Jews and Judith's faith in the dedicatory letter to his play and praised her as an exemplum of "eines waren/festen/rechtschaffenen/glaubens/starcker hoffnung gegen Gott/und rechtschaffner trewer liebe gegen irem nehisten."[68] Hans Ackermann in his *Tobias* (1539) interpreted the biblical story in even more explicitly Lutheran terms:

> Wie euch hierinn dann wird entdeckt
> Ein spiegel, klar vor augen glegt,
> Nicht das man seh auff gute werck,
> Die menschen thun (ein ieder merck),
> Und wollen selig werden mit,
> Dieselben werck die wil Gott nit,
> Nur die, do aus dem glauben sein,
> Als lieb des nehsten, nicht im schein,
> Welchs nur anzeigt allein der mund
> Und kommet nit aus herzen grund.[69]

---

[67] Tobias 2:17-18, as quoted in Martin Luther, *Die gantze Heilige Schrifft Deudsch. Wittenberg 1545*, eds. Hans Volz and Heinz Blanke, vol. 2 (Munich: Rogner & Bernhard, 1972), p. 1735.

[68] Joachim Greff, *Tragedia des Buchs Judith* (Wittenberg: Georg Rhaw, 1536), sig. Aii[v].

[69] Hans Ackermann, *Ein Geistlich und fast nutzlichs Spiel, von dem frommen Gottfürchtigen mann Tobia ... 1539*, in Hans Ackermann, *Dramen*, ed. Hugo Holstein, BLVS, 170 (Tübingen, 1884), p. 13, lines 19-28.

Both Greff and Ackermann betrayed their Lutheran sympathies in the introductory remarks; the plays themselves slavishly followed the biblical account which, as we have seen, could easily be read from a Protestant perspective. Paul Rebhun, however, in his *Susanna* (1536) expanded his brief biblical source and thereby gave a decidedly Lutheran character to his protagonist. Rebhun was doubtless familiar with Luther's reading of the union between Sara and Tobias (Tobias 8) as a model marriage, and he consequently portrayed Susanna as an exemplary wife and mother in several non-biblical scenes.[70] More importantly, Rebhun amplified the sparce biblical speeches of the heroine in order to underline the strength of her faith and her passive acceptance of her fate. After learning of her condemnation to death, Susanna remarked:

> Die weil ich dann nu soll auffgebn mein sele
> So wil ich dirs in deine hendt bevelen
> Dann du o mein Gott wirst mich nicht verlassen
> Und diser rach zur zeit dich recht anmassen.[71]

Through the same unshakable belief in God, Rebhun suggested, man would finally be saved from sin.

Luther's views on salvation were not confined exclusively to these Apocryphal dramas. The Magdeburg school dramatist Valten Voith (1487-1558) composed an allegorical play (*Ein schön Lieblich Spiel, von dem herlichen ursprung,* 1538)[72] to explicate the Lutheran concepts of Law and Grace as they had been depicted in a painting in the council room of the city hall. In this work, Voith portrayed key theological ideas, such as Law, Sin and Death, as the medieval devils of the Passion Plays who continually harassed and eventually seduced man from God. Voith, in fact, imitated the narrative disposition of biblical events from the Fall of man to the Redemption as in the passion plays, but in contrast to medieval practice, he had the allegorical figures of "Gesetz," "Sündt" and "Todt" comment on each scene. In this way, Voith demonstrated the biblical origins of Luther's ideas as he explicated them for the audience. In Voith's presentation, man was assailed by Law, Sin and Death after the Fall; the Law showed Adam his error; Sin pricked his conscience; and Death remained a terrifying reminder of the consequences of Adam's disobedience. Shortly thereafter, Adam was comforted by God's promise

---

[70] E.g., I.2 (Susanna taking leave of her husband Joachim); II.3 (Susanna giving religious instruction to her children).

[71] Rebhun, *Dramen,* p. 60, lines 13-16.

[72] The complete title of Voith's play was: *Ein schön Lieblich Spiel, von dem herlichen ursprung: Betrübten Fal. Gnediger widerbrengunge. Müseligem leben. Seligem Ende, und ewiger Freundt des Menschen aus den Historien heiliger schrifft gezogen gantz Tröstlich* in Valten Voith, *Dramen,* ed. Hugo Holstein, BLVS, 170 (Tübingen, 1884).

of a Redeemer and consequently strove to lead a pious life. But the consequences of original sin could not be eradicated through man's adherence to the Law; indeed, as Voith illustrated after Luther, the more man was governed by his conscience, the greater the temptation for him to consider his obedience to God sufficient for salvation. Voith therefore concluded his play with the Redemption so that his viewers might realize that salvation was attainable through Christ alone, not through the "false works"[73] of the Law. As Luther stated in his commentary on Galatians, man must recognize the limitations of "active righteousness," i.e., observance of the Law, and acknowledge that his salvation depended on his passive reception of God's grace through faith. This distinction between the "active righteousness" of the Law and the "passive righteousness" of faith informed the Protestant playwrights' characterizations of the Apocryphal heroes and thereby provided a theological structure for Protestant religious theater.

Whereas most Protestant dramatists depicted the triumph of faith (*sola fide*) by following the biblical disposition of events, some writers amended their sources to emphasize the passive righteousness of the hero. In Hans Sachs' 1550 tragedy, *Die Enthaubtung Johannis,* the protagonist, John the Baptist, appeared only to deliver a Lutheran oration and then became an invisible victim of the wrath of Herodias.[74] A more interesting example was offered by a Protestant dramatization of the martyrdom of St. Stephen (Acts 6-7), especially in the light of a Catholic version of the same material. In his 1592 tragedy on the protomartyr,[75] Melchior Neukirch (ca. 1540-1597), a Protestant preacher at the Petrikirche in Braunschweig, limited St. Stephen's role to the final act where he no sooner appeared than he was stoned. Neukirch had already filled the previous scenes with other events from the Acts of the Apostles, more in the tradition of the *Apostelspiel* (1550) of the Colmar dramatist and novelist, Jörg Wickram, than of the unified character dramas of other writers (e.g., Rebhun's *Susanna*). Neukirch's work contrasted sharply with a contemporary Jesuit Latin play on the same events. In the anonymous *Comoedia de S. Stephano* (MS. ca. 1600; performed in the Rhineland Province),[76] the dramatist focused primarily on the title hero: the mental anguish Stephen suffered before his conversion; his attraction to the works of charity of Jesus' apostles; and his own duties as a deacon after his baptism. Stephen's active ministry consisted of almsgiving and healing as well as preaching, and all three tasks earned him the support

---

[73] "Mit falschen wercken," Voith, p. 256, line 1259.
[74] Hans Sachs, *Die enthaubtung Johannis* in *Werke,* vol. 11, pp. 198-212.
[75] See note 30.
[76] *De S. Stephano,* ms. Koblenz Staatsarchiv, Abteilung 117, No. 718.

of heaven and the enmity of two German-speaking devils. Stephen's martyrdom was thus seen as the culmination of a lifetime devoted to Christ rather than as a sudden test to assess the strength of his faith. Good works as evidence of a Christian's belief played a central role in Catholic theology, and Counter-Reformation dramatists took great pains to portray such active righteousness on the stage.

Sixteenth-century Jesuit playwrights vied zealously for Christian souls in several towns throughout the Holy Roman Empire and the Netherlands in which Protestant missionaries had made significant gains (i.e., Augsburg; Liège). To this end, they frequently adapted biblical, hagiographical and secular topics in which a clear distinction could be drawn between the teachings of Rome and Wittenberg. Where Protestant playwrights were eager to expose the valuelessness of the Law for salvation, Catholic dramatists sought to establish it as both an ethical and spiritual guide for the audience. Ecclesiastical law thus assumed as much significance for Catholic writers as Mosaic Law had held for the Jews, and, as in the Old Testament, transgressions against the Church were severely punished with death and eternal damnation. The *ecclesia militans* of the Counter-Reformation had replaced Christ as the guarantor of man's salvation.

The contrast between Catholic and Protestant concepts of the Law were especially apparent in Jesuit plays on Old Testament subjects. The fathers continued to compose dramas on Joseph, Esther, Susanna, Judith and Tobias until the suppression of the order in 1773 by Pope Clement XIV, for these topics provided excellent examples of Christian virtues.[77] But some of their Old Testament plays on Apocryphal subjects, such as the martyrdom of Eleazar (2 Maccabees 6:18-31; 4 Maccabees 5:1-7, 23) combined moral instruction with a uniquely Catholic view of salvation. The Bavarian Jesuit, Jacob Pontanus (1542-1626), who taught in the order's schools in Dillingen and Augsburg, belonged to the militant generation of proselytizing Jesuits in the post-Tridentine years. In his 1587 tragedy, *Eleazarus Machabaeus*,[78] he provided a Catholic response to Luther's denigration of the Law. Since his drama was based on events from two Apocryphal books (supplemented by material from Josephus' *Antiquities of the Jews*), Pontanus may have hoped to challenge the popular

---

[77] See note 58. For examples of the way in which Jesuit dramas on these Apocryphal heroes were presented, see the program sheets to *Victrix Fiducia Bethuliae. Sigreiches Vertrawen auff GOTT* (Munich, 1679) and *Anna Tobiae Mater ex Luctu Laeta* (Landshut, 1715) reprinted in E. M. Szarota, *Das Jesuitendrama im deutschen Sprachgebiet. Eine Periochen-Edition*, vol. 2, part 1 (Munich: Fink, 1980), pp. 163-73, and vol. 3, part 2 (Munich: Fink, 1983), pp. 1597-1604.

[78] Jacob Pontanus, *Eleazarus Machabaeus*, in his *Poeticarum institutionum libri III (1594)*, editio tertia (Ingolstadt: Adam Sartorius, 1600), pp. 507-56.

Protestant dramas derived from the same collection. As in the
Apocryphal Susanna story, Pontanus' protagonist was threatened
because of an injustice perpetrated against him. Eleazar , the eldest and
most pious member of the Jewish community, refused to submit to the
new Roman religion promulgated by the Seleucid king, Antiochus IV,
Judea's most recent conqueror. Antiochus had already managed to persuade the majority of the Jewish leaders to join him despite Eleazar's continued observance of Judaic Law. Disturbed by Eleazar's stubborn
fidelity, the traitorous Jews sought to ingratiate themselves with
Antiochus by forcing the elder's conversion. Eleazar was brought to trial
and soon condemned for his refusal to eat pork and honor the Roman
gods. Hopeful that Jewish youths would be inspired by his martyrdom,
Eleazar entrusted his fate to God as he was burned alive.

The circumstances of the plight of Judea and Eleazar suggested an
immediate parallel to the popular Protestant Judith dramas. (Judith did
not become a familiar figure on the Jesuit stage until the mid-seventeenth
century.)[79] The reasons for the subjugation of the Jews and the Jewish
reaction to it differed, however, and therein lay the source for Pontanus'
criticism of the Protestants. The Assyrians had been motivated by
imperial ambitions to rule Judea (Judith 2:1-13); religious differences
between the Assyrians and the Jews were of little consequence to
Holofernes as long as the Jews acknowledged him as their leader. In Pontanus' tragedy, however, the religious conflict was central to Antiochus'
destruction of Judea and persecution of Eleazar. In the foreword to his
play, Pontanus referred to the sixteenth-century tyrants (''saeculi nostri
Antiochos'')[80] who threatened the survival of the Church. Because of the
religious distinction between Antiochus and the Jews, there can be little
doubt that Pontanus was thinking of the rift between Catholics and
Lutherans. The Jewish leaders who had already foresworn their
ancestors' faith represented two types of Catholics who had similarly
abandoned the Church for Protestantism. The traitor Leontius had
joined Antiochus since Judaic laws were much too strict. Dionysius had
also abandoned Judaism but for political reasons: he hoped to advance
his own ambitions by allying himself with the victorious tyrant. Leontius
represented the average Catholic who ignorantly rejected ecclesiastic
laws for the apparent freedom of justification by faith alone. Dionysius,
clearly driven by the same amoral impulse, reflected the Machiavellian
shifts of allegiance that town councils and princes made to Protestantism
for their own secular advantage.

---

[79] Johannes Müller cited only two Judith plays before 1640; eleven between 1640 and
1700, and four in the eighteenth century, Müller, p. 115.

[80] Pontanus, *Eleazarus*, p. 509.

In contrast to his faithless countrymen, Eleazar upheld the supremacy of Mosaic law. Whereas Judith had rejected the Law for it threatened faith by engendering despair, Eleazar defended it, for man could only be saved by his obedience to its precepts. Eleazar's refusal to abjure Jewish Law, as evidenced by his spitting out the pork which Antiochus had so viciously forced into his mouth, was Pontanus' response to the passive righteousness of the Protestant protagonists. Eleazar did not earn the heavenly reward prophesied for him in the final scenes solely by faith but also by the demonstration of his obedience and love of God through martyrdom. By his self-sacrifice, Eleazar hoped to atone for the sins of his people. His actions as dictated by the Law were based on rational decisions to preserve his own spiritual welfare and that of his homeland. By analogy, Catholic youths were now encouraged to display their religious fervor by observing ecclesiastical rules:

> Tragoedia, praeterquam quod rarum et admirabile Catholicae iuventuti exemplum ad imitandum proponit, quantisque animis pro avita religione, sanctissimisque caeremoniis propugnandum sit docet, etiam saeculi nostri Antiochos, depingit.[81]

For Pontanus, Jewish Law was a preliminary stage in the development of Church law; the elimination of pork from the diet was merely a prefiguration of ecclesiastical customs concerning abstinence. Pontanus' protagonist acted, therefore, as a spokesman for a beleaguered Church. The martyr Eleazar strove not only to repulse the heretical tenets of his opponents, but also to prove the validity of ecclesiastical law.

Both Catholic and Protestant dramatists, then, inserted contrastive paradigms for eternal salvation into their biblical plays. Their respective interpretations of man's participation in or absence from the process of salvation significantly influenced their choice of dramatic topics and characterizations of their protagonists. Whereas Protestant playwrights preferred biblical plots in which man was rewarded for his passive subordination of his soul to God's care, Catholic writers, especially the Jesuits, who used the stage as a Counter-Reformation weapon, were attracted to hagiographical and historical themes in which man's obedience to the Church guaranteed his salvation. Although this division between Catholic and Protestant drama was not always evident—both sides did after all use the same biblical personages for moral instruction— theological assumptions about the nature of salvation informed their respective preferences. Sixteenth-century religious playwrights consequently established the antithetical model of the passive Protestant hero and the active Catholic protagonist suggested by their respective

---

[81] *Ibid.*

theologies. As we shall see, these same qualities continued into the seventeenth century in the tragedies of Vondel and Gryphius. Vondel, who, as a Mennonite and later as a Catholic, emphasized the importance of man's free will for salvation, favored topics in which his protagonists were confronted with a decisive choice. The Lutheran Gryphius reacted against this practice and introduced the passive Protestant hero into his Christian historical drama.

## The Education of Fallen Man

In addition to suggesting the manner in which salvation occurred and the attributes which the candidate for God's grace must display, humanist religious playwrights further upheld the idea that the moral education of a Christian best prepared him for the attainment of heaven. From a theological perspective, this assumption was fundamentally unsound, for both Catholic and Protestant agreed, regardless of their divergent stance on free will, that man was ultimately saved by God's grace. But sixteenth-century dramatists, bent on the mass education of citizens to defend and rule a Catholic or Protestant town, were not disturbed by— or, in some cases, even aware of—their implicit linking of moral education with salvation. Hieronymus Ziegler implied in his Abel iustus (1559) that Abel's continued obedience to his parents, and by extension, the practice of the same virtue by the schoolboy audience would guarantee salvation.[82] Similarly, Protestant writers suggested that the viewers' acquisition of the patience of the beggar Lazarus or the conjugal fidelity of Esther could gain them an eternal crown.[83]

The theological problem was additionally complicated by the dramatists' intentional avoidance of the ineluctable consequences of

---

[82] Hieronymus Ziegler, Abel iustus. Tragoedia (Ingolstadt: Alexander & Samuel Weissenhornius, 1559), sig. B 3.

[83] In the verse prologue to his Spiel vom reichen Manne und armen Lazaro (1590), the Magdeburg schoolmaster, Georg Rollenhagen, advised:

So wird hier auch gezeiget an,
Wie sich haltn sol ein armer Man,
Das er sein armut also trag,
Das er an Gott mit nicht verzag,

Georg Rollenhagen, Spiel vom reichen Manne und armen Lazaro, ed. Johannes Bolte, Neudrucke deutscher Literaturwerke des XVI. und XVII. Jahrhunderts, 270-273 (Halle: Max Niemeyer, 1929), p. 9, lines 27-34. Similarly, Valten Voith directed his audience to the moral significance of his Esther figure (1537):

Zur andern Köngin [Esther] kert euch hin,
Zu irer tugend gebt mut und sinn
Und folget ir, das ist mein rat,
Die Gottes wort stets seer lieb hat!

Voith, Dramen, p. 159, lines 83-86.

original sin. If, because of the Fall, man possessed a natural proclivity for evil, how then could he ever be educated sufficiently so that he might gain favor in God's eyes? For Protestant writers whose theology was grounded in the absolute depravity of man, such a dilemma was theologically insoluble, especially since they had denied any positive abilities (e.g., free will) to man. Indeed, the whole foundation of Luther's soteriology rested on corrupt man's recognition of his helplessness and sinfulness under the Law and his consequent need for God. As Luther had remarked about the Fall in his 1535-1536 lectures on Genesis:

> Let us learn, therefore, that this is the nature of sin: unless God immediately provides a cure and calls the sinner back, he flees endlessly from God and by excusing his sin with lies, heaps sin upon sin until he arrives at blasphemy and despair. Thus sin by its own gravitation always draws with it another sin and brings on eternal destruction, till finally the sinful person would rather accuse God than acknowledge his own sin.[84]

Following Augustine,[85] the Reformer further noted on this occasion that children were especially inclined to evil. As Adam attempted to hide his shame from his Creator (Genesis 3:8-10), so did children hope to conceal their guilt from their parents through excuses and lies.[86]

Christian humanists attempted to reconcile man's nature with their belief in his moral improvement by extolling the salutary benefits of a religious education. Christian writers essentially adopted two positions on man's educability. The first was typified by Erasmus in his oration *De pueris* (1529); the second by more conservative writers like Ludovicus Vives[87] and Christopher Hegendorphinus.[88] In the former instance, Erasmus betrayed his sympathy for the classical assumption espoused by Plutarch, Quintilian and Quattrocento theorists that man possessed an

---

[84] As quoted in *Luther's Works*, vol. 1, *Lectures on Genesis, Chapters 1-5*, ed. Jaroslav Pelikan (St. Louis: Concordia, 1958), p. 175. The original reads: "Discamus igitur naturam hanc peccati esse, quod, nisi Deus statim medicinam faciat et revocet peccatorem, fugit sine fine a Deo, et excusando mendaciter peccatum, peccatum peccato addidit, donec veniat ad blasphemiam et desperationem. Sic peccatum pondere suo semper secum trahit aliud peccatum et facit aeternam ruinam, donec homo peccator tandem Deum potius accuset, quam ut agnoscat peccatum suum." *WA*, 42, pp. 130-131.

[85] Augustine, *Confessiones* 1.7.11-12.

[86] "Haec peccati natura etiam in pueris cernitur, qui saepe deprehensi in ipso facto tamen satagunt, quo parentibus aliud persuadeant et se excusent. Sic simpliciter solent homines, etiam cum deprehensi tenentur, tamen conantur elabi, ne confundantur, sed videantur boni et iusti. Hoc venenum etiam per peccatum in naturam instillatum est ...." *WA*, 42, p. 127.

[87] Ludovicus Vives, *De tradendis disciplinis* (1531).

[88] Christopher Hegendorphinus, *Christiana studiosae iuventutis institutio* (1526) and *De instituenda vita et moribus corrigendis iuventutis* (1529). Hegendorphinus, who blamed negligent parents for evil children, believed in the power of religious instruction to tame ill-mannered youths: "iuventutem nulla alia re quam divino verbo domare posse." Hegendorphinus, *Christiana*, sig. aiiᵛ.

inborn aptitude and propensity for the acquisition of virtue.[89] On the basis of this postulate, Erasmus was able to argue persuasively that an evil or poorly educated child did not so much demonstrate man's congenital bestiality, but rather the negligence of his parents. Since Erasmus was eager to convince his readers of the benefits of parental guidance and public education, he prudently played down the consequences of original sin. Although he acknowledged its existence and its utility for explaining why a child was more prone to forget good behavior than bad, he overlooked its theological significance and noted that evil children were produced by schools not by nature.[90]

Such a blatant neglect of original sin rarely appeared in humanist writing without further refinement; Erasmus' arguments were atypical of most Nothern educational writers. A more guarded and consequently more influential approach to the question of man's educability was offered by Vives in his *De tradendis disciplinis* (1531). Vives also believed that education would have a civilizing effect on man—it distinguished him from beasts—but, in contrast to Erasmus, he underscored the religious significance of good schooling. Man must not only be trained for social reasons, but so that he might be able to serve God; man in fact required God to imbue his life with meaning.[91] To accord with this pious outlook, Vives acknowledged man's natural proclivity for evil because of the Fall, but then quickly tempered this pessimism with a firm belief in the ability of man's reason to control such excesses.[92] Vives' middle position between the dangerously pagan—from the sixteenth-century perspective—Erasmus and the bleakness of Luther's theology became the foundation for the pedagogical arguments of the humanist school dramatists. Ziegler acknowledged in his *Abel iustus*, which had opened with Adam's account of the Fall, that a child's evil tendencies could easily be controlled by a good education.[93] Similarly, Protestant writers such as

---

[89] Plutarch, Περὶ παίδων ἀγωγῆς (*De liberis educandis*); Quintilian, *Inst. orat.* 1.3. For a survey of important Italian pedagogical treatises at Erasmus' disposal, see the introduction to Erasmus, *Declamatio de pueris statim ac liberaliter instituendis,* ed. Jean-Claude Margolin (Geneva: Droz, 1966), pp. 101-3.

[90] "christiana philosophia nobis prodidit, quae docet hanc ad mala pronitatem insedisse nobis ex humanae gentis principe Adamo. Quod ut falsum esse non potest, ita verissimum est maximam hujus mali partem manare ex impuro convictu pravaque educatione, praesertim aetatis tenerae et in omnia flexilis." Erasmus, *De pueris,* p. 419.

[91] Ludovicus Vives, *De tradendis disciplinis* (1531) in his *Opera omnia,* vol. 6 (Valencia, 1782), p. 245.

[92] Vives, *De tradendis disciplinis,* p. 262.

[93] In I.4, Adam and Eve imparted moral instruction to their two sons:
Nostro periculo [original sin] fugere discite malum
Formate mentes sedulo vestras sacris
Sentenciis, vitaeque preceptis bonis.
Ziegler, *Abel iustus,* sig. C 3ᵛ-C 4.

Paul Rebhun and Hans Sachs, with their careful catalogue of lessons exemplified by each character, suggested God's salvation was possible for those who followed their counsel.[94]

Vives' resolution of the contradiction between original sin and education was particularly helpful for Catholic writers. With the establishment of reason as a moral corrective, Vives suggested that pious behavior could raise man up to God.[95] For Counter-Reformation authors battling against the Protestant emphasis on faith at the expense of reason, Vives' rationality had a particular appeal. Since man's reason could help him restrain the consequences of original sin, some Catholic dramatists, inspired by the revival of Neo-Stoicism in the late sixteenth century,[96] praised man's rational ability to endure adversity and thereby gain eternal life. In Pontanus' *Eleazarus,* reason enabled the title hero to forbear his horrible death and win God's favor. As his survivors exhorted the schoolboy audience:

> Tu perdoces parere rationi, doces
> Motus domare turbidos, praecordiis
> Ex intimis Deum diligere.[97]

To the same end, the Louvain professor of rhetoric Nicolaus Vernulaeus (1583-1649) portrayed the adventures of St. Eustachius (*Divus Eustachius sive fidei et patientiae triumphus,* 1612) whose rational response to each new misfortune ultimately gained him eternal life.[98] After each new difficulty,

---

[94] In the epilogue to his *Susanna,* Rebhun cited the following lessons: the shameful lust of old men (Susanna's accusers); the dangers of voting for immoral actions (city councilmen); God often speaks through children (Daniel); pious, unshakable chastity (Susanna); loyal husband (Joachim); proper social deportment as befits one's station (the servants): Paul Rebhun, *Dramen,* pp. 83-7. Similarly, Hans Sachs noted at the end of his 1551 play on the resurrection of Lazarus that the protagonist typified a lost sinner; his sister, Marta, represented the Christian community which prayed for the souls of all deceased sinners; and the Pharisees exemplified the enemies of the Christian church. Sachs, *Werke,* vol. 11, p. 254.

[95] Vives, *De tradendis disciplinis,* p. 256.

[96] Catholic writers maintained a guarded attitude toward Neo-Stoicism and the philosophy of Seneca. Neo-Stoicism was especially attractive to young Catholics because of the rational, moral discipline which could be derived from it. Consider, for example, the case of Martinus Del Rio who praised both the style and moral lessons of Seneca's tragedies in his *Adversaria in Senecam* (published 1576). Later, in a commentary on Seneca written after Del Rio had become a Jesuit (*Commentarius novus,* published 1595), Del Rio criticized a Stoic man's passivity in the face of both virtue and vice; in his *Cenodoxus* (1602), Jacob Bidermann similarly mocked a Stoic's dispassionate forbearance of death and his consequent neglect of his immortal soul. On Del Rio's opinions, see Maturin Dréano, *Humanisme chrétien. La tragédie latine commentée pour les chrétiens du XVIᵉ siècle* (Paris: Éditions Beauchesne, 1936); for Bidermann's critique, see *Cenodoxus* (IV.3).

[97] Pontanus, *Eleazarus,* p. 556.

[98] Nicolaus Vernulaeus, *Divus Eustachius sive fidei et patientiae triumphus* (1612) as printed in his *Tragoediae decem,* editio secunda (Louvain: Petrus Sassenus & Hier. Nempaeus, 1656), pp. 615-83.

the loss of his wealth and property; the abduction of his wife and children; and his condemnation to death, Eustachius, a Job figure whose legend was embellished with exotic episodes from Greek romance,[99] employed his reason to assuage his fears and thank God for yet another test of his faith.[100] Because of his perseverance, Eustachius was eventually reunited with his family and honored—at least to Vernulaeus' Catholic readers—with a martyr's crown. In Catholic drama, reason controlled man's propensity for evil and thereby aided his attainment of salvation.

The disharmony between man's nature and humanist pedagogical objectives was more acute for Protestant schoolmen; but, in the 1520s, a compromise between theology and education was reached. Luther essentially shared Vives' opinion that all learning should be directed toward piety, but his theology with its damning consequences for man's rational ability contradicted this humanist view. He resolved this problem by approaching it first from the perspective of a social advocate for education rather than as a theologian.[101] Since education performed a useful civil service by training men to restrain their evil impulses, Luther reasoned, it might also serve a propaedeutic function in preparing man for salvation. Later in his 1531 commentary on Galatians, he linked education to this theological view. Since the Gospel (i.e., New Testament) could not be understood without some knowledge of the Law (in both a civil and theological sense) man must be familiar with its precepts and trained to recognize his deviation from it.[102] Only when man realized

---

[99] The legend was full of the calamities, abductions, mistaken identities and discoveries which characterized the Hellenistic novels of Heliodorus and Achilles Tatius. For example, Eustachius and his family were forced to leave Rome when a plague overtook their household. While en route to Egypt, Eustachius' wife, Theophistes, was seized by the sailors for payment; having arrived in Egypt, Eustachius lost both of his sons while fording a river. He eventually led the life of a simple *rusticus* until his true identity was discovered, and he was summoned back to Rome to lead the imperial armies. During the campaign, Eustachius was reunited with his sons (now soldiers) and finally with his wife. The martyrdom of Eustachius and his family consequently seemed anticlimactic after such turmoil: because of his refusal to worship Jupiter, Eustachius was quickly stripped of his military honors and burned alive with his family in a heated brazen bull.

[100] On Eustachius' forbearance, consider the following passage:
Ut in aequor undae, sic miseriae in nos cadunt,
Succedit altera, cum prior nondum perit,
Et fortiorem sors resumit impetum
Cum saeviit: quis ergo finis, aut modus?
Tamen est ferendum, nam voluntas haec Dei est,
Et quia voluntas, quicquid obtingit placet.
Vernulaeus, p. 638.

[101] On the social implications of Luther's educational ideas, see Gerald Strauss, *Luther's House of Learning* (Baltimore and London: Johns Hopkins, 1978), pp. 41-7.

[102] "Itaque verum officium et principialis ac proprius usus legis est, quod revelat homini suum peccatum, caecitatem, miseriam, impietatem, ignorantiam, odium, con-

his sinfulness under the Law, could he begin to acknowledge his need for faith. Although these arguments created a theoretical framework for the utility of education, they were still theologically problematic. As Luther had remarked in the same commentary, and as Voith so vividly illustrated on the religious stage, the excessive observance of the Law could lead man into the false belief that such obedience resulted in salvation. In the sixteenth century when Protestants hastily attempted to consolidate their church, this theological incongruity between the Law as a prerequisite for and hindrance to salvation was left unresolved so that the more important task of man's education could take place.

The paradox in Protestant thought between man's fallen nature and his educability was more apparent in Sixt Birck's two Susanna plays (German, 1532; Latin, 1537).[103] In these works, the theological significance of Birck's religious plot contradicted the sociopolitical lessons he had incorporated into his plays. This discrepancy was especially evident in the Latin drama where Birck developed his ideas about the sociopolitical function of theater. In the prefatory note addressed to the Augsburg Town Council ("senatus"), Birck deplored the neglect of political issues on the contemporary stage. He criticized the recent religious plays of Gnapheus (*Acolastus,* 1529) and Crocus (*Joseph,* 1536) not so much because of their immoral content—to which he also objected—but because the authors were disinterested in politics.[104] Birck, who chided the Council for forcing him to write a religious play, now hoped to demonstrate the way in which politics and religion could be sensibly combined. In order to provide a model for governing a Protestant

---

temptum Dei, mortem, infernum, iudicium et commeritam iram apud Deum." *WA,* vol. 40, part 1, p. 481.

[103] *Die history von der/frommen Gottsförchtigen frouwen/Susanna* (Basel: Thomas Wolff, 1532); *Susanna/Comoedia/Tragica* (Augsburg: Philippus Ulhardus, 1537). Both reprinted in Sixt Birck, *Sämtliche Dramen,* vol. 2, pp. 3-53; 169-272.

[104] Birck criticized the Senate's disapproval of secular classical drama because of its alleged immorality; he was quick to point out that the sacred dramas of Gnapheus and Crocus were not any less offensive:

Acolastus arridebit blandius? Puto.
Sed is nec Aeschyno cedit luxuria,
Nec Pamphilo.

.....................................................

Iuvat Ioseph magis audire? Sed
Terentius nullum scortum impudentius
Petulantiusve inducit, quam sit Sephirach.

[Sephirach was the name ascribed to Potiphar's wife by Crocus in his Joseph play.] Birck, *Susanna,* pp. 179-80, lines 25-27; 38-40. In light of Birck's remarks in the dedicatory letter that education should serve a political ("salus et felicitas Reipublicae") rather than a spiritual (education of priests) end, it seems that he may have found the standard theological and moral interpretations of religious subjects too confining. For his opinions on the utility of politics, see Birck, *Susanna,* pp. 170-6.

republic, Birck shifted the traditional emphasis on Susanna's chastity to the manner in which her case was handled by the local magistrates and council. In portraying these political figures, Birck re-created contemporary legal procedures: the magistrates debated about judging Susanna according to her character or the basis of her accusers' testimony; the plaintiffs were excluded from the trial proceedings; Susanna was encouraged to petition the emperor (in this case the Assyrian king, Nebuchadnezzar, who held the Jews in captivity) in the event of an unfavorable decision; and the respective merits of mercy and punishment were discussed.[105] Susanna's behavior was particularly noteworthy in light of Rebhun's pious treatment of the same subject a few years before (1536). Where Rebhun had followed Scripture and allowed Susanna to call out to heaven for assistance, Birck dispensed with the prayer and portrayed his heroine's absolute confidence in the power of judicial law (Themis) and her right of appeal to preserve her from an erroneous verdict.[106] But having devoted the greatest portion of his play to the judicial milieu of Susanna's trial, Birck reverted to the biblical narrative in the final act. With the appearance of the young prophet Daniel to interrogate the elders and acquit Susanna, the tone of the play switched markedly from politics to religion. Contrary to Birck's pronouncements in his preface, the politicians were ultimately ineffectual, for without the intervention of the young prophet Daniel, Susanna would have been executed. Birck's trial scene had doubtless contributed to the political education of the audience; but in purporting to extol republican virtues and train citizens for the state, Birck had actually exposed man's fallibility and need for God.

Birck never really reconciled this disharmony between moral, political man and man's natural propensity for evil. In his *Judith* (German/Latin, 1539), where Birck adhered more closely to the biblical source, the Jewish leaders were as unable as Susanna's judges to reach a correct decision, and Judith's assistance was needed to ward off their despair.[107] Nevertheless, several other plays reflected Birck's confidence in political man's ability to act in accordance with his faith: *Sapientia Solomonis* (posthumously published, 1591) extolled Solomon as "regis typus sapientis, et justi et pii,"[108] and *Ezechias* (1539) illustrated God's reward

---

[105] Birck, *Susanna*, III. 3; IV. 5; IV. 8, pp. 213-7; 227-33; 240-2.
[106] Birck, *Susanna*, IV. 8, pp. 241-2.
[107] Birck, *Judith*, III. 11, pp. 355-9.
[108] [Sixt Birck], *Sapientia Solomonis*, ed. Elizabeth Rogers Payne, Yale Studies in English, 89 (New Haven: Yale University, 1939), p. 128. With a few modifications, Birck's play was acted before Queen Elizabeth I by the Westminster School boys in 1565-66.

of the prudent king, Ezechias, who had entrusted the fate of beleaguered Jerusalem to heaven (2 Chronicles 32). In his *Ezechias*, Birck had also attributed the erroneous counsel of some of the king's advisers to original sin for exhorting the monarch to capitulate to the Assyrians. But his emphasis on Ezechias' power to avoid such lapses led him to remark that men could similarly overcome misfortune through patience and prayer:

> So merckend hie ir Christen all
> Wann in dem Creutz zu dem abfall
> Sich nayget unser blödigkeit
> Wir sollen sein zum bett berait
> Wie der küng Ezechias that. [109]

Birck's dramas thus reflected the incongruity between his Protestant belief and his educational aspirations in two respects: the inevitable fallibility of any political system administered by fallen man; and the implicit suggestion that adherence to Christian principles (e.g., Ezechias) would free man from evil and thereby lead to eternal life. As Birck's dramas demonstrated, the practical but paradoxical compromise which Luther had devised between education and his theology resulted in the composition of religious plays whose moral and secular goals clashed with their theological meaning.

In sixteenth-century humanist religious drama, then, theology was subordinated to morality. Theology was, of course, still evident in the soteriological paradigms which the dramatists had contributed to strengthen the faith of the viewers. But, as in the case of the appended allegorical interpretations, the christological sense of the plot was regarded as equal to the literary, moral and even the ecclesiastical levels. The humanist playwrights' certainty of man's educability, moreover, induced them to play down any theological issues which undermined this belief. Catholic writers who ascribed some importance to man's participation in his salvation through free will and reason had little difficulty harmonizing this theological tenet with their pedagogical aims. But Lutheran playwrights, convinced of man's unrestrained proclivity for evil, were forced to create an inadequate compromise between secular and religious intentions. As we noted first in Luther and then in Birck, the insufficiency of this resolution was apparent from the contradiction between theology and man's educability and, more importantly, from the possible conclusion that moral acts contributed to salvation. When

---

[109] Sixt Birck, *Ezechias. Ain nutzliche kurtze Tragedi Wie man sich in Kriegs Nöten gegen Gott halten soll (1539)* in his *Sämtliche Werke,* vol. 1, ed. Manfred Brauneck (Berlin: Walter de Gruyter, 1969), p. 9.

theology replaced morality as the predominant function of religious drama in the seventeenth century, however, both of these problems would be settled. Where Vondel created Christian tragedy by depicting the plight of fallen man, Gryphius' historical dramas revealed the vanity of the political world and man's consequent dependence on God for salvation.

# CHAPTER THREE

# THE BIBLICAL TRAGEDIES OF JOOST VAN DEN VONDEL

Joost van den Vondel (1587-1679) has long occupied a hallowed place in seventeenth-century Netherlandic literature. In his seventy years as a writer, Vondel variously practiced epic and lyrical poetry, political satire, religious polemic, hagiography and literary criticism, but his literary fame chiefly rested with his dramas. Written between 1612 and 1668, these thirty-two works were comprised of eight translations from Graeco-Roman and humanist theater and twenty-four original plays with plots derived from classical mythology, ancient, medieval and Renaissance history, hagiography and, above all, the Old Testament. Because of the extent and variety of this production, Vondel has understandably been grouped by his admirers with Shakespeare (although his piety more appropriately allied him with Milton) while his strict adherence to neo-classical form, especially in his work after 1648, suggested resemblances to Corneille and Racine. Similarly, within the context of seventeenth-century Netherlandic culture, Vondel's poems and dramas have been accounted among the highest artistic achievements of the Dutch Golden Age, worthy to stand alongside the paintings of Rembrandt and the economic miracle of the Dutch Republic.[1] Yet, as so frequently occurs with the canonization of a poet into a cultural symbol, his literary-historical significance has been adjusted, if not distorted, to accord with the nationalistic fervor of his interpreters. The dramas upon which Vondel's reputation rested did not so much contain the spirit of the Dutch Renaissance as the intimate reflections of an exceptionally pious poet about man's troubled relationship to his Creator.

Despite the propensity of cultural historians to consider Vondel the arch-representative of Dutch seventeenth-century drama, literary interpreters have long acknowledged Vondel's anomalous position in Netherlandic theater history. Although many of Vondel's plays were enthusiastically received by Amsterdam audiences during the mid-

---

[1] The view of Vondel as the literary representative of the Dutch Golden Age was especially promoted by Johan Huizinga, *Holländische Kultur im siebzehnten Jahrhundert,* trans. Werner Kaegi (1961; Frankfurt a. Main: Suhrkamp, 1977), pp. 93-8. With the nationalistic fervor of the 1930s, Heinz Haerten regarded Vondel as the quintessential Baroque genius who synthesized "die volkstümlich-gebärdenhaften und gelehrt-rhetorischen Überlieferungen." Heinz Haerten, *Vondel und der deutsche Barock* (Nymegen: Druck und Kommissions-verlag der zentralen Druckerei, 1934).

seventeenth century, popular interest in the dramas written after the 1650s, when many of the poet's masterpieces were composed, declined sharply. Clerical opposition to Vondel's religious plays contributed greatly to his absence from the stage, but the public's marked preference for bloody revenge dramas, secular historical plays and peasant comedies rather than biblical tragedy further accelerated his isolation from the repertoire. Indeed, Vondel's uniqueness in Dutch drama was due to his preference for religious subjects rather than the romantic tragedies and the social satires of his contemporaries. Sixteen of Vondel's twenty-four original dramas were based on Old Testament and hagiographical topics. Several minor contemporaries of Vondel also composed biblical dramas, but Vondel's religious plays remained a unique phenomenon both for their quantity and their neo-classical structure. Paradoxically the works of the chief figure of seventeenth-century Dutch theater were the least representative of that era's lively and varied dramatic production.

The atypicality of Vondel's religious theater has, however, contributed significantly to his exalted status in Dutch literature; the more he deviated from common practice, the greater his artistry was apprized. But this emphasis on the extraordinary aspects of Vondel's genius has obscured his relationship to the Latin and vernacular tradition of Renaissance religious drama. Instead of regarding Vondel as an extension of sixteenth-century biblical theater, it has become a common practice to contrast his complex tragedies to the less sophisticated Rederijker and humanist Latin dramas of the sixteenth century.[2] Indeed, Vondel's artistic prowess is believed to have been evidenced by his ability to adapt the simple piety of medieval and humanist sacred drama to the form of Graeco-Roman theater. Because of his clear superiority to the sixteenth century, it has, moreover, been argued that Vondel's tragic vision was similarly unique. Accordingly, in recent years, three different interpretations have been devised to underscore his distinctiveness in tragedy. In each instance, a literary or philosophical model has been employed to illuminate Vondel's concept of that genre. G. Bomhoff (1950) borrowed categories from twentieth-century existentialism and phenomenology to suggest that the tragic conflict between a biblical protagonist and God arose from man's fundamental need to exercise his free will.[3] Vondel's tragedies consequently reflected the historical conflict between medieval

---

[2] B. H. Molkenboer, *De jonge Vondel* (Amsterdam: Parnassus, 1950), pp. 163-5, and Kåre Langvik-Johannessen, *Zwischen Himmel und Erde. Eine Studie über Joost van den Vondels biblische Tragödie in gattungsgeschichtlicher Perspektive* (Oslo: Universitetsforlaget, 1963), pp. 9-111.

[3] J. G. Bomhoff, *Vondels drama. Studie en pleidooi* (Amsterdam: Ploegsma, 1950), pp. 5-26.

and Renaissance thought which the new humanist glorification of man had inspired. J. Poulssen (1963) and K. Langvik-Johannessen (1963) similarly imported terminology from European intellectual history to explicate the dramas. Drawing on art-historical categories, Poulssen suggested that Vondel's tragic heroes failed because they could not tolerate the imperfection ("chiaroscuro") of their souls.[4] Langvik-Johannessen likewise analyzed Vondel's protagonists in terms of the opposition between spirit and flesh in order to demonstrate the way in which this conflict was resolved in the plays. For this reason, it was argued, Vondel's works proved the hypothesis that Baroque literature arose through a synthesis of the spirit (medieval culture) and the flesh (the Renaissance).[5]

There have also been occasional forays into psychoanalysis (G. Kazemier)[6] and juridical and legal history (J. Vandervelden)[7] to explicate various plays, but for the most part, Vondel criticism has been predominantly historical and philosophical rather than literary. W. A. P. Smit filled this lacuna with his three-volume analysis of all the dramas (1956-1962).[8] In an attempt to create a proper literary-historical context for his interpretations, Smit reconstructed seventeenth-century neo-classical dramatic theory and closely demonstrated to what extent Vondel adhered to its principles. Smit's emphasis on the formal and structural aspects of the plays did not, however, explicate Vondel's concept of tragedy and many of his problematic characterizations. Moreover, Smit applied his poetological model too strictly to the evaluation of the works; Vondel's failure to create a unified dramatic whole in accordance with Aristotle was often unjustly regarded as a shortcoming in a writer for

---

[4] J. Poulssen, "Tragiek van Vondels glans. Bijdrage tot de beschrijving ener dichter-lijke eigenheid," *Raam,* 2 (1963), 83-108. For a typological survey of the light-dark imagery in Vondel's dramas, see Lieven Rens, "Beelden van duisternis in Vondels drama,"*SpL,* 10 (1966-67), 1-15, and Lieven Rens, "Het clair-obscur in Vondels drama," *SpL,* 12 (1969-70), 81-175.

[5] Langvik-Johannessen, pp. 108-112.

[6] G. Kazemier, "Over de psychologie van Vondels Jefta," *NTg,* 33 (1939), 18-29, and, more recently, Lieven Rens, "Prolegomena bij een psychoanalytische interpretatie van Vondels drama," in *Visies op Vondel na 300 jaar,* eds. S. F. Witstein and E. F. Grootes (The Hague: Martinus Nijhoff, 1979), pp. 270-88.

[7] Jos. Vandervelden, *Staat en recht bij Vondel* (Haarlem: H. D. Tjeenk Willink, 1939). Vandervelden was the master of the discursive, essayistic approach to Vondel's works within the broad intellectual context of seventeenth-century Europe. See his *Vondels wereldbeeld* (Utrecht: Het Spectrum, 1948), and *Vondel's schoonheid* (Amsterdam: Lieverlee, 1952). This reduction of Vondel to a compendium of philosophical ideas was more successful with the didactic epic poems than with the drama.

[8] W. A. P. Smit, *Van Pascha tot Noah. Een verkenning van Vondels drama's naar continuiteit en ontwikkeling in hun grondmotief en structuur,* 3 vols. (Zwolle: W. E. J. Tjeenk Willink, 1956-1962).

whom poetic rules were merely a convention.[9] Despite the utility of his literary readings, Smit's study was weakened by his tendency to regard Vondel as an individual dramatist and not as a practitioner of the long-established tradition of humanist sacred theater.

The literary-historical approach which follows is intended to rectify the shortcomings of the previous Vondel criticism. Instead of attributing the uniqueness of Vondel's dramatic works solely to his artistic talent, his distinctive style will be shown to have arisen from his adaptation of earlier motifs in Renaissance religious drama. In this manner, several problems which have vexed Vondel scholars can be better understood. Vondel's relationship to humanism and medieval culture will no longer be interpreted on the basis of philosophical categories, but in light of the dramatic praxis of both eras. Moreover, his debt to neo-classical dramatic theory, which Smit had too narrowly assessed, will be clarified by aligning Vondel's critical adaptation of the classical and Renaissance tradition to the theological arguments of his plays.

The purpose of the following discussion therefore is twofold. First, it will be argued that Vondel's approach to biblical drama was grounded in the tradition of sixteenth-century religious theater. Despite his experimentation with different tragic styles, be they Rederijker, Roman or Greek, all of Vondel's biblical plays were written to reinforce the piety of his Christian audience. Secondly, it will be suggested that Vondel's concept of biblical (or Christian) tragedy can only be fully understood through an analysis of his critical reception of humanist religious drama. Whereas previous commentators have examined Vondel through the introduction of philosophical or aesthetic models, I shall regard the texts essentially as religious plays whose primary function was the dissemination of theological truths. The artistry of Vondel's religious drama did not lie so much with his adaptation of biblical topics to neo-classical forms but with his sophisticated portrait of fallen man and the nature of his faith.

Vondel's composition of biblical drama extended over a fifty-year period in which he progressed from the neo-classical form of the humanist (i.e., early seventeenth century) Rederijkers[10] to Aristotelian

---

[9] This criticism of Smit was first made by Poulssen, pp. 15-28. Smit does not really respond to Poulssen's observations in his review of that book (*NTg*, 58 (1965), 91-9) though he quite rightly objects to Poulssen's arbitrary use of the confusing terms "Barok" and "maniërisme" to describe Vondel's "dichterlijke eigenheid."

[10] The influence of Senecan language in Rederijker theater was apparent, for example, in Jacob Duym's *Ghedenck-boeck* (1606) which contained his vernacular adaptation of Daniel Heinsius' tragedy *Auriacus sive libertas saucia* (1602) on the assassination of William the Silent: *Het moordadich stuck van Balthasar Gerards*. In the 1610s the dramas of Abraham de Koning and Guilliam van Nieuwelandt also betrayed the gradual influence of classical

tragedy. The stylistic development evidenced by the dramas was matched by Vondel's increasingly complex presentation of his theological ideas. To organize the tragedies under convenient headings, it has been fashionable to note distinctions between characterizations or style. Thus, for example, T. De Jager[11] and J. Noë[12] suggested that all Vondel's heroes before 1648 were innocent victims of injustice whereas all protagonists after that time brought about their own destruction. Smit likewise noted Vondel's progression from the mystery play-symbolic mode of *Het Pascha* (1612) to the emblematic portraits of good versus evil (ca. 1640) and finally to the Aristotelian tragedies of the 1650s and 1660s.[13] In keeping with the theological intention of the tragedies, however, the following discussion will examine those aspects of humanist religious dramas with which Vondel was most concerned: the visual representation of divine justice; the typological interpretation of biblical events and, most importantly, the use of drama as a mirror for the education of man. For this purpose, three different periods in Vondel's dramatic development have been selected for analysis. First, Vondel's initial reception of sixteenth-century theory and praxis in *Het Pascha* (1612) will be described in order to determine to what extent these early works adumbrated his subsequent theory of biblical tragedy. Secondly, Vondel's adaptation of the sixteenth-century tradition will be assessed through an examination of the problematic tragedies of 1640: *Joseph in Dothan* and *Joseph in Egypten*. In each of these works, Vondel challenged the sixteenth-century assumption about the use of drama as a moral exemplum by casting doubts on man's ability to imitate virtue. Finally, in *Jeptha* (1659), Vondel developed this critical attitude toward man's imperfections fur-

---

style and form in works written for the Rederijker chambers in Amsterdam and Antwerp respectively. For an analysis of these late Rederijker writers, see: K. Poll, *Over de tooneelspelen van den Leidschen rederijker Jacob Duym* (Groningen, 1898), and A. A. Keersmaekers, *De dichter Guilliam van Nieuwelandt en de Senecaans-classieke tragedie in de zuidelijke Nederlanden* (Ghent: Secretarie der Academie, 1957).

[11] Th. De Jager, "Vondel of de majesteit," *Roeping*, 16 (Nov.-Dec. 1937), pp. 69; 112.

[12] J. Noë, *De religieuse bezieling van Vondels werk* (Tielt: Lannoo, 1952), pp. 67; 82-3.

[13] Smit detected three different structures in Vondel's plays: "symbolisch-emblematisch"; "exemplarisch-emblematisch"; and the neo-classical "contrasterend-uitbeeldend." Where dramas in the first category (*Het Pascha; Maeghden*) exemplified Divine Providence, the second group (e.g., *Lucifer*) designated conflicts between good and evil. In keeping with Aristotelian prescriptions, the last plays focused on the reversal of fortune and downfall of the hero. Though these categorizations aptly described the plays in general, Smit's emphasis on form resulted primarily in an analysis of structure rather than of the problematic content. Moreover, Vondel's occasional reversion to an earlier dramatic structure such as humanist tragedy for *Adam in ballingschap* and possibly to John the Baptist plays (e.g., Jacob Schoepper's *Ectrachelistis*, 1546) for the Achiman-Urania conflict in *Noah* weakened Smit's argument about Vondel's turn to Aristotle in the 1660s.

ther. Through the adaptation of his biblical topics to the prescriptions of Greek tragedy, Vondel juxtaposed divine justice to man's limited perception of it and thereby established a basis for Christian tragedy.

## Vondel and the Religious Drama of the Renaissance

Vondel's relationship to Renaissance religious drama can be easily established since he himself composed his first two plays *Het Pascha* and *Hierusalem verwoest* within that tradition. Indeed, a quick overview of Vondel's dramatic topics from 1612 to 1662 would appear to suggest that Vondel never abandoned the sixteenth-century canon. Several of his subjects had been treated many times in sixteenth-century humanist theater: the Fall of Man, Joseph, Moses, Jeptha, Samson, David and Absalom, the fall of Jerusalem and Catholic martyr dramas, but as will be seen, it would be unjust to regard these works simply as variations of sixteenth-century plays. Similarly, Vondel's prefaces to his biblical dramas appeared to retain the moralistic purpose of sixteenth-century drama regardless of the neo-classical style in which it was written. Just as God had punished the disobedient Jews for the crucifixion of Christ in *Hierusalem verwoest* (1620), so did He promise to destroy sinful mankind in *Noah* (1667). Whereas Vondel retained such common motifs as God's punishment of evil throughout his works, other characteristics of sixteenth-century drama were discarded. The distinction between Vondel's debt to and deviation from sixteenth-century praxis ultimately determined his unique concept of Christian tragedy.

When dealing with Vondel's relationship to Renaissance drama, it is first important to recall the various types of plays and theories which were attributed to the Renaissance at the beginning of the seventeenth century. There were essentially three traditions at Vondel's disposal, the vernacular drama of the Rederijkers, the Latin school plays of the Christian humanists, and late sixteenth-century French biblical tragedy. The closing years of the 1590s had also witnessed the development of the Senecan tragedies of P. C. Hooft on two fateful Greek romances, *Achilles en Polyxena* (written 1597) and *Theseus en Ariadne* (written 1602) and the rise of the elitest Senecan closet dramas of the accomplished classical scholars, Daniel Heinsius and Hugo Grotius. But these two movements had at best only a minimal effect on Vondel's first play.

There is, however, sufficient evidence to suggest that Vondel was familiar with Latin school theater, French religious drama and especially with the contemporary praxis of Rederijker theater.[14] Indeed, *Het Pascha*

---

[14] W. J. M. A. Asselbergs, *Pascha problemen* (Hilversum: P. Brand, 1940), pp. 4-16.

(on Moses and the flight of the Jews from Egypt) has generally been regarded solely as a Rederijker play.[15] As a member of the Brabantine Rederijker chamber "'t Wit Lavendel," Vondel had had the opportunity to participate in the famous Haarlem festival in 1606 where many Rederijker dramas had been performed. The festival also acted as a meeting place for many Rederijker dramatists from various guilds throughout Holland and young Vondel, who had proudly carried his chamber's standard during the public parade, no doubt learned firsthand about the latest developments in that dramatic style. Not surprisingly, formal traces of Rederijker praxis reappeared in *Het Pascha*: the use of the allegorical figure Fama to report events not represented and the designation of each act as "deel" instead of the humanist "bedrijf." But Vondel did not so much intend to continue as to break away from the stringent Rederijker style. To be sure, the moralistic tenor of Rederijker religious drama with its repertoire of topics from medieval mystery cycles— Abraham and Isaac, St. John the Baptist—and miracle plays (e.g., the miracles and parables of Jesus)[16] appealed to Vondel as a pious Mennonite student of Scripture. From a literary standpoint, however, Vondel preferred to ally himself with recent achievements in Latin, Netherlandic and French humanist dramas and thereby distinguish himself from his Rederijker contemporaries.

In his eagerness to surpass previous Rederijker practices, Vondel first derived inspiration from Latin religious comedy. This important tie to the humanist tradition has often escaped notice because of the difficulty in ascertaining the extent of Vondel's knowledge of Latin around 1610. There is no accurate account of Vondel's training in Latin before he engaged an English tutor in 1613 to help him with the study of classical texts.[17] Vondel no doubt had had a rudimentary background in Latin at the Calvinist school in his birthplace, Cologne, but instruction there had been primarily conducted in Dutch and German. His acquaintanceship with school theater did, however, begin in Cologne, for his older sister, Clementia, had played the title role in a drama on Moses' Egyptian mother (ca. 1594-1595). A few years later (ca. 1597-1598), Vondel attended a performance in Utrecht by the students of the local Latin school of a humanist drama on David and Goliath.[18] To be sure, atten-

---

[15] Langvik-Johannessen, p. 74; Molkenboer (pp. 163-74) justly noted Vondel's deviation from Rederijker praxis as well as the similarities.

[16] For an overview of Rederijker topics in the sixteenth century, see W. M. H. Hummelen, *Repertorium van het Rederijkersdrama 1500-ca. 1620* (Assen: Van Gorcum, 1968).

[17] Molkenboer, pp. 307-10.

[18] Vondel recorded his earlier theatrical experiences in the preface to *Salmoneus* (1657): *WB*, V, pp. 712-3. The Latin drama may have been written by Gabriel Jansenius (ca. late 16th century), as Molkenboer asserted (p. 57), but it is unlikely that a drama by this

dance at a Latin play, particularly at a public performance before the city hall where a large portion of the audience was unfamiliar with the language, cannot be a gauge of Vondel's comprehension of the text. But his exposure to school drama in both Cologne and Utrecht does suggest that he was at least familiar with the five-act structure and explicit moralistic aims of the genre.

Despite the uncertainty about Vondel's understanding of Latin, previous Latin treatments of the Moses material were probably familiar to him. In 1562, Cornelius Laurimannus, Macropedius' successor to the rectorship of the Hieronymus school in Utrecht, published a "comoedia tragica" on the Jews' flight from Egypt, *Exodus sive transitus maris rubri*.[19] Given the numerous formal and structural similarities between the Latin drama and *Het Pascha*, it is likely that Vondel may have known this play. Both works were classified as tragicomedies; both displayed the five-act structure of biblical school drama with choruses after every act; and both dramas were introduced by lenghty prefaces in prose in which the authors commented *in extenso* about the utility of religious theater. Moreover, both Laurimannus and Vondel introduced a trio of Jewish leaders, who did not appear in the biblical account, to lament the misery of the Jews and later to celebrate when the promised salvation arrived. The dramas also shared a contemporary political application. Whereas the Catholic Laurimannus envisioned Moses as a papal figure protecting his church (the Israelites) from the dangers of heresy (the Egyptians with their false gods),[20] the Mennonite Vondel regarded Moses as the Dutch prince Maurice defending his fellow Protestants from the tyranny of Spain. There were also a few parallel scenes between the two works, such as Moses' soliloquy on pastoral life before the burning bush episode (Exodus 3; 4:1-23) and the encounter between Moses and the Pharaoh's magicians (Exodus 7:10-13),[21] but the common Biblical source may well have suggested the similar mode of exposition. Nonetheless, the connections between the two plays certainly support the hypothesis that Vondel

---

school rector from Aalst (Flanders), *Monomachia Davidis cum Goliath* (first printed 1600), would have been performed in Utrecht a few years earlier. It is more likely that Vondel may have seen Jacob Schoepper's *Monomachia Davidis et Goliae* (printed Dortmund, 1550), itself perhaps the model for Jansenius' play. More puzzling than the work's identity, however, is the absence of any record that a David and Goliath play was performed in Utrecht in the late 1590s. The performances recorded dealt only with Judith, Joseph (1597) and the Magdalene (1598, 1599). See A. Ekker, *De Hieronymusschool te Utrecht* (Utrecht, 1863), p. 75.

[19] Cornelius Laurimannus, *Exodus sive transitus maris rubri* (Louvain: Antonius Bergagne, 1562).

[20] Laurimannus, fol. 61-62[v].

[21] Cf. Laurimannus, fol. 17[v]-18[v] (Act II, scene 1) and *WB*, I, pp. 178-83, lines 1-140, and Laurimannus, fol. 30[v]-32[v] and *WB*, I, pp. 212-6, lines 865-1022.

was familiar with Laurimannus' play and possessed a sufficient Latin knowledge to benefit from the study of it.

Vondel's deviation from Laurimannus' school drama, however, is more noteworthy than the similarities. Like many sixteenth-century playwrights, Laurimannus had drawn on late medieval and contemporary vernacular theater for several characterizations. Pharaoh, for example, was frequently impelled to resist the Jews' pleas for freedom by his evil adviser Symbulus, a descendant of the medieval devil figure. Laurimannus also introduced two allegorical characters reminiscent of vernacular Rederijker theater to embody public opinion in both the Egyptian and Israelite camps: "populus Israelis", "populus Aegyptius." Furthermore, Laurimannus retained the epic narrative mode of much sixteenth-century school drama by beginning with Moses' birth in the first act and belaboring the confrontation between the Pharaoh and Moses in the remaining four. In contrast, Vondel dispensed with allegorical characterization and organized his plot in a more unified and economical manner. Instead of recounting each of the twelve plagues in exhausting detail, Vondel summarized them in the second-act chorus and focused instead on contrastive characterizations of Moses and Pharaoh. Both men were so burdened by the responsibilities of leadership that they yearned for a rustic existence,[22] and both were subjected to soul-wrenching hardships. But where Moses had endured the slavery of Jews through the power of faith, the desperate Pharaoh reacted to the plagues and the eventual death of his son with a call for vengeance. Such a purposeful juxtaposition of characters, atypical of both contemporary Rederijker drama and humanist comedy, betrayed Vondel's debt to the Senecan tradition of biblical tragedy. Indeed, Vondel's careful elaboration of Pharaoh's downfall recalled similar tyrannical rulers, such as Thyestes and Oedipus, in Seneca's plays. Despite an occasional borrowing from Rederijker theater and a plot reminiscent of school comedy, *Het Pascha* was written in the Senecan style of humanist tragedy.

Vondel's familiarity with Seneca was most likely based on Renaissance imitations of the Roman's plays in contemporary Netherlandic and French theater. Jacob Duym, a Rederijker dramatist from Leiden, had translated Seneca's *Troades* into Dutch in 1600 as *Den spiegel des hoochmoets,* but without any of its numerous choruses.[23] A more exacting imitator of Senecan form was P. C. Hooft, but his *Achilles en Polyxena* and *Theseus en Ariadne,* both written around 1600 and published in 1614-1615, dealt with mythological rather than religious subjects. In fact, the only Senecan

---

[22] Cf. Laurimannus, fol. 17v-18v and *WB*, I, p. 207, lines 733-748.
[23] See note 10 above.

religious dramatists in the northern Netherlands between 1600-1610 were Hugo Grotius and the Leiden schoolmaster Rochus Honerdus. The latter had actually been working on a Moses tragedy, *Moses legifer seu Nomoclastes* around 1610, but it was never published.[24] Given Vondel's proximity to vernacular traditions rather than Latin praxis, it is unlikely that he had studied Grotius' *Adamus exul* (1601) or *Christus patiens* (1608). Rather, Vondel most probably derived his knowledge of Senecan religious tragedy from late sixteenth-century French theater. He had a solid command of French—an epistolary poem to "mon singulier Amy" Jean Michiels van Vaerlaer prefaced *Het Pascha*—and, a few years later (1616), he translated several long religious works of Guillaume Du Bartas into Dutch.[25] The piety which had attracted Vondel to Du Bartas may also have drawn him to French biblical tragedy.[26] Robert Garnier's *Les Juifves* (1583) on Nebuchadnezzar's conquest of Jerusalem most certainly inspired some of the scenes in Vondel's next play, *Hierusalem verwoest* (1620). Consequently Vondel may have also been familiar with other Senecan French tragedies such as Jean de La Taille's *Saül le furieux* (1572) and *La famine, ou les Gabéonites* (1573) and Antoine de Montchrestien's *Aman* (1601) and *David* (1601).[27] Regardless of the provenance of Vondel's technique, however, the form and structure of *Het Pascha* did suggest that the author was familiar with three different types of humanist drama: Latin school comedy, Netherlandic imitations of Seneca by both Rederijkers and the Italianate poet Hooft and French biblical tragedy. A brief overview of Vondel's borrowings from each of these traditions reveals the stylistic novelty of *Het Pascha*. Where Dutch religious drama had hitherto been confined to the allegorical expositions of the Rederijker and Latin school theater, Vondel introduced the contemporary Senecan vogue. Similarly, where Dutch Senecan imitators (e.g., Duym; Hooft) formerly had dealt primarily with mythological topics, Vondel replaced their pagan content with a religious plot. *Het Pascha* was thus a Netherlandic confirmation of the tradition of Renaissance religious drama in which biblical episodes were adapted to the form and language of classical theater.

---

[24] J. IJsewijn, "Annales theatri Belgo-Latini. Inventaris van het Latijns toneel uit de Nederlanden," in *Liber amicorum G. DeGroote* (Brussels, 1980), p. 50. The manuscript of *Moses legifer* was last known to be in the private possession of J. H. Hoeufft (d. 1843).

[25] Vondel translated Du Bartas' *Les Pères* (a portion from his *Seconde semaine ou l'enfance du monde*) in 1616 as *De vaderen* and, from the same work, *La Magnificence de Salomon,* in 1620 as *De heerlyckheyd van Salomon*. On this relationship, see A. Hendriks, *Joost van den Vondel en G. de Saluste Sr. du Bartas* (Leiden, 1892).

[26] Asselbergs, p. 9.

[27] For a brief analysis of these works, see J. S. Street, *French Sacred Drama from Bèze to Corneille* (Cambridge: Cambridge University, 1983), pp. 67-72 (De la Taille); 83-90 (Garnier); 111-3 (Montchrestien).

In light of Vondel's stylistic debt to humanist theater, it is not surprising that the programmatic preface to *Het Pascha* should retain many sixteenth-century arguments on the utility and goals of religious drama. Indeed, similar theoretical introductions had been a common practice among Latin school playwrights, and Vondel most likely adapted this technique to accord with his composition of a humanist religious drama in the vernacular. Many of Vondel's ideas on the moral function of drama were probably drawn from the Rederijkers rather than the Latin humanists, but since there was a considerable overlap between these two schools it is impossible to attribute Vondel's arguments to a single source. Both groups had promoted the visual effectiveness of religious drama over the spoken and written words: Vondel was especially eager that his talking pictures ("een levende schoon-verwighe schilderije")[28] clarify religious lessons which his Christian audience otherwise would be unable to comprehend. The moral utility of theater was likewise defended by the familiar arguments about the stage as a mirror (or theater) of the world from which men could learn to distinguish between good and evil behavior.

Religious arguments from the Rederijker and humanist traditions were also introduced. The primary function of religious drama, Vondel asserted, was the instilling of piety into the hearts of the faithful.[29] To this end, the salvation of mankind would be represented through the prefigurative Old Testament allegory of the Jewish liberation. In keeping with sixteenth-century humanist practice, Vondel further explicated the spiritual allegory of *Het Pascha* in the choral epilogue: just as Moses freed the Jews from Egypt, so would Christ one day preserve all men from sin through the blood (Red Sea) of the Redemption. But, the most distinctive feature of the introduction was Vondel's incorporation of Renaissance dramatic praxis into his defense of the genre. To support the idea that the Bible contained several plots worthy of dramatic adaptation, Vondel referred to topics which had often already been treated in the Dutch, Latin and French stage: The Good Samaritan (Zacharias Heyns),[30] the prodigal son (Gulielmus Gnapheus, Robert Lawet),[31]

---

[28] *WB*, I, p. 164. On the visual effectiveness of theater (after Horace, *Ars poetica* 179), see chapter 2, note 30.

[29] "tot prijs van den heylighen ende ghebenedijden Name Godts," *WB*, I, p. 166.

[30] Zacharias Heyns' play on the Good Samaritan was performed at the Haarlem Rederijker festival of 1606 in which Vondel participated; Heyns wrote the play in reply to the question "wat den mensche mach wecken om den armen te troesten ende zijne naesten bij te staen," Asselbergs, p. 7.

[31] Gulielmus Gnapheus, *Acolastus* (1529); Robert Lawet, *Twee schoone rethoryckelicke speelen // van zinnen ende vanden Verlooren // Zoone ... 1583*, ms. cited in Hummelen, p. 53.

Lazarus and the Rich Man (D. V. Coornhert),[32] the fall of Jerusalem (Robert Garnier) and the death of Saul (Jean de la Taille). Without naming any authors, Vondel adroitly aligned himself with the tradition of Renaissance religious drama in order to defend his first play from the censure of his fellow poets and to underscore his humanist transformation of the Rederijker style.

Vondel's debt to the sixteenth century was not only evident in the preface but also in the drama itself. In keeping with his avowed intention to explicate the hidden mysteries of the Moses story for his audience, Vondel provided several allegorical interpretations of his play. Sixteenth-century writers had frequently analyzed their biblical dramas according to the fourfold method of Scriptural exegesis: the playwrights not only represented the biblical events but they also appended an allegorical, tropological (or moral) and anagogical (spiritual) reading to their texts. Although Vondel did not classify the different levels of allegory in *Het Pascha* in this manner, it is clear that four such interpretations could be derived from the play. Vondel himself explicated the spiritual (anagogical) significance of the Jew's flight from Egypt. The anagogical level was adumbrated in the preface through Vondel's reference to the typological correspondence between Old and New Testament. He expanded this parallel further in the play itself by composing emblematic episodes so that Moses' prefiguration of Christ would be immediately apparent. In the opening scene, for example, Moses was portrayed as a watchful shepherd over his flocks, a duty which foreshadowed his subsequent function as a leader of Israel. At the same time, the contemporary Christian, who through religious worship was trained to perceive correspondences between the Old and New Testament, would have instantly recognized Moses as Christ, the Good Shepherd, the savior of mankind from sin (Luke 15:3-7). Vondel, moreover, provided an allegorical checklist in the final chorus lest the true meaning of the Paschal offering be obscured by the plot.[33] Thus, Pharaoh was equated with Satan, the Jewish captivity with man's enslavement to sin and the Paschal Lamb with Christ, the sacrificial offering necessary for the salvation of man. In view of the prominence given to the anagogical reading, it is clear that Vondel entitled his play *Het Pascha (The Paschal Feast),* rather than the obvious *Exodus* of Laurimannus or *Moses* of Rochus Honerdus, to underline its christological significance. Although the drama also contained a political-allegorical and tropological message, the

---

[32] D. V. Coornhert, *Comedie vande Rijckeman* (1582).
[33] *WB,* I, pp. 256-60, lines 2055-2202 (the final chorus).

Redemption of man, rather than the liberation of the Jews, was its primary lesson.

In addition to the anagogical reading, Vondel also took pains to interpret the play as a political allegory of the late sixteenth-century Netherlands. In a poem appended to the published text of 1612, Vondel likened Pharaoh to Philip II of Spain, the Jewish bondage to Spanish tyranny and Moses to the House of Nassau.[34] In the tradition of Rederijker and Latin plays on the assassination of William the Silent (1584)[35]— the latest version *Het moordadich stuck van Balthasar Gerards* (1606) by the Senecan Rederijker Jacob Duym—Vondel now apotheosized the Dutch leader by likening him to Moses. It has been suggested by some critics that Vondel had separated the political allegory from the biblical play so as not to profane Holy Scripture.[36] On the contrary, Vondel was eager to regard the Dutch attainment of independence as a righteous act of God, and at the end of the poem he called on divine justice to destroy all enemies of the state.[37] Moreover, Vondel had interspersed his views on the ideal king and the dangers of tyranny throughout the play. The shepherd image of Moses in the opening scene, which had anagogically prefigured his savior role, was also used allegorically on the same occasion to decry the abuse of kingship. Moses' lament for his fellow Jews referred not only to their slavery, but also to the Pharaoh's misrule:

> Tyran! och! oft ghy eens begrijpen mocht int minst,
> Dat herderlijck beroep den Koninghlijcken dienst
> Beteecken t'eenemael, ghy bleeft niet zoo versteenight,
> Zaeght ghy den Scepter met den Herder-staf vereenigt:
> Het Herder-ampt vereyscht, dat hy syn kudde hoet,
> De Koning dat hy t'volc heerscht met een wijs gemoet,
> Den Herder moet syn kud voor des wolfs tanden vrijen,
> De Koningh weeren al d'uytheemsche tyrannijen,
> Dat d'Herder-staf geen Lam voor d'ander stoot noch sla,
> En elck Inwoonder hoort den Scepter even na,
> D'een vlies voor d'ander komt de weyde niet ten goeden;
> Zoo hoort t'Rijck op te staen, om yeghelijc te voeden:[38]

Similarly, Pharaoh's spiritual blindness was intimated by his disregard for the populace and his unconditional exercise of power—familiar characteristics of the stock Senecan tyrant. In a world in which religion and

---

[34] *WB*, I, pp. 261-4.

[35] On these dramas on William the Silent, see B. A. Vermaseren, "Humanistische drama's over de moord op de vader des vaderlands," *TNTL*, 68 (1951), 31-67.

[36] Smit, vol. 1, p. 60.

[37] *WB*, I, p. 263, lines 67-68:
Help God! de wraeck is u, ghy zult hier namaels eyssen
Het dier vergoten bloedt met een ghekromde Zeyssen.

[38] *WB*, I, p. 180, lines 53-64.

politics were inseperably intertwined, Vondel followed the humanist practice of using religious drama to support a political argument.

Moral instruction had always been the primary function of religious drama. In *Het Pascha*, however, ethical lessons were subordinated to the predominant political and soteriological goals. The tragic fate of the Pharaoh had, of course, served as a negative exemplum to remind the viewers of the dangers of disobedience. But more importantly, Vondel introduced three Jewish leaders as positive models for the ideal Christian's reaction to misfortune.[39] Whereas one elder, Corach, yearned for death to escape misfortune, the pious Iosua urged his fellow Jews to atone for their former sins for which they were now suffering. Since all hardship was sent from God to strengthen the virtuous and punish sinners, the Jews were now enjoined to anticipate the liberation which they would one day certainly attain. To emphasize the tropological significance of this scene, Vondel concluded it with the arrival of Moses and his promise of triumph. As in sixteenth-century biblical drama, the moral education of the Christian was effected by the visual representation of just rewards and punishments.

Vondel's adherence to Renaissance religious drama was thus reflected in *Het Pascha* in three ways: (1) his introduction of a religious topic to a classical dramatic structure; (2) his ascription of an allegorical, tropological and anagogical interpretation to the play and (3) his overt depiction of divine justice. All three aspects would subsequently be revised to accord with Vondel's notion of Christian tragedy. In this first drama, Vondel did not so much retain Rederijker theater as adapt its traditional religious subject to the new Senecan humanist style in the vernacular. In later works, Vondel continued to connect religious topics to the form and theory of Greaco-Roman tragedy. Indeed, Vondel measured his own artistic achievement and that of his fellow playwrights against classical standards. In 1615, he praised the biblical tragedy of his fellow Rederijker in the Brabantine chamber, Abraham de Koning, *Iephthahs ende zijn eenighe dochters treur-spel,*[40] by noting its debt, if not its superiority to the ancients:

> *Euripides* voor langhs dede al d'Aenschouwers weenen
> Doen *Iphigenia* bebloeden zijn Toonneel,
> En als een schoone Bloem van haren groenen steel
> Geblixemt nederviel, gelijck een schauw verdwenen:
>
> Doch *Koning* doet niet min wanneer hy't oud voorhenen
> Droef Schouw-Spel ons vernieut, en 't Maegdelijcke bloed

---

[39] *WB*, I, pp. 189-202. This scene was probably based on Laurimannus, fol. 27-28ᵛ.

[40] Abraham de Koning, *Iephthahs ende zijn eenighe dochters treur-spel* (Amsterdam: Paulus van Ravesteyn, 1615).

Van *Iephthahs* weerdste pant, uytstort als eenen vloed,
Dan stervet al met haer, dan bersten schier de steenen.

Zoo werd een oud geschicht vergetelheyt ontogen,
En levend'wederom gebootst voor yders oogen,
Zoo een uytheemsche daed met onze stof bekleed.[41]

Vondel likewise regarded his own plays as moral equivalents, if not improvements, of pagan classical models. The Old Testament Joseph was extolled as a Christian Hippolytus in *Joseph in Egypten* (1640) while Ursula (*Maeghden,* 1639) was characterized as a Christian Amazon in the tradition of Penthesilea.[42] But after Vondel studied the formal sophistication of Greek tragedy in the late 1630s, his attitudes toward ancient theater changed. He was no longer so much concerned with the ethical qualities of his figures as with the adaptation of formal attributes of Greek tragedy. In contrast to the Renaissance playwrights who had established an ethical competition between ancient and Christian theater, Vondel later attempted to rival the ancients aesthetically. As will be seen, this subordination of ethics to the Aristotelian prescriptions for tragedy set the stage for Vondel's neo-classical transformation of biblical drama.

Vondel's subsequent deviation from the tradition of sixteenth-century Christian humanist drama was further evinced by the breakdown of the synthesis of the political, moral and spiritual interpretations of a single play. Political allegories were henceforth associated with mythological plots (*Palamedes,* 1625, on the execution of Johan van Oldenbarnevelt), and historical subjects (*Maria Stuart,* 1646, on the persecution of Catholics). As Vondel's interest in the aesthetics of tragedy increased, the ethical utility of drama also degenerated into a theoretical commonplace for Vondel's arguments against the Calvinist opponents of theater. The later Vondel did not so much seek to teach as to cast doubts on the possibility of man's educability. The spiritual significance of the biblical event was likewise removed from the play. Although Vondel would refer to the Redemption in other religious dramas, *Het Pascha* was the only biblical play in which such salvation was actually represented.[43] Similarly, because of the absence of the Redemption, divine justice subsequently became a problematic concept. Where *Het Pascha* had ended justly with virtue rewarded and sin condemned, Vondel later focused on punishment alone.

---

[41] *WB,* I, p. 472.
[42] *WB,* IV, p. 150 (Joseph); *WB,* III, p. 711 (Ursula).
[43] In the martyr plays *Maeghden* (1639) and *Peter en Pauwels* (1641), however, the protagonists gained an eternal crown; in contrast, such rewards were absent in *Samson* (1660) and *Noah* (1667) where destruction accompanied the promise of grace.

*Het Pascha* thus occupied a unique position in the canon of Vondel's biblical plays, for it contained all the attributes of sixteenth-century drama which he later transformed: the representation of divine justice, the ethical utility of sacred theater and the christological significance of the Old Testament. The pious Vondel did not, of course, deny the existence of any of these elements; he objected rather to the unsophisticated manner in which such concepts had been portrayed on the stage. In contrast to the sixteenth century, Vondel later emphasized the complexity of the relationship between God and fallen man. For a contemporary Christian, Vondel realized that divine justice was seldom, if ever apparent, that perfect virtue was unattainable and that the concept of salvation defied all reason. Nonetheless, he glorified the mysterious faith which impelled men to trust in Providence, embrace virtues and hope for the grace of the Redemption. This unbridgeable gap between God's justice and man's faulty perception of it, between the imitation of virtue and man's fallen state and between the promise of a Redeemer and man's despair became the showplace for the downfall of Vondel's tragic heroes.

### The Joseph Plays: The Christian Ideal in a Fallen World

Vondel's deviation from Renaissance dramatic praxis was first apparent in the three Old Testament tragedies of 1640: *Gebroeders, Joseph in Dothan* and *Joseph in Egypten*. Drawing on plots which had been treated by sixteenth-century playwrights, Vondel transformed the tendentious didactic dramas of the previous century into tragedies about the evil consequences of man's Fall. In all three works, the Christian humanist assumptions about man's educability, the justice of God and the certainty of salvation were severely tested. Vondel did not intend to refute these assumptions, for as the theoretical prefaces to these dramas made plain, he shared them as well. Rather, he hoped to qualify these humanist ideals by assessing the difficulty or ease with which fallen man could live accordingly. Vondel's discovery of the complexity of this struggle between man and God led to his revision of humanist religious drama.

Vondel's break from the Renaissance tradition was not an explicit program of reform. Indeed, his critical reception of Renaissance drama can only be perceived through a comparative analysis between the biblical plays of 1640 and earlier humanist treatments of the same material. The two Joseph tragedies are especially well suited for this purpose, for this Old Testament subject had been adapted many times by several humanist dramatists.[44] Vondel himself had been attracted to the subject by several previous versions, and his two plays were written with an eye to both his contemporaries and predecessors. His interest in Joseph had first been aroused by his close friend Hugo Grotius. Vondel greatly admired Grotius' 1635 Latin tragedy *Sophompaneas* on Joseph's reunion with his brothers (Genesis 42-45) since it was intentionally modeled on Greek drama. Having recently discovered Greek theater through Grotius' assistance, Vondel eagerly translated the play (Dutch title: *Sofompaneas*, 1635) so as to rival the ancients in the vernacular. Accordingly, the emotional denouement between Joseph and his brother was deemed an accomplished imitation of Euripides: "en doet alle toezienders zo schreyen en tot water smelten van beweegelijckheid, dat de treurspeelder den wijzen Euripides (die in het harteroeren boven anderen uitsteeckt) niet en durf wijcken."[45]

Although Vondel's friendship with Grotius had first directed him to Joseph, his two original plays of 1640 were inspired by the multipartite Joseph dramas of his contemporaries. Jan Tonnis (1607-1672?), a former member of Vondel's Mennonite community in Amsterdam, had published a trilogy in Groningen in 1639, *Iosephs droef en bly-eynd'-spel*,[46] on the entire Joseph story from the sale of the hero by his brothers to Joseph's triumphant reunion with Jacob in Egypt. In the same year, Jacob Libenus (1603-1678), a Flemish Jesuit, published two tragedies, *Josephus venditus* and *Josephus agnitus,* which he had written for the Jesuit schools in Mechelen and Antwerp.[47] As is evident from the titles, the first, which had already appeared in a 1634 anthology of Jesuit drama,[48] dealt with Joseph's enslavement and the second with his reunion with his brothers. Vondel was doubtless familiar with the work of his fellow Dutchman Tonnis; he also maintained close ties to the Jesuits—he con-

---

[44] On the sixteenth-century Latin school stage in the Netherlands, Joseph plays were written by Cornelius Crocus (1536), Georgius Macropedius (ca. 1540) and Cornelius Schonaeus (1590). For a recent account of these works as well as the Joseph plays produced in Germany, see Jean Lebeau, *Salvator Mundi: l' "exemple" de Joseph dans le théâtre allemand au XVI<sup>e</sup> siècle*, 2 vols. (Nieuwkoop: B. de Graaf, 1977).

[45] *WB,* III, p. 434.

[46] Jan Tonnis, *Iosephs droef ende bly-eynd'-spel* (Groningen: A. Eissens, 1639). On Tonnis, see H. F. Wijnmann, "Jan Tonnis, de schrijver van *Josephs droef en bly-eind spel,"* *Vondel-Kroniek,* 11 (1940), 172-81.

[47] There are no records of any performance of Libenus' plays, but they were probably read in the schools in Mechelen and Antwerp. On the former, see Raymond van Aerde, *Het schooldrama bij de Jezuieten, bijdrage tot de geschiedenis van het tooneel te Mechelen* (Mechelen: H. Dierickx-Beke, 1937). For a brief comparison of Libenus' *Josephus venditus* with *Joseph in Dothan,* see L. van den Boogerd, *Het Jezuietendrama in de Nederlanden* (Groningen: J. B. Wolters, 1961), pp. 147-50.

[48] *Selectae patrum Societatis Jesu tragoediae,* vol. 2 (Antwerp: Ioan. Cnobbarus, 1634).

verted to Catholicism in 1641[49]—whose theater he subsequently praised in his 1661 *Tooneelschilt*, an apologia for drama.[50] The extensive treat-ment of the Joseph material by Tonnis and Libenus therefore may well have inspired Vondel to supplement his translation of Grotius with two other plays to form a triptych.[51] Since Grotius had written the final chapter, Vondel focused on the two episodes which previous Joseph dramatists had often portrayed: the sale of Joseph by his brother and Joseph's precarious career at the Egyptian court in the service of Potiphar and his seductive wife. In composing his trilogy Vondel thus aligned himself with prior dramatizations and thereby established a basis of comparison for his own interpretations of the popular material.

Vondel's interpretation of Joseph was initially based on Grotius' characterization of him in *Sophompaneas*. In the dedicatory letter of 15 July 1634 to his close friend Gerardus Vossius, the prominent Netherlan-dic humanist,[52] Grotius explicated the reasons for his fondness for the Joseph character. The composition of this tragedy was closely related to the personal hardships which Grotius had suffered since his 1619 imprisonment for his sympathies with the condemned Land's Advocate, Johan van Oldenbarnevelt. With the assistance of his clever wife, Grotius had escaped from prison in 1621 and taken up residence in Paris where he subsisted on a meager pension from Louis XIII. While in prison, Grotius drew comfort from the study of Greek tragedy, especially from Euripides' *Phoenissae,* and he published a Latin translation of it in Paris in 1631.[53] In the prose prologue to that work, Grotius extolled the

---

[49] The date of Vondel's conversion to Catholicism has been the subject of a heated debate between Catholic and Protestant critics. Molkenboer suggested 1639: B. H. Molkenboer, "Wanneer werd Vondel Katholiek?" *Vondel-Kroniek*, 3 (1932), 82; W. A. P. Smit made the more reasonable suggestion that Vondel converted in 1641, the date when Vondel's conversion was recorded in the *Litterae annuae* of the Jesuits: W. A. P. Smit, "Vondel en zijn bekering," *NTg*, 29 (1935), 264. I agree with Smit's argument that Vondel was attracted to Roman Catholicism since the Church had appealed to the hope of the Mennonite Vondel for universal peace ("pax ecclesiastica"): Smit, "Beker-ing," pp. 258-9.

[50] *WB,* IX, p. 386.

[51] The idea of a dramatic trilogy may have been suggested to Vondel through his reading of the three Joseph plays of Theodorus Rhodius (ca. 1570-1626), a schoolteacher in the Palatinate, whose works Vondel could have known through the 1625 Strasbourg edition. Rhodius' plays were entitled: *Josephus venditus, Josephus servus* and *Josephus princeps.* Libenus' *Josephus venditus* (1634) had most likely been inspired by Rhodius' play of the same name, for both dramatists employed the pathetic, declamatory style of Seneca. On Rhodius, see Paul Stachel, *Seneca und das deutsche Renaissancedrama* (Berlin: Mayer & Müller, 1907), pp. 120-36.

[52] On Vossius see the excellent biography: C. S. M. Rademaker, *Life and Work of Gerardus Joannes Vossius (1577-1649)* (Assen: Van Gorcum, 1981).

[53] *Euripidis Tragoedia Phoenissae.* Emendata ex manuscriptis & latina facta ab Hugone Grotius (Paris: Jacobus Ruart, 1630). In the following discussion, I have quoted from: Euripides, *Tragoedia Phoenissae.* Interpretationem addidit H. Grotii et al. Ludovicus Casp. Valckenaer (Leiden, 1802) .

therapeutic effect of tragedy, for its ability to arouse and purge the emotions had helped him to endure the difficulties which Fate had ordained.[54] Grotius ascribed a similar effect to Joseph's potential as a tragic protagonist. In the letter to Vossius, Grotius established Joseph as a model for those men who, like himself, did not despair of God's guidance during times of persecution.[55] Just as Joseph was eventually rewarded for his perseverance through his rule in Egypt and reunion with his family, so had Grotius likewise been assisted by the Swedish crown. He regarded his appointment as Swedish ambassador to Paris (1634) as an achievement comparable to Joseph's attainment of the administration of Egypt. In the *Sophompaneas*, Grotius consequently dispensed the consolatory advice which he had always derived from tragedy. Through the demonstration of virtue rewarded, Grotius was able to inspire the perseverance man required to endure misfortune and trust in God.

In the translator's preface to *Sofompaneas*, Vondel similarly noted the consolatory effect which Joseph's fate would have on the viewer. Joseph was intended to serve as "een zuivere spiegel der eerst verdruckte, maer namaels gekroonde deughd en Godtvruchtigheid."[56] Since his wife had recently died in 1635, Vondel himself urgently required solace. The translation of *Sophompaneas* was also able to free him from the sorrow he experienced when his mentor, Grotius, had once again been constrained to leave the Netherlands after a brief return from exile in 1632. Confident of the righteousness of God, Vondel was comforted by this exemplum of justice vindicated, and he therefore attempted to overcome his grief through dramatic composition.

In keeping with his affection for Grotius, Vondel further developed other aspects of *Sophompaneas* which would subsequently influence his 1640 portrait of Joseph. Besides the interpretation of Joseph as an example of Divine Providence, Vondel was also struck by the hero's political acumen.[57] Grotius had presented Joseph as a masterful statesman who not only resolved his familial conflicts but also averted the dangers of civil war in Egypt. In a non-biblical episode, Grotius portrayed Joseph's fair and able handling of a peasant revolt against the provincial landowners whose selfish appropriation of grain had resulted in widespread famine.[58]

---

[54] "Ego in carcerem conjectus ab his, qui me ignorabant, post sacras meditationes existimavi remedium mihi posse aliquod et a tragoedia praestari; quam affectuum non tantum movendorum, sed et movendo purgandorum causa institutam, a summis magistris proditum memineram." *Tragoedia Phoenissae* (ed. 1802), p. x.

[55] Hugo Grotius, *Tragoedia Sophompaneas* (Amsterdam: Gulielmus Blaeu), pp. 6-7.

[56] *WB*, III, p. 433.

[57] *WB*, III, p. 435.

[58] Grotius, *Sophompaneas,* pp. 28-34 (Act III, scene 1).

Moved by the plight of the starving peasants whose desperation had driven them to heed the advice of greedy agitators and occupy the city of Coptos, Joseph ordered the landowners imprisoned, dispersed grain to the needy and sentenced their rapacious leaders to the mines. Vondel consequently regarded Joseph as a lover of justice and peace whose wisdom might well be an apt model for contemporary politicians. Moreover, Vondel was especially moved by the emotions which Joseph's reconciliation with his brothers unleashed. Mindful of Grotius' concept of the cathartic effect of tragedy, Vondel similarly hoped that his style would rival Euripides and free his viewers from their subservience to their passions.[59]

Vondel continued his admiration for Grotius in *Joseph in Dothan* by retaining the three qualities he esteemed in *Sophompaneas*: the unchangeable and just nature of Divine Providence, the importance of peace and the emotional effect of drama. In the dedicatory letter to Ioachim van Wickevort, Vondel underlined Joseph's significance as an exemplum "hoe Gots voorzienigheit zich hier van wel weet te dienen, tot uitvoeringe van zijn verborgen besluit."[60] Several misfortunes assailed Joseph in the play—his brothers' hatred, his imprisonment in the well, Ruben's reluctance to save him and his sale into slavery—but Vondel took special pains in each instance to dispel any doubts about Providence which such injustices might provoke. In the opening scene, a chorus of angels prophesied Joseph's eventual triumph over his brothers; shortly thereafter, Joseph, who had been troubled by a nightmare about his brothers' enmity, was heartened by an angel's promise that God would never abandon him. The same angel chorus reaffirmed God's justice and Joseph's immunity from danger at the end of each of the following acts by praising the hero's constancy and virtue and foretelling the glory of his subsequent rule in Egypt:

> Daer zal men, in dat prachtigh hof,
> Wiens naeldepunt Godts hof beschiet,
> Zien, hoe de Nijl, de groote vliet,
> ............................................
> De Kroon met zeven tacken buight,
> Voor zyne Godtheit, voor zijn hooft,
> 't Welck aller wyzen glans verdooft.[61]

Vondel thus established a firm connection between *Joseph in Dothan* and *Sophompaneas* by referring to Grotius' portrait of Joseph the statesman to

---

[59] *WB*, III, p. 434.
[60] *WB*, IV, p. 74.
[61] *WB*, IV, pp. 128-9, lines 1176-1178; 1180-1182.

demonstrate the necessity for and benefits of a steadfast belief in divine justice.

Vondel also ascribed additional themes from *Sophompaneas* to his first Joseph drama. Vondel, who shared Grotius' opinion on the emotional impact of tragedy, was especially desirous of creating scenes to achieve this effect. He was especially moved by the animosity which the brothers had displayed toward Joseph and by the shortsightedness of parents like Jacob who had allowed their excessive affection of one child to evoke envy between siblings. This fraternal hatred was also imbued with a contemporary political significance borrowed from Grotius' play: Vondel encouraged his readers to acquire Joseph's ability to deal fairly and mercifully with their enemies. The imitation of such Christ-like behavior was seen as the only means whereby civil war between contemporary Christians could be avoided.[62] As in *Sophompaneas*, Joseph was conceived as a political exemplum whose sagacity and pacifism might well resolve the religious and political turmoil of the mid-seventeenth century.

Although Vondel restated Grotius' characterization in the dedicatory letter, these views were not reflected in the play. The affirmation of divine justice dominated the choral songs, but the actual representation of virtue rewarded was withheld. Where Grotius had joyfully concluded his work with Joseph's revelation of his true identity to his brothers, Vondel's dramas ended with the enslavement (*Joseph in Dothan*) and imprisonment (*Joseph in Egypten*) of the hero. Similarly, Vondel also refrained from importing his political interpretation of the Joseph story into the play. Where the choruses of *Het Pascha* had echoed the patriotic fervor voiced in the appended political poem, Vondel's hopes for a united Christian Europe in *Joseph in Dothan* were restricted to the preface. The emotional effect of the Joseph story which Vondel had initially noted was likewise transformed in the drama. The injustice which Joseph had been forced to experience at the hands of his brothers was certainly as poignant as Vondel suggested, but as will be seen, the emotional impact of *Joseph in Dothan* lay elsewhere. The inability of the willing but fearful Ruben to save his younger brother and his subsequent lamentation about Joseph's loss produced the moving climax of the play. The pathetic weeping of the well-intentioned Ruben rather than the righteous indignation caused by

---

[62] "gelijck noch hedensdaeghs onder de Christenen, die, gebroeders en leden eens lichaems zijnde, en zich luttel aen Iosephs verdriet keerende, den onnoozelen dagelix vangen verkoopen en leveren aen hunne allerbitterste en gezwore erfvyanden; wanneer ze, d'een den anderen verradende en vernielende, liever de poorten van Christenrijck voor den Ismaëlleren open zetten, dan malkanderen toegeven en ondergaen." *WB*, IV, p. 74.

the brothers' sale was the primary source of the emotional upheaval in Vondel's tragedy.

Paradoxically, the reason for the discrepancy between Vondel's purported intentions and the drama itself were related to his fondness for Grotius. Vondel did not merely borrow Grotius' interpretation of Joseph to establish the chronological connection between his own play and *Sophompaneas*; he also modeled *Joseph in Dothan* on Grotius' youthful tragedy *Christus patiens* (1608).[63] Indeed, the parallels between the latter work and Vondel's drama were so numerous that *Joseph in Dothan* appeared to be an intentional though unacknowledged imitation of *Christus patiens*. A comparison of the goals and characterizations in both works can in fact clarify the reasons for the incongruities between Vondel's preface and his text.

Grotius' *Christus patiens* was in many respects an innovative drama. Written during Grotius' active political career as Attorney General for the new Dutch Republic, it was primarily an elitist tribute from a precocious youth to his literary mentor Joseph Scaliger. Having dealt with man's Fall in his first play, *Adamus exul* (1601), Grotius was eager to supplement that work with an account of the Passion and Redemption in *Christus patiens*. Besides the obvious religious lesson, Grotius intended that his new drama would resolve several literary problems about religious tragedy which had hitherto been avoided or mishandled by previous playwrights. His first concern related to the dramatization of the Passion as a tragedy. Since the Passion culminated with the Redemption of man, its denouement could hardly be construed as sorrowful. As a student of Graeco-Roman drama and Renaissance poetics, however, Grotius well knew that tragedies could end happily; both Euripides (*Iphigenia among the Taurians*) and Seneca (*Hercules Oetaeus*) had provided precedents for such dramas.[64] Secondly, Grotius was eager to demonstrate that the Passion could be successfully adapted to the form and language of Senecan tragedy. To this end, he modeled his play on the recently discovered Byzantine drama ΧΡΙΣΤΟΣ ΠΑΣΧΩΝ which

---

[63] On *Christus patiens* as a literary work, see Christian Gellinek, *Hugo Grotius* (Boston: Twayne, 1983), pp. 15-20, and A. Eijffinger's introduction to the play in *De dichtwerken van Hugo Grotius. Oorspronkelijke dichtwerken*, Tweede deel, Pars 5 A & B, ed. B. L. Meulenbroek (Assen: Van Gorcum, 1978), pp. 23-36.

[64] Grotius most likely knew Julius Caesar Scaliger's revision of the medieval formulation that all tragedies end sadly: "ut nequaquam sit quod hactenus professi sunt, Tragoediae proprium, exitus infelix: modò intus sint res atroces." Julius Caesar Scaliger, *Poetices libri septem*, ed. August Buck, Faksimile-Neudruck der Ausgabe von Lyon 1561 (Stuttgart and Bad Cannstatt: Frommann, 1964), p. 145. There is little doubt that Grotius conceived of his title hero as a christianization of the Hercules figure in *Hercules Oetaeus*: Eijffinger, p. 32.

sixteenth-century writers had ascribed to the fourth-century Church father Gregorius Nazianzenus.[65] Where the Greek author had focused almost exclusively on the lamentations of the Virgin Mary before the cross, Grotius expanded the drama to include the reactions of the apostles, the Jews and the Romans. Similarly, in contrast to the Greek dramatist, who had slavishly strung together quotations from Euripides, Grotius hoped to illustrate that Senecan language could be inventively combined with a Christian subject. In this way Grotius intended not only to surpass secular tragedy and the Byzantine model, but also to assess the effect of the Redemption on mankind.

Vondel betrayed his debt to Grotius' *Christus patiens* in both the preface and text of *Joseph in Dothan*. In the dedicatory letter, Vondel shared Grotius' competitive attitude toward Graeco-Roman drama and the Byzantine passion play; he proudly noted the similarities between Joseph's stormy relationship with his brothers and classical precedents for fraternal strife. Just as Polynices and Eteocles had vied for Thebes (Euripides' *Phoenissae*) and Atreus and Thyestes for kingship (Seneca's *Thyestes*), so did the brothers compete with Joseph for their father's affection.[66] Vondel, moreover, took pains to extol the supremacy of his biblical plot to the pagan parallels, for "de heilige, boven andere geschiedenissen, altijt voor zich brengen een zekere goddelijcke majesteit en aenbiddelijcke eerwaerdigheit, die nergens zoo zeer dan in treurspelen vereischt worden."[67] As in *Het Pascha,* Vondel eagerly replaced a pagan with a sacred subject so that biblical truths would be enhanced by the neo-classical form.

Since Vondel and Grotius were both engaged in the familiar humanist practice of joining religious topics to a classical style, their use of the competitive imitation trope was hardly accidental. More importantly, Vondel's close ties to *Christus patiens* were illustrated by his political interpretation of the Joseph material. Vondel's hope that Joseph's pacifism would induce contemporary Christians to avoid internal disputes recalled the preface to *Christus patiens*. On that occasion Grotius had pleaded with Petrus Ianninus, the French legate to the Dutch States General, to persuade Henri IV to mediate an end to the Dutch war with Spain. Troubled by the internecine conflict between Catholics and Protestants, Grotius dramatized the Passion, for the Redemption was the only belief

---

[65] For a discussion of the Renaissance reception of the Byzantine play, see chapter 1, pp. 55-6.
[66] *WB*, IV, p. 73.
[67] *WB*, IV, pp. 73-74.

all Christians still shared.[68] His reference to Christ's death, like Vondel's warning about fraternal jealously, was thus designed to promote the Erasmian ideal of a united Christendom, lest the present political and religious strife destroy the principles of that faith forever.[69]

The close connection between *Christus patiens* and *Joseph in Dothan* was evidenced further by several parallels between the plays. In the first place, both men had written works in which the apparently tragic fate of the protagonist was subsequently revealed as an occasion for joy. Secondly, each writer assigned the main figure a minimal role; they were not so much interested in the fate of the titular hero as in the reaction of the other characters to his misfortune. To this end, they established a sharp contrast between the divinely protected protagonist—Christ or Joseph—and the other figures who were too blinded by fear or sorrow to discern the justice of God behind the victim's fate. Where tragedy had previously been determined by the downfall of the protagonist, Vondel and Grotius aroused a tragic response through their depiction of mankind's misperception of the truth.

Vondel initially applied Grotius' portrait of Christ to his hero. In both tragedies, the opening act was devoted to the protagonist's recognition of imminent suffering and his painful decision to endure it. Grotius presented Jesus' agony in Gethsemane where Christ's all-too-human fears clashed with his acknowledgment of the necessity of his death. On the one hand, Jesus recoiled in the foreknowledge of his fate ("horresco nefas"),[70] but shortly thereafter he declared his willingness to die for the salvation of man ("sponte festino mori").[71] Following his model, Vondel took pains to emphasize Joseph's biblical role as a descendant of Christ. The entire first act with its chorus of angels who comforted the innocent hero was an iconographic prefiguration of the New Testament scene in which angels ministered to Jesus (Matthew 4:11). To underscore this parallel, the chorus foretold that the Redeemer of man would one day arise from Joseph's house:

---

[68] On his sacred plot Grotius commented: "Haec eadem est quae sola Christianorum mentes adeo dissociatas atque divulsas, et tanto inter se odio certantes quanto amore deberent, ferme invitas adhuc continet, neque in immensum a se invicem discedere patitur." Grotius, *Christus patiens* (1978), p. 55.

[69] Erasmus' pacificism was especially evident in his *Querula pacis* where the promotion of peace was associated with true Christianity: "Quisquis Christum annuciat, pacem annunciat. Quisquis bellum praedicat, illum praedicat, qui Christi dissimillimus est," in *Ausgewählte Werke*, vol. 5, ed. Werner Welzig (Darmstadt: Wissenschaftliche Buchgesellschaft, 1968), p. 382. On parallels between the pacificism of Erasmus and Grotius, see G. J. de Voogd, *Erasmus en Grotius* (Leiden: Ned. Uitgeversmaatschappij, 1946), pp. 51-79; 135-68.

[70] Grotius, *Christus patiens* (1978), p. 75. line 90.

[71] Grotius, *Christus patiens* (1978), p. 79, line 133.

Waer van ghy, eedle spruit, het wercktuigh strecken moet,
En leggen d'eersten steen en grontsteen, aen den voet
Van 't stamhuis, 't welck, eerst laegh van top en naeuw besloten,
Ten leste met zijn hooft, de starren komt te stooten,
En reickende voorby den op- en ondergangk,
Het aerdrijck en den doot en afgront houdt in dwangk:[72]

Furthermore, like Grotius' hero, Joseph imperiled his life for the sake of peace even though he had foreseen in a dream that his brothers would harm him. But Vondel did not limit his imitation of Grotius to these christological parallels. Indeed, these similarities alone did not demonstrate the influence of *Christus patiens*, for Joseph's prefigurative role had been a familiar topic since late antiquity. Rather, Vondel's adaptation of Grotius' concept of tragedy provided the strongest evidence for the close relationship between these two works.

As a devout Christian, Grotius had realized that the Redemption was fundamentally untragic. Christ himself had proclaimed his joy at liberating sinful man from the outset. Since tragedy could not be based on the fate of the protagonist, Grotius evoked a tragic mood by recounting the lamentations of the Virgin, the apostles and the chorus of Jewish women. Peter wept because of his inability to save Jesus despite his earlier bravado; Judas likewise voiced his pangs of conscience for the betrayal. Following his Byzantine model, Grotius presented the Virgin's outcries before the cross; similarly, the Jewish women despaired because of their disbelief that Jesus could rise from the dead as he had promised. Such grief was, however, ultimately revealed as vain and unnecessary by the Virgin's prophecy of Christ's triumph. Although she had been severely affected by her son's death, her extraordinary status as the Mother of God freed her from the false illusions which had obscured the truth:

Maiora iam prospicio, et ante oculos meos
Omne est futurum. Nate tu vadis pias
Nunc inter animas maior: assurgit tibi
Sanctus parentum populus et coelum suo
Debet nepoti. Iam tuos mors pallida
Sequitur triumphos, dum remolito novus
Exis sepulchro. non diu terris tamen
Spectandus, en mox totus ad patrem redis.[73]

Tragedy was no longer understood as Christ's death, but as man's inability, that is his fear, despair and blindness, to perceive the significance of the Redemption and to rejoice.

---

[72] *WB*, IV, p. 79, lines 21-26.
[73] Grotius, *Christus patiens* (1978), p. 189, lines 1415-1422.

Grotius' concept of tragedy was adapted by Vondel for *Joseph in Dothan*. In general, Vondel had based the structure of his work on the middle acts of Jacob Libenus' *Josephus venditus*. In contrast to the biblical account, Libenus had only involved three brothers in the plot to eliminate Joseph: Simeon and Levi were the instigators; and Ruben, having rejected their murderous plan, was easily outwitted and consequently unable to save his younger brother from the others. Inspired by Grotius, Vondel now assigned four of Joseph's brothers a specific role from *Christus patiens*: Simeon and Levi represented the indecisive Pilate and the vengeful Caiphas eager to execute Christ for his opposition to the Law. Ruben's failure to rescue Joseph recalled St. Peter's denial of Christ, and the fears of yet another brother, Judas, about divine punishment foreshadowed his namesake's despair in the New Testament. In keeping with Joseph's christological role, his sale into slavery was presented as a prefiguration of the Passion.[74]

Vondel's imitation of *Christus patiens* thus reflected a major shift in his concept of religious drama. From Grotius' play, Vondel had learned to create a work in which the tragedy did not arise from the fate of the titular protagonist, but from the reaction of the other characters to it. The lugubrious plaints of St. Peter, Judas and the Virgin Mary served to instill the audience with faith by purging them of sorrow and despair. At the same time, the grief which St. Peter and Judas voiced in their tirades because of their denial and betrayal of Christ illustrated man's desperate need for the forgiveness of the Redemption. Vondel similarly juxtaposed the enmity of Joseph's brothers to the love which he bore them. Through the prefigurative interpretation of Joseph, Vondel was able to suggest that the weaknesses of his brothers would one day be forgiven. Indeed, when viewed together, the entire trilogy—*Joseph in Dothan*, *Joseph in Egypten* and *Sofompaneas*—clearly demonstrated the triumph of justice and the pardon of sinners. In their tragedies, Grotius and Vondel contrasted the fundamental sinfulness of fallen man to the grace of the Redemption and thereby strengthened the faith of the viewer.

In his adaptation of *Christus patiens*, Vondel appeared to retain many of the characteristics of Renaissance religious drama which he had espoused in *Het Pascha*. Joseph, an Old Testament figure, was regarded as a prefiguration of Christ; God's justice, though absent from the stage, was present in the prophetic angel chorus, and Joseph's forbearance provided Christian viewers with an exemplum of the correct behavior when

---

[74] Smit, vol. 1, pp. 336-8. Although Smit noted the christological parallels in the Joseph play, he did not mention its connection to the *Christus patiens*.

afflicted by misfortune. This apparent similarity was, however, altered considerably by Vondel's focus on the faults of the brothers. Where Grotius, in the tradition of sixteenth-century religious dramatists, had been eager to proclaim the salvation, Vondel exposed man's unceasing propensity for sin. To this end he significantly changed the characters of his "apostle" figures, Judas and Ruben. In Grotius' play, St. Peter and Judas lamented sins they had already committed;[75] in *Joseph in Dothan*, Vondel stressed the ineluctability of sin by allowing Judas and Ruben to err several times. Indeed, the failings of these two brothers were so pronounced that Vondel scholars have been obsessed with the determining which of the two was the weakest.[76] But their respective strengths as well as their assigned prefigurative roles (an equally stormy debate still rages about whether Judas or Ruben represented St. Peter)[77] were not Vondel's main concerns. Rather, he introduced both figures to portray the tragedy of man's fallen state and to question the humanists' confidence in the educability of man.

Vondel's characterization of Judas and Ruben was far more complex than that of Grotius' sinful disciples. In contrast to the unrestrained hatred of Simon and Levi, Judas and Ruben had both learned to accept Jacob's fondness for Joseph regardless of their personal misgivings about such excessive love. Judas tried to dissuade Simeon and Levi from their murderous plan by ascribing Jacob's favoritism to his senility;[78] Ruben similarly remarked that old men often doted on their youngest sons.[79]

---

[75] Grotius, *Christus patiens* (1978), pp. 89-97, lines 236-344 (St. Peter); pp. 113-9, lines 518-537; 544-587 (Judas).

[76] The modern debate was initiated by A. M. Verstraeten, *Studiën over Vondel en zijn Josef in Dothan* (Ghent, 1886); Verstraeten argued (p. 48) that Ruben had acted nobly in his attempt to save Joseph from the enmity of the brothers; in contrast, Judas had treated Joseph shamefully by selling him to the Arabs. W. A. P. Smit countered this interpretation in his article, "Judas en Ruben in Vondels *Joseph in Dothan*," *NTg*, 41 (1948), 97-107. Smit suggested that Judas was not so much weak as flawed (pp. 97-100); on the other hand, Ruben was a weakling who only defended Joseph with words (p. 105). Smit's praise of Judas, however, hardly squared with his final association of him with Judas Iscariot. A more reasonable and less subjective argument was proposed by Robert Antonissen: like a tragic hero, Ruben's final lamentations did not serve to illustrate his weakness but to move the audience to pity. See R. Antonissen, "Over Vondels *Joseph in Dothan*," in *European Context: Studies in the History and Literature of the Netherlands,* eds. P. K. King and P. F. Vincent (Cambridge: Modern Humanities Research Association, 1971), pp. 132-50.

[77] Smit cleverly resolved this problem with his assertion that Judas and Ruben were both St. Peter and Judas Iscariot, except at different times, Smit, vol. 1, p. 106. In the first three acts, Smit argued, Judas represented his New Testament namesake while Ruben's actions recalled St. Peter; in the last two acts, however, this configuration was reversed. For an opposing interpretation of the ending, see Antonissen, p. 146.

[78] *WB*, IV, p. 85, line 181.

[79] *WB*, IV, p. 95, lines 381-389.

But Judas and Ruben subsequently defended their brother in a considerably different manner. Mindful of Jacob's deathbed prophecy (Genesis 49) about the hegemony of Judas' house, Vondel absolved Judas from any malicious complicity in his brother's demise.[80] Judas was portrayed as a God-fearing man who regretted his agreement to the murder plot. He had, in fact, initially disapproved of the scheme but Simon and Levi had easily persuaded him of its advantages. Later, however, Judas was tormented by moral scruples, and he negotiated the sale of Joseph to the Arabs in order to appease his guilt. But Judas' pursuit of virtue was only temporary: his pangs of conscience did not prevent him from retaining a portion of the Arab money (''bloetgelt''), nor from swearing to conceal the truth from Jacob. Although his rescue of Joseph was motivated by his fear of God, Judas was still susceptible to the temptations of wealth and cruelty which afflicted all men.

Ruben was Vondel's most sophisticated characterization in the early biblical plays. The motivations for his problematic actions were much more intricate than the fearful misgivings of the guilty Judas. Ruben was at once pious and timid, sympathetic and selfish, blind to his weakness and grand in his downfall. At a time when Vondel seemed obsessed with simple virtuous heroes like Ursula (*Maeghden,* 1639) and Joseph,[81] Ruben's psychological crisis brought the inimitable stature of an Aristotelian tragic hero to the stage. Indeed, Ruben's role fulfilled most of the prescriptions of Aristotelian tragedy as it had been interpreted by late Renaissance commentators like Daniel Heinsius.[82] He was neither completely virtuous nor totally evil; his pride was tempered by his lack of courage, and his downfall resulted from his hesitation and inability to overcome fear and selfishness.[83] Ruben, moreover, illustrated two closely related Aristotelian principles integral to the structure of tragedy: peripeteia or the sudden reversal of fortune and anagnorisis, the resultant recognition or discovery of the true state of affairs.[84] At the moment when Ruben believed he would finally rescue Joseph from the well, Judas sold him to the Arabs. After this discovery (the simplest kind of Aristotelian recognition), Ruben then recognized his own responsibility

---

[80] Smit, vol. 1, pp. 351-3.

[81] Both Noë (p. 72) and Smit (vol. 1, p. 317) suggested that such one-dimensional characterizations prevented Vondel from re-creating the heroic grandeur of true tragedy. Cf. Antonissen, pp. 146-7. Although Antonissen made some valuable remarks about Ruben, his belief that the fall of an innocent victim such as Joseph was far graver than the traditional crisis of the tragic hero (p. 142) was too subjective a judgment to convert Joseph into a tragic protagonist.

[82] Daniel Heinsius, *De tragoediae constitutione liber* (Leiden: Elsevier, 1643).

[83] Heinsius, chapter 9, *passim.*

[84] Aristotle, *Poetics,* chapter 11; Heinsius, chapter 7.

for this tragic turn of events. Had he not hesitated to save Joseph from the well into which, to gain time, he had originally suggested he be placed, he could have prevented the fateful sale. Finally, Ruben's mourning over Joseph's cloak and his graphic description of Jacob's future sorrow recalled the tragedy of Sophoclean and Euripidean heroes whose desperate lamentations could never obliterate their guilt.

As in the case of Judas, Vondel based his characterization of Ruben on Jacob's final words (Genesis 49) about the future of his family. Despite his preeminent status as the eldest, Ruben was forbidden to succeed his father as head of the family since he had once defiled his father's bed by sleeping with one of his concubines (Genesis 35:22). Such questionable behavior had led Jacob to describe his eldest as "unstable as water" (Genesis 49:4). In the play, Vondel provided additional evidence for Jacob's opinion. Ruben lost every opportunity to save Joseph because of his unwillingness to challenge the murderous verdict of his brothers. Although Ruben heartily condemned their recommendation of fratricide, he was too terrified by his younger brothers to carry out his pious intentions. Indeed, Ruben's defense of Joseph seemed motivated more by the fear of his father than by any fraternal compassion. He devised the plan that Joseph be imprisoned in the dry well, rather than killed, so that he could later free him and gain Jacob's favor.[85] But when Ruben had his chance, fearful of his brothers' sudden return, he decided to wait until the cover of night, a delay which caused the shortsighted Ruben to lose Joseph forever. Ruben was predictably disconsolate after learning of the sale, but despite his acknowledgment of his lack of courage, he continued to blame his brothers for the tragedy which he could have and should have averted. He denied his earlier desire to help Joseph and held Judas responsible for the loss. Ruben's ambiguous character was apparent even after his mournful weeping over the blood-stained cloak of his brother. On the one hand he angrily refused to accept his share of the money earned through the sale, but shortly thereafter, he fearfully agreed to lie about Joseph's death to his father. In contrast to Judas' expedient solution to the Joseph problem, Ruben struggled to act virtuously and failed.

Ruben's fall did not result from any inherent evil, but from his inability to pursue the course of action which he perceived to be morally correct. He was not at all corrupt like the pernicious Simon and Levi; indeed, he reproved them for their vices:

> Een schrickelijck gedroght. het broet, niet veer van hier,
> In 't grondelooze hol een heiloos slagh van jongen.
> Het knaeght zijn eigen hart, van spijt schier toegewrongen.

---

[85] *WB*, IV, p. 104, lines 636-648.

Het aengezicht ziet dootsch. het keert de blicken dwars
Van yeder af, van't licht van lach en blydschap wars.[86]

Unlike Judas he did not agree to the plot and he countered his brothers'
murder scheme with a plea for mercy rather than punishment. Surrounded by such blatant cruelty, Ruben's defense of virtue could not
help but arouse the audience's sympathy for his cause. His behavior was,
in fact, much more verisimilar and hence accessible to the audience than
Joseph's exemplary virtue. Whereas Joseph clearly enjoyed the
benevolence of heaven, Ruben was constrained to act without the benefit
of divine assistance. Because of this difference, any anxiety which the
viewers might have felt for the titular hero was diverted to Ruben and
his internal struggle to act as righteously as he intended. Each time
Ruben neglected his brother the audience was not outraged but dejected
by his indecisiveness and hopeful that he would regain his courage.

In *Joseph in Dothan*, Vondel, then, established two distinct types of
tragic response. In keeping with the sixteenth-century tradition, the sale
of the pious Joseph revealed the enmity of the world toward the chosen
man of God. The hero was a paragon of virtue and God's presence was
manifested by the prophecies of his angels about future salvation. The
tragedy of Ruben, however, was grounded in the ambiguous world of
Greek tragedy. Ruben was neither exemplary nor depraved, but he
lacked the resolve to renounce his worldly fears and trust in God. He was
in effect an apt metaphor for fallen man who yearned for virtue but was
unable to attain it because of original sin. In opposition to the tragedy
of the virtuous hero, Vondel juxtaposed the tragedy of fallen man and
thereby underscored the unbridgeable gap between God and the world
which had been cleft by sin.

Vondel continued his dual approach to tragedy in *Joseph in Egypten*
(1640) which completed the trilogy of Joseph plays. This drama was
based on Genesis 39 where the hero's early days at the Egyptian court
in service to Pothiphar were recounted. For his tragedy, Vondel focused
on the encounter between Joseph and Potiphar's wife in which the Jewish
youth defended his chasity from the seductive wiles of his mistress. As
one might expect, this incident had been especially popular in the
misogynistic world of sixteenth-century school drama, but Vondel was
the first Dutch religious playwright to dedicate an entire work to this
episode.[87] In Cornelius Crocus' comedy, *Joseph* (1535; printed 1536), for

---

[86] *WB*, IV, p. 96, lines 434-438.

[87] In his *Josephus servus* (ca. 1625), Theodorus Rhodius presented Joseph's downfall at
Pharaoh's court; he followed Cornelius Crocus' disposition of the events (*Joseph*, 1536)
with the seduction scene in the second act and Joseph's liberation from prison at the end.
In contrast, Vondel focused solely on the episode with Potiphar's wife.

example, Joseph's rebuke of Potiphar's wife was linked to his subsequent imprisonment under false charges of adultery and, more importantly, to his pardon from the Pharaoh many years later. For Crocus, as for most of the humanist Joseph dramatists, the significance of this particular event was not so much Joseph's defense of his virtue as the illustration of virtue rewarded.

This frank pedagogical intention was absent from Vondel's tragedy. As in *Joseph in Dothan*, divine justice was evidenced only by the chorus of angels who predicted Joseph's rejection of Potiphar's wife and his ultimate release from prison. Typological motifs were likewise sounded in the dedicatory letter to Ioan Victorijn where Joseph was designated "een schets en schaduwe"[88] to accord with the character in the previous plays. But, as in *Joseph in Dothan*, the presence of these traditional devices in such a reserved manner indicated that Vondel's main purpose lay elsewhere. In contrast to the humanist Joseph presentations, Vondel did not wish to educate through example, but to probe the difficulties which fallen man would experience in his struggle to accept and obey the word of God.

Vondel first betrayed his theological plan to focus on the crisis of Christian man in his prefatory remarks about the imitation of classical models. He confessed to Victorijn that, through his concentration on the episode with Potiphar's wife, he hoped to provide a Christian equivalent to Euripides' tragedy *Hippolytus*.[89] To be sure, this particular plot was an important chapter in Vondel's trilogy. But, having honored Grotius in *Joseph in Dothan*, Vondel now sought to please him further by imitating his favorite Greek tragedian. As we have seen, Vondel had adopted the humanists' critical stance toward Graeco-Roman literature in *Joseph in Dothan*; he now hoped to surpass the achievements of the ancients by substituting Christian plots similar to the pagan models. In this instance, the excellence of the religious material did not arise from the morality it espoused but from the superior humanity of the protagonist. A pious reader would have doubtless been impressed by the chastity which Euripides' *Hippolytus* strove to uphold; indeed, in the sixteenth century the Hippolytus character of both Euripides and Seneca had been sanctioned by Christian schoolmen because of his virtuous misogyny.[90] But

---

[88] *WB*, IV, p. 152. Victorijn, a close friend of Vondel and a member of the Brabantine Rederijker chamber, was an ardent student of the classics as well as a lawyer and dramatist. On Victorijn as a playwright, see the introduction to P. Minderaa, ed., *I. P. V. Goliath. Treurspel (1629)* (Leiden: Brill, 1963), pp. 1-14.

[89] *WB*, IV, p. 150.

[90] Gulielmus Xylander noted the moral utility of the Hippolytus figure in his 1558 preface to Melanchthon's translations of Euripides: "Disputat ... argute Phaedra, voluptatum specie homines seduci, ut mala bonis praeferant. Multa sunt huiusmodi de sup-

to Vondel's mind such unnatural behavior could hardly serve as an adequate deterrent to a profligate life. The efficacy of a moral exemplum did not lay exclusively in the representation of a specific virtue, but rather in the struggle of the virtuous man to act morally.[91] Euripides' *Hippolytus* was consequently considered ineffectual in two respects: first, Hippolytus' chastity had arisen not from his love of virtue but from his natural aversion to women; secondly, Hippolytus' purity and the lust of his stepmother, Phaedra, for him had been caused not by their own inclinations but by the desire of two warring goddesses, Aphrodite and Artemis, to suppress the influence of the other. In accord with his concept of the ideal exemplum, Vondel replaced this superficial pagan model with an all-too-human Joseph. The assaults of Potiphar's wife (unnamed in the Bible, but called Jempsar by Vondel) on his virtue were portrayed as real threats since Joseph himself was susceptible to a woman's charms. He did not reject Jempsar out of unfeeling self-righteousness but because he believed that adultery undermined the social order. In sharp contrast to Hippolytus' disavowal of the need for women,[92] Joseph defended the utility of marriage as the guarantor of the security and continued existence of the state. As the chorus of angels remarked after the failed seduction attempt,[93] Joseph himself would harness his natural passion through his marriage to Assenat (Genesis 41; 45). The Christian Hippolytus was consequently deemed superior to his pagan prototype, for he had been forced to undergo the same temptations which afflicted all men since the Fall.

In his eagerness to compose a Christian critique of Euripides, Vondel had significantly altered the characterization of the exemplum. Indeed,

---

plicio, quod Deus malis tandem irroget, cum virtus et ipsa demum suum inveniat praemium," *CR,* XVIII, col. 283-284. Language from Seneca's *Hippolytus* reappeared in Joseph's rejection of Potiphar's wife on the sixteenth-century school stage (Stachel, pp. 38-9), and Vondel's translation of this same play was published in 1628. In the early seventeenth century, the Hippolytus story was recast into tragedies on the unfortunate Crispus, who, having rejected the advances of his step-mother, was falsely accused of rape and executed by his father, Constantine the Great. The Crispus material was especially popular on the Catholic stage: the Italian Jesuit, Bernardinus Stephonius (*Crispus,* Rome, 1601; Antwerp, 1634) introduced the subject to his order's repertoire where it flourished: Joachim Müller, *Das Jesuitendrama in den Ländern deutscher Zunge,* vol. 2 (Augsburg: Benno Filser, 1930), p. 103; in Louvain, Nicolaus Vernulaeus produced a *Crispus* in 1628. For a brief account of this work, see the introduction to *Henry VIII: A Neo-Latin Drama by Nicolaus Vernulaeus,* ed. Louis A. Schuster (Austin: University of Texas, 1964), p. 41.

[91] Vondel went to great lengths to show that his Joseph "stock nochte block was," especially after being subjected to the lust of a passionate woman while he was still "in de bloem en hitte zijner jaeren." *WB,* IV, p. 151.

[92] Euripides, *Hippolytus* 616-668.

[93] *WB,* IV, p. 201, lines 1225-1236.

to follow Vondel's arguments to their logical conclusion, any unequivocally positive models were fundamentally flawed since they, like
Hippolytus, were too unnatural to arouse any sympathy from the
audience. Vondel's sensitivity to the psychological complexity of the
exemplum was reflected further in his concern with the viewer's ability
to identify with the crisis of the protagonist. He no longer believed that
the customary humanist presentation of a pious or a sinful man would
suffice to induce the audience to imitate the former and avoid the latter.
The mere illustration of divine justice through the bestowal of rewards
for virtue and eternal damnation for sin failed to account for the complexity of the moral choices with which man was confronted. Where
sixteenth-century humanists had assumed that piety could be attained
and sin avoided through a solid religious education, Vondel emphasized
man's natural proclivity for evil. Since all men were already oppressed
by sin because of the Fall, the triumph of man over temptation was
regarded as a heroic accomplishment. Conversely, the victory of evil was
viewed as man's willing submission to his sinful nature. The
characterization of Joseph in *Joseph in Egypten* was consequently inspired
by Vondel's attempt not only to surpass the ancients but also to criticize
the Renaissance tradition of religious theater in which man's fallen state
had been obscured by pedagogical goals.

Despite the progressiveness of his arguments in the dedicatory letter,
Vondel was unable to break away completely from the standard
Renaissance characterization which he implicitly criticized. As befitted
his age and his station, the Egyptian Joseph displayed a greater
familiarity with worldly matters than he did as a child in the earlier play.
But his status as the chosen favorite of God had not changed at all. The
chorus of angels still watched over the entire play: they intimated the
eventual triumph of "'s helts godtvruchtigheit";[94] warned of Jempsar's
unrestrained passion; and, in their closing remarks, removed any doubt
that the imprisoned Joseph would one day be freed. Though consistent
with the first play, this careful incorporation of divine providence
detracted from Vondel's intention to humanize the exemplary hero.
Whatever temptations Jempsar might have offered, Vondel had already
removed by casting Joseph as the unshakable virtuous hero. Besides the
pious reassurances of the chorus, Joseph's disinterest in Egyptian women
was apparent from his reluctance to watch the young handmaidens
engaged in the religious celebration to Apis. As Joseph explained to the
astonished Potiphar, such a firm resolve was grounded in his Jewish faith

---

[94] *WB*, IV, p. 157, line 26.

according to whose precepts any promptings toward unchaste behavior were avoided:

> Vertrouw, belieft het u, mijn heer, dat wy Hebreen,
> Veel meer dan eenigh volck, de bloem der jaeren wyden
> De kuischeit; om wiens wil wy heilighlijck vermyden
> Gelegentheit en plaets, die ons verrucken zou,
> Door't loncken op een maeght, of een gehuwde vrouw.[95]

Joseph's subsequent interview with Jempsar must be read in light of his indifference. Regardless of Vondel's theoretical intentions, Joseph never once gave any indication that Jempsar's advances weakened his resistance. On the contrary, Joseph displayed the same righteous fervor of God's spokesman which had characterized his predecessor on the humanist stage. He lectured Jempsar on the dangers which adultery posed to the state and the shameful punishment which both of them would incur should he accede to her wishes. Having failed to dissuade her with rhetorical arguments he finally resorted to the traditional condemnation of the temptress' deceitful tears. Although Vondel had attempted to acquit his hero of misogyny, Joseph's praise of marriage did not suffice to broaden his customary role as an exemplum. Like his youthful counterpart in *Joseph in Dothan*, the Egyptian Joseph had been characterized as an ethical model free from the internal strife of the Greek tragic hero whom Vondel so greatly admired.

Vondel's failure to distinguish Joseph's behavior from the tradition did not, however, mean that his tragedy merely imitated earlier plays. On the contrary, *Joseph in Egypten* raised the same problematic questions about man's ability to embrace virtue as *Joseph in Dothan*. To underscore the similarities between the two works, Vondel constructed several structural and thematic parallels. Besides the exemplary character of Joseph, Vondel introduced the fundamentally good man who wavered between virtue and sin. Like Ruben in the first play, Potiphar was torn between two poles: his excessive love for Jempsar and his paternal affection for Joseph. Ruben had, of course, belonged to the true religion of the Jews, but although Potiphar did not share this belief, Vondel did not condemn him. Rather, Vondel betrayed his sympathies for Grotius' promulgation of religious toleration[96] by regarding Potiphar's fidelity to Egyptian rituals as a sign of piety.

Having established Potiphar's probity, Vondel used him to illustrate the dangers which beset all men who struggle to lead a virtuous life. The deceitful Jempsar posed the greatest threat, for Potiphar's passion

---

[95] *WB*, IV, p. 178, lines 602-606.
[96] See note 69 above.

prevented him from recognizing that her own ardor had waned. The same credulity with which he believed the arguments of Jempsar's clever nurse about her mistress' temporary frigidity foreshadowed his own subsequent blindness about Joseph's alleged rape of his wife. More notably, Potiphar's debate with Joseph about the nature of the Hebrew religion reflected the doubts of all men about God's justice. Joseph rebuked Potiphar's enthusiasm for the pomp surrounding the feast of Apis with an account of the history of the Jews. But Potiphar countered by charging the Hebrews with barbarism for praising Abraham and his willingness to sacrifice his son to God. Potiphar's inability to conceive of such irrational behavior revealed not only the difference between Egypt and Israel but also the central problem with the Judaeo-Christian religion. Faith was not defined as the rational allegiance to a set of customs, such as the cult of Apis, but as man's unconditional obedience to God. As Joseph asserted, the evidence of faith lay in man's readiness to withhold nothing from his Creator, regardless of the unnaturalness of the demand:

> Uit dwang, noch lantsgewoont, noch eerzucht, noch yet menschelijx:
> Maer om te toonen, dat hy niet bezat yet wenschelijx,
> 't Geen stont te weigeren den rechten Eigenaer,
> Die 's mans gehoorzaemheit beproefde op dat autaer;[97]

Potiphar's blindness to the true state of his marriage and to Joseph's denial of the rape thus reflected his fundamental misperception of the truth behind appearances: his error was simply summed up by the opening chorus: "de dingen zijn niet als zy schynen."[98] Just as Potiphar was unable to detect the falsity behind the pomp of the festival to Apis, so too did he fail to discern the truth behind the apparently barbaric sacrifice of Isaac.

In his characterization of Potiphar, Vondel thus continued the practice he had borrowed from Grotius in *Joseph in Dothan* of juxtaposing an imperfectly pious figure to the exemplum. Potiphar's subservience to Jempsar warranted the same disapprobation from the audience as Ruben's reluctance to save his brother. Both men were essentially virtuous, but because of these weaknesses they fell considerably short of the perfection of an exemplary figure. Potiphar and Ruben did not desire to harm Joseph, but they were unable to save him because they were flawed. To underscore this connection further, Vondel ended *Joseph in Egypten* with the same tragic tableau of the first play. Just as Ruben had moved the audience with his tears of contrition and self-reproach, so did

---

[97]  *WB*, IV, p. 177, lines 575-578.
[98]  *WB*, IV, p. 161, line 159.

Potiphar arouse the viewer's sympathy with his pitiable admission that he was now forced to hate the man he so dearly loved: "'k Moet haten, dien ick niet kan laten te beminnen."[99] Vondel also established an iconographic parallel between the two closing scenes. In *Joseph in Dothan*, Ruben, whose position as the eldest had made him the surrogate father, anticipated Jacob's lament over Joseph's bloody cloak. Potiphar, who likewise harbored paternal feelings for Joseph, expressed his sorrow while holding the cloak which Joseph had allegedly left behind after the rape. The similarities between these two scenes were, moreover, devised for the same theological lesson. In combining their faults and virtues, Vondel transformed these figures into representations of good men impaired by original sin. The tragedy of the exemplum Joseph was joined with the tragedy of these imperfect characters whose weakness betrayed the afflictions which beset all men since the Fall.

The two Joseph plays thus denoted a new stage in Vondel's concept of religious drama in which he deviated sharply from the simplistic Renaissance style of *Het Pascha*. The ethical significance of the traditional exemplum was discarded in favor of a theological argument. Influenced by Grotius' version of Christian tragedy in *Christus patiens*, Vondel amplified the customary representation of divine justice. In contrast to the Renaissance tradition, the Joseph tragedies were not written to portray the righteous reward of the hero and the punishment of the persecutors. Rather, Vondel was interested in the demonstration of justice behind the appearance of chaos and persecution. In the Joseph plays, Vondel fulfilled this paradoxical intention through the introduction of consolatory choruses of angels who attested at every crisis to the righteousness of God. At the same time, however, through his characterization of Ruben and Potiphar, Vondel exemplified the obstacles which fallen man had to overcome in order to comprehend this justice. God's Providence was indeed present, but man's acceptance of it was complicated by the weakness of his faith. Where Ruben was hindered by his reluctance to suppress his worldly fears for the sake of virtue, Potiphar faltered because of his inability to distinguish between truth and appearance. Vondel did not change the traditional role of divine justice, but the extent to which fallen man could perceive and accept it.

This new orientation on man's response was further reflected in Vondel's adaptation of the typological significance of the Joseph figure. On one level, the relationship of Ruben and Potiphar to Joseph mirrored the connection between fallen man and his Redeemer. Just as Ruben and

---

[99] *WB*, IV, p. 208, line 1390.

Potiphar could have prevented personal tragedy had they defended Joseph from his enemies, so could contemporary man avoid damnation through his adherence to Christ. Moreover, in *Joseph in Egypten*, Vondel supplemented the typological view by attributing human characteristics to the protagonist. Joseph was no longer regarded merely as an exemplary Old Testament prefiguration of Christ but as a normal man subject to the same temptations of the flesh as Potiphar. As we have seen, Vondel's retention of Joseph's prefigurative role seriously hampered the successful execution of this plan, but his eagerness to make the exemplum more accessible to the audience significantly revised the traditional characterization.

Vondel's new approach toward divine justice and Joseph's prefigurative role was closely connected to his criticism of the exemplum. He was no longer so much preoccupied with the lessons which an exemplum imparted as with the effect of such teachings on the audience. Vondel still heeded the Renaissance injunction that drama, especially religious drama, should teach specific moral precepts and persuade the audience to accept them. But unlike his predecessors in this genre, Vondel was primarily concerned with the interrelationship between exemplum and viewer. Through his characterization of Ruben and Potiphar, Vondel questioned the ability of fallen man to acquire the virtues which the exemplum possessed. At the same time, he attempted, albeit unsuccessfully (*Joseph in Egypten*), to illustrate the complexity of the exemplum's moral behavior. Where the moralistic playwrights of the Renaissance had been content to represent their characters as personifications of pedagogical ideas, Vondel provided a sophisticated view of fallen man and his efforts to lead a virtuous life in a deceitful world.

### Vondel's Neo-Classicism

Vondel's transformation of the tradition of Renaissance religious drama was incited by his discovery of Greek tragedy. At the advice of Grotius and other enthusiasts for ancient Greek literature, Vondel began the serious study of Greek theater in the late 1630s and he published his first translation of a Greek play, Sophocles' *Electra,* in 1639.

For the past twenty years Vondel had been engaged in the reading and translation of ancient drama.[100] Having acquired a thorough knowledge of Latin in the late 1610s, Vondel, like many of his contemporaries, regarded Seneca as the master of tragic diction. In keeping with the

---

[100] On Vondel's relationship to Graeco-Roman literature, see the brief survey: A. M. F. B. Geerts, *Vondel als classicus bij de humanisten in de leer* (Tongerloo: St. Norbertus, 1932).

Senecan rage, many religious dramas were composed in that style especially in French (La Taille, Montchrestien) and Latin (Grotius, Heinsius, Rochus Honerdus), but the otherwise pious Vondel was an exception. His single Senecan tragedy with religious overtones, *Hierusalem verwoest* (1620), dealt with the fall of Jerusalem to the Romans. This work had in fact been conceived as a tribute to both Seneca and his contemporary imitators. Since *Troades* (on the sack of Troy by the Greeks) had long been considered Seneca's best drama—the young Grotius had enthusiastically designated it "regina tragoediarum"[101]—tragedies on the fall of cities quickly came into vogue. As a consequence, Jerusalem was besieged many times on the humanist stage by Babylonians under Nebuchadnezzar, Romans under Titus and even Crusaders under Godfrey of Bouillon.[102] In each instance, sinful men, be they Jews or Arabs, were punished by God for their recalcitrance and blindness to His Word. Vondel subsequently applied a Christian interpretation to his translation of *Troades* (*De Amsteldamsche Hecuba*, 1626) and Seneca's *Hippolytus* (1628), for they not only portrayed the mutability of fortune but also Christian virtues such as fortitude and chastity. But when he returned to biblical tragedy in the late 1630s after a detour into satirical (*Palamedes*, 1625) and historical (*Gysbreght van Aemstel*, 1637) drama, he dispensed with Senecan theater completely. Despite the continued composition of Senecan religious dramas by his contemporaries, Vondel discovered that his concept of biblical tragedy could only flourish under the aegis of the Greeks.

Literary fashion rather than theology had initially dictated Vondel's rejection of Senecan tragedy. In 1630, Grotius, who had assisted Vondel's early forays into classical literature, published his Latin translation of Euripides' *Phoenissae,* and with one swift stroke he destroyed the hegemony of Seneca. In the programmatic preface to that work Grotius, following Horace (*Ars poetica* 285-291), extolled the virtues of Greek theater over its Roman imitators. Seneca was not criticized overtly— Grotius was unwilling to disown his dramatic *iuvenalia*[103]—but he did not hesitate to make plain that the Roman tragedy which survived exceeded the requisite amount of *gravitas* for tragic composition: "tragoediae iis

---

[101] J. A. Worp, *De invloed van Seneca's treurspelen op ons tooneel* (Amsterdam, 1892), p. 48. Worp's citation referred to Vondel's claim in the preface to his *Amsteldamsche Hecuba* (Dutch translation of *Troades*) that "Het wyse en geleerde breyn van eenen [Grotius] ... heeft de Latijnsche Troas vereert met den tytel van *Regina tragoediarum.*" *WB*, II, p. 533.

[102] The most famous late Renaissance drama on Godfrey of Bouillon's conquest of Jerusalem was presented at the Jesuit school in Munich (1596) with a cast of hundreds. The ms., *Drama de Godefrido Bullone* is preserved in the Bayerische Staatsbibliothek, clm. 549 and clm. 19757₂.

[103] Grotius' first play *Adamus exul* (1601) was published when he was only eighteen; his second, *Christus patiens* in 1608.

factae temporibus, cum iam declamatorium dicendi genus vim illam masculam, quam maxime requirit tragoediae gravitas, non parum fregisset.''[104] Both Sophocles and Euripides, however, were esteemed for their avoidance of bombast as well as their individual attributes. Where Sophocles surpassed Euripides with his sublime style, the latter succeeded in provoking the strongest emotional response in the viewer.[105]

When Vondel returned to biblical tragedy in the late 1630s after his failed attempt at a religious epic on Constantine the Great, the *Constantinade*,[106] he followed the praxis and advice of his literary mentor, Grotius. He studied Grotius' Euripides translation as well as the *Sophompaneas,* and in the preface to his translation of that work, he interpreted the play in light of Grotius' remarks on Euripides. After the usual comments about the exemplary nature of the protagonist, Vondel flattered Grotius by associating him with his favorite dramatist. Just as Euripides had excelled in the arousal of emotions, especially pity, so had Grotius reduced the audience to tears when Joseph revealed his true identity to his brothers.[107] Vondel did not, however, initially share Grotius' enthusiasm for Euripides; his first published translations from Greek drama, or rather, from Latin translations of the Greek texts, were drawn from Sophocles: *Elektra* (1639) and *Koning Edipus* (1660). But Vondel was not bent on declaring his preference; even Grotius had had the wisdom to acknowledge that Sophocles and Euripides, though different in style, equalled each other in tragic skill.[108] Vondel himself praised both of them in his translations from the 1660s which had been sketched out in prose many years before: *Ifigenie in Tauren* (1666), *Feniciaensche* (1668) *Herkules in Trachin* (1668). More importantly, because of Grotius' influence, Vondel began to interpret Greek theater and to apply his conclusions to his own dramatic production.

Vondel's reception of Greek tragedy was based partly on the Netherlandic humanists' interpretation of Aristotelian and Cinquecento poetics and partly on his own concept of the function of drama. While studying the works of Sophocles and Euripides, Vondel most likely derived his knowledge of ancient theater from three sources: Grotius' preface to *Phoenissae,* Daniel Heinsius' *De tragoediae constitutione* and con-

---

[104] *Tragoedia Phoenissae* (1802), p. ix. For an analysis of this prologue's relationship to Vondel's neo-classical view of drama, see E. K. Grootes, "Het berecht voor *Jeptha* en de prolegomena van Grotius' *Phoenissae*-vertaling," in *Visies op Vondel na 300 jaar*, eds. S. F. Witstein and E. K. Grootes (The Hague: Martinus Nijhoff, 1979), pp. 236-46.

[105] *Ibid.*

[106] On this epic see J. F. M. Sterck, "Vondels epos *Constantijn,*" in his *Rondom Vondel* (Amsterdam: Wereldbibliotheek, 1927), pp. 26-40.

[107] See the earlier discussion of his play, pp. 000-000.

[108] *Tragoedia Phoenissae* (1802), p. ix.

versations with Gerardus Vossius, the famous philologist, theologian and rhetorician who had recently (1631) moved to Amsterdam from Leiden University. It is, however, difficult to determine to what extent Vondel accommodated these writers in his work around 1640, for his own tragic theory did not betray any Aristotelian traces until *Maria Stuart* (1646).[109] Besides a passing reference to Grotius' Euripidean style, Vondel still interpreted his plays in the moralistic tradition of Renaissance religious drama. In *Sofompaneas,* Joseph exemplified the justice, piety and love of peace which all contemporary princes should emulate. *Gysbreght van Aemstel* (1637) was likewise recommended to all Christians for its portrait of God's providential guidance in times of adversity. The noble Gysbreght, who like Grotius, to whom Vondel dedicated the play, had been unjustly accused of political crimes and banished from his homeland, was reassured by the archangel Raphael that his city of Amsterdam would one day dominate Europe.[110] Not surprisingly, Vondel attributed the same providential reading to his translation of *Elektra* (1639). Inspired by the lawyer and literary enthusiast, Ioan Victorijn, Vondel was drawn to this work since it demonstrated the inevitability of God's justice: "dat Gods uitgestelde straf endelijck schelmen en booswichten rechtvaerdighlijck achterhaelt."[111] Similar sentiments were voiced in the original works of 1639-40: *Maeghden* (1639), on the martyrdom of St. Ursula and her followers, portrayed the downfall of her persecutor Attila; *Gebroeders* (1640) depicted the punishment of Saul's descendants for the crimes which their ancestor perjuriously committed against the Gibeonites (2 Samuel 21), and as we have seen, the Joseph plays promised the hero's eventual triumph over his enemies. But such guarded assessments of these biblical and hagiographical dramas cannot account for the sophisticated presentation of the main figures. Vondel had clearly perceived more in Greek drama than a reaffirmation of his Christian views on Divine Providence; he had, in fact, detected the ambiguous nature of the Greek tragic hero and he subsequently adapted this characterization to accord with his own theology.

Although Vondel did not adopt Aristotelian terminology to describe his plays until the mid-1640s, and even then only peripherally until the fifties, it is nonetheless likely that he would have been familiar with interpretations of the *Poetics* before that time. Vondel's close friend, Gerardus

---

[109] *WB*, V, p. 165, where Vondel attempted to defend Maria Stuart as a tragic heroine who was neither virtuous nor evil. For a discussion of this play, see chapter 4, pp. 200-4.

[110] *WB*, III, pp. 597-9, lines 1823-1864.

[111] *WB*, III, pp. 641-2.

Vossius, has long been accredited with introducing Vondel to Aristotle's view of tragedy,[112] but since Vossius did not publish his remarks until 1647,[113] his influence on Vondel may have been limited. To be sure, in the 1630s Vondel frequented Vossius' public lectures at *Athenaeum Illustre,* the newly founded humanist institute in Amsterdam, and he may have even discussed poetic theory with him. But, in lieu of another handbook, Vondel probably turned to Daniel Heinsius' essay on tragedy, *De tragoediae constitutione.* Heinsius' treatise had first been published as a supplement to his 1611 edition of the *Poetics* and was subsequently revised in 1643. Using contemporary as well as classical examples, Heinsius offered detailed explanations of the act of tragic imitation, the arousal of emotions, their purgation and the ideal tragic style.[114] In fact, once Vossius' encyclopedic work appeared, Vondel probably still preferred Heinsius' exposition. Where Heinsius had granted contemporary religious drama an equal status with secular theater, Vossius advised against the composition of biblical plays unless they primarily dealt with political or civil matters.[115] Regardless of the source, however, Vondel was definitely attracted by the theoreticians' remarks about the characterization of the tragic protagonist. The best tragic hero was neither virtuous nor evil; although he had erred, he gained the viewer's respect and sympathy because he had not acted maliciously. The appearance of this type of figure in Vondel's plays of 1639-40 consequently revealed not only his intimate contact with Aristotle, but also his use of neo-classical theory to reform the religious drama of the Renaissance.

The first indication of Vondel's fascination with mixed characterizations appeared in the dedicatory letter to Maria Tesselscha Roemers which prefaced his *Elektra* translation. After referring to the humanists' enthusiasm for the play, Vondel praised its artful combination of passions: "in dit treurspel woelen veelerleie hartstoghten, gramschap, stoutigheid, vreeze, bekommeringe, haet en liefde, trouw en ontrouw, droefheid en blyschap, elck om't hevighste."[116] This epic variety, though

[112] Geerts, pp. 15-6; Smit, vol. 1, pp. 441-3.

[113] Gerardus Vossius, *Poeticarum institutionum libri tres* (Amsterdam: Elzevier, 1647). On the influence of Vossius' ideas on contemporary neo-classical dramatic theory, see Edith Kern, *The Influence of Heinsius and Vossius upon French Dramatic Theory* (Baltimore: Johns Hopkins, 1949).

[114] Heinsius: see especially chapters 2, 9, and 17 (1643 ed.).

[115] "plus concessero, ubi historia quidem è sacris desumitur literis; natura tamen sua argumenti est civilis. Ut si drama sit de Davide, fugiente filium Absolomum: vel item de Josepho à fratribus divendito; à Pharaone autem ad praefecturam Ægypti praefecto; inque ea dignitate à fratribus, adorato, agnitoque. Cujus argumenti est Sophompanias ....." As quoted in the "Addenda Lib. II" to Vossius, *Poet. inst.,* sig. q3.

[116] *WB,* III, pp. 641-2.

not associated here with a single character, suggested that Vondel was searching for a dramatic form with greater range than the monotonously lugubrious tragedies of Seneca or young Grotius. A few years earlier, *Gysbreght van Aemstel* had provided him with historical material for several episodes in which emotions as various as the ones listed in the *Elektra* preface were displayed: the undying love of Badeloch for her besieged husband; the noble heroism of the martyred bishop Gozewyn and the viciousness of the deceitful attackers Willem van Egmont and Diedrick van Haerlem. In *Elektra*, however, with its tightly unified plot and limited number of characters, the emotional spectrum for which Vondel was searching was embodied by the protagonist herself. In contrast to Euripides' portrayal of Electra as a bloodthirsty virago, Sophocles had ascribed human, sympathetic qualities to her as well. Thus, her vengeful fervor was tempered by her regret about the worldly pleasures she renounced to pursue her cause; her hatred for Agamemnon's assassins was moderated by her pangs of conscience about matricide; and her inhuman encouragement of Orestes in the final scene ("Verdubbel deze slagen!")[117] was balanced by her affection for him when he first arrived. Vondel's attraction to Sophocles' *Electra*, then, did not arise solely from the representation of divine vengeance but also from the characterization of the protagonist whose complexity corresponded to Heinsius' concept of the ideal tragic hero.

In the other dramas of 1639-1640, *Maeghden, Gebroeders* and the two Joseph plays, Vondel expanded the traditional one-dimensional characterization of the Renaissance religious dramatists to accord with his reading of Greek tragedy. In all these works, however, the neo-classical tragic hero was not the innocent titular protagonist but rather the flawed or weak figures around him. As we have seen, although Ruben and Potiphar were impaired by their lack of faith, their faults did not detract from the poignancy of their personal tragedies. Similarly, *Maeghden* presented a group of characters who mirrored Heinsius' definition of the tragic hero. In this drama on the martyrdom of St. Ursula before the gates of Cologne, Vondel devoted several scenes to the reaction of the Cologne citizens who witnessed her death at the behest of their besieger, Attila. Although the citizens had hitherto withstood the offensive of the Huns, they were pessimistic about victory. Before Ursula's arrival, the archbishop and the mayor had long despaired of any assistance and, indeed, of the whole enterprise of defending Christianity from the Hun; the capture of Ursula and her companions merely intensified their sorrow and further undermined their faith in the justice of

---

[117] *WB*, III, p. 701, line 1494.

Divine Providence. But Ursula's courageous defense of the Church and her bloody martyrdom inspired the citizens to repulse the pagans; her spirit not only urged them on into battle but, after their victory, she promised future prosperity for the city. The crisis of the beleaguered citizens thus fulfilled the prescriptions for a neo-classical tragic hero: they erred because of their despair of divine aide, but their faith prevented them from abjuring God and total capitulation to the Hun.[118]

Vondel established a similarly varied characterization in *Gebroeders* through the figure of David. In this work, Vondel portrayed the harsh punishment which the Gibeonites imposed on the Jews in retribution for the crimes of Saul against them. Since David's hesitation to fulfill their demands and execute Saul's descendants was linked to the continuation of a famine in Israel, he had little choice but to exact this just vengeance. Vondel's approach to this biblical episode was strongly influenced by his study of Greek tragedy. Jean de La Taille had published a tragedy on the same material, *La Famine, ou les Gabéonites* (1573), in the declamatory style of Seneca. But where La Taille had focused on the necessity of retribution,[119] Vondel concentrated on David's crucial decision to accede to the Gibeonites' demand. The reason for this expansion of David's role most likely arose from Vondel's new insight into Sophoclean characterization. Indeed, specific elements of the Gibeonite plot reflected events in *Oedipus rex,* the model tragedy for Aristotle.[120] The famine recalled the plague which afflicted Thebes, and the insistence of the high priest Abjathar and the chamberlain Benajas to save Israel mirrored similar warnings from Teiresias and Creon. David himself did not, of course, suffer from the same grievous crimes as Sophocles' hero, but he was equally flawed. Vondel had, in fact, weakened the Jewish king by attributing sympathetic characteristics to him. David was a virtuous ruler, eager to

---

[118] The double plot of *Maeghden*—the Huns' siege of Cologne and the confrontation between Attila and Ursula—has always been interpreted as a major flaw of the work: Noë, p. 68 and Smit, vol. 1, p. 262. The reaction of the Cologne citizens to the martyrdom was, however, a clever expansion of an otherwise limited plot so that the audience could be instructed in the best manner for them to endure misfortune.

[119] La Taille's David hardly displayed any signs of the psychological crisis which afflicted Vondel's hero; his reply to the Gibeonites' demands for the innocent lives of Saul's descendants was a mere: "Hé, soyez plus humains." Indeed, La Taille's king was more concerned that his people might think he executed the descendants of his old enemy out of hatred, and not "pour le bien public," than he was with the nature of the Gibeonites' request. For this crucial scene (Act III, lines 505-640) see Jean de La Taille, *Saül le furieux. La Famine, ou les Gabéonites,* ed. Elliot Forsyth (Paris: Marcel Didier, 1968), pp. 125-32. For a brief structural comparison of La Taille's tragedy with Vondel's work, see A. Kluyver, "De wraak der Gibeonieten," *TNTL,* 47 (1928), 38-42.

[120] Both De Jager (p. 87) and Noë (pp. 69-71) suggested that *Gebroeders* could be read as a Sophoclean fate tragedy, but their emphasis on the brothers' innocence obscured the harsh Old Testament concept of retributive justice which was evidenced by their death.

retain God's favor for his people; but, as a man, he was shocked by the excessiveness of the Gibeonites' request. He exhorted them to temper their vengeance and act mercifully toward the victims whose innocent lives they claimed. But David's propensity for mercy ("genade"), though admirable to the seventeenth-century Christian audience, contradicted the Old Testament law of retribution and consequently imperiled his relationship to God. Despite his piety, David was willing to ignore God's command to appease his sense of justice; his fear of the evil consequences for himself and Israel, however, induced him to obey. In contrast to La Taille, Vondel's David was not simply the executor of the Divine Will but a Christian version of the Greek tragic hero whose piety and faith were endangered by his all-too-human nature.[121]

In 1639-1640 Vondel, then, adapted the mixed characterization of the Greek tragic hero for his religious plays. The reasons for his introduction of this Greek element were at once both literary and theological. In the former instance, Vondel hoped to give an individual stamp to familiar religious topics by focusing on the effect which these events had on men who were neither virtuous nor malicious. In *Maeghden*, he expanded the traditional humanist martyr play by examining St. Ursula's death from the perspective of the beleaguered citizens of Cologne. *Gebroeders* transformed La Taille's Senecan drama of retribution into a study of man's perception of divine justice, and the two Joseph plays juxtaposed the flawless hero to his weak admirers. But literary emulation was not the predominant reason for Vondel's attraction to the Greek tragic hero. Such a character also corresponded to the spiritual state of the contemporary Christian viewer who, though marred by original sin, remained hopeful of salvation. In adapting these neo-classical characterizations for religious theater, Vondel thus intended to establish a spiritual bond between the mixed characters on the stage and his equally imperfect audience so that his viewers might recognize the true state of their souls.

Vondel was, then, clearly acquainted with the mixed characterization of the tragic hero in the late 1630s, well before his first reference to such a figure—indeed, to Aristotelian theory at all—in the dedicatory letter to

---

[121] Some critics, notably Smit and Langvik-Johannessen, followed Vondel's suggestion (*WB*, III, p. 803) that David's hesitation to have the brothers killed recalled Christ's doubts in Gethsemane; as a consequence they viewed David as a prefiguration of Christ: just as Christ's death redeemed man, so did David's accession to the Gibeonites' demands preserve Israel. In contrast to Christ, however, David did not die, nor did his execution of the descendants really alleviate the turmoil which would beset Israel in the future (see the dire prediction of Armoni before his death: *WB*, III, pp. 871-2, lines 1626-1652). For a discussion of the christological parallels, see Langvik-Johannessen, "Das Problem der christlichen Tragödie bei Vondel," *Jahrbuch der Grillparzer Gesellschaft*, 12 (1976), 142-3; Smit, vol. 1, pp. 298-9.

*Maria Stuart* (1646). The fact that he had omitted any comments on neo-classical theory before this time did not necessarily imply that he was unfamiliar with it.[122] Indeed, when Vondel did cite theoretical prescriptions, his remarks were either at odds with the play itself or too vague to cast much light on its interpretation. Instead of explicating the work, he used neo-classical ideas to defend his dramas from criticism. In *Maria Stuart,* for example, Vondel's argument about the mixed characterization of the title figure was primarily added to disguise the author's unabashed enthusiasm for the martyred Catholic queen:

> De tooneelwetten lijden by Aristoteles naulicks, datmen een personaedje, in alle deelen zoo onnozel, zoo volmaeckt, de treurrol laet spelen; ... waarom wy, om dit mangel te boeten, Stuarts onnozelheit en de rechtvaerdigheit van haere zaeck met den mist der opspraecke en lasteringe en boosheit van dien tijdt benevelden, op dat haer Kristelijcke en Koningklijcke deugden, hier en daer wat verdonckert, te schooner moghten uitschijnen.[123]

The unpopularity of this figure in the Protestant Netherlands had even induced Vondel to falsify the place of publication (now Cologne rather than Amsterdam) and the name of the publisher as he did with several of his candid Catholic writings in the early 1640s.[124] Since his actual presentation of Mary Stuart bordered on panegyric, she did not consequently arouse the requisite fear and pity of tragedy. By regarding her as an Aristotelian heroine, however, Vondel at least hoped to persuade future detractors that his drama was not as laudatory as it seemed.

Vondel's most complete exposition of neo-classical drama theory was contained in the essays which prefaced his three plays in the 1650s: *Lucifer* (1654), *Salmoneus* (1657) and *Jeptha* (1659). Each tragedy had been introduced by an address to friends of the theater[125] in which Vondel defended the composition and performance of drama from literary and religious critics. Accordingly, Vondel's arguments were proposed not so much to illuminate the work at hand as to persuade the readers of its validity. In *Lucifer* and *Jeptha,* Vondel took special pains to align his religious plays

---

[122] Cf. Smit, vol. 1, pp. 442-3.

[123] *WB*, V, p. 165.

[124] E. g., *Altaergeheimenissen ontvouwen in drie boecken door I. V. V.* (1645) and *De Heerlyckheit der Kercke ... door I. V. V.* (1663). The Amsterdam printer, Blaeu, may have been responsible for both works, though the latter may have also been printed in Antwerp. On the text history, see the commentary of Molkenboer: *WB*, IV, pp. 642-3, and the remarks of H. W. E. Moller, *WB*, IX, pp. 982-3.

[125] The exact titles were quite similar: "Berecht aen alle Kunstgenooten en Begunstigers der Tooneelspelen" (*Lucifer*); "Berecht aen alle kunstgenooten en voorstanders van den Schouburgh" (*Salmoneus*); "Berecht aen de begunstelingen der toneelkunste" (*Jephta*).

to Aristotelian rules. He had doubtless been distressed by the criticisms leveled against neo-classical religious drama in the *Poeticarum institutionum* of Vossius. In that work, the great philologist had adopted an ambivalent position on religious drama. On the one hand, as an encyclopedic compiler of the literary tradition, Vossius had carefully accorded the religious tragedies which already existed, such as Grotius' *Sophompaneas* and Vondel's *Gebroeders*, a place in his treatise. Where Vondel was praised for his adherence to biblical truth, Grotius' Joseph drama was praised as a model biblical play because of its portrait of the ideal politician. In prescribing rules for future dramatists, however, Vossius did not advocate biblical drama: "non modo est ludere in sacris, ac sacrorum imminuere majestatem sed etiam mentibus humanis inserere opiniones incertas subinde et falsas."[126] For fear of sacrilege, religious drama was thus conveniently excluded from the canon of acceptable neo-classical practices.

In *Lucifer*, Vondel countered this charge in two ways. First, in his dedicatory letter to Emperor Ferdinand III, he followed Vossius' preferences and ascribed a political reading to the play. Instead of warring among themselves, Christian rules were advised to refrain from pursuing their Luciferian ambitions and to unite against the Turk.[127] Secondly, in the introductory essay, Vondel addressed Vossius' claim about the moral danger of religious drama through a unique combination of sixteenth-century and seventeenth-century arguments. He first adopted the familiar stance of the Christian humanists about the moral and rhetorical utility of drama. Religious theater not only offered positive and negative exempla of Christian ethics, but also imparted lessons in rhetoric and decorum. Having assuaged Vossius' moral scruples, Vondel subtly introduced Aristotelian terminology on catharsis so as to suggest that religious dramas could be composed in the tragic style which Vossius had recommended. He then concluded his remarks with another direct attack. Since Vossius was so troubled by the potentially sacrilegious effect of religious drama, Vondel reminded his readers that even plays which appeared to abuse Christianity could be morally useful. As the legend of St. Genesius attested—Vondel may have known Jean Rotrou's recent drama, *Le Véritable Saint Genest* (1647)—a man's mockery of Christ may

---

[126] Vossius, "Addenda Lib. II," sig. q 2$^v$.

[127] Such pacifist intentions had long been the wish of many humanist dramatists: see note 69 above. Sixt Birck was the first playwright to yearn for a united and peaceful Christendom; in preface to his Latin *Judith* (ca. late 1530s), he followed the tradition of Erasmus and called on Christian princes, especially Charles V, to cease hostilities and lead a crusade against the Turks. On Birk and Erasmus see: J. Lebeau, "Sixt Bircks *Judith* (1539), Erasmus und der Türkenkrieg," *Daphnis*, 9 (1980), 679-98.

well result in his conversion.[128] The Roman mime, Genesius, had suddenly embraced Christianity while satirizing the behavior of Christian martyrs and was subsequently executed for his new belief. By cleverly turning Vossius' argument against him, Vondel thus hoped to gain a respectable place for religious tragedy in neo-classical theater.

Vossius' remarks about the spiritual dangers of religious theater accorded fully with the objections of conservative Calvinist preachers. Vondel's preface to his next play, *Salmoneus* (1657), on that hapless character's disastrous attempt to imitate Zeus, addressed these critics directly. After the premiere of *Lucifer* on 2 February 1654, these churchmen had successfully persuaded the Amsterdam town council to prohibit future performances of that work. Indeed, the preachers argued that religious drama should be the responsibility of the Church rather than independent playwrights.[129] To this end, they endorsed the moralistic drama of the Rederijkers where the allegorical figures left no doubt about their interpretation. In opposition to this religious party, Vondel cited the customary moral arguments for the utility of theater. He then attacked allegorical drama by resorting to a neo-classical point about the superior effect of verisimilar characterizations for ethical instruction.[130] As in *Lucifer*, Vondel's references to Aristotelian elements was primarily intended to provide a general apology for theater rather than a specific explication of his play.

---

[128] See the discussion in chapter 1 on Jacob Bidermann's *Philemon Martyr*, pp. 48-51.

[129] Such conservatism was by no means new: the argument that biblical drama profaned the Word of God—and therefore should be banned—had already been employed against sixteenth-century religious playwrights. Sixt Birck, for example, felt obliged to refute similar criticisms in his *Beel* (1539) by mocking the pious intentions of his opponents: although they called for the restriction of sacred topics to sermons, they themselves were infrequent churchgoers and avid spectators of bawdy Shrovetide plays. Sixt Birck, *Beel* in *Sämtliche Dramen,* vol. 1, ed. Manfred Brauneck (Berlin: Walter de Gruyter, 1969), pp. 168-9, lines 27-45. Similarly, in the preface to his *Ophiletes* (on Matthew 18:23-35), Hieronymus Ziegler took pains to refute such objections, as Vondel would later do, with classical and patristic references to the moral utility of theater: H. Ziegler, *Ophiletes* (Basel: Ioan. Oporinus, 1551), p. 52.

[130] Vondel did not reject allegorical drama completely because of its moralistic end. His comments about the utility of tragedy, however, suggested that he deemed the neo-classical style superior to the *sinnekens* of the Rederijkers: "De treurstyl ... arbeit om de menschen weeck in den boezem te maecken, schildert de hartstoghten naer het leven af, leert naer voorvallende gelegenheit den toom des Staets vieren of aenhaelen, en elck zich zacht aen een anders ongeluck spiegelen." *WB*, V, p. 715. Moreover, Vondel's association of allegorical drama with the pagan worship of Dagon in *Samson* (1660) further implied his critical distance to that particular tradition. Despite the fact that certain Philistines ("Vorst") voiced Vondel's favorable opinion of drama (*WB*, IX, pp. 202-3, lines 668-698), the triumph of the neo-classical, Christian hero Samson over the Philistines suggested that the Aristotelian style was preferred. Cf. Smit, vol. 3, pp. 166-7, who argued that Vondel's criticism was limited to contemporary church performances of drama.

The connection between the introductory essay and the text of *Jeptha* was much closer than in the previous two works. *Jeptha* was Vondel's most programmatic play, for it had been specifically written to demonstrate that a biblical topic could easily be adapted to neo-classical form. In this case, however, Heinsius replaced Vossius as the target. In his *De tragoediae constitutione,* Heinsius had sharply criticized the biblical dramas of George Buchanan (1506-1582), *Baptistes* (published 1577) and *Jephthes* (published 1554), for their structural deficiences and inelegant style. *Jephthes* was especially subjected to Heinsius' censure, for he considered *Baptistes* beneath contempt.[131] Vondel hoped to avoid Buchanan's errors by composing his Jeptha tragedy to accord with contemporary readings of Aristotle. He thus introduced several neo-classical traits: the mixed characterization of Jeptha, use of peripeteia and tragic recognition, limiting the action to twenty-four hours and catharsis. Although Vondel ascribed these characteristics to the play, he did not always explicate their relationship to the plot. Structural and formal aspects were easily recognizable: the drama turned from joy to sorrow and the three unities were strictly observed. But in the case of catharsis, Vondel offered several different interpretations—moderation, purification and instruction—without explaining how the dramatic events incited any of these reactions.[132] Vondel's neo-classicism in this work, therefore, did not so much serve as proof for his mastery of dramatic theory as evidence for his argument against Heinsius, Vossius and the preachers in favor of religious theater.

In the 1660s, Vondel continued to compose religious tragedies which betrayed his familiarity with contemporary theory. But in contrast to the previous decade, Vondel no longer recorded his debts. On the basis of his prefatory remarks alone, Vondel in fact appeared to have reverted back to the tragic dramas of punishment in which sinners were damned

---

[131] Heinsius, chapter 17, pp. 200-11.

[132] Vondel essentially followed the Renaissance commentators' (Robortello; Castelvetro) moral transformation of Aristotelian tragedy into a school for the passions. Aristotle's concept of catharsis as purification, whereby man learned to control (''maetigen'') his emotions, had arisen in reaction to Plato's belief that all emotions were evil and should consequently be purged. Vossius had noted this controversy in his *Poet. inst.* (II.13.20): ''Ille [Plato] putabat tragoedias esse affectuum flabellum. Aristoteles verò censet esse remedium'' (p. 65), but he did not explain how this process occurred, an omission which Vondel later repeated. In adapting Vossius' vague idea of catharsis, Vondel primarily hoped to demonstrate that neo-classical precepts and sacred topics could successfully be combined. His own limited understanding of catharsis was further evidenced by his ascription of a non-Aristotelian didactic lesson to his definition: catharsis not only moderated the emotions (Vossius), but also liberated man from error (''d'aenschouwers van gebreken zuiveren''; cf. Donatus' ''vita fugienda''). For Vondel's opinions on catharsis, see *WB,* VIII, p. 777.

for their crimes. David (*Koning David in ballingschap/Koning David herstelt,* 1660) was castigated for his adulterous relationship to Bathsheba by the death of Absalom. Adonias (*Adonias,* 1661) was executed for his revolutionary ambitions, and man was ousted from Paradise (*Adam in ballingschap,* 1664) and later destroyed (*Noah,* 1667) for his disobedience to God. As in the case of the dramas of 1639-1640, Vondel now omitted neo-classical references, for he was engaged in defending the validity of theater elsewhere (e.g., *Tooneelschilt,* 1661). In both periods, his silence did not imply that Vondel was unfamiliar with contemporary theory, nor did it suggest that he had dispensed with its principles. The recognition of the extent of Vondel's limited neo-classicism is, however, essential for determining his unique concept of religious theater. Tragedy for Vondel cannot be defined by adherence or deviation from neo-classical rules,[133] but only by the theological purpose of his drama.

When Vondel's religious plays are examined in light of their theological goals, his selective adaptation and transformation of neo-classical practices becomes apparent. Certain formal attributes (e.g., peripeteia) were inherent in many religious plots, but other attributes, such as mixed characterizations and catharsis, necessitated the author's reinterpretation of the biblical material. As we have seen, Vondel was drawn to mixed characterizations because they allowed him to create a bond between the audience and the imperfect hero. But Vondel was not content merely to permit his viewers to recognize their fallen state. Having familiarized himself with catharsis, Vondel was eager to liberate man from his spiritual infirmity. To this end, he transferred the pity and fear which a perfect tragedy necessarily aroused into a Christian context. For Aristotelian commentators like Heinsius and Vossius, pity and terror were both incited so that the audience could be freed from the debilitating effect of these emotions.[134] In the dramas of 1639-1640, however, audiences were primarily motivated by pity since the characters were designed to win the viewer's sympathy with their predicament. Terror or fear was experienced only mildly and in the traditional sense Heinsius had outlined, viz., that such misfortunes might one day burden the viewer.[135] In the tragedies after 1648, however, terror was once again

---

[133] See my criticism of W. A. P. Smit above, pp. 97-8.

[134] Heinsius took pains to describe the psychological-physiological process whereby man could be incited to temper his emotions: Heinsius, chapter 2, pp. 10-13; in contrast, Vossius shared Heinsius' view but merely summarized the desired tragic effect: "Percellit auditorem facti ipsius atrocitas, et rei indignitatem auget dignitas personarum. Eò autem percellere animum vult, ut eum hisce affectibus expurget." Vossius, II.13.20, p. 65.

[135] Heinsius, chapter 9, pp. 74-6.

equally joined to pity not simply to control emotions but to reveal the complexity of Christian faith.

Vondel's interpretation of catharsis and, by extension, the purpose of religious drama, can best be understood by determining the nature of tragedy in these later plays. In all the religious tragedies, Vondel set up a basic conflict between God and man in which God tested the faith of his believers. Man's soul was endangered by temptation, but if he repulsed it, he gained eternal life. This simple structure did not, of course, originate with Vondel, for it had informed the structure of the school plays of the previous century. The nature of the test which he devised, however, separated him from the tradition. Where earlier dramatists had chiefly portrayed the seduction of man by evil,[136] Vondel's test was initiated by God. A biblical simile can best illustrate this point. Vondel essentially subjected his protagonists to the same crisis which God imposed on Abraham (Genesis 22) when He demanded the sacrifice of his son. Abraham's willingness to comply with God's command was an act of faith and obedience which took precedence over his love for Isaac. In a similar manner, Vondel tested the spiritual strength of his characters by depicting their reaction to God's demand for absolute obedience. Their refusal to accede to His Will led predictably to their downfall. But at the same time, their objections to the apparent injustice and irrationality of God's actions aroused the sympathy of the audience to such a degree that the play itself revealed the spiritual weaknesses of the viewer. By inducing the audience to pity the recalcitrant sinner, Vondel helped them perceive their own fundamental sinfulness. Such goals were already evident in Vondel's characterization of Ruben and Potiphar. But in the dramas of the 1650s and 1660s, this act of identification between character and spectator served to underscore the irreconcilability of faith and reason. In his later works, Vondel moved away from the strictly ethical counsel imparted by a figure like Ruben to a theological representation of the paradox of faith.

To achieve this end, Vondel shifted the character configuration he had developed in the late 1630s. Instead of focusing on the innocent exemplum—Joseph, Ursula, Sts. Peter and Paul[137]—whose constancy guaranteed their salvation, he made the sinful figures the titular heroes. Ideal exempla still played a major role in many of the later plays, but

---

[136] Consider, for example, the seductive power of Herodias over Herod in Jacob Schoepper's *Ectrachelistis* (1546) where she assuaged the fears of the guilt-stricken tetrarch with declarations of her undying passion and assurances of the Baptist's foolishness. Jacob Schoeper, *Ectrachelistis* (1546; Cologne: Maternus Cholinus, 1562), Act III, scene 4, sig. C 6ᵛ-D.

[137] *Peter en Pauwels* (1641).

only as a virtuous contrast to the protagonist. In this way Vondel not only directed the viewer's attention to the sinner, but he also emphasized the improbability that his fallen hero could ever attain the perfection of the exemplum.

Secondly, in keeping with his theological aim, Vondel dispensed with the one-sided classification of the protagonist as a condemnable sinner. In order to emphasize the parallel between his tragic hero and the equally fallen spectator, Vondel placed his protagonists in dramatic situations in which, despite their former errors, they might still avoid damnation. Several of Vondel's later heroes had already erred or contemplated evil before the drama began. For example, the character of Lucifer, curious about the development of God's new favorite, man, had already dispatched his henchman, Apollion, to earth to assuage his jealous urges.[138] Salomen (*Salomen,* 1648) had already introduced pagan gods into Jerusalem to please his mistress Sidonia; Samson (*Samson,* 1660) had been seduced by Delilah; and Jeptha had already decided to fulfill his rash oath to sacrifice his daughter. Similarly, all men stepped onto the world stage tainted with original sin and hence with a marked propensity for evil from which they could only be saved by divine grace. In the course of each play, Vondel's fallen characters were confronted with a choice between repentance and sin which resembled the decisions all men were constrained to make in order to gain God's favor. The fact that such choices often offended both the hero's and the audience's sense of justice confirmed the fundamental sinfulness of man. But through the depiction of the downfall of the sympathetic sinner, Vondel terrified the audience into moderating their pity for the protagonist. The arousal of the viewer's emotions served to remind him of his distance from his Creator, indeed of the frequent disharmony between faith and reason, so that he might be incited to obey God's laws. Catharsis was thus understood as the liberation of man from those human, natural and consequently sinful

---

[138] As Belzebub remarked about Apollion's mission in the opening scene:
Vorst Lucifer zondt hem, tot dezen toght bequaem,
Naer 't aertrijck, op dat hy eens nader kennis naem'
Van Adams heil en staet, waer in d'Almogentheden
Hem stelden.                                    (*WB,* V, p. 618, lines 3-6)
Lucifer's curiosity has long been thought to reflect his own incipient jealousy of man though the presense of such evil before the revolt raised theological questions about its origins. In accordance with his portrait of Lucifer as a "middle hero," divided between good and evil, Smit avoided the theological issue and suggested that Lucifer had been forced by the other more evil angels to investigate Adam's state: Smit, vol. 2, p. 92. More recently, Peter King wisely noted the illogical theology of Vondel's play and suggested that his excessive fidelity to poetic norms may have induced him to avoid troublesome questions about the nature of evil and the revolt. See P. King, "Vondels *Lucifer.* Een mislukt theologisch toneelstuk," in *Visies op Vondel na 300 jaar,* pp. 231-4.

reactions which prevented his unimpeded submission to God's Will. In the tragedies of the Catholic Vondel, as in the Old Testament, faith had to be confirmed by obedience before God's favor could be won and salvation granted.

### "Jeptha": The Establishment of Christian Tragedy

A close examination of *Jeptha* (1659) can best illustrate Vondel's sophisticated presentation of theological truths in Aristotelian garb.[139] Of all the biblical tragedies, Vondel regarded this work as his most complete imitation of classical tragedy. It was written in fact to demonstrate that Heinsius' and Vossius' objections to neo-classical religious tragedy were unfounded. Accordingly, Vondel took great pains to include as many formal neo-classical motifs as his plot could reasonably contain. He adhered strictly to the Aristotelian obsession with the three dramatic unities, especially to the unity of time, for Heinsius had criticized earlier Jeptha dramas (Buchanan) for spanning a two-year period as the Bible had recorded. Vondel also took care to include not only the requisite peripeteia, but also two different occasions of tragic recognition: Jeptha's perception of his error and, on a simpler level, his wife's discovery of her daughter's death. He was especially proud of his clear and verisimilar style which decorously accorded with each character's role. More importantly, Jeptha conformed to the mixed characterization of the ideal tragic hero; indeed, the Catholic biblical commentators Jacob Salianus and Nicolaus Serarius, whom Vondel consulted, were themselves perplexed by the ambiguity of Jeptha's actions.[140] On the one hand, Jeptha may have erred by rashly swearing to sacrifice to God the first living thing he encountered after his defeat of the Ammonites; conversely, Jeptha was esteemed as a righteous judge by St. Paul who consequently ranked him with Abraham, Moses and David (Hebrews 11:32). Vondel thus had the opportunity to focus alternately on his hero's piety and his flaws in order to arouse the appropriate pity and terror in the audience. For this reason, he attributed a cathartic significance to the events he portrayed. By suggesting that all tragedies tempered and purified the audience's emotional

---

[139] *Jeptha* has often been accorded a major place in Vondel criticism. Bomhoff (pp. 67-108) believed that this play exemplified Vondel's tragic view of man's inability to assert his will in the world. Langvik-Johannessen held that the play demonstrated the tragedy which necessarily ensued when man relied on his own conscience: "die Ereignisse werden subjektiviert und in den Menschen verlegt" (pp. 171-2). In contrast to these philosophical readings, Smit suggested a structural analysis in light of the play's preface, its model, *Jephthes* (1554) of George Buchanan, and contemporary Catholic interpretations of the biblical story, Smit, vol. 2, pp. 240-379.

[140] Jacob Salianus, S. J., *Annales Ecclesiastici Veteris Testamenti*, vol. 2 (Paris, 1620), and Nicolaus Serarius, S. J., *Iudices et Ruth explanati* (Mainz, 1609).

reaction to the play, Vondel intimated that the viewers of *Jeptha* would be better prepared to withstand rationally and soberly whatever misfortunes might subsequently befall them. But this cathartic interpretation was never explicitly connected to *Jeptha*. On the contrary, as his depiction of the events demonstrated, Vondel did not arouse emotions in order to teach men to control them but, rather, to induce his Christian audience to lament their fallen state, recognize the paradoxical relationship between faith and reason and to evince their belief through their unreserved submission to God's will.

In order to clarify his theological argument, Vondel structured the entire work around the character of Jeptha and his interpretation of the oath. As in the previous Jeptha dramas which Vondel undoubtedly knew—George Buchanan's *Jephthes sive votum* whose subtitle Vondel had borrowed and the tragedy of his Rederijker friend Abraham de Koning, *Iephthahs ende zijn eenighe dochters treur-spel*—there was little doubt that Jeptha had acted wrongly in sacrificing his daughter Ifis. The question of the righteousness of the oath itself had been left unresolved, for it was merely a device to facilitate the demonstration of other points. In Buchanan's tragedy, Jeptha's inhuman suppression of his love for his daughter and his obstinate refusal to reflect soberly on the consequences of the oath precipitated the tragedy. Buchanan was not so much interested in the theological problems of oaths—indeed, before the Inquisition, he attested that all oaths must be fulfilled[141]—but in Jeptha's tragic and irrational resolution of his psychological conflict. De Koning had much simpler ambitions. Although he noted the foolishness of Iephthah's oath and his observance of it in the prefatory letter,[142] his primary purpose was the illustration of the mutability of the world. Iephthah's varied fortunes— his rise from his outcast status as an illegitimate child to his victory over the Ammonites and his fateful execution of his daughter—were intended, in the usual Senecan fashion, to prepare man for his future afflictions. Vondel likewise left the question of the oath unresolved—the theological commentators themselves could not decide on this question[143]—and focused on Jeptha's reaction to his dilemma. In this way, Vondel not only avoided a ticklish theological question (if the oath were evil, why did Jeptha conquer his enemies?) but he also set up the framework for his subsequent demonstration of the irreconcilability of faith and reason.

---

[141] On the question of oaths and the concept of tragedy in Buchanan's play, see James H. McGregor, "The Sence of Tragedy in George Buchanan's *Jephthes*," *HumLov*, 31 (1982), 120-40, especially, pp. 135-40.

[142] De Koning claimed that Jephta had sworn ''een zotte belofte'' which consequently made his fall an excellent example "van d'ongestadicheyt deser bedrieglijcker Werelt." Abraham de Koning, *Iephthahs ende zijn eenighe dochters treur-spel*, sig. *2.

[143] Smit, vol. 2, pp. 277-81.

Despite Vondel's prefatory announcement of his mixed characterization of Jeptha, the virtuous and malicious sides of the protagonist were not immediately apparent. In contrast to *Salomen* and *Lucifer* where the primary sin of the titular heroes was explicated in the introduction and mirrored in the play, *Jeptha* lacked any such preliminary guidelines. Of course Vondel no doubt assumed that his audience was already familiar with the orthodox stance on this episode, but given the confusion of the theologians, introductory remarks from the author would have been in order. Smit's suggestion that Vondel may have concealed the lesson of *Jeptha* from his Protestant readership because of his criticism of Jeptha's "Protestant" (i.e., subjective) interpretation of the oath might certainly be valid,[144] but it still does not acount completely for the purpose of the tragedy. Nor does it suffice, as Smit further argued,[145] to view the play exclusively as a moral condemnation of self-righteousness. Had Vondel desired to convey this straightforward lesson, he would have picked a less ambiguous figure and certainly one who did not recognize his faults in the end. Indeed, Jeptha's transformation from a severe judge to a contrite sinner in the final act did not merely illustrate neo-classical recognition, but it also provided a key insight into his fundamental piety.

I should like to suggest that Vondel's refusal to interpret Jeptha's character was closely connected to the programmatic neo-classical intention of his tragedy. Had Vondel elected to make censorious remarks about his protagonist at the outset, the audience would have been prejudiced against him. Vondel knew that Jeptha held an ambiguous status theologically and, in withholding his judgment, he carefully navigated between positive and negative evaluations of him. At the same time Vondel hoped that the viewers would consequently be able to sympathize with Jeptha's plight so that his fall and subsequent remorse might terrify them into avoiding his error.

In keeping with his mixed characterization, Vondel slowly introduced the audience to Jeptha by focusing in the first two acts on the two characters who contrasted most sharply with him: his wife Filopaie and his daughter Ifis. Filopaie, whose Greek name signified her love for her daughter, was presented in the opening scene as a proud woman whose overconfidence in Jeptha and in her daughter's beauty endangered her faith in God. Indeed, as was evident from her conversation with the reproving chamberlain (*Hofmeester*), Filopaie had already replaced God with her worship of her husband and child. Flushed with the joyful tidings that Jeptha would return triumphantly, Filopaie believed herself

---

[144] Smit, vol. 2, pp. 358-9.
[145] Smit, vol. 2, p. 357.

immune from sorrow and misfortune; Jeptha himself had once again demonstrated his invincibility ("een Godt, geen sterflijck mensch").[146] Filopaie likewise anticipated Ifis' imminent return from the mountains where, unknown to Filopaie, she had gone to prepare herself for Jeptha's sacrifice, and she looked forward to entertaining the suitors who would doubtless woo such a beautiful daughter. Vondel clearly juxtaposed Filopaie's irrepressible happiness to the sober remonstrances of the chamberlain ("Niets staet hier stil. geen blyschap is volkomen"),[147] to exploit the irony of Filopaie's ignorance of the oath and the sacrifice. But, at the same time, he created a negative representation of excessive love and pride which anticipated Jeptha's subsequent self-righteousness. Just as Filopaie naively believed that Ifis would live a long life and one day care for her parents, so did Jeptha hold that God would never permit the unnatural sacrifice of Ifis to occur. In both instances Filopaie and Jeptha had ascribed their own will to God by rationally determining His necessary course of action.

In the opening act Filopaie had served to direct the audience's attention to the vices which would subsequently lead to the downfall of the protagonist. But where Filopaie had foreshadowed Jeptha's pride, Ifis provided a spiritual contrast to her father's piety. In the introduction Vondel had suggested that Ifis' willingness to die cast her as a *praefiguratio Christi*. In contrast to the Catholic theologians who argued that Jeptha's daughter shared in his sin by complying with her father's wishes,[148] Vondel took pains to emphasize her innocence. She was instead a model of filial obedience—a second Isaac—whose eagerness to die differed sharply from Jeptha's reluctance to kill her. Vondel in fact expanded Ifis' christological role by underscoring her willingness to suffer for whatever injury she might have caused him; indeed, she promised to unburden him of sorrow and guilt:

> Nu vader, draegh uw hartewee geduldigh.
> Ben ick, och arme, aen uw elende schuldigh,
> Aen uw verdriet? vaer voort, en strafme vry.
> Ontlast uw ziel: ick neem de schult op my,
> En op mijn ziel, dan is de strijt ten ende.
> Gy blijft gepaeit, ick vaere uit deze elende.[149]

By establishing these parallels to Christ, Vondel did not so much intend to suggest Jeptha's salvation as to associate him with Adam, the archetype for fallen man. As the scribe (*Wetgeleerde*) pointed out, like

---

[146] *WB*, VIII, p. 783, line 83.
[147] *WB*, VIII, p. 784, line 89.
[148] Smit, vol. 2, p. 287.
[149] *WB*, VIII, p. 802, lines 623-628.

Adam's brief reign in Paradise, Jeptha, who had once attained the pinnacle of victory, now fell because of the oath. The reason for Jeptha's demise, his pride, likewise recalled Adam's attempt to usurp God's role in Paradise. Where Ifis' pious submission to her fate resulted from her exemplary obedience, Jeptha's alleged obligation to fulfill the oath arose from his own subjective interpretation of God's will.

But Vondel was not content to dismiss Jeptha as a typical victim of excessive *superbia*. To be sure, Jeptha had deluded himself into dismissing God and the Law, regarding himself as the savior of his people and providing his own justification for Ifis' death. But Jeptha did not act out of jealousy or malice, as Lucifer had done in Vondel's earlier play, but out of excessive self-serving piety. Jeptha suffered from an Abraham complex, and his tragedy followed from his eventual recognition of the distinctions between himself and his ancestor. In his debate with the scribe about the righteousness of the execution, Jeptha explicated the reasons why he was obliged to fulfill the oath: he viewed himself as another Abraham who was required to demonstrate his faith by his obedience to God's command. Jeptha was consequently grieved not only by the impending loss of his daughter, but also by the possibility that he might fail to satisfy God as Abraham had done:

> Dat ick Godt verongelijcke,
> Zoo't hart hem niet gehoorzaeme, en dit blijcke
> Door't offer, hem belooft voor d'overhant.
> Ick steecke in schult: belofte is een verbant.
> Hier staet mijn ziel geketent, en gebonden[150]

The reprehensibility of Jeptha's obstinate refusal to heed the sound advice of his religious counselor was thus tempered by his sincere fear of offending God. In keeping with his identification with Abraham, moreover, Jeptha subsequently hoped that Ifis like Isaac would ultimately be spared. Ifis herself encouraged Jeptha to draw his inspiration from Abraham, so that his faith might be proved.[151] Even the fourth-act chorus continued the parallel between Abraham and Jeptha as if to reassure the audience that a man as faithful as Jeptha would surely not be tested in vain.[152] But Jeptha's obsession with Abraham, his rationalization of the sacrifice as yet another occassion for man to evince his obedience to God resulted in tragedy. Jeptha's excessive piety was thus connected to his proud delusion that he could dictate rules to God and thereby comprehend Him by mortal standards.

---

[150]  *WB*, VIII, p. 818, lines 1059-1063.
[151]  *WB*, VIII, p. 834, lines 1496-1498.
[152]  *WB*, VIII, p. 839-40, lines 1655-1694.

Vondel was also eager to demonstrate that Jeptha's misguided piety arose from his misconception about obedience and man's role in salvation. Nor only had Jeptha wrongly reasoned that the oath was merely a test of obedience, but his confidence in this judgment prevented him from averting the tragedy. Indeed, Jeptha's pride forced him to adopt a passive, mournful attitude toward the impending execution which contrasted sharply with Ifis' joyful anticipation. Where Ifis' strength arose from her willful agreement to the sacrifice, Jeptha was weakened by his false belief that faith could only be proven by man's passivity. In his conviction that God would reward the faithfulness of His servant, as He had so often in the past, Jeptha neglected his obligation as father and judge. He placed his interpretation of these duties above the Law of Moses, which forbade human sacrifice, concealed the truth from Filopaie and risked the disapprobation of the populace for his deed. In characterizing Jeptha as a false Abraham, the Catholic Vondel demonstrated that obedience to God was not based on man's passive belief—a decidedly Protestant view—but on his willful submission to His commands.

Vondel devoted the opening scenes of the last act to Jeptha's recognition of his error and, in contrast to previous dramatic treatments, Jeptha's "conversion" to the orthodox Law of Moses which he had lately shunned. The sudden transformation of the protagonist after his barbarous execution of Ifis has long been deemed a major weakness in the play.[153] Such an act was considered improbable and indecorous for a figure so obsessed with his own righteousness. But this conversion scene persuasively demonstrated that Jeptha's tragedy was not due so much to his eagerness to contradict as to please God. When God did not interrupt the sacrifice of Ifis, Jeptha, who had modeled his own actions on Abraham, perceived that he had blindly confused God's will with his own: "Nu gaen te spa, te spa mijne oogen open."[154] With the same pious exactitude with which he had earlier sought to obey God, Jeptha now resolved to seek the forgiveness of the High Priest whose advice he had formerly neglected. To underscore the fact that Jeptha's contrite resolution was related to Jeptha's fundamentally pious nature, Vondel reintroduced Filopaie to contrast their reactions to Ifis' death. Whereas Jeptha recognized his error and sought God's forgiveness, Filopaie, who had earlier replaced God with her admiration for her husband and daughter, was unable to recover from the tragic turn of events. Despite the admonitions of the court priest (*Hofpriester*) to forbear, Filopaie who had based her happiness on transitory objects, succumbed to despair:

---

[153] Smit, vol. 2, p. 367.
[154] *WB*, VIII, p. 841, line 1707.

> Mijn hoop en toeverlaet is doot.
> O weerelt, vol veranderingen!
>     Wat is het aerdtsch betrouwen broos!
> Nu treur ick droef, en kinderloos.[155]

Although Filopaie's pride had earlier foreshadowed Jeptha's own conceit, each represented a different type of *superbia*. Where Filopaie's blindness arose from a reprehensible immoderate love of the world, Jeptha's overconfidence resulted from his misconception that God could be measured by human standards.

In his characterization of Jeptha, Vondel thus exposed the inability of fallen man to comprehend God and worship him through the use of human reason. True faith such as that evinced by Ifis did not question God's commands, for it was grounded in the firm conviction that God was always just. In contrast, Jeptha's lamentation about the necessity of Ifis' death betrayed the weakness of his faith; he consequently attempted to bolster his spirits by justifying the execution through the comparison with Abraham. Vondel further demonstrated the disharmony between faith and reason by arousing the audience's sympathy for Jeptha's plight. If they mourned for Jeptha's impending loss of his daughter, their sorrow was later tempered by their recognition that Jeptha acted out of pride. If they considered God unjust or if they pitied Jeptha's vain efforts to understand Him, their emotions were subsequently moderated with their realization that man could never know God completely. In short, Vondel provoked the audience to bemoan Jeptha's fate, so that they might perceive similar errors in their own belief and thereby resolve to amend them. He depicted the incongruity between faith and reason, between man's unconditional obedience and his human doubts, not to indict the Creator but to reveal man's inability to resolve these oppositions on account of sin. Because of the Fall, Vondel reminded his audience, man was blinded to Divine Providence until God deigned to reward his faith with understanding and eternal life. By explicating the seemingly paradoxical nature of Christian faith, Vondel thus hoped to free his audiences from the obstacles to their own belief and ultimately to their own salvation.

As a pious Christian, Vondel shared the humanists' belief in divine justice, the Redemption, and the education and improvement of man's spiritual life. But, in contrast to sixteenth-century religious dramatists,

---

[155] *WB*, VIII, p. 849, lines 1947-1950. In light of her excessive grief, Filopaie's acknowledgment that God was testing her patience through Ifis' death (lines 1954-1956) did not necessarily mean that she had the ability to overcome her attachment to the world and her grief. Vondel may have well allowed Filopaie to voice her belief in God lest the audience be too stricken by her sorrowful loss and likewise despair.

he was especially sensitive to the fact that the world frequently did not correspond to this ideal view; even the most pious man was often tempted by despair because of injustice and evil. At the same time Vondel was acutely aware that man's doubts about God's justice arose not so much from his weakened faith as from his misperception of Him because of the Fall (''het treurspel aller treurspeelen).[156] Since man's misunderstanding of God might well shake his faith, Vondel established two goals for his religious plays. First, man was reminded of his fallen state and the resultant alienation from God and thereby induced to regard his misperception of Providence as a necessary consequence of the Fall. Secondly, man was instructed in the irreconcilability of faith and reason and thereby urged to accept, rather than question, God's direction of the world which he could only partially, if at all, perceive. As Vondel sharpened his dramatic skills on Graeco-Roman models and neo-classical theory, he conveyed his theological points through the adaptation of mixed characterizations and tragic catharsis. His christianization of these two aspects of neo-classical theory significantly contributed to his clear exposition of man's fallen state, the difficulties inherent in man's belief and ultimately to man's renewal of his resolution to obey God. Faith was no longer merely a virtue to be imitated, as it had been in the sixteenth century, and most certainly not a virtue which could be rationally understood. In Vondel's world, faith was painfully won, tenuously held, constantly assailed and frequently lost. Vondel's sensitivity to the complexity of belief thus established religious tragedy as a uniquely sophisticated literary genre in which man was at once reminded and consoled about his distance from his Creator.

---

[156] *WB*, X, p. 97 (*Adam in ballingschap*).

# CHAPTER FOUR

# ANDREAS GRYPHIUS AND THE SANCTIFICATION OF HISTORY

Seventeenth-century German Baroque dramatists were obsessed with the chaos of human history. The devastation of the Thirty Years War and the political and social upheaval which ensued induced writers such as Martin Opitz, Andreas Gryphius and Daniel Casper von Lohenstein to seek historical parallels to the catastrophe for their own works. Mindful of the Renaissance injunction to derive tragic plots from history, these three Silesian dramatists did not hesitate to present atrocities from the past to terrify, amaze and ultimately to console contemporary audiences. To this end, they selected their subjects either from the literary tradition of bloody Renaissance drama or from contemporary chronicles about equally fearful events in seventeenth-century history. Roman, Byzantine and Turkish tyrants—all modeled on Seneca's characterization of the ever-popular Nero—strutted across the Baroque stage threatening, tormenting, raping, sodomizing and finally beheading their political and religious opponents whose unshakable resistance thwarted their lust and ambition. War, revolution, intrigue, martyrdom, seduction and sorcery became the commonplaces whereby Baroque tragedians attempted to reassure their audiences that their contemporary misfortunes, though seemingly unbearable, were in fact incomparable to the torments of the past.

Among the three major Silesian dramatists, Andreas Gryphius (1616-1664) occupied a unique position in literary history. He was at the same time an innovative lyric poet, dramatist and orator as well as a Baroque polymath equally familiar with such diverse subjects as political theory, anatomy and Egyptology. As a lyricist, Gryphius produced the most poignant expressions of hopelessness and destruction which the Thirty Years War had wreaked throughout the Holy Roman Empire. His religious *Son- undt Feyrtags- Sonnete* (1639) transformed the devotional sermon poem into an anguished confession by fallen man of his own sinfulness and yearning for Christ. His achievements in poetry were also matched by his accomplishments as a playwright. Gryphius' knowledge of European Renaissance and Baroque drama resulted in the translation and original composition of tragedies and comedies which differed radically in style and theme from the humanist theater of the previous generation. His dramas now adhered to the formal prescripts established by Martin Opitz (1597-1639) in his *Buch von der deutschen Poeterey* (1624) about the meter, language and subject of both comedy and tragedy. In contrast to the moralistic and religious theater of the humanists, Gryphius introduced a new secularized type of historical tragedy in which religion and politics were granted equal importance.

The novelty of Gryphius' plays has, however, obscured their relation-ship to the humanist tradition which fostered them. As a consequence, the literary-historical place of Gryphius' tragedies has frequently been misrepresented. Prior arguments about Gryphius' debt or deviation from sixteenth-century or even contemporary dramatic praxis have tended to glorify his superiority to the models he is known to have followed or to bolster his reputation as the founder of modern German tragedy.[1] But this ahistorical or biased approach has resulted in an unjust assessment of both the dramatic tradition and Gryphius' relationship to it. The

---

[1] Gryphius' relationship to the dramatic tradition of tragedy has generally been con-fined to his ties to contemporary Jesuit, Netherlandic and French theater. The situation is considerably better for the comedies where connections have been made to Hans Sachs (*Herr Peter Squentz*), the *commedia dell'arte* (*Horribilicribrifax*) and Philippe Quinault (*Verliebtes Gespenst*). For a survey of the secondary literature on the comedies, see Karl-Heinz Habersetzer, "Auswahlbibliographie zu Andreas Gryphius," *Text und Kritik*, 7/8 (1980), 125-8. In contrast, modern studies on the literary-historical context of the tragedies is still based on outdated information or aesthetic assumptions about seventeenth-century drama developed over fifty years ago. Gryphius' relationship to the Jesuits was first examined from a positivistic standpoint by Willi Harring, *Andreas Gryphius und das Drama der Jesuiten*, Hermaea, 5 (Halle: Max Niemeyer, 1907); his conclusions still inform con-temporary writers on the subject, who, in their eagerness to praise the artistry of Gryphius, have spoken disparagingly of the didacticism of Jesuit theater: see E. M. Szarota, *Geschichte, Politik und Gesellschaft im Drama des 17. Jahrhunderts* (Bern and Munich, 1976), pp. 63-4. Verbal similarities between Gryphius and Dutch drama were compiled by R. A. Kollewijn, *Über den Einfluß des holländischen Dramas auf Andreas Gryphius* (Heilbronn, 1880), and Gustav Schönle, *Deutsch-niederländische Beziehungen in der Literatur des 17. Jahrhunderts* (Leiden: Universitaire Pers, 1968), pp. 33-109. As in the case of Jesuit drama, critical literature on the relationship between Vondel and Gryphius has focused for the most part on establishing the greatness of one author at the expense of the other. Since Gryphius imitated Vondel's least accomplished plays, *Maeghden* and *Maria Stuart*, it was not difficult for some German critics to praise the artistic sophistication of the Sile-sian. See, for example, Willi Flemming's comments on the complexity of Gryphius' characterizations in *Catharina von Georgien* in his article "Vondels Einfluß auf die Trauerspiele des Andreas Gryphius," *Neophilologus*, 14 (1929), 113-5. In a radical view of Gryphius' uniqueness as a dramatist, Erik Lunding proposed that Vondel's tragedy did not wield any influence on the German playwright: Erik Lunding, *Das schlesische Kunstdrama: eine Darstellung und Deutung* (Copenhagen: P. Haase, 1940), pp. 44-51. In the hands of Vondel scholars, however, the differences between the dramatists were presented so as to imply Vondel's superiority to the German. For Lieven Rens, Vondel created a harmonious synthesis of religious and secular issues while Gryphius' hyperbolic language suggested an "antithetische, getormenteerde barok, die na hem spoedig in extremen zal ontaarden." See Lieven Rens, "Over het probleem van de invloed van Vondel op de drama's van Andreas Gryphius," *HZM*, 20 (1966), 262.

objective of the following discussion therefore is to clarify Gryphius' connection to the dramatic tradition and to interpret his three major historical tragedies, *Leo Armenius* (1650), *Catharina von Georgien* (1657), and *Carolus Stuardus* (1657; 1663) within the context of humanist dramatic theory and praxis. I should like to suggest here that Gryphius' tragedies can only properly be understood in the light of the dramatic models which inspired him and to which he subsequently reacted. In this way it will be argued that Gryphius' critical revision of contemporary drama and its humanist antecedents formed the basis for his own distinctive contribution to religious theater. Instead of inaugurating a new era in German theater, Gryphius attempted to amend the dramatic practice of the past by restoring the centrality of Christ to the humanist stage.

Since Gryphius had deemed his debt to the dramatic tradition to be negligible, his contemporaries and subsequent literary critics unequivocally accepted his judgment . Such disclaimers of literary roots were not uncommon among ambitious *literati* and Gryphius was no exception. In the 1650 preface to his first historical tragedy *Leo Armenius,* Gryphius proudly declared his drama's independence from foreign models.[2] Twenty years earlier Martin Opitz had provided a German tragic idiom in his translation of Sophocles' *Antigone* and Seneca's *Troades*.[3] After careful study of much contemporary tragedy, especially Jesuit and Netherlandic theater, Gryphius now attempted to outstrip Opitz by adapting the latter's reforms to an original dramatic work. He also strengthened the uniqueness of his writings by distinguishing himself from the contemporary tradition. In the same 1650 preface, Gryphius promised a new type of martyr tragedy in his second drama, *Catharina von Georgien*, which would amend the faults he had perceived in Corneille's *Polyeucte*.[4]

Gryphius' inventiveness was likewise extolled by his contemporaries who, following humanist practice, applauded him as the German

---

[2] "Ein ander mag von der Außländer Erfindungen den Nahmen wegreissen und den seinen darvor machen: Wir schliessen mit denen Worten/die jener weitberühmbte und lobwürdigste Welsche Poet uber seinen vördergiebel geschrieben:
  Das Hauß ist zwar nicht groß: doch kennt es mich allein:
  Es kostet frembde nichts: es ist nur rein und mein.
As quoted in Andreas Gryphius, *Trauerspiele II,* ed. Hugh Powell (Tübingen: Max Niemeyer, 1965), p. 4. All future references to this play are based on this edition.
[3] *Des Griechischen Tragoedienschreibers Sophoclis Antigone Deutsch gegeben durch Martinum Opitium* (1636) and *L. Annaei Senecae Trojanerinnen/Deutsch übersetzt und erkläret durch Martinum Opitium* (1625). Both translations were printed in Martin Opitz, *Weltliche Poemata,* Erster Teil (Breslau, 1638; Frankfurt a. Main: Thomas Götze, 1644). Subsequent references to these works will be drawn from the facsimile edition of the 1644 text, ed. Erich Trunz (Tübingen: Niemeyer, 1967).
[4] Gryphius, *Trauerspiele II,* p. 4.

Sophocles and Corneille.[5] In the eyes of later critics[6] he was hailed as the first German tragedian to free drama from its preoccupation with religious and biblical subjects. The chronological sequence of the tragedies from the Byzantine court of *Leo Armenius* to the pagan Roman *aula* of *Papinianus* (1659) certainly appeared to suggest a gradual development toward secular topics. To be sure *Papinianus*, with its stoical hero, differed sharply from the Christian setting of the historical plays. But when the latter are viewed within the context of contemporary humanist praxis, it becomes clear that Gryphius was equally concerned with theological as well as secular issues. As will be seen, historical topics did not suggest Gryphius' break with the tradition of religious drama; rather, they supplied the young playwright with a new forum for theological ideas which contemporary religious dramatists no longer emphasized.

*Historical Drama as Sacred Theater*

Gryphius' preference for historical rather than the familiar biblical topics may seem an odd choice for a playwright interested in religion. Predictably, the reason for such an irregularity cannot be reduced to a simple, unqualified explanation. On the one hand, Gryphius' composition of historical tragedy reflected his adherence to the humanists' view of history as a requisite topic for tragedy. As a student of Opitz and other Renaissance theoreticians, Gryphius followed the traditional prescription that tragedies illustrate the mutability of fortune and the downfall of kings.[7] Where the requisite dethronement did not occur as in *Catharina von Georgien* and *Papinianus,* Gryphius ensured that his works portrayed

---

[5] Lohenstein praised Gryphius as "Teutscher Sophocles," and Daniel von Czepko claimed that Gryphius' dramatic achievements exceeded those of Corneille. Eberhard Mannack, *Andreas Gryphius* (Stuttgart: Metzler, 1968), p. 77.

[6] Herbert Heckmann argued that Gryphius' Papinianus represented a secularized Christian martyr: H. Heckmann, *Elemente des barocken Trauerspiels* (Munich: Carl Hanser, 1959), pp. 51-71. Similarly, Albrecht Schöne suggested that Gryphius' use of biblical typology to a political end in *Carolus Stuardus* indicated a gradual development toward secularization: A. Schöne, "Carolus Stuardus," in *Die Dramen des Andreas Gryphius,* ed. Gerhard Kaiser (Stuttgart: Metzler, 1968), pp. 167-9. Cf. Hans-Jürgen Schings' refutation of Heckmann through the comparison of Gryphius' characterization of Papinianus with the stoic and patristic views of the Christian martyr: H.-J. Schings, *Die patristische und stoische Tradition bei Andreas Gryphius* (Cologne and Graz: Böhlau, 1966), pp. 277-95.

[7] Cf. Julius Caesar Scaliger's definition of tragedy and Martin Opitz's description in his *Buch von der deutschen Poetrerey*: Scaliger: "In Tragoedia Reges, Principes, ex urbibus, arcibus, castris. Principia sedatiora: exitus horribiles." J. C. Scaliger, *Poetices libri septem,* ed. August Buck, Faksimile-Neudruck der Ausgabe von Lyon 1561 (Stuttgart and Bad Cannstatt: Frommann, 1964), p. 11 (Book I, chapter 6). Martin Opitz: "Die Tragedie ist an der maiestet dem Heroischen getichte gemeße ... weil sie nur von Königlichem willen/Todtschlägen/verzweiffelungen ... handelt." Martin Opitz, *Buch von der deutschen Poeterey,* ed. Cornelius Sommer (Stuttgart: Reclam, 1970), p. 27.

the "blutschanden/kriege vnd auffruhr/klagen/heulen/seuffzen" prescribed by Opitz.[8] Secondly, Gryphius' selection of a historical subject
accorded with another humanist practice, that is, the use of tragedy for
political instruction. He was especially intrigued by the idea of kingship
and the characteristics and responsibilities of a good monarch toward the
people.[9] As a staunch defender of the divine right of kings propounded
by his Leiden university teacher, Claudius Salmasius, and his lesser
known German acquaintances, Johann Boecler, a professor in
Strasbourg, and Georg Schönborner, his Silesian patron, Gryphius
explored the problems of tyrannicide and revolution in his historical
tragedies. He vehemently condemned regicide and the subject's right to
revolt in *Leo Armenius, Carolus Stuardus* and *Papinianus* and juxtaposed the
exemplary virtues of a patriotic ruler to the conceit of a depraved tyrant
in *Catharina von Georgien.*

But Gryphius was not motivated solely by theoretical precepts and
political concerns. His preference for historical tragedy was also
grounded in his belief that this type of play best represented his
theological point, namely the necessity of faith for spiritual salvation.
The downfall of kings had long been regarded by Christian humanists as
a metaphor for the vanity of all temporal pursuits[10]—indeed, the transitory nature of the world had been a biblical commonplace[11]—but
Gryphius' acknowledgment of this fact induced him to represent the
manner in which Christian man could preserve himself from such chaos
through faith. Accordingly, in his historical tragedies, Gryphius juxtaposed the immorality of the worldly politician with the ideal Christian.
In *Leo Armenius* the reign of the ambitious revolutionary Michael Balbus,
though temporarily successful, was doomed to disappear as quickly as he
had attained power. The hapless end of Oliver Cromwell and the other
Parliamentarians was similarly foretold in *Carolus Stuardus* as proof of the
futility of their machinations against Charles I. Conversely, the tragic
protagonists, Leo, Catharina and Charles, who had perceived the transitoriness of the temporal world and hence the limitations of secular pursuits, withdrew completely from politics to prepare for death. The
development of the hero from a worldly, if not immoral, monarch into
a humble Christian with his gaze fixed on a heavenly crown remained

---

[8] Opitz, *Buch,* p. 27.

[9] Gryphius' politics have been examined closely by Hans Kuhn, "*Non decor in regno*:
Zur Gestalt des Fürsten bei Gryphius," *OL,* 25 (1970), 126-50, and Gustaf K.
Schmelzeisen, "Staatsrechtliches in den Trauerspielen des Andreas Gryphius," *Archiv für
Kulturgeschichte,* 53 (1971), 93-126.

[10] See the discussion on divine justice above, chapter 2, pp. 63-6.

[11] See Ecclesiastes, *passim.*

the foundation of Gryphius' tragic vision. The inclusion of sophisticated political and historical arguments thus intensified the contrast between the valuelessness and chaos of history and the eternal peace of salvation. By representing the changeable nature of the political world, Gryphius thus dispensed the requisite lessons for the survival of the *Christianus politicus* in it as he simultaneously revealed the dependence of the *politicus* on God's grace for eternal life.

The exposure of the falsity of the temporal world and the necessity of salvation significantly influenced Gryphius' preference for historical topics. His choice of a specific subject was, however, more directly related to his views of contemporary theatrical practice. *Leo Armenius*, *Catharina von Georgien* and *Carolus Stuardus* were each conceived as a critical response to particular abuses which Gryphius had perceived in the composition of historical drama for a Christian audience. At the root of Gryphius' criticism lay his belief that historical drama must not only impart political instruction but also lead man toward Christ. For this reason Gryphius considered certain dramatic practices especially inappropriate. First, he disliked plays which portrayed a historical world in the Christian era which failed to note the significance of the Redemption for mankind; Gryphius rectified this shortcoming in *Leo Armenius* where the critical final act focused on the salvation of the protagonist. Secondly, Gryphius disapproved of the use of secular and religious drama for the sole purpose of instilling Christian virtue in the audience; *Catharina von Georgien*, for example, demonstrated that eternal salvation depended less on the ethics man practiced than on the extent of his faith. Finally in *Carolus Stuardus*, Gryphius distanced himself from the biased application of religious arguments to support a political goal. Martyred historical figures such as Charles I were not so much to be regarded as modern postfigurations of Christ but as sinful men unworthy of the parallel between themselves and their Savior.

Gryphius' preference for historical drama was thus motivated by literary, political and, most importantly, theological reasons. It is not surprising therefore that Gryphius displayed an interest in religious as well as historical drama: he translated Joost van den Vondel's biblical tragedy *Gebroeders* (1640) and Nicolaus Caussin's hagiographical play *Felicitas* (1620) as literary exercises in the 1640s while developing his own concept of tragedy diction. His son Christian Gryphius regretted the loss of an original biblical tragedy on Saul and the Gibeonites while preparing an edition of his father's work in 1698. But Gryphius' avoidance of biblical and hagiographical drama may be grounded deeper in his religious beliefs than has hitherto been supposed. Unlike the humanist biblical dramatists, Gryphius was not interested in explicating the Word of God or in reducing it to a set of moral guidelines. Nor did Gryphius desire to imitate Vondel and transform religious crises into christianized Greek tragedy. For the devout Lutheran, Gryphius, the Word existed as God's direct revelation of himself to man. Because of its divine origin, the Word did not require any amplification or embellishment to convince man of its validity and of the need for faith.[12] Gryphius consequently dispensed with any further explication and concentrated instead on the effect of the Word on mankind. More specifically, Gryphius focused on the Word's manifestation of itself through Christ and the effect of Christ on human history. Where biblical dramatists with their marked preference for Old Testament prefigurations of Jesus (e.g., Abraham, Joseph, David) were content to foreshadow the miracle of the Redemption through their protagonists, Gryphius preferred to represent the effect of the Redemption on characters throughout Christian history. Just as the earlier biblical plays had assured audiences of the promise of salvation, so did Gryphius' historical tragedies promise the salvation of all men through the grace of Christ.

The soteriological intent of Gryphius' historical dramas thus allied his work to the biblical and hagiographical plays of the previous century. He was, of course, familiar with the recent reforms of Martin Opitz and the Netherlandic Aristotelians, Daniel Heinsius and Gerardus Vossius, about the nature and function of tragedy but, in practice, Gryphius' works betrayed several similarities to sixteenth-century religious theater. He had, moreover, been initially inspired by the dramas of the Jesuits and the early Vondel (before 1650) who themselves were rooted in the Renaissance tradition. But Gryphius' ties to the humanists were limited to the spirituality rather than the ethical utility of their plays. He was not as interested in the morality which the dramas conveyed as in the faith which determined the actions of a virtuous Christian. Besides their obvious political lessons, Gryphius' historical tragedies were written to restore the Christocentric world view of the biblical dramatists which their ethical bias had obscured and to maintain the necessity of faith for man's salvation.

---

[12] Luther's notion of the clarity of the Word whereby it legitimated its own ability to interpret itself was central to his argument with Erasmus on free will. Where the latter asserted that the meaning of the Word (''scriptura'') was often obscure, Luther suggested that the true Word of God needed no further interpretation since its meaning was always clear, *WA*, 18, p. 606. On the concept of the Word in Luther's theology, see Heinrich Bornkamm, ''Das Wort Gottes bei Luther,'' in his *Luther. Gestalt und Wirkungen* (Gütersloh: Gerd Mohn, 1975), pp. 147-86.

*Gryphius and Humanist Religious Drama*

Gryphius shared the humanists' concept of the sacred function of religious theater. As the heirs to the humanist tradition, the Jesuits supplied Gryphius with dramatic models which he then revised in accordance with his Protestant faith. His work thus resembled the religious theater of both the humanists and the Lutheran playwrights of the sixteenth-century. From the humanists, Gryphius inherited the bond between history, tragedy and truth as well as their concept of the consolation of divine justice. From the Lutherans, Gryphius borrowed the theological emphasis on salvation *sola fide* and replaced the humanist drama of justice with the Protestant drama of justification.

Gryphius' dramatic representation of history was based on the humanist religious playwrights' equation of history with spiritual truth. Since the fourth century A.D., tragedy had been associated with secular history and the fall of kings. The Terentian commentator Aelius Donatus had established history as a major characteristic of tragedy; Quattrocento Senecan editors likewise classified tragic plots as historical ("'de historica fide'")[13] and regal ("'heroicae fortunae in adversis comprehensio'"),[14] and both J. C. Scaliger and Opitz applied the same rules to sixteenth- and seventeenth-century dramatic praxis. Humanist religious dramatists, however, broadened the concept by designating spiritual truth the primary characteristic of *historia*. History was no longer understood solely as a chronicle of secular events but as Christian truth. In the verse prologue to his 1559 tragedy on John the Baptist, for example, the Protestant dramatist Daniel Walther (ca. mid-1500s) praised the moral significance of his work, for in contrast to the profane plots of classical tragedy, his drama contained the truth of Sacred Scripture.[15] Gryphius similarly offered a spiritual truth in his historical tragedies to supplement the secular plot whose falsity he had exposed. Spiritual truth thus supplanted historical truth as the basis for Gryphius' Christian tragedy. *Cardenio und*

---

[13] See the commentary of Benedictus Philologus in *L. Annei Senecae Tragoediae pristinae integritati restitutae per exactissimi iudicii viros* (Paris: Badius, 1514), sig. Aa vi.

[14] *Ibid.*

[15] Walter noted in his verse prologue:

Es ist nicht ein leichtfertigs Spiel
   Dergleichen hin und wider viel/
Man lieset bey den Comicis
   Und den Heidnischen Tragicis/
Sondern diese Tragedia
   Ist eine ware Historia
Daran gar nicht zu zweifeln ist.

Daniel Walther, *Eyne Christliche und jnn heiliger Schrifft gegründte Historia/von der entheuptung Johannis Baptistae/in ein Tragoediam gestalt* (Erfurt: Georg Bawmann, 1559), sig. Aiv^v-Avii.

*Celinde* (1657) with its fictional romantic plot, non-regal characters and ethical orientation could consequently be classified as a tragedy, for it revealed the true transitory nature of the world.

Gryphius also shared the humanists' belief in the consolatory effect of religious drama. The concept of consolation had had a complex development in both sixteenth-century dramatic theory and praxis. All of Gryphius' tragedies, in fact, betrayed similarities to the three main types: the religious dramatists' consolation of justice, the Neo-Stoic consolation of injustice and the Protestant consolation of faith. In humanist religious drama, the playwrights took pains to assure the audience that the misfortunes which beset the virtuous men onstage were only temporary. Cornelius Crocus ended his 1536 comedy on Joseph's fateful encounter with Potiphar's wife not with his imprisonment but, two years later, with his elevation to chief minister of Egypt.[16] Similarly, the Liège schoolmaster, Gregorius Holonius, concluded his tragedy on the bloody martyrdom of St. Catherine of Alexandria with her triumphant entrance into heaven.[17] The glorification of virtue doubtless consoled sixteenth-century audiences that their righteous behavior would be similarly rewarded. In humanist dramatic praxis, consolation was thus dispensed through the visual demonstration of divine justice: the persecutors and the sinners were punished by the fires of hell and the faithful attained an eternal crown. Gryphius' martyr tragedies, *Catharina von Georgien* and *Carolus Stuardus* both displayed clear reminiscences of this consolation of justice in the choruses and the final scenes. As the two martyrs gained salvation through the strength of their faith, the audience was comforted with reminders that God's justice would ultimately prevail.

In sixteenth-century dramatic theory consolation was also provided in the opposite manner, namely through the representation of injustice. This type of consolation had developed out of the humanists' interpretation of Senecan tragedy and it was chiefly applicable to secular, i.e., Graeco-Roman, drama. Whenever this type was appropriated by religious dramatists for a Christian audience, however, it was reinterpreted to accord with the consolation of justice. Gryphius himself was no exception, and in his 1650 preface to *Leo Armenius*, his christianization of this pagan concept of consolation became apparent. Gryphius had doubtless derived the Senecan concept of consolation from the preface to Martin Opitz's German translation of Seneca's *Troades* (1625); indeed, he clearly knew this work since on the same occasion he hoped his own

---

[16] Cornelius Crocus, *Joseph* (1536; Antwerp: Ioan. Steelsius, 1538).
[17] Gregorius Holonius, *Catharina. Tragoedia de fortissimo S. Catharinae virginis ... certamine* (Antwerp: Ioan. Bellerus, 1556).

tragedy would surpass Opitz's achievement. Inspired by several Senecan commentators, especially by the Saxon philologist Georg Fabricius (1516-1571) and the Flemish Jesuit Martinus Antonius Del Rio (1551-1608), Opitz had conceived of the utility of tragedy as the strengthening of man's spirit in preparation for future misfortune.[18] The witnessing of such hapless occurrences as the fall of Troy (Seneca's *Troades*) was held to be particularly beneficial for the release of harmful emotions (e.g., pity and fear) and the development of *constantia,* the hardening of man's resolve to forbear. The consolation arose from the fact that we, unlike the unfortunates onstage, have been spared such calamity. Our own present immunity thus assuaged our fears as it prepared us to endure adversity more effectively:

> Wer wird nit mit grösserem Gemüte als zuvor seines Vatterlandts Verterb und Schaden/den er nit verhüten mag/ertragen/wann er die gewaltige Statt Troja/an welcher/wie die Meynung gewesen/die Götter selbst gebawet haben/siehet im Fewer stehen/und zu Staube und Asche werden?[19]

Gryphius sympathized with Opitz's concern that his fellow Silesians urgently required moral exempla of constancy; *Catharina von Georgien* was written in part to provide such a model.[20] But Gryphius' conception of the utility of tragedy was more complex than Opitz's philological interpretation. In the 1650 preface Gryphius suggested that his tragedies would free men from "allerhand vnartigen und schädlichen Neigungen"[21] through their depiction of the transitoriness of the world ("vergänglichkeit menschlicher sachen").[22] Clearly Gryphius, himself no stranger to Renaissance dramatic theory, ascribed a cathartic function to his plays. His notion of tragic catharsis differed, however, from Opitz's psychological reinforcement of the terrified viewer. Gryphius did not claim that the audience of *Leo Armenius* would subsequently be able to endure lesser hardships, nor did he remark that man possessed the ability to control his fears. Rather, Gryphius suggested that by observing the vanities of the world, man would be liberated from its evil effects. Since Gryphius had imbued his historical plays with a religious

---

[18] On Opitz's relationship to the late sixteenth-century reception of Seneca, see Hans-Jürgen Schings, "Seneca-Rezeption und Theorie der Tragödie. Martin Opitz' Vorrede zu den *Trojanerinnen,*" in *Historizität in Sprach- und Literaturwissenschaft,* eds. Walter Müller-Seidel, et al. (Munich: Fink, 1974), pp. 521-37.

[19] Opitz, *Trojanerinnen,* p. 315.

[20] On the political significance of *Catharina von Georgien,* see E. M. Szarota, *Künstler, Grübler und Rebellen. Studien zum europäischen Märtyrerdrama des 17. Jahrhunderts* (Munich and Bern: Francke, 1967), pp. 205-7.

[21] Gryphius, *Trauerspiele II,* p. 3.

[22] *Ibid.*

significance, the "vnartigen und schädlichen Neigungen" were doubtless understood as sin. Tragic catharsis therefore served to free man from the alluring but false pleasures of the world and to redirect his attention toward an eternal, heavenly God. This lesson was reinforced through the consolatory suggestion in the *Leo Armenius*, for example, that sinners like the tyrannical Leo who have renounced the world, might be saved through Christ. In the tradition of sixteenth-century religious drama, the assassination of the Byzantine emperor christianized Opitz's neo-classical interpretation by promising salvation for all men who believed in the power of the Redemption.

Gryphius thus adapted the sixteenth-century consolation of justice to the prescriptions of Reanaissance theory. He did not, however, represent a just universe in the same unsophisticated manner of many religious dramatists. Gryphius disapproved of a visual confirmation of a providential God for his Protestant viewers. Choruses of angels who assuaged the audience's fears about the execution of a Christian martyr, as in the *Felicitas* (1620) of the French Jesuit, Nicolaus Caussin, were absent from Gryphius' stage. Although the heavens were silent, they were by no means empty. To support this view, Gryphius reverted to the Christocentric concept of consolation which underlay Lutheran school drama in the sixteenth century. As a general rule, sixteenth-century Catholic humanists had assumed that consolation could be imparted through the restoration of justice. But Protestant writers revised this view to accord with their theology. Because of man's fallen state, consolation could only be afforded through the grace of Christ. In the face of the inescapable hardships of the world and its seemingly inexplicable misfortunes, the presence of God or his angels did not suffice to calm man's fears. On the contrary, the wrathful face of God reminded the sinner of his own inability to preserve himself from eternal damnation. Consequently, man's true consolation could only be found if he were to place his fate entirely in Christ's hands. Like the three Apocryphal heroes of sixteenth-century Lutheran theater, Susanna, Judith and Tobias, salvation for Gryphius' tragic protagonists could only be won through the unconditional surrender of their souls to Christ. In the tradition of his Lutheran predecessors, Gryphius transformed the humanists' consolation of justice in order to underline the significance of faith—*consolatio fidei*—for man's salvation.

Gryphius' debt to the humanist tradition of religious drama was thus qualified by his Protestant beliefs. He was not merely content to imbue his historical plots with Christian truth nor to illustrate God's providential guidance of the universe. Rather, the most significant occurrence in Gryphius' view of human history was the Redemption of mankind, for all events derived their meaning from it. Through Christ's intervention in history, the martyrdom, revolution and tyranny in Gryphius' tragedies were not solely painful tests of virtue, but a testament to man's belief in salvation.

In his historical tragedies, Gryphius also sought to amend the faults he had perceived in humanist dramatic praxis. His disenchantment with earlier religious theater was based on his concept of the soteriological function of sacred drama. Each of his historical tragedies had been written to remind Protestant audiences of the significance of faith and to attest to the salvation which Christ had bestowed on man through the Redemption. To underscore this theological truth, Gryphius retained Luther's pessimistic notion of human nature and dispensed with the humanists' optimism about man's educability.[23] Because of original sin, man, society and history were inevitably flawed. Humanist religious dramatists had, of course, shared this belief in the consequences of the Fall, but unlike Gryphius, they had also provided practical solutions to control, if not overcome, this cursed inheritance. In his 1529 oration *De pueris* Erasmus had casually dismissed the vexing problem of original sin by suggesting that a strong moral education would suffice to free man from its consequences.[24] Similarly, Gulielmus Gnapheus had intimated in his *Acolastus* (1529) that the misbehavior of the prodigal son might well have been obviated by a better (i.e., humanist) education. Such optimism deviated sharply from Gryphius' more radical idea that all human undertakings were imperfect and vain:

> Ein Irrlicht ists was Euch O sterbliche! verführet
> Ein thöricht Rasen das den Sinn berühret.
> Wil jmand Ewig seyn wo man die kurtze Zeit
> Die Handvoll Jahre die der Himmel euch nachsiht
> Diß Alter das vergeht in dem es blüht
> In Vnmuth theilt vnd in Vergängligkeit?[25]

Indeed, as long as man remained in the world, he would be deceived, tormented and even reformed only to fall again because of his spiritual frailty. The urgency of Gryphius' reliance on Christ must be seen against this backdrop of man's fundamental depravity. His critique of religious drama was thus directed against the two practices which interfered with the communication of this message: (1) the exclusive use of drama as a pedagogical tool for instilling social mores, and (2) the subordination of

---

[23] See chapter 2, pp. 86-7.

[24] For a quotation of the relevant passage, see chapter 2, note 90.

[25] From the opening monologue of the allegorical *Ewigkeit* figure: Gryphius, *Trauerspiele III,* ed. Hugh Powell (Tübingen: Max Niemeyer, 1966), p. 139, lines 9-14.

the christological interpretation of biblical plays to ethical concerns. In his tragedies, Gryphius responded to both of these practices by exposing the limitations of man's educability and emphasizing Christ's unique role in human history.

Gryphius was further troubled by the humanists' exclusion of the soteriological significance of their biblical plots from their plays. In keeping with medieval practice, humanist religious playwrights had regarded many of the biblical events they portrayed as allegories of the Redemption.[26] Old Testament figures such as Abraham, Joseph and David retained the same typological function they had had in patristic literature as prefigurations of Christ; New Testament parables such as those of the Lost Sheep, the Prodigal Son, and the Good Samaritan, were similarly interpreted as paradigms of man's salvation. The allegorical significance of these biblical episodes was not, however, an intrinsic part of the play. Sixteenth-century dramatists preferred to separate the actual narration of the biblical events from their interpretation by confining the allegorical reading to their own ancillary remarks in the prologue, epilogue or dedicatory letter.

In contrast to this practice, Gryphius incorporated the christological meaning of the dramatic events into the work itself. The key historical episode in each of his tragedies now assumed both a literal and allegorical significance; indeed, the allegorical meaning was essential for a correct interpretation of the tragic plot. The assassination of Leo Armenius, the martyrdom of Catharina von Georgien and the execution of Carolus Stuardus were not merely portraits of the downfall of kings but also allegories of the Redemption. Moreover, the characters themselves, rather than the playwright, illustrated the spiritual significance of their actions. Leo's embrace of the true Cross, Catharina's longing for Christ as her bridegroom and Carolus Stuardus' reflections on his Christ-like death established the basis for Gryphius' emphasis on the Redemption. In response to the humanist tradition, Gryphius shifted the focus from man to Christ, from education to salvation and from earth to heaven. The moralistic biblical drama of the sixteenth-century writers and their descendants in the seventeenth-century Jesuit and Netherlandic theater was now replaced by sacred historical drama which, like the Bible, revealed to man the miracle of the Redemption.

*Gryphius' Dramatic Apprenticeship*

Gryphius' critical revision of sixteenth- and seventeenth-century literary praxis was not an explicit program of reform. With few exceptions,

---

[26] See chapter 2, pp. 66-74.

objection he ever made about seventeenth-century drama was directed against the romantic subplot in Pierre Corneille's martyr tragedy, *Polyeucte* (1643). In the 1650 preface to *Leo Armenius*, Gryphius complained that the romantic bond between the wife of the martyr, Pauline, and the Roman general, Sévère, dominated the drama to such an extent that the glory of Polyeucte's martyrdom was obscured.[27] *Catharina von Georgien* was subsequently written as a replique to demonstrate the superiority of heavenly to earthly love. Otherwise there was little historical evidence about which tragedies Gryphius himself had studied. He was of course familiar with the two works he had translated, Nicolaus Caussin's *Felicitas* and Joost van den Vondel's *Gebroeders.* His knowledge of Caussin may have also extended to the Jesuit's other four tragedies included in the volume Gryphius is known to have owned.[28] His familiarity with the works of other tragedians can only be demonstrated indirectly: his *Leo Armenius* was most likely inspired by the *Leo Armenus* (1625?; 1656) of the English Jesuit Joseph Simons;[29] and the numerous verbal similarities between the three historical tragedies and the plays of P. C. Hooft and Joost van den Vondel (before 1650) suggest that Gryphius was also well read in Netherlandic theater.[30]

Despite the paucity of direct references it is possible to assess Gryphius' reaction to the contemporary tradition of both religious and historical drama. The two main influences on Gryphius' tragedies—the theater of the Jesuits and the Netherlands—had produced both kinds of plays, and in both instances Gryphius objected to their praxis. His first three historical tragedies differ so markedly from Jesuit and Dutch work in the same genre that one can safely regard the *Leo Armenius*, *Catharina* Gryphius himself remained silent about his contemporaries. The only

---

[27] Gryphius did not refer directly to Corneille's drama, but rather described his reaction to the plot: "vnd desselben Werck schlechten ruhmbs würdig achten/welcher vnlängst einen heiligen Märterer zu dem Kampff geführet /vnd demselben wider den grund der warheit eine Ehefraw zu geordnet/welche schier mehr mit jhrem Bulen/als der Gefangene mit dem Richter zuthun findet/und durch mitwürckung ihres Vattern eher Braut als Wittbe wird.'' *Trauerspiele II*, p. 4. Szarota briefly discussed *Catharina von Georgien* as an anti-*Polyeucte* in *Künstler, Grübler und Rebellen*, p. 191.

[28] Harring, p. 30.

[29] On Joseph Simons see J. A. Parente, Jr., "Tyranny and Revolution on the Baroque Stage: The Dramas of Joseph Simons," *HumLov*, 32 (1983), 309-24, and William H. McCabe, *An Introduction to Jesuit Theater*, Diss. Cambridge 1929; rpt. ed. Louis J. Oldani (St. Louis: Institute of Jesuit Sources, 1983), pp. 131-265.

[30] In addition to the references cited in note 1 on Gryphius and Dutch theater, see Theodore Weevers, "Vondel's Influence on German Literature," *MLR*, 32 (1937), 1-23; Clarence K. Pott, "Holland-German Literary Relations in the Seventeenth Century," *JEGP*, 47 (1948), 127-38; Edward Verhofstadt, "Vondel und Gryphius: Versuch einer literarischen Topographie," *Neophilologus*, 53 (1969), 290-9; Ferdinand van Ingen, "Die Übersetzung als Rezeptionsdokument: Vondel in Deutschland-Gryphius in Holland," *Michigan Germanic Studies*, 4 (1978), 131-64.

*von Georgien*, and *Carolus Stuardus* as responses to the tradition, if not to specific plays. The critical awareness which Gryphius displayed in his brief remarks about Corneille similarly informed his original compositions. Thus, *Leo Armenius* was written to counter Joseph Simons' historical tragedy, *Leo Armenus*. *Catharina von Georgien* not only refuted *Polyeucte*, but also the entire tradition of humanist martyr drama to which *Polyeucte*, Caussin's *Felicitas* and Vondel's *Maeghden* (1639) belonged. Finally, *Carolus Stuardus* was conceived as a refutation of Vondel's *Maria Stuart* (1646) and the unabashed invention of parallels between political martyrs and Christ's passion.

The extent of Gryphius' knowledge of the sixteenth-century tradition of drama can never be determined, but the Jesuit and Netherlandic plays by which he was inspired and to which he reacted had developed out of humanist dramatic praxis. In the early seventeenth century Jesuit playwrights were producing biblical, hagiographical and historical dramas in their schools to glorify the achievements of the Catholic Church. Since the 1560s Jesuit school playwrights had shared the humanist view that religious subjects were morally superior to the fictive plots of ancient dramatists.[31] Although the Jesuits recognized the pedagogical utility of their plays as exercises in Latin language and rhetoric, the value of their works lay in their ability to convey Catholic Church dogma and ethics to the largest possible audience. Since the Church's interest was both religious and political, the Jesuits did not distinguish between sacred and secular topics. All Jesuit plays were fundamentally religious dramas in which the Church's stance in politics and ethics was variously conveyed. Gryphius' first two tragedies, *Leo Armenius* and *Catharina von Georgien* were written in reaction to this unreserved assimilation of secular and religious goals. Whereas *Leo Armenius* was directed against the Jesuits' secular (i.e., ecclesiastical rather than Christocentric) view of history, *Catharina von Georgien* was aimed at the trivial transformation of the martyr play into a mirror of virtue for daily Christian life.

Seventeenth-century religious drama in the Netherlands had likewise developed under the aegis of the humanists. In the hands of accomplished

---

[31] See, for example, the verse prologue to a 1577 Jesuit play on Esther:
  Venimus huc Christo auspice, ut spectaculum
  Vobis novum exhibeamus, tragicocomicos
  Non fabulam, quales Plauti et Terenti
  Ac caeterorum sunt pleraeque fabulae
  Vanae, profanae, et impudicae ac lubricae
  Vobis daturi sumus at historiam sacram
  Verissimamque, sumptam è sacris Bibliis
*Hester comoedia sacra,* ms. Bayerische Staatsbibliothek, clm. 524, fol. 3.

classical scholars such as Hugo Grotius and Daniel Heinsius and later Joost van den Vondel, biblical drama was molded into an exclusive art form which corresponded to the humanists' unique interpretation of Aristotelian tragedy. Indeed, some Netherlandic dramatists like the peripatetic Benedictine Jacob Cornelius Lummenaeus à Marca of Ghent (1570-1629) dispensed with the ethical tradition of school theater altogether in favor of religious plays which unintentionally reintroduced the immorality of classical tragedy along with its style.[32] Although Gryphius' first dramatic venture had been a translation of Vondel's religious tragedy, *Gebroeders*, his attraction to Dutch theater primarily lay in their historical dramas. As a student of political theory, Gryphius had been intrigued by the problem of tyrannicide which Hooft had dramatized in his *Geeraerdt van Velsen* (1613). But it was Vondel's historical tragedies with their mixture of religion with hagiography and politics which wielded the strongest influence over Gryphius. Gryphius' *Papinianus* betrayed similarities to *Palamedes* (1625); the *Leo Armenius* contained parallels to *Gysbreght van Aemstel* (1637), but Vondel's *Maeghden* and *Maria Stuart* with their Catholic equation of religion and history aroused the strongest reaction. Whereas Vondel's fervor for his new Catholic faith induced him to extol the policies of the *ecclesia militans,* Gryphius demonstrated the significance of man's faith rather than his Church to preserve him from damnation. *Catharina von Georgien* and *Carolus Stuardus* revealed the inability of man's temporal achievements to grant him eternal salvation.

Gryphius' first dramatic venture coincided with his exposure to Netherlandic theater. During his studies at the University of Leiden (1638-1644), when Gryphius was at the peak of his poetic activity—he published no fewer than five poetry collections in that six-year period— Dutch drama flourished at the newly constructed *Stadsschouwburg* in

---

[32] Lummenaeus' biblical tragedy, *Amnon* (Ghent: Cornelius Marius, 1617) provided vivid descriptions and frank declarations of the uncontrollable incestuous lust of the title hero for his sister, Thamar:

> Heu caeca rabies! heu mihi! perii miser,
> Et restat aliquid semper in manes meos
> Ut vidi, ut aeger occidi, ut malus furor
> Abstulit amantem! perdidit fratrem Soror,
> Nutuque ocelli, cuspide et iaculo magis
> Strictim et potenter cordis effodis sinum
> Vitamque penitus, sanguinemque hausit meum.
> ..................................................
> o Dea! o sidus meum!
> Thamara! quid obstas? Thamara! o fatum meum
> Crudele! morior! morior! et nunquam, tuis
> Si non ab oculis, ulla me adspiciet salus.      (sig. A 4v-A 5)

Amsterdam. The plays of Vondel, whose historical tragedy *Gysbreght van Aemstel* had been written for the opening of the new theater, dominated the stage in the early 1640s. Within the space of a few years (1639-1641) Vondel published six plays: two martyr tragedies *Maeghden* and *Peter en Pauwels* (1641) to glorify his new allegiance to Roman Catholicism; a translation of Sophocles' *Electra* and three biblical dramas (*Gebroeders, Joseph in Dothan* and *Joseph in Egypten*) in which religious plots were adapted to tragedy. *Gebroeders* was his most popular work in the early 1640s. It was performed eight times during April, the month of its premier in Amsterdam, and it is not surprising that a successful poet such as Gryphius would have been inspired to translate it.[33] A classical form of vernacular German tragedy did not yet exist, and Gryphius no doubt hoped to import the Dutch model to fire the imaginations of the Empire's *respublica litteraria*.

Gryphius probably worked on the translation after seeing a performance of the play in Amsterdam (1641-1642), for his own text contained stage directions. His German translation was, in fact, presented at the St. Elizabeth gymnasium in Breslau in 1652.[34] But Gryphius himself never included his version in any of his completed works during his lifetime (1657; 1661); *Die sieben Brüder* was first published in 1698 in the edition which Christian Gryphius, Andreas' son, prepared for the press. The reasons for Gryphius' reluctance to print his translation are difficult to determine. He may have been embarrassed about the uninspired quality of the work ("in Eyl gesetzte Dolmetschung").[35] A more probable explanation was the fact that Gryphius himself had his own dramatization (now lost) of the same biblical plot in progress and that publication of Vondel's tragedy might possibly have detracted from his own achievement.

It is not too difficult, however, to detect the reasons for Gryphius' attraction to the Vondel text. *Die sieben Brüder* was the only biblical drama which Gryphius composed, but in light of his subsequent production and especially his first tragedy, *Leo Armenius*, Gryphius' enthusiasm for the work was clearly due to more than its contemporary popularity. An investigation of *Gebroeders* can not only explicate the reasons for Gryphius' choice, but it can also clarify the uniqueness of Gryphius' own translation within the tradition of seventeenth-century religious drama.

It will be recalled that Vondel derived his plot for *Gebroeders* from the Bible (2 Samuel 21) and Josephus' account of the same events in the

---

[33] Henri Plard, "Die sieben Brüder/Oder die Gibeoniter," in *Die Dramen des Andreas Gryphius*, ed. Gerhard Kaiser (Stuttgart: Metzler, 1968), p. 306.

[34] Mannack, p. 53.

[35] *Trauerspiele III*, p. ix.

*Antiquities of the Jews* (VI. 12). In order to alleviate the famine which was afflicting Israel, King David had been constrained to execute seven descendants of Saul in retribution for Saul's crimes against the Gibeonites. The tragedy arose from two different angles each reflective of Vondel's tragic vision in 1639-1640. On one hand, Vondel betrayed his Senecan origins in several scenes in which the mothers of the doomed brothers mourned the impending fate of their children. As in his play *Hierusalem verwoest* (1620), Vondel resurrected Seneca's bleak notion of tragic fate in *Troades* to arouse the audience's sympathy for the victims of misfortune. At the same time, Vondel introduced a new concept of the tragic protagonist which he had derived from his recent study of Sophocles' *Electra*. In the preface to that work, Vondel turned away from Seneca's lamentations and embraced Sophocles' drama of justice.[36] Electra's vengeance testified to the tragedy which will inevitably befall all men who, like Clytemnestra and Aegisthus, have acted immorally. David's insistence on justice, despite his own doubts and the cries of outrage from the wives and mothers of the victims, was doubtless conceived as a Christian equivalent to Electra's sense of righteousness. Vondel divided his attention between the victims and their executioner and thereby underscored the severity of God's justice. Man was no longer encouraged to vent his emotions for the victims of an unjust fate but rather like David to contain his human misgivings and submit to God's will.

Gryphius' exacting—if not slavish—translation of Vondel's drama does not leave much opportunity for analyzing his opinion of his Dutch model. There was only one major addition, the character of the ghost of Saul, to function as a verse prologue and epilogue to the work. But this recasting of the Dutch text provides an important clue for Gryphius' attraction to this particular play. Gryphius' introduction of the ghost of Saul was more than a convention of Senecan practice;[37] it betrayed his own unique interpretation of the events. In keeping with Opitz's view of tragedy, Gryphius regarded the execution of Saul's descendants as an exemplum of the downfall of kings. The ghost of Saul admonished all men about the dire consequences of challenging God's order and warned them that their kingdoms could also be imperilled through sin. Saul consequently served as an illustration of both an evil ruler and of the transitory nature of all political order. Indeed, Gryphius' interest in kingship and the rule of a religious state—a theme which would recur five years

---

[36] See the discussion on Vondel's *Elektra* above, chapter 3, pp. 135-6.

[37] On Gryphius' possible imitation of sixteenth-century Senecan characterizations of Saul, see van Ingen, pp. 151-3.

later in his own *Leo Armenius*— probably drew him to Vondel's work as
well. Like the melancholy Byzantine emperor Leo in the later work,
David was plagued by the trials of his office. His sense of mercy—an
attribute of the ideal Renaissance king[38]—was gravely offended by the
Gibeonites' harsh demand for the blood of Saul's descendants. But this
human aspect of the uncertain ruler and his subsequent fulfillment of
God's Will constituted Gryphius' own conception of the ideal Christian
monarch. As a divinely anointed ruler, David was obliged to maintain
the physical and spiritual security of the state. His decision to accede to
the demands of the Gibeonites represented the harmonious interaction
between the Will of God and the well-being of the populace to which all
Christian monarchs should aspire. David's initial misgivings about the
offering reflected an apolitical human side to the ruler which anticipated
the discomfort which Gryphius' regal protagonists would later experience
on the throne. But his recognition of God's pleasure in the survival of his
chosen people induced David to uphold the Gibeonites' decision. The
transitory nature of the world, the signature of Gryphius' historical
tragedies, was absent from Vondel's portrait of the Jewish theocracy, but
the burden of the crown foreshadowed the crisis which would ensue when
man rather than God directed the future of the state.

Gryphius' admiration for Vondel's portrait of the ideal king was not
the sole reason for the addition of the ghost to justify David's actions.
Saul's presence helped to resolve an inconsistency in the play which had
resulted from Vondel's own remarks on his protagonist. In his dedicatory
letter to Gerardus Vossius for the 1640 edition of the tragedy, Vondel
anticipated the objections which many religious critics would raise
against his characterization of David.[39] David's initial reluctance to fulfill
God's commandment might be construed as self-pity and disobedience.
To prevent this misinterpretation, Vondel noted David's inclination for
mercy—he had after all mourned for the defeat of Saul and his sons—and
the crisis which God's ordinance would spark in such a sensitive soul.
Indeed, Vondel argued that David's hesitation recalled Abraham's anxiety about the sacrifice of Isaac and, more significantly, Christ's prayer
to his father in the garden of Gethsemane to preserve him from the trial
of the crucifixion. David's acquiescence to the divine oracle was conse-

---

[38] As Erasmus noted in his *Institutio principis christiani* (1515), a good king was never
vengeful; rather, he took pains to act justly and mercifully so as to maintain the people's
favor: "Princeps qui volet odium suorum effugere, ac benevolentiam alere, quae sunt
odiosa, delegat aliis, quae plausibilia, per se faciat." As quoted in Erasmus, *Ausgewählte
Werke*, vol. 5, ed. Werner Welzig (Darmstadt: Wissenschaftliche Buchgesellschaft, 1968),
p. 262.

[39] *WB*, III, pp. 799-805.

quently likened to the obedience of Abraham and Jesus, to the former's sacrifice of Isaac and God's sacrifice of his son. Within this typological context, David himself thus appeared as a prefiguration of Christ; the execution of Saul's descendants as the martyrdom of Jesus; and Saul's earlier crimes against the Gibeonites as the postfiguration of the Fall of Adam.[40]

Vondel's association of David with Christ was not an accidental comparison. As an ancestor of Jesus, David had long been thought to display Christ-like characteristics. Episodes from David's life, such as his triumphal entry into Jerusalem with the Ark of the Covenant, were believed to foreshadow events in Christ's passion (in this instance, Christ on Palm Sunday).[41] But where the christological parallel to Gethsemane adequately justified David's quandary, it did not follow that the execution of the innocent brothers necessarily anticipated the Redemption of man. Rather, as Saul's son Armoni predicted, the injustice wreaked on Saul's descendants would one day be avenged by the destruction of David's kingdom and the Babylonian captivity of the Jews:

> Indem Asch/Brand und Mord/Reich gegen Reich sich setzt/
> Und Heer sich gegen Heer/Stadt gegen Stadt verhetzt
> Altäre gegen Chor/und Tempel und Altare
> Des Arons Mandelstab/des Arons Schild durchfahre.
> Des Davids eignes Haus/durch Auffruhr/Schwerdt und Brand
> Verfall in einen Weh-Noth-Angst-und Jammer-Stand/
> Und schmacht in Dienstbarkeit für fremder Herren Thüre/
> Das Isai die Macht des Regiments verliehre.[42]

Instead of preserving Judea from danger as Christ had saved man, the execution only alleviated the present famine. David's offspring would one day be subject to the same sufferings which were now being borne by Saul's descendants. Vondel did not by any means intend that the curse of Armoni justify the previous crimes of Saul or cast doubt on the rectitude of David's decision. The end of the famine clearly indicated the righteousness of David's action. As in the *Elektra*, Vondel was primarily interested in the representation of justice; Jewish Law with its system of rewards and punishments for adherence to or deviation from God's commands was aptly suited to his reading of Sophocles. As a prefiguration of Christ, David anticipated the era when men would be freed from sin

---

[40] *Ibid.* On the christological significance of Vondel's play, see Kåre Langvik-Johannessen, "Das Problem der christlichen Tragödie bei Vondel," *Jahrbuch der Grillparzer Gesellschaft*, 12 (1976), 142-5.

[41] For previous christological interpretations of David in humanist drama, consider, for example, Jacob Schoepper, *Monomachia Davidis et Goliae* (Dortmund: Melchior Soter, 1550) where David's slaying of Goliath foreshadowed Christ's liberation of mankind from sin (sig. F 6).

[42] *Trauerspiele III,* p. 124, lines 91-98.

by mercy, but as a Jewish monarch he was still part of the unending Old Testament cycle of crime and retribution. The execution of the brothers was not, then, to be construed as a foreshadowing of the Redemption, as Vondel's introductory remarks seemed to suggest, but rather as part of the harsh justice of Jewish Law.

Gryphius must have noted the disharmony in Vondel's play, for his addition of the ghost of Saul served to underscore the significance of divine vengeance for a sinner's crimes. Having dispensed with Vondel's problematic preface, Gryphius refrained from establishing any christological parallels between David and Jesus. David's preference for mercy rather than punishment might have anticipated Christian *caritas*, but Gryphius did not draw attention to this connection. David's unwavering obedience to Old Testament law rather than his prefigurative role was what attracted Gryphius to the work. In the world before the Redemption, Gryphius did not perceive any escape from God's vengeance and the instability of human existence foretold by the condemned Armoni. David's just action would only be followed by subsequent crimes which would entail future punishments; only Christ could free man from his inevitable relapse into evil. In the post-Redemption era of Gryphius' historical dramas, however, the grace of God would finally be revealed to all men through Christ's forgiveness of sin.

Gryphius' inclusion of the ghost of Saul reflected a key distinction between himself and Vondel which was developed further in his original dramas. Saul's interpretation of the dramatic events in the prologue detracted from Vondel's emphasis on David's hesitation and choice in the play itself. The main point of Vondel's work had been man's acceptance of the harsh necessity of God's will; man's inability to measure the justice of God's decisions by his own standards of reason and fairness was shown to lead ultimately to disobedience. David's admirable display of mercy from a human and political standpoint, as evidenced by his unwillingness to accede to the Gibeonites' demands, was thus perceived as a failing in the eyes of God. In the course of the play David had to learn to act against his human nature and harden himself against the lamentations of the mothers of Saul's descendants. He was constrained by the famine in Israel and the divine oracle to submit to God's will, and the difficulty he experienced in obeying underscored the unbridgeable distance between himself and God.

Gryphius alleviated David's crisis by setting the whole play in the cosmological framework of God's vengeance on the sinner Saul. The ghost already announced in the prologue that his crimes against the Gibeonites would be avenged:

Das Volck/auf das/ich unbesonnen wüttet/
Rufft noch mit seinem Winseln mich hervor/
Und liegt dem höchsten Gott im Ohr/
Der meinen Meineid/und mein Rasen
An dem was übrig ist/an meinem Blut wird rächen.[43]

David's spiritual doubts about the correct course of action now seemed to arise more from weakness than from his human inclination for mercy and forgiveness. His long debate with both the high priest Abjathar and his chief adviser Benajas about the righteousness of the sacrifice lost its urgency, if not its purpose, since the prologue had already testified to God's preordained plan of vengeance. In Gryphius' adaptation, then, David was transformed from an all-too-human king into a passive instrument of divine justice. As we shall see, the resignation of Gryphius' David, reminiscent of the submissiveness of the Apocryphal heroes of sixteenth-century Protestant theater, would shortly become the basis for the characterization of his own tragic protagonists.

### Tyranny and Salvation: "Leo Armenius"

Although Gryphius did not translate another Dutch play, the shadow of seventeenth-century Netherlandic drama always hung over his own tragedies. Whereas the political arguments of Hooft occasionally reappeared in Gryphius' works, the dramas of Vondel supplied him with inspiration for both emulation and reform. *Catharina von Georgien* and *Carolus Stuardus* were both conceived in reaction to two Vondel texts, *Maeghden* and *Maria Stuart*. These two Vondel works were in turn related in form and content to the tradition of Latin humanist theater which, in the early seventeenth-century, was dominated by the dramas of the Catholic orders, the Benedictines, the Augustinians and, most importantly, the Jesuits. Since Jesuit drama provided the common denominator for both Gryphius and Vondel, Gryphius' historical plays can be regarded at one and the same time as a response to both the Netherlandic and Catholic traditions. In establishing Gryphius' relationship with Jesuit theater, it is consequently possible to determine the extent of his critique of Vondel. Gryphius' reception of the Jesuit theater is thus central to his interpretation of contemporary dramatic praxis as well as the humanist tradition from which it was derived.

The Jesuits had been active during Gryphius' childhood in the 1620s in his native Silesia, but the disruptions of the Thirty Years War

---

[43] *Trauerspiele III*, p. 77, lines 76-80.

prevented him from attending any of their school performances.[44] His real familiarity with Jesuit theater probably began in Danzig between 1634 and 1646. In this flourishing commercial center where religious toleration prevailed, Gryphius, a student at the Protestant *Academisches Gymnasium,* came into contact with many Calvinist and Catholic intellectuals. His *Lissaer Sonette* collection (1637) betrayed the influence of the Polish Jesuit poet Mathias Casimir Sarbiewski (1595-1640), and he may have even traveled to the Jesuit school at nearby Braunsberg to attend theatrical performances there. In Danzig, Gryphius also acquired a copy of the 1621 Cologne edition of the *Tragoediae sacrae* (originally published, Paris, 1620) of the French Jesuit Nicolaus Caussin whose martyr drama *Felicitas* he later translated. Gryphius' next exposure to Jesuit drama may have occurred during his travels through France in 1644-1645, but there is no reliable record of his wanderings there.

In Italy, however, which Gryphius reached in the winter of 1645-1646, he became acquainted with many Jesuits in Rome. Gryphius may have attended dramatic performances at both the Italian and English Jesuit colleges especially since his sojourn there coincided with their traditional Shrovetide presentations. Indeed, it is generally believed that Gryphius must have been inspired to write his first tragedy after seeing a performance of *Leo Armenus* by Jesuit author Joseph Simons while in Rome.[45] But according to the play list of the English college, Simons' tragedy was performed once the previous February in 1645 and not repeated (an Italian tragedy *David e Absolone* was presented in 1646).[46] There is little doubt, however, that Gryphius knew the text intimately. There are several for-

---

[44] For a brief survey of Jesuit theater in Glogau, see Hermann Hoffmann, *Die Jesuiten in Glogau* (Breslau: Kommissionsverlag der schlesischen Volkszeitung, 1926), pp. 79-96. The Jesuits established their school in Gryphius' native Glogau in 1625 and began dramatic productions in 1629. It is unlikely that Gryphius would have seen the Jesuits' 1629 Corpus Christi play and the 1630 Good Friday pageant since he was then living in Driebitz with his Protestant stepfather who had been forced to leave Glogau by the Catholic administration. There are no records of Jesuit dramas in Glogau in 1631 when Gryphius again returned there. From spring 1632 to May 1634, Gryphius studied at the Protestant gymnasium in Fraustadt where he did not have any opportunity to encounter Jesuit theater.

[45] Gryphius' presence at a Roman production of Simons' *Leo Armenus* was first suggested by Jacob Zeidler, *Studien und Beiträge zur Geschichte der Jesuitenkomödie und des Klosterdramas,* Theatergeschichtliche Forschungen, 4 (Hamburg, 1891), p. 118., reiterated in Victor Manheimer, *Die Lyrik des Andreas Gryphius. Studien und Materialien* (Berlin, 1904), p. 140 and became an unquestioned assumption after Harring's 1907 comparison between Gryphius and Simons. Cf. H. Plard, "De heiligheid van de koninklijke macht in de tragedie van Andreas Gryphius," *Tijdschrift van den Vrije Universiteit van Brussel,* 2 (1960), 217-20, and Gerhard Kaiser, "Leo Armenius," in his *Die Dramen des Andreas Gryphius* (Stuttgart: Metzler, 1968), pp. 5-8.

[46] Suzanne Gossett, "Drama in the English College, Rome, 1591-1660," *English Literary Renaissance,* 3 (1973), 92.

mal similarities between Simon's and Gryphius' works, notably their use of Byzantine sources and non-historical characters.[47] But, most importantly, both dramatists presented revolution and the dilemma of the revolutionary as God's avenger in an equally complex manner. Political intrigue was, in fact, the main issue in all five of Simons tragedies, and Gryphius, fresh from the lectures of Claudius Salmasius at Leiden, may have known the other plays, some of which had been presented at the English college in the 1630s and 1640s.[48] Since Gryphius did not see a performance of *Leo Armenus*, he must have had access to a manuscript copy of it (Simons drama was first printed in Liège, 1656) and may have thereby encountered Simons' four other tragedies, all of which had been written many years before for the Jesuit school at St. Omer.[49]

In order to determine the reasons for Gryphius' attraction to the Jesuit work, it is necessary to understand the main points of Simons' own production.[50] Born in Portsmouth into a merchant family, Simons was converted to Catholicism in Portugal and later studied theology in the Low Countries. He spent the early part of his career after his ordination as a teacher of poetry and rhetoric at the English College in St. Omer. Simons was subsequently called to Rome in the mid-1640s (did he know Gryphius?) as the head of the English College and finally to England as Provincial General where he converted the future James II (then Duke of York) to Catholicism. His dramatic career was, however, confined to St. Omer between 1622 and 1631. There, in his capacity as rhetoric instructor, Simons composed five tragedies which not only enjoyed a favorable reception at St. Omer but also in Switzerland and Italy.[51] Like many successful Jesuit school plays, Simons' dramas were circulated among the Jesuit colleges in manuscript by both wandering teachers and enthusiastic visitors from other schools. The chronology of Simons' life

---

[47] Harring, pp. 68-74.

[48] Simons' *Zeno* (ca. 1631) was performed at the Jesuits' English College in Rome in 1634 when Simons was supposedly teaching theology in Liège (Gossett, p. 92).

[49] For a synopsis of St. Omer theater, see William H. McCabe, "The Play-List of the English College of St. Omers, 1592-1762," *Revue de littérature comparée*, 17 (1937), 355-75. McCabe's work is especially important since he provides the dates of composition and performance for all Simon's plays: *Vitus* (1623); *Theoctistus* (1624); *Leo Armenus* (? 1624-29); *Zeno* (1631).

[50] The most complete version of Simons' life is contained in Henry Foley, *Records of the English Province of the Society of Jesus*, vol. 1, First Series (London, 1877), p. 272, n. 52. Foley's account subsequently provided the basis for the DNB entry (Vol. 18, pp. 257-8).

[51] A slightly altered version of *Zeno* was presented at the Jesuit school in Lucerne in 1642 with the new title *Wol-Bewärte Tugend Pelagii. Umb welcher wegen ihme Zeno der Lasterhafttige Kayser/hat lassen das Leben nehmen*. This perioche, whose relationship to Simons' work has hitherto been overlooked, is reprinted in E. M. Szarota, *Das Jesuitendrama im deutschen Sprachgebiet: eine Periochen-Edition*, vol. 2, part 1 (Munich: Fink, 1980), pp. 491-502.

is uncertain between 1631 when he stopped teaching at St. Omer and 1647 when he was sent to Italy, but his tragedy *Zeno* was performed in Rome in 1634, *Leo Armenus* in 1645 and *Mercia* (on an episode in English medieval history) in 1648. If Gryphius' exposure to Simons was limited to manuscript versions of the plays, it is likely that he may have also known the others and most certainly *Zeno* (performed ten years before Gryphius arrived), Simons' other drama on Byzantine revolution.

Simons had come of age during the heyday of Elizabethan and Jacobean drama. Although he spent many years in exile at English colleges on the continent, his Latin plays contained numerous reminiscences of vernacular English theater. Dumb shows, masques, plays-within-plays and the frequent appearance of vengeful ghosts were all adapted by the Jesuit to serve the didactic ends of his order's theater. But, more importantly, besides these formal similarities, Simons inherited the contemporary English playwrights' love of imbroglio and intrigue. This attraction in turn effected a major change in Simons' approach to the customary themes of Jesuit drama. On the surface, the subjects of Simons' five tragedies recalled the traditional tyrant and martyr plays of the early Counter-Reformation. The Jesuits never tired of the tyrant-martyr configuration, for it could easily be applied to any religious, political or social issue. Enemies of the Church were conveniently characterized as ruthless tyrants who well deserved eternal damnation while the martyrs they persecuted gained an eternal reward. Simons, however, shifted the emphasis in his plays from the confrontational aspects of the commonplace tyrant-martyr plot to the machinations the persecutors devised to entrap the Catholic defenders. In his first two tragedies, *Vitus* on the martyrdom of St. Vitus (1623) and *Mercia* (1624) on the martyrdom of Sts. Ruffinus and Ulfadus, Simons devoted the greater portion of each play to the clever intrigues of the tyrant's courtiers. Religious differences between tyrant and martyr (pagan versus Christian) were almost completely disregarded; the enmity the martyr incurred arose not from his defense of Christ, but from his enemies' fears that they might lose their wealth and power because of the Christian's influence at court. Simons retreated from the traditional militancy of Jesuit drama, and thereby redirected his viewers to the complexities of leading a Christian life in a deceitful world.[52]

Simons' transformation of the proselytizing tone of Jesuit theater significantly influenced his presentation of political revolution in the Byzantine dramas *Zeno* and *Leo Armenus*. Contrary to popular belief, early seventeenth-century Jesuits were not a fanatical religious organization

---

[52] Parente, *Simons*, pp. 321-4.

bent on attaining political power at any cost. The portrait of the Jesuit as an amoral intriguer with a copy of Machiavelli in one hand and a dagger in the other, though admittedly true in some instances such as the ill-conceived Gunpower Plot of 1605, was more a propagandistic fiction of the Protestant opposition than a reality. Indeed, under pressure from the Papacy, the Jesuit General Claudio Aquaviva had published two injunctions against tyrannicide (1610; 1614) in an effort to dissuade the order from active and embarrassing political involvement.[53] This new conservatism among the Jesuits was in turn reflected in Simons' characterizations of the revolutionaries in his Byzantine plays.

Simons essentially relied on two devices to demonstrate his critical attitude toward political revolution and tyrannicide. The first of these, his problematic portrait of the revolutionary, was derived from his knowledge of Elizabethan revenge tragedy. In plays such as Thomas Kyd's *Spanish Tragedy* (ca. 1585) and Beaumont's and Fletcher's *The Maid's Tragedy* (ca. 1611), the apparent justice of an avenger's bloody action against his immoral enemy was shown to be incompatible with the biblical principle that vengeance belonged to God alone (Romans 12:19). The avenger's usurpation of God's role resulted in his madness and death, a fate equally as unfortunate as that of the men he slew in God's name. By transferring this dilemma to his political revolutionaries, Simons similarly cast the righteousness of their actions into doubt. He further bolstered his criticism of the revolutionaries by providing a model in the plays for an alternative Christian response to injustice. Just as St. Vitus and the English martyrs (*Mercia*) had earlier borne the tyranny of their oppressors with fortitude, so did a few courtiers in the Byzantine plays display similar courage by relying on God's intervention for the alleviation of tyranny.[54] Although the punishment of the wicked king may indeed be justified, Simons enjoined his audience to avoid the deceptive allure of political power and devote their lives to strengthening their faith in God.

A closer examination of Simons' *Leo Armenus* will demonstrate the complexity of his portrait of political revolution. In Simons' cited source, Caesar Baronius' *Annales ecclesiastici* and in the Byzantine chronicles of Cedrenus and Zonaras which he most likely also consulted, the conflict

---

[53] Aquaviva addressed his decree of 1610 against the promulgation of tyrannicide to the French Jesuits whose reputation had recently been harmed by the assassination of Henri IV by the Catholic fanatic François Ravaillac. To counteract the increasing tendency to categorize all Jesuits as revolutionaries, Aquaviva forbade any writing on tyrannicide or in favor of the temporal power of the Pope in 1614.

[54] Consider, for example, the virtuous behavior of the courtier Pelagius (*Zeno*), who, having fallen from power as a result of a court intrigue, commended his soul to Christ before his execution (IV.3; IV.4).

between the harsh emperor Leo the Armenian and his general Michael Balbus was presented in a purely political context.[55] Balbus, whose military help had been instrumental in securing the throne for Leo from the befuddled Michael I Rhangabe, felt insufficiently rewarded for his assistance and consequently plotted to seize power for himself. Leo had by no means been an exemplary ruler, though credited with introducing many domestic reforms, and his fervent iconoclasm had induced him to persecute many orthodox believers. Simons likewise conceived of the conflict between Leo and Balbus as a political power struggle; the iconoclasm controversy merely served to underscore Leo's own godlessness. Indeed, Simons used the iconoclasm isue not to support Balbus' schemes but to expose its questionable political nature.

In the opening scene, Simons established three different courses of action for his viewers to consider. Leo had summoned his courtiers to entertain him with a debate on whether a king, wine or God was stronger.[56] Leo himself had just mercilessly condemned six icon-worshippers to death ("sex catholici") so there was little doubt that he had placed all his hopes on earthly power. In contrast, the courtier Papias strongly defended the supremacy of God. The future revolutionary, Balbus, however, endorsed the potency of wine, for it had always been a more effective means to secure control over men than brute force. The Machiavellian Balbus dispensed with God to attain the power he craved; invoking Fortuna to favor his schemes, he exploited every opportunity to win support for his ambitious goals. When he learned that an oracle had predicted that Leo would fall by the hand of a certain Michael, he immediately regarded himself as the chosen "minister coeli" and "vindex Dei";[57] when Leo enjoined him to illustrate the power of wine in a drama, Balbus used the occasion to stage an assassination attempt which, however, failed (III.2); when Papias despaired of the justice of the emperor's decision to slay him for neglecting to guard the imprisoned Balbus, the latter quickly persuaded him to carry out a second assassina-

---

[55] C. Baronius, *Annales ecclesiastici*, vol. 9 (Antwerp: Plantin, 1612), pp. 697-700. Simons had consulted Cedrenus and Zonaras already for the historical background to *Zeno*; he probably referred to them as well for *Leo Armenus* since Baronius himself based his account on the same Byzantine chronicles. Despite the belief of Kaiser (p. 6) and Szarota (*Geschichte, Politik und Gesellschaft*, p. 65) that the iconoclasm of Simons' Leo made him an enemy of the Church worthy of Balbus' punishment, the debate upon image-worship was never a major issue in the Jesuit play. As a careful reader of the Byzantine sources, Simons knew very well that Balbus himself was also an iconoclast.

[56] Simons I.1 recalled the debate at King Darius' court (1 Esdras 3-4) about the respective strengths of wine, women, politics and the truth. Sixt Birck wrote a German play on this plot, *Zorobabel*, in 1538.

[57] Joseph Simons, *Leo Armenus*, in his *Tragoediae quinque* (Liège: Ioan. Mathias Hovius, 1656), pp. 464-5.

tion attempt so both of them could be freed (V.2). Where Leo had used
military force, viz., Balbus' armies, to triumph over his predecessor and
maintain his rule, Balbus relied on his wits and the influence of Fortune
to secure his political goals.

Simons had thus presented a political revolution whose leader was just
as condemnable as the tyrant he had overthrown. To be sure, Leo
deserved the punishment which he received through God's self-appointed
instrument; his bloodthirstiness had already resulted in the slaughter of
many innocent victims, several of whom had been persecuted for their
orthodox (i.e., Catholic) beliefs. But Leo's guilt did not by any means
absolve Balbus from falsely usurping God's role. Simons took great
pains to demonstrate that Balbus did not act for the benefit of the state
or the Church but solely to appease his own ambitions. Balbus, whose
schemes were concealed in the first two acts by his clever tongue, was
finally compelled to act openly not by any specific injustice of Leo, but
by the fear that Leo's son Sabatius would prevent him from ever gaining
the throne:

> Inauspicato cujus incepto puer
> Absente Balbo, jussus Imperii notas
> Capessere haeres! O probrum! O nulli scelus
> Viro ferendum! Balbus Imperii comes
> Submissa puero genua provolvam duci?
> Senex puello? Pronus Acherontem polus
> Citius adoret.[58]

Simons was not at all interested in promoting revolution; rather, he was
concerned with presenting a pessimistic portrait of history in which
man's sole comfort was his faith in divine justice. Simons' tragedies were
all designed to impart this consolatory advice by portraying the downfall
of tyrants and the triumph of martyrs. God was indeed present in the
world, and His justice would ultimately prevail, but Simons exhorted
man only to believe in, and not to assume, God's avenging role.
Gryphius would subsequently share Simons' idea that man's actions
appeared to occur in an unending cycle of crime and retribution. But
whereas Simons believed that man could only endure injustice through
prayer, Gryphius provided a more optimistic solution by emphasizing
the effect of the Redemption on human history.

Gryphius approached Simons' tragedy with the insecurity of a begin-
ner but the daring of an ambitious playwright. He was at the same time
an admirer of Simons' politics as well as a critical reader of the text.
Gryphius adapted Simons' portrait of the court and the characterizations

---

[58] Simons, *Leo Armenus*, p. 465.

of the tyrant and the revolutionary only to reinterpret them in accordance with his faith. Where Simons had written a historical drama so that God's justice could ultimately be perceived, Gryphius imbued the same historical events with an ahistorical Christian significance. Gryphius' reaction to Catholic theater did not arise from any doctrinal or soteriological difference between the two churches but rather from his objections to the Church's limitations of Christ's role in man's salvation.

Gryphius' presentation of Leo's Byzantine court aptly illustrated his guarded imitation of the Jesuit text. Simons, following his Senecan model, had characterized the court as a locus of instability. Not only did revolution and betrayal appear to prevail, but language itself was sorely abused in the process. Intriguers in Simons' tragedies triumphed because their enemies believed in the sincerity of their oaths. Balbus, for example, successfully managed to escape Leo's wrath only because he swore that of all the "Michaels" at court, he would be the least likely to fulfill the oracle's prediction to assassinate him (I.3). Gryphius similarly portrayed Balbus as an accomplished master of language whose rhetorical skills could incite the conspirators to action (I.1).

Gryphius' use of language was not confined to the commonplace trope about the deceit of the court; it also contributed to his concept of the instability of all human existence. In contrast to Simons' exciting, melodramatic tragedies in the Elizabethan style, Gryphius relied on language alone to create the tension of his play. In the opening acts, the audience is never certain whether the conspirators or Leo are defending a just cause, and it is this very insecurity which gives the drama its energy. Simons made it clear from the outset with the appearance of the ghost of Leo's dead enemy, the exiled patriarch Tarasius (I.2), that no matter how questionable Balbus' actions may later seem, Leo did indeed deserve God's punishment. Gryphius, however, reserved the introduction of the same ghost until the third act to prevent his audience from interpreting the work on a literal, superficial level. The first act chorus warned of both the beneficial and destructive aspects of language and thereby challenged the viewers to discern the difference themselves:

> Lernt/die jhr lebt/den zaum in ewre Lippen legen!
> In welchen heil vnd schaden wohnet/
> Und was verdammt/vnd was belohnet.
> Wer nutz durch wortte such't/sol jedes wort erwegen.[59]

---

[59] *Trauerspiele II*, p. 25. On Gryphius' use of language in *Leo Armenius*, see W. Barner, "Gryphius und die Macht der Rede. Zum ersten Reyen des Trauerspiels *Leo Armenius*," *DVLG*, 42 (1968), 325-58; Peter Schäublin, "Andreas Gryphius' erstes Trauerspiel *Leo Armenius* und die Bibel," *Daphnis*, 3 (1974), 1-40, and Manfred Beetz, "Disputatorik und Argumentation in Andreas Gryphius' Trauerspiel *Leo Armenius*," *Zeitschrift für Literaturwissenschaft und Linguistik*, 38-39 (1980), 178-203.

To complicate this hermeneutical challenge, Gryphius allowed Leo and Balbus to offer conflicting interpretations of their past achievements and their present discontent. Each man claimed to be a more courageous and more competent statesman than the other, and each devised his own convenient notion of their friendship. Balbus attributed the reasons for his revolt to Leo's ingratitude toward him while Leo accused the revolutionary of violating his fealty to the throne. Gryphius extended the interpretive problem into other areas of the first two acts as well. Since Gryphius dispensed with Simons' presentation of Balbus' first unsuccessful assassination attempt, Balbus could only be brought to trial by cunningly constructing a circumstantial case against him. To this end, Leo's adviser, Exabolius, entrapped Balbus into admitting his dissatisfaction with the emperor by feigning similar feelings (I.4); other courtiers likewise presented hearsay evidence to ensure Balbus' condemnation to death (II.1). Balbus, however, exploited the absence of any firm proof by proclaiming the injustice of the verdict and by calling on the Furies to avenge him (II.6). Indeed, his vehement oration in favor of justice created yet another interpretative problem, for immediately thereafter Leo followed the advice of his wife and postponed the execution. The audience consequently remained uncertain whether the pleas of Leo's spouse (who objected to the sacrilege of executing Balbus on Christmas Day) or the fear of retribution drove the emperor to make such a fateful decision. Gryphius purposely directed his reader toward the instability of the court and the uncertainty of all human understanding so that the potential liberation from such anxiety through Christ in the later acts might appear all the more glorious.

In addition to the problematic use of language, Gryphius further developed Simons' implicit parallel between the revolutionary and the tyrant. But, as in the case of the court, Gryphius expanded the immorality of both Leo and Balbus into a means to christianize Simons' tragic view of history. On the literal level, Gryphius' Balbus appeared to be nothing other than a reflection of a younger Leo. Indeed, the ties between their political careers were so strong that the play could be viewed as an exemplum of the inevitable misfortunes of kingship. Both men were ambitious warriors; both seized the throne by force and treachery. When considered together, each character seems to embody one part of a diptych in which the unending instability of history is portrayed. Simons had been content to limit the bond between Balbus and Leo to their godless quest for political power; Gryphius, however, broke out of this historical continuum by illustrating the consequences of Christ's intervention in human history.

Gryphius' Christian transformation of Simons' tragedy occurred shortly before the assassination of the emperor in the fifth act. As has often been noted, the fourth-act chorus was atypical of the others in the drama: where the first three choruses had each provided a moral commentary to the preceding act, the fourth "Reyen" functioned as a separate scene inserted between the two acts in which the priests and virgins triumphantly proclaimed the miracle of the Incarnation. Up until this moment, Gryphius had closely followed Simons' disposition of the events and, like Simons, had taken great pains to avoid any reference to Christ. Here, however, Gryphius drew a sharp distinction to the Jesuit by supplanting Simons' Old Testament concept of God as an angry avenger with the Christ child through whose grace sinful mankind will be redeemed. With the birth of Christ, the old order of the Law in which men lived in fear of each other and God's wrath, the old order of vengeful punishment practiced by Balbus and Leo, was replaced by the promise of salvation through Christ's mercy. Man was henceforth guaranteed the possibility of Redemption provided he accept Christ as his savior.

Gryphius' juxtaposition of the Old Testament (Law) ethics of the first four acts with the New Testament (Grace) in the last was firmly grounded in his Lutheran faith. Just as Luther had argued that the Law served to remind us of our own sinfulness,[60] so did Leo react to the ghost of Tarasius (III.3) who condemned him under the Law:

> Kürtzt Er der Fürsten jahr?
> Oder lehrt er nur durch zeichen
> Wie man sol der grufft entweichen?
> So ists! er pflegt vns zwar zu drewen:
> Doch pflegt jhn auch sein zorn zu rewen.[61]

Similarly, at the moment of his death, Leo warned the assassins from slaying him, a sinner, in such a holy place lest they commit a sacrilege:

> denckt/rufft er/an das Leben/
> Das sich für ewer Seel an dieser Last gegeben.
> Befleckt deß Herren Blut/das diesen stamm gefärbt
> Mit Sünder blut doch nicht. Hab ich so viel verkärbt/
> So schont vmb dessen Angst/den dieser stock betragen/
> An JESUS Söhn-Altar die grimme Faust zu schlagen/[62]

It does not, however, follow that Leo's embrace of the True Cross

---

[60] For a summary of Luther's views of the Law, see *WA*, vol. 40, part 1, pp. 40-52. See also the discussion above on sixteenth-century Protestant drama, chapter 2, pp. 78-9.

[61] *Trauerspiele II,* pp. 52-3.

[62] *Ibid.*

immediately resulted in his redemption.[63] The potentiality of salvation was available through the presence of Christ in the world on Christmas. The fact that the blood of the dying Leo mixed in with the sacrificial body and blood of Christ on the altar does not suggest that Leo was necessarily forgiven for his crimes, but rather that a sinner such as Leo might potentially be saved by the grace of Christ. Gryphius thus retained the basic form of Simons' traditional tyrant drama but for a different end. Where Simons had been content to remind his audience of the harsh and inescapable justice of God, Gryphius comforted his viewers with the promise of Christ's forgiveness for all sinners.

In accordance with the pedagogical tendency of Jesuit theater, Simons conceived of Leo's downfall primarily as an exemplum of impiety punished ("impietas punita").[64] From this moralistic perspective derived from sixteenth-century humanist drama, the tyrant Leo and the revolutionary Balbus were both condemnable for their blasphemous disrespect for God. There was no mention of the possibility of forgiveness, of Christ's love for the lost sheep, of grace dispensed and salvation won. It was rather a merciless Old Testament world dominated by an angry God in which men were compelled to obey the Almighty or be lost forever. To describe this situation in Luther's terms, it was a world ruled by the Law in which good men realized their helplessness without God. Simons alleviated this discontent by suggesting that man's adherence to the precepts of the Church could ensure him salvation. Balbus' young son Theophilus, for example, illustrated the ideal Catholic response: he was devoted to both the Virgin Mary and his father, Balbus, but was remarkably naive about the latter's ambitions.[65] Personal piety rather than worldly glory was clearly the virtue Simons hoped his schoolboy audience would acquire. For the Lutheran Gryphius, however, the practice of virtue was an inadequate consolation for fallen man whose only hope lay in the merciful love and forgiveness of Christ. In contrast to the Jesuit play in which ecclesiastical precepts were enforced with the same

---

[63] Cf. Kaiser, p. 24. It is indeed true that the messenger's narrative of the assassination suggested that Leo's death could be interpreted allegorically as a parallel to Christ's sacrificial suffering. But this allegorical significance of the event did not mean that, on a literal level, the historical Leo was necessarily saved. Indeed, in the end, Leo seemed to adhere more to the precepts of the Law: his final words were an admonition to the conspirators to avoid sacrilege rather than a clear admission of faith in Christ. Leo's recognition of his own sinfulness as well as of the salvation accessible to man through Christ did not mean he *had been* saved, but rather that he *could* be saved through God's mercy.

[64] The full title of Simons' play was: *Leo Armenus seu impietas punita.*

[65] Theophilus was clearly intended as a pious exemplum for the schoolboy audience. In establishing Theophilus as a contrast to Balbus, however, Simons altered historical fact by casting the youth as an image-worshipper.

severity as the Law of Moses, Gryphius demonstrated the victory of Christ over the Law by promising salvation to a tyrant.

Gryphius thus rejected Simons' historical drama because of the Jesuit's concern with justice rather than justification. To Gryphius' mind, the former was typical of the Old Testament world of Vondel's *Gebroeders*, and in his translation of that work, Gryphius emphasized the righteousness of God's Will. In the Christian era, however, Gryphius no longer regarded historical events exclusively as acts of God's Providence or anger, but as occasions to reveal the influence of the Redemption on human history. Having illustrated the miraculous effect of grace on the sinful Leo, Gryphius now turned to its workings on Christian martyrs. As in the case of *Leo Armenius*, Gryphius once again dispensed with the customary moralistic interpretation of the martyr figures in humanist drama and reestablished Christ's central role in preserving these heroes from damnation.

### Protestant Martyrdom: "Catharina von Georgien"

Martyr drama in the mid-seventeenth century was primarily practiced by Catholic school playwrights to inspire the youths in their charge to emulate the virtue of courageous saints. The martyr plays themselves had originated in the sixteenth century as part of the humanists' efforts to adapt religious subjects to the form and language of classical theater.[66] As school theater, martyr dramas contributed to the moral education of Christian youths as it trained them in rhetoric and public speaking. The plays varied in literary quality from dramatized hagiographical legends with an awkward Plautine frame to serious attempts to establish a pantheon of Christian heroes reminiscent of, but superior to, the ancients. Despite these differences, the main impetus for the composition of the plays was not so much literary as practical. In the religious and political upheaval of the holy wars which raged throughout Europe in the mid-sixteenth century, models for the ideal behavior of a persecuted Christian were desperately needed to encourage the members of churches to defend their respective faiths. In this regard the plays hardly differed from the numerous prose martyrologies which were compiled in the sixteenth century: John Foxe's *The Book of Martyrs* (1563)[67] for the English Protestants,

---

[66] For a study of the beginnings of humanist martyr drama, see J. A. Parente, Jr., "Counter-Reformation Polemic and Senecan Tragedy: The Dramas of Gregorius Holonius (1531?-1594)," *HumLov*, 30 (1981), 156-80.

[67] John Foxe had originally compiled records of early Christian martyrdom in his *Commentarii rerum in ecclesia gestarum* (1554), enlarged this same work in 1559 and appended recent martyrdoms (e.g., William Tyndale, d. 1536) for the 1563 collection in *The Acts and Monuments of the Church.*

Jean Crespin's *Histoire des martyrs* (1554)[68] for the Calvinists, and the hagiographies of Laurentius Surius[69] and Aloysius Lipomanus[70] for the Catholics.

The composition of martyr dramas served a dual purpose. First, the impressionable youths were inspired to die for their church by the glories which awaited them in heaven.[71] As in the early Church, the acts of the martyrs were now related to the faithful in order to train and establish a cadre of unshakable defenders. The martyr dramas frequently retained the miracles of the prose sources—painless tortures, retinues of angels guiding the saints into heaven—to stimulate the audience not only to endure but also to proselytize for the faith. The second aim of the plays was far more realistic: the schoolboys were reassured that the sufferings they might one day endure would have been ordained by a just God.[72] Once again arguments from the patristic literature on Christian martyrdom reappeared in the plays. The inevitability of human suffering was not to be regarded as evidence of an indifferent or even absent God but rather as a test of the strength of a Christian's faith. Every martyr drama consequently testified to the presence of divine justice—not unlike the martyr's testimony for Christ—for it was from this basis that the central virtues of fortitude and constancy derived their validity.

In the hands of the Jesuits, the martyr was established as the quintessential warrior of the Counter-Reformation. All martyrs were, of course, distinguished because of the nature of their deaths, but in keep-

---

[68] Jean Crespin, *Histoire des martyrs* (first printed 1554).

[69] Laurentius Surius, *Historiae seu vitae sanctorum iuxta optimam Coloniensem editionem,* 7 vols. (Cologne, 1570-81).

[70] Aloysius Lipomanus, *De vitis sanctorum,* Pars prima et secunda (Louvain: Petrus Zangrius, 1565).

[71] In the verse prologue to his *Laurentias* (1556), Holonius exhorted his audience to emulate the heroism of the martyr:

Nam quisquis ipsos laudat Heroas sacros,
Mage laudat ipsum, qui sacros facit, Deum,
Sed hinc et ista prodit utilitas gravis,
Ut qua Beati sydera adierunt via,
Constante per varias cruces Christi Fide,
Et Charitate fervida, et Spe gloriae,
Petamus iisdem aulam Dei vestigiis:
Eadem et ipsi sancta subeamus via.

Gregorius Holonius, *Laurentias* (Antwerp: Ioan. Bellerus, 1556), sig. Aiiiv-Aiiii.

[72] In the Latin poem appended to his German play, Zacharias Zahn explicated the consolatory purpose of his tragedy on St. Stephen Protomartyr:

Hoc opus idcircò scripsi de Martyre sancto,
    Ut maneant nobis sub cruce summa salus.
Quem deus affligit, deus hunc pater adiuvat ultrò
    Et pro tristitiis gaudia saepe parat.

Zacharias Zahn, *Tragoedia lapidati Stephani* (Mühlhausen: Andreas Hantzsch, 1589), sig. K 3v.

ing with the Tridentine revival of the cult of the saints, these Church heroes quickly acquired other attributes as well. Two favorite Jesuit martyrs, St. Eustachius and St. Catherine of Alexandria, for example—whose popularity lasted well into the eighteenth century—were appreciated equally for their courage and their relevancy to the sixteenth-century intellectual scene. St. Catherine was esteemed for both her learning and chastity;[73] similarly St. Eustachius had the triple appeal of being a warrior, a converted pagan (conversion was always encouraged especially in areas with a mixed Catholic-Protestant population) and an exemplum of *patientia* similar to the Neo-Stoic ideal.[74] As defenders of the Church, the dramatists emphasized the martyr's superhuman ability to overcome any misfortune. The Christian virtue of humility was rarely endorsed, and the martyr's strength appeared to derive more from his temerity than from his faith. The Catholic Church was less interested in the martyr's imitation of Christ's passion—an exemplum of a passive hero, to be sure—than in the adaptation of classical heroic virtues for ecclesiastical ends.[75] For Catholic writers, the christological parallel of the martyr's death was consequently minimized, if not eliminated, so that audiences might aspire to achieve the secular goals of the Church.

The martyr drama with which Gryphius was familiar in the mid-seventeenth century had been produced by Catholic authors in France, Italy and the Netherlands for the glorification of Rome. The Jesuits Joseph Simons and Nicolaus Caussin provided the customary Counter-Reformation bravado. Pierre Corneille, a former student of the Jesuits at their Collège de Clermont, imbued his martyr heroes, Polyeucte and Théodore,[76] with equally militant fervor, and Joost van den Vondel betrayed the uninhibited enthusiasm of a recent convert in *Maeghden* (on St. Ursula and the ten thousand virgins) and *Peter en Pauwels*. In contrast, Gryphius' *Catharina von Georgien* was written to counter the Catholic reduction of martyr drama to a representation of Christian heroics for the sake of the Church. The martyr was no longer conceived as an extraordinary individual of limitless courage but as fallen man who was constrained by circumstances to die for his faith. For Gryphius, the martyr's confrontation with death was not so much an occasion for the triumph of courage as for the recognition of his own sinfulness and need for

---

[73] Besides presenting numerous dramas on St. Catherine, the Jesuits sponsored several public orations in her honor on her feast day (November 25). See, for example, the entries in the diary of the Munich rector in 1596 and 1598: ms. Bayerische Staatsbibliothek, clm. 1550, fol. 12ᵛ; 26ᵛ.

[74] See the above discussion of Nicolaus Vernulaeus' tragedy on St. Eustachius, chapter 2, pp. 89-90.

[75] Holonius, *Laurentias*, sig. Aii-Aiii.

[76] *Théodore, vierge et martyre* (1645).

Christ's grace. Where Catholic writers limited martyrdom to a specific historical event, Gryphius used the martyr to explicate the significance of the Redemption for man's salvation.

Despite confessional differences, Gryphius developed his dramatic skills through a close translation of Caussin's *Felicitas*. As in the case of *Gebroeders*, Gryphius' work with this traditional genre induced him to develop his own concept of the martyr play a few years later. For this reason, the *Felicitas* translation has generally been regarded as a useful basis for comparison of Catholic and Protestant martyr drama.[77] Whereas the Catholic protagonists generally experienced a painless death as a reward for their zeal, Gryphius' characters were considered genuine heroes because of the suffering they were forced to endure. But such distinctions—often inspired by Protestant prejudices about Catholic drama—failed to account for Gryphius' attraction to Caussin's work in the first place. His choice of the Caussin tragedy was not accidental; on the contrary, Felicitas and her sons displayed unwavering fortitude before their persecutors that would later be associated with Gryphius' own martyr heroes.

Gryphius' interest in *Felicitas* primarily arose from Caussin's presentation of his protagonist. The *Felicitas* was not typical of the Jesuit repertoire, and the material itself was seldom presented in their schools.[78] What popularity the legend had was not so much due to Felicitas as to her seven sons whose enthusiasm for death could easily enflame the hearts of the schoolboy audiences. Felicitas herself was the paragon of the Catholic mother, at once tearful and joyous at the martyrdom of her children. But Jesuit restrictions about the appearance of female characters on the stage hindered the Felicitas legend from gaining international notoriety.[79] The unusual emphasis on the protagonist's lamentations rather than on her martyrdom further limited the dramatic development of the material. The graphic descriptions of each son's death also increased the plot's tedium. In contrast to popular martyrs such as St. Catherine of Alexandria and St. Vitus who seldom experienced the afflictions of the world in their haste to leave it, Felicitas was a passive figure forced to endure seven martyrdoms before her own. Felicitas' exemplary forbearance of this torment rather than the triumph of her

---

[77] Lunding, pp. 16-25; Henri Plard, "Beständige Mutter/Oder Die Heilige Felicitas," in *Die Dramen des Andreas Gryphius*, ed. Gerhard Kaiser (Stuttgart: Metzler, 1968), pp. 327-30.

[78] Joh. Müller cited only four performances of plays on St. Felicitas between 1597 and 1771: Johannes Müller, *Das Jesuitendrama in den Ländern deutscher Zunge vom Anfang (1555) bis zum Hochbarock (1665)*, vol. 2 (Augsburg: Benno Filser, 1930), p. 107.

[79] See Chapter 1, note 73.

sons; her patient endurance of misfortune rather than the martyrdom itself, dominated Caussin's work and distinguished it from the traditional martyr play. Where other martyrs had attacked, Felicitas defended; where others proselytized, Felicitas endured; where others died, Felicitas mourned. Caussin's Felicitas was not so much a fiery martyr designed to inspire the audience, but rather to console them with lessons in forbearance.

In light of Gryphius' subsequent conception of the martyr, the reasons for his attraction to the Jesuit are immediately apparent. Felicitas exemplified the ''Bewehrte Beständigkeit'' which Catharina would later display during her persecution. Both women shared other virtues besides constancy: *eloquentia* to defend the tenets of their faith; *prudentia* to see through the wiles of the court and recognize the valuelessness of the world; and *castitas,* the unassailable virtue which coupled with their physical beauty confounded their male persecutors. As prisoners of pagan tyrants, both Felicitas and Catharina were subjected to hardships which tested the strength of their faith. Gryphius appreciated Felicitas' heroism and believed that the virtues which Felicitas and other Catholic martyrs displayed were worthy of emulation. In contrast to the Jesuits, however, he perceived the inability of these virtues to secure man's salvation. The performance of Gryphius' translation of the *Felicitas* at the Elisabeth Gymnasium in Breslau in 1653 therefore recalled the humanists' sixteenth-century presentations of classical drama. Although the characters might at times act offensively, the elegance of their language and their general moral significance justified the production of such works on the school stage. In *Felicitas*, Caussin demonstrated the eternal rewards which awaited all martyrs for their obedience to the Church. In Gryphius' martyr tragedies, however, the heroes would later be forced to acknowledge their sins and the impossibility of any reward without Christ.

Gryphius thus shared the Catholic moralistic conception of the martyr character. Such similarities were not surprising, for Gryphius was well versed in the writings of St. Basil, Justin Martyr and Prudentius who had contributed to the establishment of the early Christian martyr cult.[80] His criticism of the martyr drama tradition was directed toward its application to ecclesiastical rather than soteriological ends. Gryphius objected to the transformation of the martyr into a Catholic demigod whose glorious death justified the seventeenth-century Church's imperial hegemony in

---

[80] For references from Gryphius' writings to St. Basil's *Oratio in 40 martyres,* Justin Martyr's *Apologia pro christianis I & II,* and Prudentius' *Peristephanon,* see Schings *Patristische und stoische Tradition,* pp. 297-8.

Europe. *Felicitas* did not offend in this way. Caussin's introduction of the allegorical figure of "ecclesia militans" in two of his four choruses, though clearly intended as a representative of Rome, was easily assimilated by Gryphius into "die streitenden Kirchen," a symbol for all persecuted churches. But Caussin's other martyr dramas did not maintain this neutrality. *Theodoricus* and *Hermenigildus* portrayed the Arian (i.e., Protestant) persecution of orthodox Christianity and the eventual defeat of the heretics by Rome.[81] Still stronger panegyrics of Catholic heroism were devised by Vondel in the years surrounding his conversion from Anabaptism to Catholicism. Gryphius, who had hitherto esteemed Vondel's plays, was now wary of the sudden fervour of *Maeghden* and *Peter en Pauwels*; *Catharina von Georgien* and *Carolus Stuardus* gauged the extent of his disapproval.

*Maeghden* has customarily been viewed as a crude adaptation of the naive and old-fashioned mystery play to the structure of classical tragedy.[82] The hagiographical account of the martyrdom of St. Ursula and her ten thousand virgin followers at Cologne had been a popular topic in both the visual arts and in meditational literature since the twelfth century,[83] but Vondel's first hagiographical work broke sharply with both the medieval tradition and the Jesuits who preserved it in their schools. Whereas Ursula resembled the fervent virgin heroines of the Jesuits' drama, the characterization of her persecutor, Attila, preserved the work from the banality of most martyr plays. Vondel was not content to portray the mere confrontation between the saint and the tyrant; rather, his play provided a philosophy of history which, in true Counter-Reformation fashion, reconfirmed the supremacy of the Roman Church.

The desire of a pagan lover for a Christian virgin had been a common topic in Catholic hagiography and the Jesuits exploited this material for their martyr plays in the early seventeenth century.[84] Generally, the Jesuit heroines also possessed other qualities such as the love of learning, which justified their appearance on the school stage. Virgin martyrs, such as Saints Dorothea, Catherine of Alexandria and Cecilia were not portrayed primarily because of their chastity but rather on account of

---

[81] Szarota, *Geschichte, Politiek und Gesellschaft*, pp. 25-37.

[82] W. A. P. Smit, *Van Pascha tot Noah. Een verkenning van Vondels drama's naar continuiteit en ontwikkeling in hun grondmotief en structuur*, vol. 1 (Zwolle: W. E. J. Tjeenk Willink, 1956), p. 258.

[83] On the medieval sources to *Maeghden*, see Rosa Schömer, "Über die Quellen zu Vondels Maeghden," *Festschrift der Nationalbibliothek in Wien*, 1926, pp. 734-44.

[84] Vondel, for example, presented the verse letters of virgin martyrs to both Christian and pagan recipients in his *Brieven der Heilige Maeghden, Martelaressen* (1642); this work was a christianization of Ovid's *Heroides* which Vondel was translating into Dutch about the same time.

their role in local and ecclesiastical history.[85] Patron saints of local churches or cities such as Ursula of Cologne also insured certain martyrs a
place in the repertoire and Vondel's *Maeghden* belonged to this *laus urbis*
tradition.

Vondel intended that his portrait of Ursula commemorate his birthplace, Cologne, and the continued existence of the bishopric. To this
end, he retained the simplistic hagiographical characterization of the
virgin. Informed in a dream of her impending death in Cologne, Ursula
eagerly welcomed her fate and permitted her followers to leave should
they be unwilling to perish with her. She never once deviated from fulfill-
ing God's prophecy; indeed, she hastened to display her bravery so that
the beleaguered Christians of Cologne who witnessed her death might be
inspired to emulate her.[86] Ursula's martyrdom also served to instruct the
citizens of Cologne in God's justice and, under the banner of Ursula's
ghost, to inspire them to oust the Huns from their territory. The besieged
citizens needed the reassurance from heaven that their obedience would
reap palpable rewards for their homeland. Ursula thus recalled the
heroines of Jesuit theater whose triumphs were designed to banish the
audiences' fears and to propel them into action.

Vondel's characterization of Ursula's persecutor, Attila, considerably
expanded the tyrant's customary role. The insatiable passion of the
pagan prefects, governors and emperors for Christian virgins had frequently served to emphasize the martyr's chastity and to illustrate the
satanic depravity of the heathens. Sexual perversity (such as the brutal
removal of the saint's breasts) was often employed by the tyrants as
punishment for the women who refused to accede to their desires.[87]
Vondel's Attila was likewise inflamed with lust for the virgin, but his passion was intricately intertwined with his military and political leadership
role among the Huns. Having been smitten by the noble beauty of the
virgin, Attila halted his advance on Cologne and devoted his energies to
winning Ursula as his bride. Torn between his allegiance to the Huns
and his love for a Christian woman, the raging tyrant of hagiography and

---

[85] St. Catherine's popularity on the school stage was primarily due to her exemplary
explication and defense of the tenets of Christianity. In contrast, the Protestant dramatist
Balthasar Thamme composed his 1594 tragedy on St. Dorothea for a birthday performance in honor of the Duchess of Anhalt-Saxony, Dorothea Maria, at the royal palace
in Altenburg.

[86] See the discussion of the relationship between Ursula's death and the siege of Cologne above, chapter 3, pp. 136-7.

[87] Such atrocities were often illustrated and described in gruesome detail; see, for
example, Antonius Gallonius, *De ss. martyrum cruciatibus* (Rome, 1594) and his *Trattato
degli instrumenti di martirio, e delle varie maniere di martoriare usate da' gentili contro christiani*
(Rome, 1591).

Jesuit theater had been transformed into a pitiful ruler constrained by fate to destroy the object of his love. As a heathen, Attila was doomed by his blindness to Christianity to perish so that the Church could achieve its destined victory; as a monarch, Attila was compelled to destroy every threat to the preservation of his kingdom. The classical heroism of Attila, whose reluctant suppression of his passion recalled P. C. Hooft's Achilles (*Achilles en Polyxena*, 1597), was revealed as misplaced and ineffectual in the new Christian world of Ursula and her followers. The downfall of Attila did not so much arise from a moral failing as it had in Jesuit drama, but from his inability to detect the invalidity of the laws of the Huns in the age of Christianity.

*Maeghden* has long been regarded as Gryphius' model for *Catharina von Georgien* because of the similarities between the dramatic conflicts and the characterization of the tyrant.[88] Both tragedies related the misfortunes of female prisoners whose physical beauty had enraptured their captors. The political tyranny of Attila and Chach Abas was paradoxically complemented by the women's tyrannical hold over their wooers. Indeed, the passion with which the tyrants coyly approached the objects of their affection far exceeded the lustful infatuation of the hagiographical tyrant (such as Marcus Aurelius in *Felicitas*) with a woman martyr. The passion of traditional tyrants was quickly transformed into a lasting anger when the women rejected their advances.[89] Attila and Chach Abas were, however, forced by reasons of state to execute the women. The high priest Beremond accompanied Attila to the execution lest the hesitant tyrant succumb to his passion and spare the Christian. Similarly, Seinelcan, Chach Abas' closest adviser, reminded him of the threat which Catharina posed to the state; her continued imprisonment not only increased Chach Abas' hopeless passion but it also endangered Persian security since Russia had sworn to avenge any mistreatment of the Georgian queen. Both Beremund and Seinelcan referred their kings to the noble example of the ruler who slew his beloved lest his passion for her endanger his civilization.[90]

---

[88] See, for example, Kollewijn, pp. 19-22; Flemming, pp. 111-8, and Clemens Heselhaus, "Catharina von Georgien," in *Das deutsche Drama*, vol. 1, ed. Benno von Wiese (Düsseldorf: August Bagel, 1958), pp. 57-8.

[89] The wrath arising from the unrequited passion of a pagan admirer was commonplace in medieval hagiography; it first appeared in a religious play in Hrotsvitha von Gandersheim's comedy on the martyrdom of Sapientia by the emperor Hadrian (*Sapientia*), continued into vernacular hagiographical theater (e.g., "Das Dorotheaspiel," ca. 1340) and later into early humanist drama: *Chiliani equitis Comoedia gloriosae parthenices et martyris Dorotheae agoniam passionemque depingens* (Leipzig: Wolfgang Monacen, 1507). On the medieval Dorothea play, see Heinrich Schachner, "Das Dorotheaspiel," *ZDP*, 35 (1903), 157-96.

[90] Cf. *WB*, III, p. 751, lines 969-990 and *Trauerspiele III*, p. 174, Act II, lines 297-322.

Ironically, the tyrants' adherence to their councilors' advice did result in the weakening and eventual destruction of their states. Attila's siege was halted by the ghost of Ursula who predicted his bloody death; Catharina likewise foretold the end of Persia to the mournful Chach Abas who regretted both the injustice of his deed and his inextinguishable love for the martyr.

Despite these superficial similarities, Gryphius differed sharply from Vondel's approach to the hagiographical material. His Christocentric concept of drama induced him to redefine the function of the martyr play. First, Gryphius revised the standard characterization of the martyr as a Christian hero. Ursula's yearning for death, though typical of Jesuit heroines, differed radically from Felicitas' patient forbearance of injustice. Where Felicitas had suffered to gain her heavenly reward, Ursula had been assured of a martyr's crown in a vision. Gryphius' critique of the martyr in *Catharina von Georgien* could thus be directed at her predestined sanctity (Ursula) as well as the exclusive merit of her virtue (Felicitas). In her preparation for death, Catharina would realize the sinfulness of her life and her need for Christ's grace to gain salvation. Secondly, Gryphius transferred the martyr play from the temporality of human history to the atemporality of salvation history. Where the martyrdom of Felicitas and Ursula glorified the Roman Church's victory over paganism, Catharina's death promised eternal redemption for all sinners. For Catholic writers, the early church martyrs justified the hegemony of Rome. For the Lutheran Gryphius, the temporal triumph would be revealed as a defeat without Christ's intercession. In restoring Christ's central role to martyr drama, Gryphius transformed martyrdom from a heroic assault on paganism to a metaphor for the existence of fallen man.

Gryphius structured the plot of his drama to juxtapose the worthlessness of human endeavors to the benefits which awaited man through Christ and his grace. In the course of the play, Catharina herself had to learn, along with the reader, the significance of the Redemption for man's history. When Catharina first appeared on the stage, she was still entangled in the political world which resulted in her imprisonment. She reflected on the familiar theme of the transitoriness of all earthly power, and like a virtuous queen, feared for the preservation of her son and her kingdom. Until this point Catharina had led an active political life; she had not only avenged the death of her husband by a deceitful plot to entrap his murderer (Catharina had lured her guilty brother-in-law back to Georgia with a promise of marriage and then had him ambushed en route), but she had also endangered her own safety by offering to negotiate a peace treaty with the untrustworthy Chach Abas. During her seven-year incarceration, Catharina resisted the Chach's amorous advances and fluctuated between hope and despair that a political solution might be devised to mend the rift between the two kingdoms.

Gryphius' tragedy focused on Catharina's final hours in which she discovered the futility of politics and dedicated herself to Christ. In the opening act, two episodes served to illustrate that the queen was still beset by worldly cares. First, her handmaiden Salome presented Catharina with some fresh roses she had just gathered from the palace garden. Catharina immediately interpreted them as an emblem of her own loss of political power and her imprisonment. Just as the rose inevitably lost its petals and pricked its admirer with its thorns, so had Catharina lost her crown and languished in prison.

> O Blumen welchen wir in Warheit zu vergleichen!
> Die schleust den Knopff kaum auff/die steht in voller Pracht
> Beperl't mit frischem Taw. Die wirfft die welcke Tracht
> Der bleichen Blätter weg. Die edlen Rosen leben
> So kurtze Zeit/vnd sind mit Dornen doch vmbgeben.
> Alsbald die Sonn' entsteht/schmückt sie der Gärte Zelt;
> Vnd wird in nichts verkehrt so bald die Sonne felt.[91]

Shortly thereafter Catharina related her dream from the previous evening in which she experienced an indescribable sensation of pleasure after being stripped of her earthly raiment. She immediately associated the pleasurable sensation with the sudden appearance at Chach's court of the Russian ambassador who had come to restore her to her throne. The prospect of freedom after such a long imprisonment led Catharina to interpret her political success as God's reward for her loyal defense of her kingdom and her Christian religion. God's kindness toward her had been manifested by the success which the Russian ambassador and her son Tamaras enjoyed in securing Chach Abas' promise to release her. In other words, Catharina regarded her impending liberation as a visible manifestation of God's justice in the world:

> HERR das dein' arme Magd noch vnverletzt gestanden;
> Ist dein/nicht Menschen Werck. Der Cörper ist in Banden;
> Doch find der Geist sich frey/der durch vil Creutz bewehrt
> Doch/weil du für vns wachst/durch keine Glut verzehrt![92]

Catharina's fidelity to her God and homeland, like the adherence of Caussin's martyrs to the Church, had reaped a material reward.

Gryphius immediately undermined the joy of Catharina's reprieve in order to juxtapose the worthlessness of political freedom to Christ's

---

[91] *Trauerspiele III*, p. 148, Act I, lines 302-308.
[92] *Trauerspiele III*, p. 194, Act IV, lines 53-56.

liberation of mankind from sin. Compelled by Chach Abas—who had broken this pledge to free his prisoner—to choose between him and death, between an earthly kingdom and her immortal soul, Catharina realized the insignificance of politics in the eyes of God. In her long debate with the Persian adviser. Imanculi (IV.2), Catharina defended the basic tenets of Christianity, the miracles of Christ's Redemption and the Resurrection, and thereby acknowledged the primacy of faith over obedience. Where Catharina had previously attributed her release from prison to her tenacious defense of "Kirch und Vaterland," she now believed that the only true liberation from human misfortune lay in the saving power of faith. Through her declaration of Christ's role in history, Catharina was able to offer a soteriological rather than a political interpretation of the dream she had described in the first act:

> Vmbsonst sind Meurab/Reuß vnd Tamaras bemüht
> Zu wenden vnser Leid das vnauffhörlich blüht/
> Und täglich fruchtbar wird. Der endlich an vns setzte
> Und auß den Dornen riß/vnd (wie es schin) verletzte;
> Ist (Zweifels ohn) der Tod. Die Lust die vns empfing
> Als der geschwinde Sturm der Wetter vberging
> Zilt auff das seel'ge Reich das JEsus uns erworben.[93]

Her fear for the security of Georgia was now replaced by her fear for her "durch Schuld beflecktes Blut,"[94] and her love for her son and her people was now supplanted by her love for Jesus through whose grace her sins would be forgiven. In choosing martyrdom, Catharina was not so much eager to defend her faith and crown, as to show her loving gratitude to her Redeemer Christ, "dem der sich selbst für vns ließ in ein Holtz erheben."[95] Through the careful delineation of Catharina's development from a defender of Georgia to a martyr for Christ, Gryphius dispensed with the exclusive use of the martyr as an exemplar of heroic virtues and transformed the martyr play into a representation of the significance of the Redemption.

Gryphius' Christocentric approach to his work also effected a major change in the customary historical function of the martyr play. In contrast to *Maeghden* with its origins in medieval legend, Gryphius' tragedy presented an elaborate—to some minds too elaborate—portrait of Georgian history in the early seventeenth century. The recent martyrdom of Queen Catharina of Georgia-Gurgistan in 1624 certainly appeared to have a greater historical relevance for the beleaguered

---

[93] *Trauerspiele III*, p. 203, Act IV, lines 363-369.
[94] *Trauerspiele III*, p. 200, Act IV, line 270.
[95] *Trauerspiele III*, p. 205, Act IV, line 425.

citizens of Silesia than any play based on the early Church or medieval chronicles.[96] Yet in contrast to Catholic martyr dramatists, Gryphius did not limit himself to the historical utility of his work; rather *Catharina von Georgien* was intended to reveal the insignificance of history from the perspective of eternity. Vondel and the Jesuits had subscribed to a progressive concept of human history, derived from humanism, in which Christianity (i.e., the Catholic Church) succeeded to antique culture without rejecting its partial utility for man's spiritual development. From the perspective of Caussin and Vondel in the seventeenth century, the dramatization of a martyr's triumph over his persecutors visibly confirmed the fulfillment of Christ's promise of the eternal reign of his Church. Gryphius' view of man's historical development, however, was not based on humanism but on the Scriptures.[97] In his fallen state, man had lived under the severity of the Law of Moses until Jesus re-created the possibility of salvation through his sacrificial death. History itself— like the tumultuous events in Georgia—was a changeable series of progress and regression, a vicious circle from which man could only be liberated through his faith in Christ. For the Catholics, martyrdom was a single historical event in which the defender of the Church defeated the representative of a defunct pagan culture. As noted previously, Attila's tragedy did not arise so much from his amorality, as from his application of pagan values to a Christian age. In contrast, Gryphius conceived of martyrdom as a perennial state for fallen man who yearned for Christ's grace through faith.

Gryphius' historical *Catharina von Georgien* was thus written paradoxically to reveal the ahistorical significance of martyrdom. To be sure, Gryphius had announced his ahistorical intention at the outset by revealing the invalidity of all transitory events from the vantage point of the allegorical figure of Eternity. All earthly actions—such as the practice of virtue—only gained significance insofar as they were directed toward a heavenly goal:

> Ihr/wo nach gleicher Ehr der hohe Sinn euch steht;
> Verlacht mit ihr/was hir vergeht.[98]

The Catholic emphasis on ecclesiastical obedience for the forbearance of injustice was now replaced by the necessity of faith for man's spiritual

---

[96] On the early seventeenth-century source for Gryphius' play, see Eugène Susini, "Claude Malingre, Sieur de Saint-Lazare, et son Histoire de Catherine de Georgie," *EG*, 23 (1968), 37-53.

[97] For Gryphius' view of history and time, see Wilhelm Voßkamp, *Zeit- und Geschichtsauffassung im 17. Jahrhundert bei Gryphius und Lohenstein* (Bonn: Bouvier, 1967), especially pp. 63-100.

[98] *Trauerspiele III*, p. 141, Act I, lines 85-86.

justification. For Gryphius, true Christian history did not record human achievements but rather man's spiritual evolution from the Fall to the Redemption and ultimately to the Last Judgment. In *Catharina von Georgien*, the roses which Salome presented to Catharina[99] embodied the simultaneity of all three events from the perspective of eternity. The image of the rose itself had long been associated with martyrdom, but its application to Gryphius' historical vision considerably broadened its traditional interpretation. In the patristic literature, especially St. Ambrose,[100] the thorns of the rose at once suggested the Fall of man (each thorn represented a sin) and man's Redemption through Christ (the crown of thorns). At the same time, the rose's petals reminded man of the paradise which he had lost and the eternal bliss which he could gain through faith. In like manner, Gryphius explicated his soteriological concept of history through Catharina's spiritual growth before her death: her despair and fear under the Law; her joyful embrace of Christ's grace and her final triumph in heaven. In *Catharina von Georgien* the ecclesiastical martyr play of the Catholic humanists had been transformed into a Lutheran emblem of man's salvation history.

### *The Fall and Redemption of a Protestant King: "Carolus Stuardus"*

In contrast to the ahistorical spirituality of *Catharina von Georgien*, Gryphius' *Carolus Stuardus* appeared to be the consummate political play. The tragedy, which was first written in 1649 and revised after the Restoration in 1661,[101] frankly betrayed Gryphius' shock and indignation at the execution of Charles I. As a fervent defender of the divine right of monarchs, Gryphius exploited every opportunity to condemn the misguided actions of the English Parliamentarians and to uphold Charles' innocence. The sudden promulgation of a political stance was in itself a surprising gesture for a playright who had hitherto devoted his energies to exposing the changeable nature of the world and to extolling man's ability to free himself from it. To be sure, the political downfall of the king, itself a prescriptive rule for tragedy, aptly illustrated the whimsy of Fortuna. But Gryphius' characterization now seemed

---

[99] *Trauerspiele III*, p. 148, Act I, lines 302-318.

[100] Ambrose, *Hexameron*, III. 11.48 where he noted: "Surrexerat ante floribus immista terrenis sine spinis rosa, et pulcherrimus flos sine ulla fraude vernabat: postea spina sepsit gratiam floris, tanquam humanae speculum praeferens vitae, quae suavitatem perfunctionis suae finitimis curarum stimulis saepe compungat .... Unde cum unusquisque aut suavitate rationis, aut prosperioris cursus successibus gratulatur meminisse culpae eum convenit, per quam nobis in paradisi amoenitate florentibus spinae mentis, animaeque sentes jure condemnationis ascripti sunt." *PL*, 14, col. 188.

[101] For a comparison of the two versions, see Hugh Powell's remarks in the introduction to his edition, *Carolus Stuardus* (Leicester: Pitman, 1955), pp. lxxxiii-cxxxvii.

primarily directed to secular rather than religious ends. Gryphius no longer appeared as interested in explicating the Redemption to man as he was in defending the inviolability of majesty and in arousing universal contempt for Charles' executioners. Gryphius had, of course, included political arguments in his first two tragedies: the revolution of Balbus was portrayed as a hollow victory since tyrannicide was equally condemnable from both a political and religious perspective. Indeed, the sanctity of kings as well as tyrants was founded on the principle that God alone was empowered to remove these rulers from their thrones. Despite its sacred purpose, *Catharina von Georgien* presented geopolitical arguments about the nature of treaties and the government of a buffer state (Georgia) whose survival depended on its relations with its powerful neighbors.[102] But, in both tragedies, the historical and political lessons were over-shadowed by the transcendental framework which clarified man's tenuous relationship to the transitory world and his need for Christ. In *Carolus Stuardus*, Gryphius' heated disapproval of the revolution appeared to have led him to dispense with his explication of man's relationship to Christ and to transform the king's final hours into a secularized reenact-ment of Christ's passion.

A comparative examination of other secularized passion plays and Gryphius' work does, however, reveal differences which then allow *Carolus Stuardus* to be associated with the first two historical tragedies. As in *Leo Armenius* and *Catharina von Georgien*, Gryphius was reacting against the contemporary praxis of abusing religion by applying it to secular ends. Gryphius' Charles character cannot be considered merely a political rather than a religious martyr, for religion and politics were intricately combined within his person. As a political victim he died for the injustices perpetrated against him by an illegal band of rebels. At the same time he perished for the cause of orthodox Anglicanism since the Puritan rebels (Presbyterian and Independents) wished to punish Charles in retaliation for his earlier actions against them. Gryphius' construction of the parallel between Charles and Christ served both a political and a religious end. In his office as king, God's ordained vicar on earth, Charles acquired an aura of sanctity which corresponded to the divinity of Christ. As a man, however, Charles was subject to the same errors and sins which every man committed because of his fallen nature. Whereas the royal Charles retained his innocence because of the divinity of his office (*legibus solutus* in political theory), the human Charles needed the grace of Christ to liberate him from the sins which all men inevitably

---

[102] For an account of *Catharina von Georgien* as a political play, see Szarota, *Künstler, Grübler und Rebellen*, pp. 205-7.

commit. Through this dual perspective on Charles' nature, Gryphius reestablished the importance of the Redemption in order to refute the exclusively secular portrayal of human history.

Gryphius' unique Christocentric approach can best be demonstrated through a comparison of *Carolus Stuardus* and the work from which Gryphius borrowed several Passion motifs: Vondel's *Maria Stuart* (1646). The devout Catholic Vondel was gravely disturbed by the execution of Mary Stuart, for her loss amidst the machinations of English politics not only defeated Rome but also heralded the turmoil of Cromwell's revolution. Indeed, the fires of Vondel's heated defense of Mary Stuart were not so much stoked by her tragic death almost sixty years before (1587) as by contemporary events in England.[103] Mary's enemies were now anachronistically characterized as Puritans, Elizabeth as a usurper of Cromwell's ilk and the English lords as defenders of the populace's right to depose a king. To underscore the injustice of Elizabeth, Vondel constructed an elaborate parallel between Christ's Passion and Mary's final hours. Just as Jesus had suffered for man, so did Mary die as a sacrificial lamb for her people. She celebrated a Last Supper (''avontmael'') with her handmaidens, forgave her oppressors and commended her soul to God before her death. Moreover, in the preface, Mary was assigned a place in the typological biblical sequence which proceeded from Moses to Christ. Where Moses had foreshadowed the reign of Christ, Mary served as a postfiguration of the Passion.[104] Above all, Vondel stressed the righteousness of Mary's claim to the throne and her consequent innocence of the charges of revolution which Elizabeth had trumped up against her.

Vondel's christological references, though new to Mary Stuart plays in Northern Europe,[105] had been employed in his historical sources.[106] Similar descriptions of Charles I were published during his imprisonment and more profusely after his execution to arouse international sympathy for his plight. For this reason, it cannot be demonstrated with any

---

[103] Smit, vol. 1, pp. 416-7.

[104] *WB*, V, pp. 164-5.

[105] The first humanist drama on Mary Stuart, *Stuarta tragoedia* (1593) by Adrianus Roulerius, a Benedictine from Douai, viewed the queen more as a victim of fate and political machinations than as a christological postfiguration. For an account of Mary Stuart in the theater of the Northern Renaissance, see Karl Kipka, *Maria Stuart im Drama der Weltliteratur*, Breslauer Beiträge zur Literaturgeschichte, 9 (Leipzig: Max Hesse, 1907), pp. 63-100.

[106] Vondel's main sources were William Camden's *Annales rerum Anglicarum* (1615; 1625) and Nicholas Caussin's *Le Combat de toutes les passions, représenté au vif en l'histoire de la Reine Marie Stuart* from his *Le Cour sainte* (1627). For an account of the relationship between the sources and the text, see the commentary by J. F. M. Sterck, *WB*, V, pp. 940-3.

certainty that Gryphius' establishment of Charles as a postfiguration of Christ was due to Vondel alone. Certainly both authors shared the language of political martyrdom which their different sources contained. Besides the obvious connection to Christ, references were made to the exchange of an earthly for a heavenly crown, to their prisons as metaphors for their mortal existence and to their hope that their innocent deaths might be avenged.[107] But there were also other parallels between the texts which suggested that Gryphius (especially in the second edition) probably had Vondel's play in mind. First, Gryphius established a connection between Charles' fate and that of his grandmother, Mary Stuart, by introducing her ghost (Act II) to bemoan the bloody chronicle of English history and to warn Charles of his impending doom. Because of the Restoration, Gryphius was also able to use a historical fact to demonstrate the ultimate triumph of God's justice. Just as James I succeeded his mother's executioner in Vondel's work, so did Charles II finally gain the throne which Cromwell had so brutally wrenched from his father. Still other less important ties suggested Gryphius' debt to Vondel. The executions of Sir Thomas Wentworth, Earl of Strafford, and Archbishop Laud were mentioned in both plays as evidence of Puritan bloodthirstiness.[108] Cromwell's religious justification for his political persecution of Charles similarly recalled Elizabeth's abuse of power. But although Vondel and Gryphius agreed about the deceit and injustice of their protagonists' enemies, they differed sharply about the significance of the martyrdoms. Whereas Mary's death was presented as a crime against unadulterated innocence, Charles' execution revealed the inevitability of the guilt which even the martyr will incur as long as he remained in the world.

*Maria Stuart* was conceived as an apologetic work for a Roman Catholic heroine. By removing all doubts about Mary's innocence, Vondel vindicated his panegyrical comparison between her final hours and the Passion of Christ. But his unabashed enthusiasm, if not naiveté, about his subject produced several literary and theological problems. As a student of Aristotle's *Poetics*, Vondel of course knew that Mary did not possess the prescriptive attributes of a tragic hero who was both virtuous and flawed.[109] Her innocence in the eyes of God and the Church absolved her

---

[107] Cf. *Maria Stuart* and *Carolus Stuardus*: (1) the exchange of an earthly for a heavenly crown), *WB*, V, p. 164; *Trauerspiele I*, ed. Hugh Powell (Tübingen: Niemeyer, 1964), p. 136, Act V, line 448; (2) prison as a metaphor for human existence: *WB*, V, pp. 190-1, lines 589-594; *Trauerspiele I*, p. 136, Act V, lines 437-440; (3) hope for divine vengeance, *WB*, V, p. 196, line 755; *Trauerspiele I*, p. 81, Act II, line 282.

[108] Cf. *WB*, V, p. 215, lines 1149-1150, and *Trauerspiele I*, pp. 74-8, Act II, lines 1-160.

[109] See the discussion above, chapter 3, p. 139.

from any error. Mindful of this shortcoming, Vondel resorted to a few unsubstantiated arguments to defend his praxis. First, in his dedicatory preface to Edward of Bavaria, Vondel stated that the false accusations which Mary's opponents leveled against her would suffice to dim the luster of Mary's exemplary character. Her continued protestations against these accusations merely increased her forbearance of much injustice. Secondly, Vondel having freed his heroine from real guilt, precipitated the tragic circumstance by ascribing Mary's untimely end to her political inexperience:

> Mijn schulden hadden schult, die zulck een straf verdienden.
> Men waerschuwt al vergeefs: wien Godt zijn hoede ontzeit,
> Bemerckt den valstrick niet, die voor zijn voeten leit:
> Men wort door rampen wijs, en ondervint te spade,
> Hoe los men henedrijve op's nagebuurs genade.[110]

Mary's innocence was consequently upheld since she was now regarded as a passive victim of her own ignorance about the world; at the same time, her indifference to political events contributed to her sanctity.

Vondel also associated his heroine with the Virgin Mary. Because of her glorious death, Mary Stuart attained the special favor of her biblical namesake: "hierom blincktze nu met recht onder de zalige Martelstarren in Godts hemelsche klaerheit, aen de voeten van Maria, wiens naem zy zoo waerdigh gedragen heeft."[111] Moreover, in the first-act chorus, Vondel, borrowing from a poem by Romoaldus Scotus,[112] equated the queen to the Virgin, for both had sought comfort, albeit with various success, from their kinswoman Elizabeth (Luke 1:39-45). But this artful correspondence had a significant effect on Vondel's religious concept of her character. Mary's declaration of innocence ("ick, vroom en zonder smette")[113] no longer referred exclusively to her political but also to her spiritual state. By likening his heroine to the Virgin Mary, Vondel had acquitted her of all evil, including the most grievous of all human afflictions: original sin.[114] Consequently Mary did not require Christ for her salvation; her political innocence reflected a spiritual purity which she had always possessed. As a guiltless victim of circumstances, her martyrdom did not become an occasion for her to secure Christ's grace but rather, like the Assumption, it concluded a virtuous life which had always

---

[110] *WB*, V, p. 181, lines 336-340.

[111] *WB*, V, p. 165.

[112] Vondel imitated poem 16 in Romoaldus Scotus' collection *Summarium de morte Mariae Stuartae* (Ingolstadt, 1588).

[113] *WB*, V, p. 220, line 1286.

[114] For example, the Virgin Mary was deemed free from original sin by Augustine, *De natura et gratia* 36.42.

been devoted to Christ. In her final speech, Mary claimed that her blood would suffice to wash away her sins: "mijn bloet, het welck mijn vlecken spoel',/Gelijck een offerhant." [115] But in the context of her postfiguration of both the Virgin Mary and Christ, her self-accusations merely reinforced exemplary piety. Vondel's christianization of Mary's passion thus served an exclusively secular purpose. The religious parallels were employed to underscore the injustice of Mary's enemies and her martyrdom and thereby canonize her because of her political goals.

Vondel's application of the Passion to a political end ironically weakened his characterization of his protagonist. Though useful for his apology of Mary Stuart, the religious parallels often betrayed their own inappropriateness because of Mary's reluctance to renounce her claim to a throne which she had never possessed. The stoical calm with which she endured the removal of the baldachin over her chair and prepared for death ("De weerelt is maer rook met al haer ydelheden,/Een oogenblick, een niet.") [116] was immediately undermined by her brash declaration of her sovereignty to Elizabeth's dukes:

> Ick bezweer u by dien eeuwigh levenden,
> Ontzeght toch nu de nicht van Henderick den Zevenden,
> Elizabeths verwante en maeghschap voor altoos,
> Een boedelhoudtster van gansch Vranckrijck en Valois,
> En dit gezalfde hooft der Schotten niet een bede,
> Een nootbe, van geen Turck, noch Tarter, woest van zede,
> Oit Kristensch mensche ontzeit: [117]

Mary never really attained the sublime other-worldliness of the Jesuit martyrs but rather displayed the proud demeanor of a dishonored queen. Her doctor-confidant Burgon who witnessed the execution described Mary Stuart in worldly terms—full of majesty—even as he noted the parallels between her death and Christ's. [118] For her part, Mary never dispensed with her pride to such an extent that she could convincingly forgive her enemies. As a pious Catholic she prayed that God would bless Elizabeth and that her enemies might live in peace, but when joined to Mary's protestations of innocence and Burgon's subsequent curse of Elizabeth, such sentiments merely appeared to be pious formalities. The soteriological purpose of Christ's death had been obscured by Vondel's reduction of the Passion to a set of Christ-like actions which were intended to legitimize and sanctify a political action. Just as the legen-

---

[115] *WB*, V, p. 230, lines 1594-1595.
[116] *WB*, V, p. 219, lines 1241-1242.
[117] *WB*, V, p. 223, lines 1402-1408.
[118] *WB*, V, pp. 227-31.

dary Ursula was assured salvation because of her exemplary death, so did Mary attain eternal life not through Christ's grace, but through her own *imitatio Christi*.

Vondel's glorification of this Catholic heroine was likely considered excessive by the Protestant Gryphius, but he was not so much disturbed by Mary's religion as by the nature of her martyrdom. To be sure, Gryphius shared Vondel's political objections to the turmoil of the Cromwellian revolution and borrowed the subtitle of *Maria Stuart of Gemartelde Majesteit* for his own play, *Ermordete Majestät oder Carolus Stuardus*. Stichomythic debates in Gryphius on a subject's right to revolution against his king, such as the quarrel between Cromwell and the Scottish ambassador, recalled the argument in Vondel's play between Elizabeth's dukes and Mary's adviser, Melvin.[119] The outcome of such discussions was predictably conservative with each author condemning the persecutors of their heroes as misguided claimants to the rights which belonged to God alone. But Gryphius was not content to confine himself to a political apologia; he took great pains to distinguish between Charles' royal and private person so that the ruler's relationship to God, to whom he owed his throne, could be explored from both a political and theological perspective.

From the moment he first appeared on the stage, Charles maintained his innocence of the crimes which his enemies leveled against him. Confident in the righteousness of his claim to the throne, he comforted himself by comparing his own plight to the Pharisees' persecution of Christ. Like Christ in Gethsemane, Charles willingly accepted the hardships which God assigned to his "nicht unschuldig Blut"[120] and forgave his enemies for their blindness to the inviolability of his majesty. At the same time, he gained additional strength from his belief that God's justice would ultimately prevail. He condemned the self-seeking ambition of the Parliamentarians which prevented them from perceiving that a king's true duty lay in his preservation of the state. In the edition published after the Restoration, Gryphius intensified his portrait of Charles as an advocate of peace still further by allowing him to prophesy the destruction of the Cromwellians whose reign was based on war and sacrilege rather than civil harmony. Charles rejected offers of military assistance from the Continent where his son and wife were plotting to regain their former status lest the chaos which Cromwell unleashed lead to further bloodshed. In short, Charles typified the ideal Christian prince that

---

[119] Cf. *WB*, V, pp. 201-10, lines 903-1066, and *Trauerspiele I,* pp. 109-12, Act. III, lines 665-784.

[120] *Trauerspiele I,* p. 81, Act II, line 258.

Erasmus had envisioned in his *Institutio principis christiani* (1515).[121] Troubled by the preservation of the commonweal, Charles displayed contempt for the hollow significance of the pomp and power which he held by right and which his enemies tirelessly sought to usurp. Where Charles evinced his virtue and wisdom by his exemplary forbearance of injustice, the Parliamentarians intended to rule by instilling fear in the populace. Cromwell demanded Charles' immediate execution in the hope that further political agitation would abet his ambition; similarly, Hugo Peter, the fanatical leader of the Independants, advocated a reign of terror against the aristocrats and the bishops so as to bring about his personal dream of a classless society. In contrast, Charles patterned his rule after Christ: he entrusted the punishment of his enemies to God, forgave them and, as a martyred king, relied on Christ for salvation.

Gryphius panegyric of this Christian king was, however, tempered by his realization that the ideal prince and the real prince were two different characters. This insight was not based on any historical evaluation of Charles' actions but on Gryphius' emphasis on the fundamental sinfulness of man. Gryphius dispensed with Vondel's naive notion that the sanctity of political office could preserve a ruler from sin. On the contrary, Charles' political actions in *Carolus Stuardus* were portrayed as morally reprehensible because they compromised justice for the sake of *raison d'état*. To be sure, the sanctity of his office preserved him from censure from his subjects, but not from God. Because of the inviolability of kingship, Charles was immune to the charges of tyranny and injustice which Cromwell directed against him. Charles could, however, be held accountable before God for both his misrule and his sins. The illegality of the Parliamentarians' revolt was not so much based on Charles' innocence, but on the idea that God, not man, was empowered to punish a ruler for his crimes. To emphasize this dual concept of the king as both majesty and man, Gryphius attributed a political crime to his protagonist. In a vain effort to appease the shiftless will of the people, Charles had ordered the unjust execution of two of his advisers, Thomas Wentworth, Earl of Strafford and Archbishop Laud. Charles himself had been reluctant to accede to the demands of the populace, but political expediency had impelled him to act wrongly. In defending the sanctity of the monarchy, Gryphius exposed the fallibility of all men and thereby established the basis for his subsequent revelation of the theological significance of Charles' death.

---

[121] Charles possessed all the virtues which Erasmus hoped that his ideal prince, the young Charles V, would acquire: "Si te voles excellentem Principem ostendere, vides ne quis te propriis superet bonis, sapientia, animi magnitudine, temperantia, integritate." Erasmus, *Ausgewählte Werke,* vol. 5, p. 136.

Charles' complicity in the execution of Wentworth and Laud has frequently been overshadowed by his protestations of innocence throughout the play. But Charles "nicht unschuldig Blut" referred to the falsity of the accusations of the Parliamentarians rather than to his former deeds as ruler. In his final hours, Charles was plagued by his earlier surrender to the will of the people and even to Wentworth's pleas that his death would mend the rift between the king and the Puritans. Indeed, Charles now believed that the "arge That"[122] itself resulted in his own dethronement: "Sein Vnschuld hat den Plitz auff unser Haubt erreget."[123] Only the blood of the sacrificed Christ would suffice to absolve Charles from the heinous betrayal of friendship and loyalty: "Er wird von disem Blut uns durch sein Blut befreyen."[124] But Charles' simplistic conception of the reasons for his present dilemma fell far short of its significance in Gryphius' play. Despite Charles' assertions to the contrary, the responsibility for the martyrdom of Wentworth could not be ascribed to a single person. Rather, the executions of both Wentworth and Laud reflected Gryphius' pessimistic notion of all political events. As an Erasmian prince, Charles most certainly erred by acceding to the demands of the populace whose ignorance and changeability could reduce a weakly governed state to anarchy.[125] On the other hand, the ideal king was obliged to maintain peace and harmony within the state. Since the rival religious factions could only be appeased by Wentworth's death, Charles acted in the desperate hope that innocent blood would silence the mob. Wentworth himself had had to convince Charles that the situation necessitated his death, and his ghost appeared early in the play to exculpate the king.

> Doch klag ich werther Printz nicht über deine Treue
> Du libtest biss an End'/und trugest keine Scheue
> Zu reden vor mein Heil. Was hast du nicht versucht
> Zu retten disen Kopff? und gleichwol sonder Frucht.[126]

If any party were guilty of Wentworth's death, it would have been the rabble, but their blind instinctual behavior suggested that they were the instruments rather than the instigators of this shameful deed. Gryphius was not so much obsessed with the assignation of guilt as he was with the illustration of the fallibility of all human actions, especially those which were blasphemously justified by religion. The question of Charles' guilt

---

[122] *Trauerspiele I,* p. 116, Act IV, line 72.

[123] *Trauerspiele I,* p. 116, Act IV, line 62.

[124] *Trauerspiele I,* p. 116, Act IV, line 74.

[125] "At boni Principis partes sunt, nihil horum mirari, quae vulgus hominum magni facit, sed omnia veris malis, ac veris boni metiri." Erasmus, *Ausgewählte Werke,* vol. 5, p. 130.

[126] *Trauerspiele I,* p. 75, Act II, lines 45-48.

was ultimately not as important as Charles' recognition of his limitations as king, his sinfulness as a man and his need for Christ's mercy for salvation.

Gryphius' introduction of Charles' troubled conscience into the play was motivated by literary, political and, most importantly, theological reasons. In the first instance, Gryphius' critical transformation of Vondel's *Maria Stuart* led him to create a tragic protagonist who would correspond more closely to the Aristotelian concept of the hero than the guiltless Mary. Secondly, Gryphius rejected Vondel's naive confidence in the political world by demonstrating that all political actions were inevitably flawed. To this end, Gryphius established the irreconcilability of *raison d'état* and private morality through Charles' recognition of the injustice of his actions against Wentworth and Laud. His willingness to commit a morally reprehensible yet politically justifiable act betrayed Charles' overconfidence in the power of his office. Through his subsequent fall from grace, Charles perceived the limitations of the shiftless political world whose utilitarian ethic had driven him to injustice and sin. In sacrificing two innocent men, Charles abused the divinity of his office and, consequently, by his own admission, deserved a just punishment from God.

But Gryphius was not content merely to expose the mutability of the political world. The endless cycle of crime and retribution, indeed the inevitability of change itself, assumed a Christian allegorical significance within the postfigurative context of the tragedy. Charles' inability to act in a consistently righteous manner suggested the fundamental fallibility of all men. His political identity and his blind trust in the validity of political solutions became a metaphor for original sin and man's inability to overcome it. The allegorical significance of Charles' crimes was heightened even further by his acknowledgment that only Christ's blood could free him from these sins: "Er wird von disem Blut uns durch sein Blut befreyen."[127] Through the death of Charles, Gryphius was thus able to suggest three main events in man's salvation history: the Fall, the Redemption and the Last Judgment. Charles' sinfulness represented the fallen state of man, his bloody martyrdom recalled Christ's liberation of man from sin, and the punishment of the Parliamentarians predicted by the final vengeful chorus anticipated the Last Judgment, the final triumph of Christ and his faithful over all sinners. As in *Leo Armenius* and *Catharina von Georgien*, Gryphius conceived of the moment of martyrdom not as a single glorious act of heroism but as a signature for salvation

---

[127] *Trauerspiele I*, p. 116, Act IV, line 74.

history in which the sinful burden of man's finite existence was alleviated by the blood of Christ with whom man would then be joined forever.[128]

By revealing the significance of the Redemption, Gryphius' historical dramas paradoxically exposed the intrinsic valuelessness of the temporal events they purported to portray. The basic assimulation of religious and social goals which underlay the pedagogical effectiveness of humanist drama was now transformed by Gryphius' emphasis on man's fundamental depravity. Original sin could no longer be explained away as a character flaw easily controlled by an exemplary moral education. Such optimism was completely foreign to Gryphius' dramas where even the paragons of virtue—Catharina and Charles—were exposed as helpless sinners. Conversely, social behavior could no longer be construed as a valid gauge of morality, for as long as man remained in the world he would inevitably err. History itself was consequently flawed, for it chronicled the unceasing attempts by man to secure a secular aim. Should man fail to perceive the worthlessness of this pursuit, his own salvation would be imperilled. By examining man's soul in light of his social actions, Gryphius thus broadened the gap between God and man which the humanists had attempted to bridge through moral education.

In contrast to the religious plays of the previous century, whose ethical and social concerns he shared, Gryphius chiefly ascribed a soteriological purpose to his historical tragedies. Poetry no longer fulfilled an exclusively moral end, but, most importantly, a sacred function as well. The three historical plays served equally as historical representations of actual events and as typological postfigurations of Christ's suffering and Redemption of fallen man. The angry, just God of the Old Testament still existed to condemn tyrants to hell and to incite man to acknowledge his own depravity. But the martyrdoms of Leo Armenius, Catharina von Georgien and Carolus Stuardus each exemplified Christ's promise of salvation through the forgiveness of sins. History no longer functioned exclusively as a chronicle of truth nor did poetry merely appear to be utilitarian ornament. Rather, Gryphius' historical dramas now served as a metaphor for the Bible itself because of their depiction of the triumph of Christ over the Law and of grace over sin. In Gryphius' hands, the moralistic dramas of the humanists, the Jesuits and the Catholic Vondel, were transformed into a sacred book whose study preserved man from the otherwise meaningless cycle of secular history.

---

[128] Cf. K.-H. Habersetzer's analysis of the historical sources in which Charles is portrayed as a Christ-figure; he does not however discuss Charles' guilt: *Politische Typologie und historisches Exemplum*, Stuttgart: Metzler, 1985, pp. 15-42.

## CONCLUSION

The preceding study has argued for the significance of humanist religious drama and the interpretive advantage of analyzing Baroque Christian theater in light of its Renaissance antecedents. To demonstrate these points, I have sought to establish an intellectual context for the understanding of sixteenth-century religious drama so that these texts would no longer be dismissed as uninteresting, didactic exercises of pious schoolmen, but viewed as the products of Christian humanists attuned to the main literary and theological currents of the late Renaissance. I have also attempted to clarify the often contradictory relationship between the author's literary and pedagogical objectives and his own theological beliefs. Where earlier criticism examined sixteenth-century religious theater by providing thematic or historical accounts with little regard for its literary-historical role, the present study has suggested that the Christian theater of Vondel and Gryphius can best be assessed through an investigation of its relationship to the past.

One of the chief preoccupations of religious dramatists had been the imitation of Graeco-Roman theater. Writers in both centuries had adopted a critical approach to the ancients and conceived of their religious plays as ethical improvements of a specific classical model. As a consequence, these playwrights were placed in the difficult position of defending the imitation of a classical text which they also wished to reform. This practice resulted in the paradoxical situation where the dramatists directed the viewers' attention to the immorality of the model which they simultaneously claimed to have banished from the stage. As long as morality was used as a criterion for the correct imitation of the ancients, religious playwrights were unable to achieve the ideal synthesis they sought between classical theater and Christianity. With the adoption of Aristotle's *Poetics* as an aesthetic norm in the 1620s and 1630s, however, the Christian imitation of the classics was no longer dependent on the moral reform of the model but on the adherence to specific poetological rules. Formal precepts regarding peripeteia, tragic recognition and, more importantly, mixed characterizations and catharsis were easily adapted by Vondel and Gryphius to underscore the theological purpose of their tragedies. Although their concept of catharsis as liberation from sin differed from Aristotle's original notion of emotional purgation, the christianization of his ideas rather than of a particular classical text freed seventeenth-century writers from the contradictory praxis of earlier humanists. In Baroque tragedy, the disharmony between sixteenth-century views on imitation and reform was resolved as Vondel and Gryphius developed a neo-classical form for Christian theater to equal, if not surpass, the achievements of the ancients.

Where moral scruples had complicated the sixteenth-century writers' imitation of classical theater, the didactic goals of these same religious dramatists frequently overshadowed the theological significance of their works. All humanist religious drama had been written for a soteriological purpose; the playwrights were equally eager to illustrate God's salvation of man and to propose an ethical course of action for man to follow to gain eternal life. Since the dramatists were primarily motivated by pedagogical concerns, they often simplified the act of salvation by implying that man's upright conduct rather than the grace of God earned him an eternal reward. Had the dramatists proclaimed that salvation was primarily contingent on grace, they would have deprived their young audiences of the incentive they doubtlessly needed to obey the commandments of God. The reduction of theological doctrine to practical ethics was absolutely essential for the indoctrination of Protestant and Catholic youth. Because of the distinctions between the teachings of the two churches on salvation, Catholic and Protestant schoolmen dealt with the incongruity between theology and morality with varying degrees of success. Catholic writers for whom salvation depended on the interaction between grace and free will were consequently more readily able to demonstrate that man's behavior would prepare him to receive God's grace. Indeed, with the reaffirmation of the *ecclesia militans* of the Counter-Reformation, Catholic dramatists promised salvation through compliance with the ecclesiastical rules of Rome. In contrast, Protestant playwrights could not easily reconcile Luther's belief in man's natural inclination for evil with their educational aspirations. Since fallen man could never act righteously in the eyes of God, he could not be saved through the merit of his moral actions. In the interest of education, however, Protestant dramatists overlooked the obvious contradiction between theology and morality and permitted their didactic lessons to predominate.

Vondel and Gryphius shared the earlier humanists' attitude about the moral function of sacred theater, but in contrast to their predecessors, they subordinated ethical instruction to theology. Both dramatists focused on the tragedy of man's fallen state and the seemingly unbridgeable gap between man and his Creator; at the same time, they allowed their audiences glimpses of the merciful grace of God through which righteous Christians would one day be saved. Instead of portraying the actual process of salvation, they concentrated on man's tormented existence between the Fall and the Last Judgment. Most of

Vondel's tragic heroes (especially after 1645) had already sinned once—as Adam had done in the Garden of Eden—and were now granted one last opportunity to choose between damnation and forgiveness. Gryphius' protagonists were flawed by both original sin and their fatal involvement in the unstable political world and likewise awaited salvation from God's hand. Man's role in receiving this grace varied according to the respective confessions of the writers. Where the Catholic Vondel permitted his protagonists to decide between good and evil and thereby determine their spiritual fate, Gryphius' heroes could only be preserved by their faith and through their passive submission to God's will. Since Gryphius exposed the falsity of the secular world and the limitations of all human endeavors, he was able to resolve the sixteenth-century paradox between theology and education. Gryphius may well have been the most Protestant of all religious dramatists, for his reflections on the moral utility of theater were always tempered by his acknowledgment of man's fallen state. In the 1650s and 1660s, Vondel also settled the anomalous relationship in Catholic theater between salvation and ecclesiastical obedience—a view which he had earlier espoused in his partisan dramas of the 1640s—in favor of the theological interpretation of salvation as a divine gift. Morality was still present on the Baroque stage, but the dramatists were dubious about man's ability to act accordingly and thereby prepare for, if not ensure, his eternal salvation.

Two questions naturally arise from these conclusions about the Baroque writers' adaptation of Renaissance dramatic praxis: why did these dramatists display a marked preference for theological rather than ethical issues; and what can this practice contribute to the understanding of Christian tragedy. Each of these problems can be better understood through a brief consideration of the motives which underlay the composition of seventeenth-century sacred drama. As religious poets, Vondel and Gryphius were especially concerned with the consequences of the Fall and salvation, but their piety did not really distinguish them from earlier writers. Rather, I should like to suggest that their particular interest in theology may reflect their disillusionment after the collapse of the humanist ideal of a united Christendom. Since the time of Erasmus, Northern humanists had urged the cessation of internecine warfare among Christian princes, for this practice blatantly clashed with the principles of their faith. Erasmus was disturbed by the imperial ambitions of England, France and the Italian states, especially when these Christian rulers should have united in a holy war against the Turks. Sixt Birck voiced the same fears in the preface to his *Judith* and exhorted Francis I and Charles V, as well as the restless German princes, to end hostilities and emulate his heroine's leadership against the heathens. Similarly,

Hugo Grotius objected to the French religious wars and wrote his *Christus patiens* as a reminder to all Christians of their common belief regardless of their respective allegiances. Vondel composed *Joseph in Dothan* and *Maria Stuart* in reaction to the contemporary strife on the Continent and in England while Gryphius echoed his disapproval by lamenting the folly of the foreign armies who had lately reduced the Holy Roman Empire to ruins. In the face of so much destruction, Vondel and Gryphius had little reason to believe that fallen man could ever lead a Christian existence which accorded with God's commandments. Where earlier humanists had still harbored some hope for man's capacity to reform his condition, Vondel and Gryphius were discouraged by historical circumstances to impute any such ability to the fallen world. In their religious plays, the protagonist's natural sinfulness as Adam's heir was reconfirmed as the dramatists illustrated the disharmony between God and the world which could only be restored by grace.

Baroque Christian tragedy thus arose from the playwrights' insight into the fundamentally tragic nature of human existence. The more fallen man strove for virtue, the more he realized the impossibility of attaining this goal without the assistance of God. In the shadowy, fallen world of Vondel and Gryphius, man was caught between his evil inclinations and the promise of salvation. In Vondel's Old Testament tragedies, the fulfillment of the Redemption lay in the distant future; in Gryphius' historical dramas, Christ's justice and mercy would only become apparent at the Last Judgment. The grace of God was indeed present, but the inability of man to secure this benefit through his own actions confirmed the inescapable tragedy of his corrupted nature. Through their presentation of this central theological issue in neo-classical form, Vondel and Gryphius resolved the problems which confronted earlier playwrights and thereby established their own works as the unrivaled achievements of humanist religious theater.

# BIBLIOGRAPHY

## PRIMARY WORKS

*A. Manuscripts*

The following list contains only those manuscripts which are referred to in the text.
*Acolastus* (1587). Munich. Bayerische Staatsbibliothek, clm. 2202. Fol. 674-719.
*Diarium gymnasii et lycei S. J. Monachii, 1595-1772.* Munich. Bayerische Staatsbibliothek, clm. 1550-1553.
*Drama de Godefrido Bullone* (1596). Munich. Bayerische Staatsbibliothek, clm. 549; clm. 19757$_2$ (fol. 421-553).
*Hester comoedia sacra* (1577). Munich. Bayerische Staatsbibliothek, clm. 524. Fol. 1-157.
*S. Quirinus* (no date). Munich. Bayerische Staatsbibliothek, clm. 24674. Fol. 1-45$^v$.
*De S. Stephano* (no date). Koblenz. Staatsarchiv. Abteilung 117. No. 718.

*B. Dramatic Works*

Aal, Johannes. *Tragoedia Johannis des Täufers.* Ed. Ernst Meyer. Neudrucke deutscher Litteraturwercke des XVI. und XVII. Jahrhunderts, 263-267. Halle (Saale): Max Niemeyer, 1929.
Ackermann, Hans. *Dramen.* Ed. Hugo Holstein. BLVS, 170. Tübingen, 1884.
Anon. *Theophilus* (Munich, 1596). In *Lateinische Ordensdramen des XVI. Jahrhunderts.* Ed. Fidel Rädle. Berlin and New York: Walter de Gruyter, 1979.
Avianus, Ioannes. *Adamus lapsus. Tragoedia nova.* Leipzig: Michael Lantzenberger, 1596.
Balde, Jacob. *Opera poetica omnia. Tomus VI: Dramatica.* Munich: Ioannes Luca Straubius, 1729.
Balticus, Martin. *Adelphopolae sive Josephus.* 1556; Ulm: Ioannes Antonius Ulhardus, 1579.
Bar(p)tholomaeus, Nicholaus. *Christus xylonicus.* 1529; Antwerp: Vidua Martini Caesaris, 1537.
Baxius, Nicasius. *Theophilus.* In his *Poemata.* Antwerp: Hieronymus Verdussus, 1614.
Bidermann, Jacob. *Ludi theatrales (1666).* Ed. Rolf Tarot. 2 vols. Tübingen: Max Niemeyer, 1967.
Bidermann, Jacob. *Cenodoxus.* Ed. and trans. D. G. Dyer. Edinburgh Bilingual Library, 9. Austin: University of Texas, 1974.
Bidermann, Jacob. *Philemon Martyr.* Ed. Max Wehrli. Cologne: Jakob Hegner, 1950.
Binder, Georg. *Acolastus (1535).* In *Schweizerische Schauspiele des sechzehnten Jahrhunderts.* Vol. 1. Ed. Jakob Bächtold. Zürich, 1890, pp. 171-271.
Birck, Sixt. *Sämtliche Dramen.* 2 vols. Ed. Manfred Brauneck. Berlin and New York: Walter de Gruyter, 1969;1976.
Birck, Sixt. *Sapientia Solomonis.* Ed. and trans. E. R. Payne. Yale Studies in English, 89. New Haven: Yale University, 1938.
Brechtus, Levin. *Euripus. Tragoedia Christiana (1549).* In *Lateinische Ordensdramen des XVI. Jahrhunderts.* Ed. Fidel Rädle. Berlin and New York: Walter de Gruyter, 1979.
Brulovius, Casparus. *Moses sive exitus Israelitarum ex Aegypto. Tragico-comoedia sacra.* Strasbourg: Paul Ledertz, 1621.
Buchanan, George. *Poemata quae extant. Éditio postrema.* Amsterdam: Joannes Waesberg and Elizeus Weyerstraet, 1665.
Camerarius, Joachim, trans. *Sophoclis Tragoediae septem unà cum omnibus Graecis scholiis.* Geneva: H. Stephanus, 1568.
Caussin, Nicolaus. *Tragoediae sacrae.* Paris: Nivelliana, 1620.

Chilianus Eques. *Comoedia gloriosae parthenices et martyris Dorotheae agoniam passionemque depingens.* Leipzig: Wolfgang Monacen, 1507.

*Comoediae ac tragoediae ex novo et vetere testamento.* Basel: Nicholaus Brylinger, 1541.

Coornhert, D. V. *De comedies van Coornhert.* Ed. P. van der Meulen. Assen: Van Gorcum, 1945.

Corneille, Pierre. *Théâtre complet.* Vol. 2. Ed. Maurice Rat. Paris: Éditions Garnier, n. d.

Crocus, Cornelius. *Joseph.* 1536; Antwerp: Ioannes Steelsius, 1538.

Crusius, Balthasar. *Exodus. Tragoedia sacra et nova.* Leipzig: Bartholomaeus Voigtus, 1605.

Crusius, Balthasar. *Tobias. Comoedia sacra et nova.* Leipzig: Bartholomaeus Voigtus, 1605.

Crusius, Balthasar. *Paulus naufragus. Tragoedia sacra et nova.* Altenburg, 1609.

*Dramata sacra: comoediae atque tragoediae aliquot e veteri testamento desumptae.* Basel: Ioannes Oporinus, 1547.

Duym, Jacob, *Het moordadich stuck van Balthasar Gerards (1606).* Eds. L. F. A. Serrarens & N. C. H. Wijngaards. Zutphen: W. J. Thieme, n.d.

*Egerer Fronleichnamsspiel.* Ed. Gustav Milchsack. BLVS, 156. Tübingen, 1881.

Erasmus, Desiderius, trans. *Euripidis Hecuba et Iphigenia.* Ed. Jan Hendrik Waszink. In *Opera omnia Des. Erasmi Roterodami.* Vol. I.1. Amsterdam: North Holland, 1969, pp. 193-359.

*Euripides.* 4 vols. Trans. A. S. Way. London: W. Heinemann, 1912-29.

Euripides. *Tragoedia Phoenissae.* Interpretationem addidit H. Grotii et al. Ludovicus Casp. Valckenaer. Leiden, 1802.

Fabricius, Andreas. *Jeroboam rebellans. Tragoedia.* Ingolstadt: Wolfgang Eder, 1585.

Fabricius, Franciscus, trans. *Divi Gregorii Naziazeni theologi, tragoedia Christus patiens.* Antwerp: Ioannes Steelsius, 1550.

Frischlin, Nicodemus. *Deutsche Dichtungen.* Ed. David Friedrich Strauss. BLVS, 41. Stuttgart, 1857.

Garnier, Robert. *Les Juifves.* Ed. Lucien Pinvert. Parjis: Garnier Frères, 1927.

Gart, Thiebolt. *Joseph.* In *Die Schaubühne im Dienste der Reformation.* Vol. 2. Ed. Arnold E. Berger. DLE, Reihe Reformation, 6. 1936; rpt. Darmstadt: Wissenschaftliche Buchgesellschaft, 1967, pp. 4-134.

Gnapheus, Gulielmus. *Acolastus.* Ed. and trans. P. Minderaa. Zwolse drucken en herdrucken, 15. Zwolle: W. E. J. Tjeenk Willink, 1956.

Gnapheus, Gulielmus. *Acolastus.* Ed. and trans. W. E. D. Atkinson. University of Western Ontario Studies in the Humanities, 3. London, Ontario: Humanities Depts. of the University of Western Ontario, 1963.

Greff, Joachim. *Tragedia des Buchs Judith.* Wittenberg: Georg Rhaw, 1536.

Gretser, Jacob. *Udo von Magdeburg.* Ed. Urs Herzog. Quellen und Forschungen, 13. Berlin: Walter de Gruyter, 1970.

Grimald, Nicholas. *Archipropheta. Tragoedia iam recens in lucem edita.* Cologne: Martin Gymnicus, 1548.

Grotius, Hugo. *Sacra in quibus Adamus exul (1601).* In *De dichtwerken van Hugo Grotius. Oorspronkelijke dichtwerken. Eerste deel. A en B.* Ed. B. L. Meulenbroek. Assen: Van Gorcum, 1970-71.

Grotius, Hugo. *Christus patiens (1608).* In *De dichtwerken van Hugo Grotius. Oorspronkelijke dichtwerken. Tweede deel. Pars 5a en B.* Ed. B. L. Meulenbroek. Assen: Van Gorcum, 1978.

Grotius, Hugo. *Tragoedia Sophompaneas.* Amsterdam: Gulielmus Blaeu, 1635.

Gryphius, Andreas. *Carolus Stuardus.* Ed. Hugh Powell. Leicester: Pitman Press, 1955.

Gryphius, Andreas. *Trauerspiele.* 3 vols. Ed. Hugh Powell. Tübingen: Max Niemeyer, 1964-1966.

*Heidelberger Passionsspiel.* Ed. Gustav Milchsack. BLVS, 150. Tübingen, 1880.

Heinsius, Daniel. *Herodes infanticida.* In *Danielis Heinsii Poematum editio nova.* Amsterdam: Ioannes Ianssonius, 1649.

Holonius, Gregorius. *Catharina. Tragoedia de fortissimo S. Catharinae virginis ... certamine.* Antwerp: Ioannes Bellerus. 1556.

Holonius, Gregorius. *Lambertias. Tragoedia de oppressione B. Lamberti.* Antwerp: Ioannes Bellerus, 1556.

Holonius, Gregorius. *Laurentias. Tragoedia de martyrio constantissimi Levitae D. Laurentii.* Antwerp: Ioannes Bellerus, 1556.

Honerdus, Rochus. *Thamara tragoedia.* Leiden: Ioannes Patius, 1611.

Hooft, P. C. *Achilles en Polyxena.* Ed. Th. C. J. van der Heijden. Zutphen: W. J. Thieme, 1972.

Hooft, P. C. *Geeraerdt van Velsen.* Ed. A. J. J. de Witte. Zutphen: W. J. Thieme, 1976.

Hoyerus, Michael. *Tragoediae aliaque poemata.* Antwerp: Hen. Aertssens, 1641.

Hrotsvitha von Gandersheim. *Opera.* Ed. Helene Homeyer. Paderborn: Ferdinand Schöningh, 1970.

Hunnius, Aegidius. *Iosephus. Comoediae duae.* Ed. Eduard Schroeder. Marburg, 1898.

Hunnius, Aegidius. *Ruth. Comoedia nova et sacra.* Ed. Eduard Schroeder. Marburg: R. Friedrich, 1900.

Ischyrius, Christian. *Homulus.* Ed. Alphonse Roersch. Ghent and Antwerp: La librairie néerlandaise, 1903.

Koning, Abraham de. *Iephthahs ende zijn eenighe dochters treur-spel.* Amsterdam: Paulus van Ravesteyn, 1615.

Koning, Abraham de. *Simsons treur-spel.* Amsterdam: Paulus van Ravesteyn, 1618.

*Das Künzelsauer Fronleichnamsspiel.* Ed. Peter K. Liebenow. Berlin: Walter de Gruyter, 1969.

Laurimannus, Cornelius. *Esthera regina. Comoedia sacra.* Louvain: Antonius Bergagne, 1562.

Laurimannus, Cornelius. *Exodus sive transitus maris rubri.* Louvain: Antonius Bergagne, 1562.

Laurimannus, Cornelius. *Miles Christianus. Comoedia sacra.* Antwerp: Gulielmus Silvius, 1565.

Leendertz, Pieter, ed. *Middelnederlandse dramatische poëzie.* Leiden: A. W. Sijthoff, 1907.

Libenus, Jacob. *Tragoediae in sacram historiam Iosephi.* Antwerp: Ioannes Cnobbarus, 1539.

Lorichius, Joannes. *Jobus, patientiae spectaculum in comoediam.* Marburg: Christianus Aegenolphus, 1543.

Lummenaeus à Marca, Jacob Cornelius. *Opera omnia.* Louvain: Phil. Dormalius, 1613.

Lummenaeus à Marca, Jacob Cornelius. *Amnon tragoedia sacra.* Ghent: Cornelius Marius, 1617.

Macropedius, Georgius. *Omnes Georgii Macropedii fabulae comicae.* Utrecht: Harmannus Borculous, 1552-1554.

Macropedius, Georgius. *"Rebelles" und "Aluta."* Ed. Johannes Bolte. Lateinische Litteraturdenkmäler, 13. Berlin, 1897.

Macropedius, Georgius, *Hecastus.* Ed. Johannes Bolte. In his *Drei Schauspiele vom sterbenden Menschen.* BLVS, 269-270. Leipzig: W. Hiersemann, 1927, pp. 63-160.

Moltzer, Henri Ernst, ed. *De Middelnederlandse dramatische poëzie.* Groningen, 1875.

Murer, Jos. *Sämtliche Dramen.* 2 vols. Ed. Hans-Joachim Adomatis et al. Ausgaben deutscher Literatur des XV. bis XVIII. Jahrhunderts, Reihe Drama IV. Berlin and New York: Walter de Gruyter, 1974.

Naogeorgus, Thomas. *Sämtliche Werke.* Vol. 1. *Dramen I Pammachius.* Ed. Hans-Gert Roloff. Berlin and New York: Walter de Gruyter, 1975.

Naogeorgus, Thomas. *Hamanus. Tragoedia nova.* Leipzig: Michael Blum, 1543.

Naogeorgus, Thomas. *Hieremias. Tragoedia nova.* Basel, 1551.

Naogeorgus, Thomas. *Iudas Iscariotes. Tragoedia nova et sacra. Adiunctae sunt quoque duae Sophoclis tragoediae Aiax flagellifer et Philoctetes.* N.p., 1552.

Neukirch, Melchior. *Stephanus. Ein schöne geistliche Tragedia von dem ersten Merterer.* Magdeburg: Johan Francken, 1592.

Nieuwelandt, Guilliam van. *Ierusalems verwoestingh door Nabuchodonosor, treur-spel.* Amsterdam: Anthony Iacobzoon, 1635.

Nieuwelandt, Guilliam van. *Saul tragoedie.* Antwerp: Guilliam van Tongheren, 1617.

*Noordnederlandse rederijkersspelen.* Ed. N. van der Laan. Amsterdam: N.V. Uitgevers-Mij. "Elsevier," 1941.

Papeus, Petrus. *Samarites. Comoedia de Samaritano evangelico.* Antwerp: G. Montanus, 1539.

Philicinus, Petrus. *Dialogus de Isaaci immolatione ad puerilem captum accomodatus.* 1544; Antwerp: Ioannes Steelsius, 1546.

Placentius, Joannes. *Susanna.* 1532; Antwerp: Willem Vorstermann, 1536.

Plautus. *Comoediae.* 2 vols. Ed. W. M. Lindsay. Oxford: Clarendon, 1904, rpt. 1968.

Pontanus, Jacob. *Eleazarus Machabaeus.* In his *Poeticarum institutionum libri III (1594).* Editio tertia. Ingolstadt: Adam Sartorius, 1600, pp. 507-56.

Rebhun, Paul. *Dramen.* Ed. Hermann Palm. BLVS, 49. Stuttgart, 1859.

Rebhun, Paul. *Ein Geistlich Spiel von der Gotfürchtigen und keuschen Frauen Susannen (1536).* Ed. Hans-Gert Roloff. Stuttgart: Reclam, 1967.

Rhodius, Theodorus. *Dramata sacra in quibus tragoediae VIII et II comoediae.* Strasbourg: P. Ledertz, 1625.

Rinckhart, Martin. *Der eislebische christliche Ritter (1613).* Ed. Dr. Carl Müller. Neudrucke deutscher Litteraturwerke des XVI. und XVII. Jahrhunderts, 53-54. Halle (Saale): Max Niemeyer, 1883.

Rollenhagen, Georg. *Spiel vom reichen Manne und armen Lazaro (1590).* Ed. Johannes Bolte. Neudrucke deutscher Literaturwerke des XVI. und XVII. Jahrhunderts, 270-273. Halle (Saale): Max Niemeyer, 1929.

Rollenhagen, Georg. *Spiel von Tobias (1576).* Ed. Johannes Bolte. Neudrucke deutscher Literaturwerke des XVI. und XVII. Jahrhunderts, 285-287. Halle (Saale): Max Niemeyer, 1930.

Rotrou, Jean. *Le Véritable Saint Genest.* In *Théâtre du XVIIe siècle.* Ed. Jacques Scherer. Paris: Gallinard, 1975.

Roulerius, Adrianus. *Stuarta tragoedia.* Ed. Roman Woerner. Lateinische Litteraturdenkmäler des XV. und XVI. Jahrhunderts, 17. Berlin: Weidmann, 1906.

Sachs, Hans. *Werke.* Ed. Adalbert von Keller. Vols. 10-11. BLVS 131; 136. Tübingen, 1876; 1878.

Sachse, Michael. *Stephanus. Eine schöne Tragedia.* Weissenfels: Georgius Hantzsch, 1565.

Sapidus, Joannes. *Anabion sive Lazarus redivivus. Comoedia nova et sacra.* 1539; Cologne: Ioannes Gymnicus, 1541.

Saurius, Andreas. *Conflagratio Sodomae. Drama novum tragicum.* Strasbourg: Conradus Scher, 1607.

Schoepper, Jacob. *Ectrachelistis sive decollatus Ioannes.* 1546; Cologne: Maternus Cholinus, 1562.

Schoepper, Jacob. *Monomachia Davidis et Goliae.* Dortmund: Melchior Soter, 1550.

Schoepper, Jacob. *Tentatus Abrahamus. Actio sacra comice recens descripta.* 1552; Cologne: Petrus Horst, 1564.

Schoepper, Jacob. *Ovis perdita. Parabola evangelica descripta comice.* 1553; Cologne: Maternus Cholinus, 1562.

Schonaeus, Cornelius. *Terentius Christianus seu comoediae sacrae tribus partibus distinctae.* 1592; 1599; 1602-3. Amsterdam: Laurentius, 1646.

*Selectae PP. Societatis Jesu tragoediae.* 2 vols. Antwerp: Ioannes Cnobbarus, 1634.

*L. Annei Senecae Tragoediae pristinae integritati restitutae per exactissimi judicii viros.* Paris: Badius, 1514.

Seneca. *Tragedies.* 2 vols. Trans. Frank Justus Miller. 1917; rpt. Cambridge: Harvard, 1968.

Simons, Joseph. *Tragoediae quinque.* Liège: Ioannes Mathias Hovius, 1656.

*Sophocles.* 2 vols. Trans. F. Storr. London: W. Heinemann, 1924-1928.

Spangenberg, Wolfhart. *Saul (1606).* In *Sämtliche Werke.* Vol. 2. Ed. András Vizkelety. Berlin and New York: Walter de Gruyter, 1975.

Stoa, Quintianus. *Christiana opera.* Paris, n.d.

Stymmelius, Christopherus. *Isaac immolandus.* Magdeburg: Joachim Boëlius, 1579.

Taille, Jean de la. *Saül le furieux. La Famine, ou les Gabéonites.* Ed. Elliot Forsyth. Paris: Marcel Didier, 1968.

Terence. *Comoediae.* Ed. N. E. Lemaire. Paris, 1827.

Thamme, Balthasar. *Tragicomoedia. Ein schön Christliches Spiel/von der Gottseligen züchtigen Jungfrawen Dorothea.* Leipzig: Abraham Lamberg, 1595.

Tonnis, Jan. *Iosephs droef ende bly-eynd'-spel.* Groningen: A. Eissens, 1639.

Tuilier, André, ed. *Grégoire de Nazianze. La Passion du Christ. Tragédie.* Sources Chrétiennes, 149. Paris: Les Éditions du Cerf, 1969.

Vernulaeus, Nicolaus. *Tragoediae decem.* Editio secunda. Louvain: Petrus Sassenus and Hieronymus Nempaeus, 1656.

Vernulaeus, Nicolaus. *Henry VIII.* Ed. Louis A. Schuster, S. M. Austin: University of Texas, 1964.

[Victorijn, Ioan.] *Goliath treurspel.* Ed. P. Minderaa. Leiden: Brill, 1963.

Virdungus, Michael. *Iuvenalia ... Tragoedias: Saul et Brutum* Nuremberg: Paulus Kaufmann, 1598.

Vivarius, Jacob. *Redemptio nostra. Comoedia nova.* Antwerp: Antonius Tilenius Brechtanus, 1579.

Voith, Valten. *Dramen.* Ed. Hugo Holstein. BLVS, 170. Tübingen, 1884.

Vondel, Joost van den. *De Werken.* Ed. J. V. M. Sterck, et al. 10 vols. Amsterdam: Wereldbibliotheek, 1927-1937.

Waldis, Burkard. *De parabell vam verlorn Szohn.* In *Die Schaubühne im Dienste der Reformation.* Vol. 1. Ed. Arnold E. Berger. DLE, Reihe Reformation, 5. 1936; rpt. Darmstadt: Wissenschaftliche Buchgesellschaft, 1967, pp. 114-220.

Walther, Daniel. *Eyne Christliche und jnn heiliger Schrifft gegründte Historia/von der entheuptung Johannis Baptistae/in ein Tragediam gestalt.* Erfurt: Georg Bawmann, 1559.

Weise, Christian. *Sämtliche Werke. Biblische Dramen.* Vols. 4, 5, 8. Ed. John D. Lindberg. Berlin: Walter de Gruyter, 1973; 1973; 1976.

Wickram, Jörg. *Tobias.* In *Sämtliche Werke.* Vol. 11. Ed. Hans-Gert Roloff. Berlin: Walter de Gruyter, 1971.

Wickram, Jörg. *Apostelspiel.* In *Sämtliche Werke.* Vol. 12. Ed. Hans-Gert Roloff. Berlin: Walter de Gruyter, 1968.

Zahn, Zacharius. *Tragoedia lapidati Stephani.* Mühlhausen: Andreas Hantzsch, 1589.

Ziegler, Hieronymus. *Cyrus Maior. Drama tragicum.* Augsburg: Philippus Ulhardus, 1547.

Ziegler, Hieronymus. *Christi vinea.* Basel: Ioannes Oporinus, 1551.

Ziegler, Hieronymus. *Ophiletes.* 1549; Basel: Ioannes Oporinus, 1551.

Ziegler, Hieronymus. *Regales nuptiae.* Augsburg: Philippus Ulhardus, 1553.

Ziegler, Hieronymus. *Abel iustus. Tragoedia.* Ingolstadt: Alexander and Samuel Weissenhornius, 1559.

## C. *Non-dramatic works*

Ambrose. *Hexaemeron.* In his *Opera omnia.* Vol. 1. Ed. J.-P. Migne. PL, 14. Paris, 1882.

Aquinas, St. Thomas. *Summa theologica.* In his *Opera omnia.* 2nd ed. New York: Musurgia, 1948-50.

Aristotle. *Poetics.* Trans. Leon Golden. Ed. O. B. Hardison, Jr. Englewood Cliffs, N. J.: Prentice Hall, 1968.

Augustine. *Confessions.* Ed. and trans. W. Watts. 2 vols. London: W. Heinemann, 1912.

Augustine. *De doctrina christiana.* In his *Opera omnia.* Vol. 3, part 1. Paris, 1836, cols. 13-151.

Baronius, Caesar. *Sacrum martyrologium Romanum.* Cologne: Joannes Gymnicus, 1610.

Baronius, Caesar. *Annales ecclesiastici.* 21 vols. Antwerp: Plantin, 1611-77.

Basil of Caesarea, St. "Address to Young Men on Reading Greek Literature." In *St. Basil's Letters.* Vol. 4. Trans. Roy Joseph Deferrari and Martin R. P. McGuire. Cambridge: Harvard University, 1934, pp. 365-435.

Bebel, Heinrich. *Opusculum de institutione puerorum.* Strasbourg: Schürer, 1513.

Bible. *The New Oxford Annotated Bible with Apocrypha.* Eds. Herbert G. May and Bruce M. Metzger. New York: Oxford University, 1977.

Bruni, Leonardo. *De studiis et litteris.* In *Leonardo Bruni Aretino. Humanistisch-philosophische Schriften.* Ed. Hans Baron. Leipzig: Teubner, 1928.

Busche, Hermann von dem. *Vallum humanitatis.* Cologne: Nic. Caesar, 1518.

Castelvetro, Lodovico. *Poetica d'Aristotele vulgarizzata et sposta.* 1570; rpt. Munich: Fink, 1967.

Celtes, Conradus. *Opera Hrosvite illustris virginis et monialis Germane gente Saxonica orte nuper a Conrade Celte inventa.* N.p. [1501].

Cicero. *De oratore.* 2 vols. Trans. E. W. Sutton. 5th ed. 1942; rpt. Cambridge: Harvard, 1976-77.

Crespin, Jean. *Histoire des martyrs (1619).* 3 vols. Ed. Daniel Benoit. Toulouse, 1885.

Crusius, Balthasar. *De dramatibus.* Altenburg, 1609.

Donatus, Aelius. *Commentum Terenti.* 3 vols. Ed. Paulus Wessner. Stuttgart: Teubner, 1962-3.

Erasmus, Desiderius. *Opera omnia Des. Erasmi Roterodami.* Ed. Jean LeClerc. 10 vols. Leiden, 1703-06.

Erasmus von Rotterdam. *Ausgewählte Schriften.* 8 vols. Ed. and trans. Werner Welzig. Darmstadt: Wissenschaftliche Buchgesellschaft, 1968-80.

Erasmus, Desiderius. *Antibarbarorum liber.* Ed. Kazimierz Kumaniecki. In *Opera omnia Des. Erasmi Roterodami.* Vol. I.1. Amsterdam: North Holland, 1969, pp. 1-138.

Erasmus, Desiderius. *Declamatio de pueris statim ac liberaliter instituendis.* Ed. and trans. Jean-Claude Margolin. Geneva: Droz, 1966.

Foxe, John. *The Acts and Monuments of the Church.* London, 1563.

Gallonius, Antonius. *De ss. martyrum cruciatibus.* Rome, 1594.

Horace. *Satires, Epistles and Ars Poetica.* Trans. H. Rushton Fairclough. 1926; rpt. Cambridge: Harvard, 1970.

Hegendorphinus, Christopher. *De instituenda vita et moribus corrigendis iuventutis.* Paris: Chr. Wechel, 1529.

Hegendorphinus, Christopher. *Christiana studiosae iuventutis institutio.* 1526; Paris: Rob. Stephanus, 1545.

Heinsius, Daniel. *De tragoediae constitutione liber.* Leiden: Elsevier, 1643.

Josephus, Flavius. *The Jewish Antiquities.* Trans. Louis H. Feldman. 9 vols. Cambridge: Harvard University Press, 1965.

Lipomanus, Aloysius. *De vitis sanctorum.* Pars prima et secunda. Louvain: Petrus Zangrius, 1565.

Lipsius, Justus. *Von der Bestendigkeit. De Constantia.* Ed. Leonard Forster. Stuttgart: Metzler, 1965.

Luther, Martin. *D. Martin Luthers Werke. Kritische Gesamtausgabe.* 61 vols. Weimar: Hermann Böhlaus Nachfolger, 1883-1983.

Luther, Martin. *D. Werke: Tischreden.* 6 vols. Weimar: Hermann Böhlaus Nachfolger, 1912-21.

Luther, Martin. *Luthers Werke in Auswahl.* Ed. Otto Clemen. 8 vols. Berlin: Walter de Gruyter, 1966.

Luther, Martin. *Die gantze Heilige Schrifft Deudsch. Wittenberg 1545.* Eds. Hans Volz and Heinz Blanke. 2 vols. Munich: Rogner and Bernhard, 1972.

Luther, Martin. *Lectures on Genesis, Chapters 1-5.* In his *Works.* Vol. 1. Ed. Jaroslav Pelikan. St. Louis: Concordia, 1958.

Melanchthon, Philip. *Philippi Melanthonis Opera quae supersunt omnia.* Ed. Carolus Gottlieb Bretschneider. 28 vols. Halle (Saale), 1834-1860.

Minturno, Antonio Sebastiano. *De poeta (1559).* Ed. Bernhard Fabian. Munich: Fink, 1970.

Opitz, Martin. *Weltliche Poemata, 1644.* Eds. Erich Trunz and Christine Eisner. Deutsche Neudrucke, 2 . Tübingen: Niemeyer, 1967.

Opitz, Martin. *Buch von der deutschen Poeterey (1624).* Ed. Cornelius Sommer. Stuttgart: Reclam, 1970.

Plutarch. "De liberis educandis." In his *Moralia.* Trans. Frank Cole Babbitt. London: William Heinemann, 1927.

Pontanus, Jacob. *Poeticarum institutionum libri III (1594)*. Editio tertia. Ingolstadt: Adam Sartorius, 1600.

Quintilian. *Institutionis oratoriae libri XII.* 2 vols. Ed. and trans. Helmut Rahn. Darmstadt: Wissenschaftliche Buchgesellschaft, 1972.

Robortellus, Franciscus. *In librum Aristotelis de arte poetica explicationes.* Florence: L. Torrentinus, 1548.

Scaliger, Julius Caesar. *Poetices libri septem.* Ed. August Buck. Faksimile-Neudruck der Ausgabe von Lyon 1561. Stuttgart and Bad Cannstatt: Frommann, 1964.

Surius, Laurentius. *Historiae seu vitae sanctorum iuxta optimam Coloniensem editionem.* 7 vols. Cologne, 1570-81; rpt. 13 vols. Turin, 1875-80.

Vives, Ludovicus. *De tradendis disciplinis.* In his *Opera omnia.* Vol. 6. Valencia: Montfort, 1782.

Vives, Juan Luis (Ludovicus). *On Education.* Ed. and trans. Foster Watson. 1913; rpt. Totowa, N. J.: Rowman and Littlefield, 1971.

Voragine, Jacobus de. *Legenda aurea.* Ed. Th. Graesse. Dresden and Leipzig, 1846.

Vossius, Gerardus. *Poeticarum institutionum libri tres.* Amsterdam: Elzevier, 1647.

Wimpheling, Jakob. *Adolescentia.* Ed. Otto Herding. Munich: Fink, 1965.

Wimpheling, Jakob. *Pädagogische Schriften.* Ed. and trans. Joseph Freundgen. Paderborn, 1898.

## SECONDARY WORKS

A complete listing of all critical literature consulted would have been exhaustive. The following list is therefore confined to works which were especially significant for the development of the present study.

Abbé, Derek van. *Drama in Renaissance Germany and Switzerland.* Melbourne: University Press, 1961.

Aerde, Raymond van. *Het schooldrama bij de Jezuieten, bijdrage tot de geschiedenis van het tooneel te Mechelen.* Mechelen: H. Dierickx-Beke, 1937.

Aikin, Judith P. *German Baroque Drama.* Boston: Twayne, 1982.

Alexander, Robert J. *Das deutsche Barockdrama.* Stuttgart: Metzler, 1984.

Alewyn, Richard. *Vorbarocker Klassizismus und griechische Tragödie.* 1926; rpt. Darmstadt: Wissenschaftliche Buchgesellschaft, 1962.

Althaus, Paul. *The Theology of Martin Luther.* Trans. Robert C. Schultz. Philadelphia: Fortress, 1966.

Antonissen, Robert. "Over Vondels *Joseph in Dothan.*" In *European Context: Studies in the History and Literature of the Netherlands.* Eds. P. K. King and P. F. Vincent. Cambridge: Modern Humanities Research Association, 1971, pp. 132-50.

Arnold, Robert F. *Das deutsche Drama.* Munich: Beck, 1925.

Aschbach, Joseph. *Roswitha und Conrad Celtes.* Vienna, 1868.

Asheim, Ivar. *Glaube und Erziehung bei Luther.* Heidelberg: Quelle und Meyer, 1961.

Asselbergs, Willem J. M. A. *Pascha problemen.* Hilversum: P. Brand, 1940.

Backer, Augustin de, Aloys de Backer, A. Carayon. *Bibliothèque de la compagnie de Jésus. Bibliographie.* Ed. C. Sommervogel. Brussels, 1891.

Bacon, Thomas I. *Martin Luther and the Drama.* Amsterdam: Rodopi, 1976.

Baechtold, Jakob. *Geschichte der deutschen Literatur in der Schweiz.* Frauenfeld, 1892.

Bahlmann, Paul. *Die lateinischen Dramen von Wimphelings Stylpho bis zur Mitte des sechzehnten Jahrhunderts, 1480-1550.* Münster, 1893.

Bahlmann, Paul. "Jesuitendramen der niederrheinischen Ordensprovinz." *Centralblatt für Bibliothekswesen,* 15. Beiheft, 1898.

Baltzer, Otto. *Judith in der deutschen Literatur.* Stoff- und Motivgeschichte der deutschen Literatur, 7. Berlin: Walter de Gruyter, 1930.

Barner, Wilfried. "Gryphius und die Macht der Rede. Zum ersten Reyen des Trauerspiels *Leo Armenius.*" *DVLG,* 42 (1968), 325-58.

Barner, Wilfried. *Barockrhetorik. Untersuchungen zu ihren geschichtlichen Grundlagen.* Tübingen: Max Niemeyer, 1970.

Beck, Hugo. *Das genrehafte Element im deutschen Drama des XVI. Jahrhunderts.* Germanische Studien, 66. Berlin: Emil Ebering, 1929.

Beck, Hugo. "Die Bedeutung des Genrebegriffs für das deutsche Drama des 16. Jahrhunderts." *DVLG,* 8 (1930), 82-108.

Becker, Hubert. "Die geistige Entwicklungsgeschichte des Jesuitendramas." *DVLG,* 19 (1941), 269-310.

Becker-Cantarino, Bärbel. *Daniel Heinsius.* Boston: Twayne, 1978.

Beetz, Manfred. "Disputatorik und Argumentation in Andreas Gryphius' Trauerspiel *Leo Armenius."* *Zeitschrift für Literaturwissenschaft und Linguistik,* 38-39 (1980), 178-203.

Benjamin, Walter. *Ursprung des deutschen Trauerspiels.* Frankfurt: Suhrkamp, 1963.

Bentley, Jerry H. *Humanists and Holy Writ. New Testament Scholarship in the Renaissance.* Princeton: Princeton University, 1983.

Berghaus, Günter. "Andreas Gryphius' *Carolus Stuardus*—Formkunstwerk oder politisches Lehrstück?" *Daphnis,* 13 (1984), 229-74.

Bernd, Clifford Albrecht. "Conscience and Pasion in Gryphius' *Catharina von Georgien."* In *Studies in German Drama.* Eds. Donald H. Crosby and George C. Schoolfield. University of North Carolina Studies in Germanic Languages and Literatures, 76. Chapel Hill: University of North Carolina Press, 1974.

Best, Thomas W. *Macropedius.* New York: Twayne, 1972.

Best, Thomas W. *Jacob Bidermann.* New York: Twayne, 1975.

*Bibliotheca Belgica.* 6 vols. Ed. Marie-Thérèse Lenger. Brussels: Culture et Civilisation, 1964-1970.

Bielmann, Joseph. "Die Dramentheorie und Dramendichtung des Jakobus Pontanus, S.J." *LJGG,* 3 (1928), 45-85.

Böckmann, Paul. *Formgeschichte der deutschen Dichtung.* 1949; rpt. Darmstadt: Wissenschaftliche Buchgesellschaft, 1973.

Bomhoff, J. G. *Vondels drama. Studie en pleidooi.* Amsterdam: Ploegsma, 1950.

Bonger, H. *Leven en werk D. V. Coornhert.* Amsterdam: G. A. van Oorschot, 1978.

Boogerd, L. van den. *Het Jezuietendrama in de Nederlanden.* Groningen: J. B. Wolters, 1961.

Borcherdt, Hans Heinrich. *Das europäische Theater im Mittelalter und in der Renaissance.* Hamburg: Rowohlt, 1935.

Borinski, Karl. *Die Poetik der Renaissance und die Anfänge der litterarischen Kritik in Deutschland.* Berlin, 1886.

Bornkamm, Heinrich. *Luther and the Old Testament.* Trans. Eric W. and Ruth C. Gritsch. Philadelphia: Fortress Press, 1969.

Bornkamm, Heinrich. *Luther. Gestalt und Wirkungen.* Gütersloh: Gerd Mohn, 1975.

Bot, P. N. M. *Humanisme en onderwijs in Nederland.* Utrecht: Spectrum, 1955.

Boyle, Majorie O'Rourke. *Christening Pagan Mysteries.* Toronto: University of Toronto, 1981.

Bradner, Leicester. "A Checklist of Original Neo-Latin Dramas by Continental Writers Printed before 1650." *PMLA,* 58 (1943), 621-33.

Bradner, Leicester. "The Latin Drama of the Renaissance (1340-1640)." *Studies in the Renaissance,* 4 (1957), 31-70.

Brett-Evans, David. *Von Hrotsvit bis Folz und Gengenbach. Eine Geschichte des mittelalterlichen deutschen Dramas.* 2 vols. Berlin: Erich Schmidt Verlag, 1975.

Brinkmann, Hennig. *Anfänge des modernen Dramas in Deutschland.* Jena: Walter Biedermann, 1933.

Brinkschulte, Eduard. *Julius Caesar Scaligers kunsttheoretische Anschauungen und deren Hauptquellen.* Bonn: Peter Hanstein, 1914.

Brom, Gerard. *Vondels geloof.* Amsterdam: N.V. De Spieghel, 1937.

Browning, Barton W. "The Development of Vernacular Drama." In *German Baroque Literature. The European Perspective.* Ed. Gerhart Hoffmeister. New York: Ungar, 1983.

Buchwald, Reinhard. *Joachim Greff. Untersuchungen über die Anfänge des Renaissancedramas in Sachsen.* Probefahrten, 11. Leipzig: R. Voigtländer, 1907.

Burger, Heinz Otto. "Dasein heisst eine Rolle spielen: Barockes Menschentum im

Spiegel von Bidermanns *Philemon Martyr* und Weises *Masaniello.*'' *GRM,* 42 (1961), 365-79.

Butler, Sister Mary Marguerite. *Hrotsvitha: The Theatricality of Her Plays.* New York: Philosophical Library, 1960.

Casey, Paul F. *The Susanna Theme in German Literature.* Abhandlungen zur Kunst-, Musik- und Literaturwissenschaft, 214. Bonn: Bouvier, 1976.

Clark, S. L. and David Duewall. "Give and Take: Good, Evil and Language in Rebhun's *Susanna.''* *Euphorion,* 75 (1981), 325-41.

Cohen, Gustave. *Écrivains Français en Hollande dans le première moitié du XVIIe siècle.* Paris: Édouard Champion, 1920.

Creizenach, Wilhelm. *Geschichte des neueren Dramas.* 3 vols. Halle (Saale), 1893, 1901, 1903.

Curtius, Ernst Robert. *European Literature and the Latin Middle Ages.* Trans. Willard R. Trask. New York: Harper and Row, 1953.

De Jager, Th. "Vondel of de majesteit." *Roeping,* 16 (Nov./Dec. 1937), 5-167.

De Molen, Richard L., ed. *Essays on the Works of Erasmus.* New Haven: Yale, 1978.

Dilthey, Wilhelm. *Weltanschauung und Analyse des Menschen seit Renaissance und Reformation.* Leipzig and Berlin: B. G. Teubner, 1914.

Dittrich, Paul. *Plautus und Terenz in Pädagogik und Schulwesen der deutschen Humanisten.* Diss. Leipzig 1915. Leipzig: Böhme und Lehmann, 1915.

Döring, August. *Geschichte des Gymnasiums zu Dortmund.* Dortmund, 1874.

Dréano, Maturin. *Humanisme chrétien. La tragédie latine commentée pour les chrétiens du XVIe siècle.* Paris: Éditions Beauchesne, 1936.

Duckworth, George. *The Nature of Roman Comedy.* 5th ed. Princeton: Princeton University, 1971.

Duhr, Bernhard. *Geschichte der Jesuiten in den Ländern deutscher Zunge.* 3 vols. Freiburg i. Breisgau: Herder, 1907-1913.

Dürrwächter, Anton. "Passionsspiele auf dem Jesuiten- und Ordenstheater." *Historisch- politische Blätter,* 126 (1900), 551-69.

Dürrwächter, Anton. "Aus der Frühzeit des Jesuitendramas." *Jahrbuch des historischen Vereins Dillingen,* 9 (1897), 1-54.

Dyck, Joachim. *Ticht-Kunst. Deutsche Barockpoetik und rhetorische Tradition.* Bad Homburg von der Höhe: Dr. Max Gehlen, 1966.

Eggers, Werner. *Wirklichkeit und Wahrheit im Trauerspiel von Andreas Gryphius.* Heidelberg: Carl Winter, 1967.

Ekker, A. *De Hieronymusschool te Utrecht.* Utrecht, 1863.

Ermatinger, Emil. *Barock und Rokoko in der deutschen Dichtung.* Leipzig: Teubner, 1926.

Flemming, Willi. *Andreas Gryphius und die Bühne.* Halle: Max Niemeyer, 1921.

Flemming, Willi. *Geschichte des Jesuitentheaters in den Ländern deutscher Zunge.* Schriften der Gesellschaft für Theatergeschichte, 32. Berlin: Selbstverlag der Gesellschaft für Theatergeschichte, 1923.

Flemming, Willi. "Vondels Einfluss auf die Trauerspiele des Andreas Gryphius." *Neophilologus,* 13 (1928), 266-80; 14 (1929), 107-20; 15 (1930), 184-96.

Flemming, Willi. *Andreas Gryphius. Eine Monographie.* Stuttgart: W. Kohlhammer, 1965.

Foley, Henry. *Records of the English Province of the Society of Jesus.* Vol. 1, first series. London, 1877.

Francke, Otto. *Terenz und die lateinische Schulcomoedie in Deutschland.* Weimar, 1877.

Froning, R. *Das Drama des Mittelalters.* Deutsche National Litteratur, 14, parts 1-3. Stuttgart, 1891.

Galdon, Joseph A. *Typology and 17th-Century Literature.* The Hague and Paris: Mouton, 1975.

Garin, E. *L'Éducation de l'homme moderne. La pédagogie de la Renaissance (1400-1600).* Trans. J. Humbert. Paris: Fayard, 1968.

Garrer, A. H. *Schonaeus. Bijdrage tot de geschiedenis der latijnsche school te Haarlem.* Haarlem, 1889.

Geerts, A. M. F. B. *Vondel als classicus bij de humanisten in de leer.* Tongerloo: St. Norbertus, 1932.

Geisenhof, Erika. "Die Darstellung der Leidenschaften in den Trauerspielen Andreas Gryphius." Diss. Heidelberg 1957.

Gellinek, Christian. *Hugo Grotius.* Boston: Twayne, 1983.

George, David. *Deutsche Tragödientheorien vom Mittelalter bis zu Lessing.* Munich: Beck, 1972.

Gerlach, Kurt. *Der Simsonstoff im deutschen Drama.* Germanistische Studien, 78. Berlin: Ebering, 1929.

Gerrish, B. A. *Grace and Reason. A Study of the Theology of Luther.* Oxford: Clarendon Press, 1962.

Gillespie, Gerald. "Andreas Gryphius' *Catharina von Georgien* als Geschichtsdrama." In *Geschichtsdrama.* Ed. Elfriede Neubuhr. Darmstadt: Wissenschaftliche Buchgesellschaft, 1980, pp. 85-107.

Gillet, Joseph E. "Über den Zweck des Dramas in Deutschland im 16. und 17. Jahrhundert." *PMLA,* 32 (1917), 430-67.

Gillet, Joseph E. "Über den Zweck des Schuldramas in Deutschland im 16. und 17. Jahrhundert." *JEGP,* 17 (1918), 69-78.

Gillet, Joseph E. "The German Dramatist of the Sixteenth Century and his Bible." *PMLA,* 34 (1919), 465-93.

Gilmore, Myron. *Humanists and Jurists: Six Studies in the Renaissance.* Cambridge: Harvard University, 1963.

Gmelin, Hermann. "Das Prinzip der Imitatio in den romanischen Literaturen der Renaissance." *Romanische Forschungen,* 46 (1932). 83-360.

Goedeke, Karl. *Grundriss zur Geschichte der deutschen Dichtung.* Vols. 2 & 3. Dresden, 1886-87.

Gombert, Ludwig. *Johannes Aals Spiel von Johannes dem Täufer und die älteren Johannesdramen.* Germanistische Abhandlungen, 31. Breslau: M. & H. Marcus, 1908.

Goppelt, Leonhard. *Typos. Die typologische Deutung des alten Testaments im neuen.* Gütersloh, 1939; rpt. Darmstadt: Wissenschaftliche Buchgesellschaft, 1973.

Gossett, Suzanne. "Drama in the English College, Rome, 1591-1660." *English Literary Renaissance,* 3 (1973), 60-93.

Griffin, Nigel. *Jesuit School Drama. A Checklist of Critical Literature.* London: Grant and Cutler, 1976.

Grootes, E. K. "Het berecht voor *Jeptha* en de prolegomena van Grotius' *Phoenissae*-vertaling." In *Visies op Vondel na 300 jaar.* Eds. S. F. Witstein and E. K. Grootes. The Hague: Martinus Nijhoff, 1979, pp. 236-46.

Guggisberg, Hans R. *Basel in the Sixteenth Century.* St. Louis: Center for Reformation Research, 1982.

Günther, Otto. *Plautuserneuerungen in der deutschen Litteratur des XV.-XVII. Jahrhunderts.* Diss. Leipzig, 1885. Leipzig, 1886.

Habersetzer, Karl-Heinz. "Auswahlbibliographie zu Andreas Gryphius." *Text und Kritik,* 7/8 (1980), 125-8.

Habersetzer, Karl-Heinz. *Politische Typologie und historisches Exemplum. Studien zum historisch-ästhetischen Horizont des barocken Trauerspiels.* Stuttgart: Metzler, 1985.

Haerten, Heinz. *Vondel und der deutsche Barock.* Nymegen: Druck und Kommissions-verlag der zentralen Druckerei, 1934.

Hagendahl, Harald. *Latin Fathers and the Classics. A Study of the Apologists, Jerome and Other Christian Writers.* Göteborgs Universitets Årsskrift, 64, no. 2. Göteborg: Elanders, 1958.

Hagendahl, Harald. *Augustine and the Latin Classics.* Stockholm: Almquist and Wiksell, 1967.

Hamel, Anton Gerard van. *Zeventiende-eeuwsche opvattingen en theorieën over litteratuur in Nederland.* The Hague: M. Nijhoff, 1918.

Hankamer, Paul. *Deutsche Gegenreformation und deutsches Barock.* Stuttgart: Metzler, 1935.

Happ, Alfred. "Die Dramentheorie der Jesuiten. Ein Beitrag zur Geschichte der neueren Poetik." Diss. Munich 1922.

Harring, Willi. *Andreas Gryphius und das Drama der Jesuiten.* Hermaea, 5. Halle (Saale): Max Niemeyer, 1907.

Hartelust, J. *De dictione Georgii Macropedii. Accedunt Macropedii Petriscus, et al.* Utrecht: J. van Boekhoven, 1902.

Hartfelder, Karl. *Philipp Melanchton als Praeceptor Germaniae.* Monumenta Germaniae Paedagogica, 7. Berlin, 1889.

Hase, Karl von. *Das geistliche Schauspiel.* Leipzig, 1892.

Hathaway, Baxter. *The Age of Criticism: The Late Renaissance in Italy.* Ithaca: Cornell University, 1962.

Heckmann, Herbert. *Elemente des barocken Trauerspiels.* Munich: Carl Hanser, 1959.

Heitner, Robert. "The Dutch Example." In *German Baroque Literature. The European Perspective.* Ed. Gerhart Hoffmeister. New York: Ungar, 1983.

Hendriks, A. *Joost van den Vondel en G. de Saluste Sr. du Bartas.* Leiden, 1892.

Herford, Charles. *Studies in the Literary Relations of England and Germany.* Cambridge, 1886.

Herrick, Marvin T. *The Fusion of Horatian and Aristotelian Literary Criticism 1531-1555.* Illinois Studies in Language and Literature, 32, no. 1. Urbana: University of Illinois, 1946.

Herrick, Marvin T. *Comic Theory in the Sixteenth Century.* Illinois Studies in Language and Literature, 34, nos. 1 & 2. Urbana: University of Illinois Press, 1950.

Herrick, Marvin. *Tragicomedy. Its Origin and Development in Italy, France and England.* 1955; rpt. Urbana: University of Illinois Press, 1962.

Herrmann, Max. *Forschungen zur deutschen Theatergeschichte des Mittelalters und der Renaissance.* Berlin: Weidmann, 1914.

Herzog, Urs. "Jakob Gretsers Leben und Werk: Ein Überblick." *LJGG,* 11 (1970), 1-36.

Heselhaus, Clemens. "Catharina von Georgien." In *Das deutsche Drama.* Vol. 1. Ed. Benno von Wiese. Düsseldorf: August Bagel, 1958, pp. 35-60.

Hess, Günter. "Spektator-Lector-Actor. Zum Publikum von Jacob Bidermanns *Cenodoxus.* Mit Materialien zum literaturgeschichtlichen und sozialgeschichtlichen Kontext der Handschriften." *Internationales Archiv für Sozialgeschichte der deutschen Literatur,* 1 (1976), 30-106.

Hillen, Gerd. *Andreas Gryphius' "Cardenio und Celinde." Zur Erscheinungsform und Funktion der Allegorie in den Gryphischen Trauerspielen.* The Hague & Paris: Mouton, 1971.

Hirsch, Rudolf. "The Printing Tradition of Aeschylus, Euripides, Sophocles and Aristophanes." *Gutenberg-Jahrbuch,* 1963, pp. 138-46.

Hocking, George Drew. *A Study of the "Tragoediae Sacrae" of Father Caussin (1583-1651).* John Hopkins Studies in Romance Literatures and Languages, 44. Baltimore: John Hopkins Press, 1943.

Hoffmann, Hermann. *Die Jesuiten in Glogau.* Breslau: Kommissionsverlag der schlesischen Volkszeitung, 1926.

Holstein, Hugo. *Die Reformation im Spiegelbilde der dramatischen Literatur des sechzehnten Jahrhunderts.* Schriften des Vereins für Reformationsgeschichte, 14-15. Halle, 1886.

Holstein, Hugo. "Zur Litteratur des lateinischen Schauspiels des 16. Jahrhunderts." *ZDP,* 23 (1891), 436-51.

Horst, D. J. H. Ter. *Daniel Heinsius.* Utrecht: Hoeijenbos & Co., 1934.

Hübner, A. "Studien zu Naogeorg." *ZDA,* 54 (1913), 297-339; 57 (1920), 193-223.

Hübscher, A. "Barock als Gestaltung antithetischen Lebensgefühls." *Euphorion,* 24 (1922), 517-62; 759-805.

Hugle. Alfons. "Der Einfluss der Palliata auf das lateinische und deutsche Drama des 16. Jahrhunderts." Diss. Heidelberg 1921.

Huizinga, Johan. *Holländische Kultur im siebzehnten Jahrhundert.* Trans. Werner Kaegi. 1961; rpt. Frankfurt a. M.: Suhrkamp, 1977.

Hummelen, W. M. H. *De sinnekens in het rederijkersdrama.* Diss. Groningen. Groningen: J. B. Wolters, 1958.

Hummelen, W. M. H. *Repertorium van het rederijkersdrama 1500-ca. 1620.* Assen: Van Gorcum, 1968.

IJsewijn, Jozef. *Companion to Neo-Latin Studies.* New York: North Holland, 1977.

IJsewijn, Jozef. "Annales theatri Belgo-Latini. Inventaris van het Latijns toneel uit de Nederlanden." In *Liber Amicorum G. DeGroote.* Brussels, 1980, pp. 41-55.

Ingen, Ferdinand van. "Die Übersetzung als Rezeptionsdokument: Vondel in Deutschland-Gryphius in Holland." *Michigan Germanic Studies,* 4 (1978), 131-64.

Jacoby, Daniel. *Georgius Macropedius. Ein Beitrag zur Litteraturgeschichte des 16. Jahrhunderts.* Berlin, 1886.

Jaumann, Herbert. *Die deutsche Barockliteratur: Wertung, Umwerting: eine wertungsgeschichtliche Studie in systematischer Absicht.* Abhandlungen zur Kunst-, Musik- und Literaturwissenschaft, 181. Bonn: Bouvier, 1975.

Jöns, Dietrich Walter. *Das "Sinnenbild." Studien zur allegorischen Bildlichkeit bei Andreas Gryphius.* Stuttgart: Metzler, 1966.

Jundt, August. *Die dramatischen Aufführungen im Gymnasium zu Straßburg.* Strasbourg, 1888.

Kaiser, Gerhard. "Leo Armenius." In *Die Dramen des Andreas Gryphius.* Ed. Gerhard Kaiser. Stuttgart: Metzler, 1968, pp. 3-34.

Kappler, Helmut. *Der barocke Geschichtsbegriff bei Andreas Gryphius.* Frankfurter Quellen und Forschungen, 13. Frankfurt: Moritz Diesterweg, 1936.

Kazemier, G. "De tragische held bij Vondel." *NTg,* 37 (1943), 225-30.

Kazemier, G. "Over de psychologie van Vondels Jefta." *NTg,* 33 (1939), 18-29.

Keersmaekers, A. A. *De dichter Guilliam van Nieuwelandt en de senecaans-classieke tragedie in de zuidelijke Nederlanden.* Ghent: Secretarie der Academie, 1957.

Kemper, Raimund. "Zur Seneca Ausgabe des Conrad Celtes. Mit Beiträgen zur Geschichte seines Freundeskreises." *Leuvense Bijdragen,* 66 (1977), 257-310.

Kern, Edith. *The Influence of Heinsius and Vossius upon French Dramatic Theory.* Baltimore: John Hopkins, 1949.

Kindermann, Heinz. *Theatergeschichte Europas.* Vol. 2. Salzburg: Otto Müller, 1959.

King, Peter. "The Sacramental Thought in Vondel's Drama." *MLR,* 51 (1956), 203-14.

King, Peter. "Twee symbolische allegorieën in Vondels *Adam in ballingschap.*" *TNTL,* 72 (1954), 201-31.

King, Peter. "Vondels *Lucifer.* Een mislukt theologisch toneelstuk." In *Visies op Vondel na 300 jaar.* Eds. S. F. Witstein & E. K. Grootes. The Hague: Martinus Nijhoff, 1979, pp. 218-35.

Kipka, Karl. *Maria Stuart im Drama der Weltliteratur.* Breslauer Beiträge zur Literaturgeschichte, 9 Leipzig: Max Hesse, 1907.

Kitto, H. D. F. *Greek Tragedy.* 2nd. ed., 1950; rpt. New York: Doubleday, 1954.

Kluge, Otto. *Die Dichtung des Hugo Grotius im Rahmen der neulateinischen Kunstpoesie.* Leiden: E. J. Brill, 1940.

Kluyver, A. "De wraak der Gibeonieten." *TNTL,* 47 (1928), 33-42.

Knuvelder, G. P. M. *Beknopt handboek tot de geschiedenis der nederlandse letterkunde.* 's-Hertogenbosch: L. C. G. Malmberg, 1962.

Koch, Ludwig. *Philipp Melanchthon's Schola Privata.* Gotha, 1859.

Kölker, A. J. *Alardus Aemstelredamus en Cornelius Crocus, twee Amsterdamse priester-humanisten.* Nijmegen-Utrecht: Dekker and Van de Vegt, 1963.

Kollewijn, R. A. *Über den Einfluss des holländischen Dramas auf Andreas Gryphius.* Heilbronn, 1880.

Könneker, Barbara. *Hans Sachs.* Stuttgart: Metzler, 1971.

Könneker, Barbara. *Die deutsche Literatur der Reformationszeit. Kommentar zu einer Epoche.* Munich: Winkler, 1975.

Kramer, Wolfgang. *Vondel als barockkunstenaar.* Antwerp: De Sikkel, 1946.

Krapf, Ludwig. "Die dramatische Agitation des Jakob Bidermanns. Einige Überlegungen zum nicht-aristotelischen Theater der Jesuiten." In *Akten des V. Internationalen Germanisten-Kongresses,* 1976, pp. 124-31.

Krause, Helmut. *Die Dramen des Hans Sachs. Untersuchungen zur Lehre und Technik.* Berlin: Hofgarten, 1979.

Krummacher, Hans-Henrik. *Der junge Gryphius und die Tradition.* Munich: Fink, 1976.
Kuhn, Hans. "*Non decor in regno*: Zur Gestalt des Fürsten bei Gryphius." *OL,* 25 (1970), 126-50.
Lage, Bertha von der. *Studien zur Genesiuslegende.* Berlin, 1898-99.
Lange. Hans Joachim. *Aemulatio veterorum sive de optimo genere scribendi.* Frankfurt and Bern: H. Lang, 1974.
Langvik-Johannessen, Kåre. *Zwischen Himmel und Erde. Eine Studie über Joost van den Vondels biblische Tragödie in gattungsgeschichtlicher Perspektive.* Oslo: Universitetsforlaget, 1963.
Langvik-Johannessen, Kåre. "Das Problem der christlichen Tragödie bei Vondel." *Jahrbuch der Grillparzer Gesellschaft,* 12 (1976), 125-45.
Lebeau Jean. *Salvator Mundi: l' "exemple" de Joseph dans le théâtre allemand au XVIe siècle.* 2 vols. Bibliotheca Humanistica et Reformatorica, 20.1/2. Nieuwkoop: B. de Graaf, 1977.
Lebeau, Jean. "De la comédie des humanistes à la divine comédie: aux origines du théâtre biblique Luthérien." In *L'Humanisme allemand, (1480-1540).* Eds. Joël Lefebvre and J.-C. Margolin. Munich: Fink; Paris: Vrin, 1979. pp. 477-91.
Lebeau, Jean. "Sixt Bircks *Judith* (1539), Erasmus und der Türkenkrieg." *Daphnis,* 9 (1980), 679-98.
Lebegue, Raymond. *La Tragédie religieuse en France. Les débuts (1514-1573).* Paris: Honoré Champion, 1929.
Lenhard, Peter-Paul. *Religiöse Weltanschauung und Didaktik im Jesuitendramen. Interpretationen zu den Schauspielen Jacob Bidermanns.* Frankfurt, Bern, Las Vegas: Peter Lang, 1976.
Levinger, Helene. *Das Augsburger Schultheater.* Theater und Drama, 2. Berlin: Otto Elsner, 1931.
Leys, F. "De middelnederlandse klucht, de Romeinse komodie, de Bijbel en Georgius Macropedius: vier polen in Macropedius' *Andrisca* (1537)." *HZM,* 32 (1978), 139-54.
Lindeboom, J. *Het bijbelsch humanisme in Nederland.* Leiden: A. H. Adriani, 1913.
Loukovitch, Kosta. *La Tragédie religieuse classique en France.* Paris: E. Droz, 1933.
Lubac, Henri de. *Exégèse médiévale: les quatre sens de l'Écriture.* 4 vols. Paris: Éditions Montaigue, 1959-64.
Lunding, Erik. *Das schlesische Kunstdrama: eine Darstellung und Deutung.* Copenhagen: P. Haase, 1940.
Maassen, Johannes. *Drama und Theater der Humanistenschulen in Deutschland.* Augsburg: Benno Filser, 1929.
Manheimer, Victor. *Die Lyrik des Andreas Gryphius. Studien und Materialien.* Berlin, 1904.
Mannack, Eberhard. *Andreas Gryphius.* Stuttgart: Metzler, 1968.
Markwardt, Bruno. *Geschichte der deutschen Poetik.* Vol. 1. Berlin: Walter de Gruyter, 1964.
Maurer, Wilhelm. *Der junge Melanchthon zwischen Humanismus und Reformation.* 2 vols. Göttingen: Vandenhoeck & Ruprecht, 1967; 1969.
Maximilianus, Pater, O. F. M. *Vondelstudies.* Ed. L. C. Michels. Terheijden: De Forel, 1968.
McCabe, William H. *An Introduction to Jesuit Theater.* Diss. Cambridge 1929; rpt., ed. Louis J. Oldani. St. Louis: Institute of Jesuit Sources, 1983.
McCabe, William H. "The Play-List of the English College of St. Omers 1592-1762." *Revue de littérature comparée,* 17 (1937), 355-75.
McGregor, James H. "The Sense of Tragedy in George Buchanan's *Jephthes.*" *HumLov,* 31 (1982), 120-40.
Meerwaldt, J. O. "Het persoonlijk element in Vondels vertalingen van de Griekse tragici." *TNTL,* 57 (1938), 110-36.
Mesnard, Pierre. "The Pedagogy of Johann Sturm (1507-1589) and its Evangelical Inspiration." *Studies in the Renaissance,* 13 (1966), 200-19.
Meter, J. H. *De literaire theorieën van Daniël Heinsius.* Amsterdam: Adolf M. Hakkert, 1975.
Michael, Wolfgang F. *Frühformen der deutschen Bühne.* Berlin: Selbstverlag der Gesellschaft für Theatergeschichte, 1963.

Michael, Wolfgang F. "Das deutsche Theater und Drama vor der Reformation." *DVLG Beiheft*, 1973, 1-73.

Michael, Wolfgang F. "Luther and Religious Drama." *Daphnis*, 7 (1978), 365-7.

Michael, Wolfgang F. *Das deutsche Drama der Reformationszeit*. Bern: Peter Lang, 1984.

Michelsen, Peter. "Der Zeit Gewalt: Andreas Gryphius: *Ermordete Majestät. Oder Carolus Stuardus.*" In *Geschichte als Schauspiel*. Ed. Walter Hinck. Frankfurt: Suhrkamp, 1981, pp. 48-66.

Molkenboer, B. H. "Wanneer werd Vondel katholiek?" *Vondel-Kroniek*, 3 (1932), 63-82.

Molkenboer, B. H. *De jonge Vondel*. Amsterdam: Parnassus, 1950.

Morsbach, Charlotte. *Jakob Bidermanns "Philemon Martyr" nach Bau und Gehalt*. Diss. Münster 1935. Bottrop: Wilhelm Postberg, 1936.

Müller, Johannes. ed. *Vor- und frühreformatorische Schulordnungen und Schulvorträge in deutscher und niederländischer Sprache*. Zschopau, 1885-86.

Müller, Johannes. *Das Jesuitendrama in den Ländern deutscher Zunge vom Anfang (1555) bis zum Hochbarock (1665)*. 2 vols. Augsburg: Benno Filser, 1930.

Nachtwey, Hermann. *Die Exerzitien des Ignatius von Loyola in den Dramen Jakob Bidermanns, S. J.* Diss. Münster 1936. Bochum: Heinrich Pöppinghaus, 1937.

Nahde, Ernst. *Der reiche Mann und der arme Lazarus im Drama des 16. Jahrhunderts*. Diss. Jena 1928. Borna-Leipzig: Robert Noske, 1928.

Nessler, Nikolaus. *Dramaturgie der Jesuiten Pontanus, Donatus und Masenius*. Programm Brixen, 1905, pp. 3-37.

Nichols, Fred. "Language and Drama in Vondel's *Lucifer* and *Adam in ballingschap.*" *Review of National Literatures*, 8 (1977), 40-69.

Nieschmidt, H. W. "Emblematische Szenengestaltung in den Märtyrerdramen des Andreas Gryphius." *MLN*, 86 (1971), 321-44.

Noë, J. *De religieuse bezieling van Vondel's werk*. Tielt: Lannoo, 1952.

Norland, H. B. "Vives' View of Drama." *HumLov*, 30 (1981), 93-107.

Norland, H. B. "Grimald's *Archipropheta*. A Saint's Tragedy." *JMRS*, 14 (1984), 63-76.

Pachtler, G. M. *Ratio studiorum et institutiones scholasticae Societatis Jesu per Germaniam olim vigentes*. Berlin, 1887-94.

Parente, James A., Jr. "Counter-Reformation Polemic and Senecan Tragedy: The Dramas of Gregorius Holonius (1531?-1594)." *HumLov*, 30 (1981), 156-80.

Parente, James A., Jr. "Tyranny and Revolution on the Baroque Stage: The Dramas of Joseph Simons." *HumLov*, 32 (1983), 309-24.

Parente, James A., Jr. "Andreas Gryphius and Jesuit Theater." *Daphnis*, 13 (1984), 525-51.

Parente, James A., Jr. "The Development of Religious Tragedy: The Humanist Reception of the *Christos Paschon* in the Renaissance." *SCJ*, 16 (1985), 351-68.

Paulsen, Friedrich. *Geschichte des gelehrten Unterrichts auf den deutschen Schulen und Universitäten vom Ausgang des Mittelalters bis zur Gegenwart*. 2 vols. Leipzig, 1896-7.

Pigman, G. W., III. "Imitation and the Renaissance Sense of the Past: The Reception of Erasmus' *Ciceronianus.*" *JMRS*, 9 (1979), 155-77.

Pigman, G. W., III. "Versions of Imitation in the Renaissance." *RQ*, 33 (1980), 1-32.

Plard, Henri. "De heiligheid van de koninklijke macht in de tragedie van Andreas Gryphius." *Tijdschrift van den Vrije Universiteit van Brussel*, 2 (1960), 202-29.

Plard, Henri. "Note sur Martin Opitz et les *Troyennes* de Sénèque." In *Les Tragédies de Sénèque et le théâtre de la Renaissance*. Ed. Jean Jacquot. Paris: Éditions du centre national de la recherche scientifique, 1964, pp. 231-8.

Plard, Henri. "Sénèque et la tragédie d'Andreas Gryphius." In *Les Tragédies de Sénèque et le théâtre de la Renaissance*. Ed. J. Jaquot. Paris: Éditions du centre national de la recherche scientifique, 1964, pp. 239-60.

Plard, Henri. "Beständige Mutter/Oder Die Heilige Felicitas." In *Die Dramen des Andreas Gryphius*. Ed. Gerhard Kaiser. Stuttgart: Metzler, 1968, pp. 318-38.

Plard, Henri. "Die sieben Brüder/Oder Die Gibeoniter." In *Die Dramen des Andreas Gryphius*. Ed. Gerhard Kaiser. Stuttgart: Metzler, 1968, pp. 305-17.

Polet, Amédée. *Petrus Nannius 1500-1557*. Louvain: Librairie Universitaire, 1936.

Poll, K. *Over de tooneelspelen van den Leidschen rederijker Jacob Duym.* Groningen, 1898.
Popp, Georg. "Über den Begriff des Dramas in den deutschen Poetiken des 17. Jahrhunderts." Diss. Leipzig 1895.
Post, R. R. *The Modern Devotion.* Leiden: Brill, 1968.
Pott, Clarence K. "Holland-German Literary Relations in the Seventeenth Century: Vondel and Gryphius." *JEGP,* 47 (1948), 127-38.
Poulssen, J. "Tragiek van Vondels glans. Bijdrage tot de beschrijving ener dichterlijke eigenheid." *Raam,* 2 (1963), 1-140.
Purdie, Edna. *The Story of Judith in German and English Literature.* Bibliothèque de la revue de littérature comparée, 39. Paris: Honoré Champion, 1927.
Rademaker, C.S.M. *Life and Work of Gerardus Joannes Vossius (1577-1649).* Assen: Van Gorcum, 1981.
Rädle, Fidel. "Aus der Frühzeit des Jesuitentheaters." *Daphnis,* 7 (1978), 403-62.
Rädle, Fidel. "Das Jesuitentheater in der Pflicht der Gegenreformation." *Daphnis,* 8 (1979), 167-99.
Reckling, Fr. "Immolatio Isaac. Die theologische und exemplarische Interpretation in den Abraham-Issak Dramen der deutschen Literatur insbesondere des 16. und 17. Jahrhunderts." Diss. Münster 1962.
Reiff, Arno. *Interpretatio, Imitatio, Aemulatio. Begriff und Vorstellung literarischer Abhängigkeit bei den Römern.* Diss. Köln 1958. Würzburg, 1959.
Reinhardstöttner, Karl von. *Martin Balticus. Ein Humanistenleben aus dem sechzehnten Jahrhundert.* Bamberg, 1890.
Reinhardstöttner, Karl von. "Zur Geschichte des Jesuitendramas in München." *Jahrbuch für Münchener Geschichte,* 3 (1899), 53-176.
Rens, Lieven. *Het priester-koningconflict in Vondels drama.* Hasselt: Heideland, 1965.
Rens, Lieven. "Over het problem van de invloed van Vondel op de drama's van Andreas Gryphius." *HZM,* 20 (1966), 251-62.
Rens, Lieven. "Beelden van duisternis in Vondels drama." *SpL,* 10 (1966-67), 1-15.
Rens, Lieven. "Het clair-obscur in Vondels drama." *SpL,* 12 (1969-70), 81-175.
Rens, Lieven. "The Project on Renaissance Drama in Antwerp." *Dutch Studies,* 1 (1974), 70-88.
Rens, Lieven. *Genres in het ernstige Renaissancetoneel der Nederlanden tot 1625.* Hasselt: Uitgeverij Heideland-Orbis, 1977.
Rens, Lieven. "Prolegomena bij een psychoanalytische interpretatie van Vondels drama." In *Visies op Vondel na 300 jaar.* Eds. S. F. Witstein & E. K. Grootes. Den Haag: Martinus Nijhoff, 1979, pp. 270-88.
Roloff, Hans-Gert. "Thomas Naogeorgs *Judas.* Ein Drama der Reformationszeit." *Archiv für das Studium der neueren Sprachen,* 208 (1971), 81-107.
Roloff, Hans-Gert. "Thomas Naogeorg und das Problem von Humanismus und Reformation." In *L'Humanisme allemand, (1480-1540).* Eds. Joël Lefebvre and J.-C. Margolin. Munich: Fink; Paris: Vrin, 1979, pp. 455-73.
Rombauts, E. "Sénèque et le théâtre flamand." In *Les Tragédies de Sénèque et le théâtre de la Renaissance.* Ed. J. Jacquot. Paris: Éditions du centre national de la recherche scientifique, 1964, pp. 211-9.
Roodhuyzen, Hendrik. *Het leven van Gulielmus Gnapheus.* Amsterdam, 1858.
Rudwin, M. J. *Der Teufel in den deutschen geistlichen Spielen des Mittelalters und der Reformationszeit.* Göttingen: Vandenhoeck and Ruprecht, 1915.
Rupprich, Hans. *Die deutsche Literatur vom späten Mittelalter bis zum Barock.* Parts 1 & 2. Munich: Beck, 1970.
Salsmans, Josef. "Vondel en het Gezelschap Jesu." *Jong Dietschland,* 1908, pp. 65-76.
Schachner, Heinrich. "Das Dorotheaspiel." *ZDP,* 35 (1903), 157-96.
Schäublin, Peter. "Andreas Gryphius' erstes Trauerspiel *Leo Armenius* und die Bibel." *Daphnis,* 3 (1974), 1-40.
Schauer, Hans. *Christian Weises biblische Dramen.* Görlitz: Verlags-Anstalt Görlitzer Nachrichten und Anzeiger, 1921.

Schings, Hans-Jürgen. *Die patristische und stoische Tradition bei Andreas Gryphius.* Kölner Germanistische Studien, 2. Cologne and Graz: Böhlau, 1966.

Schings, Hans-Jürgen. "Catharina von Georgien." In *Die Dramen des Andreas Gryphius.* Ed. Gerhard Kaiser. Stuttgart: Metzler, 1968, pp. 35-72.

Schings, Hans-Jürgen. "Consolatio Tragoediae. Zur Theorie des barocken Trauerspiels." In *Deutsche Dramentheorien.* Ed. R. Grimm. Vol. 1. Frankfurt am Main: Athenäum Verlag, 1971, pp. 1-44.

Schings, Hans-Jürgen. "Seneca-Rezeption und Theorie der Tragödie. Martin Opitz' Vorrede zu den *Trojanerinnen.*" In *Historizität in Sprach- und Literaturwissenschaft.* Eds. Walter Müller-Seidel, et al. Munich: Fink, 1974, pp. 521-37.

Schmelzeisen, Gustaf K. "Staatsrechtliches in den Trauerspielen des Andreas Gryphius." *Archiv für Kulturgeschichte,* 53 (1971), 93-126.

Schmidt, P. Expeditus. *Die Bühnenverhältnisse des deutschen Schuldramas und seiner volkstümlichen Ableger im sechzehnten Jahrhundert.* Forschungen zur neueren Literaturgeschichte, 24. Berlin: Alexander Duncker, 1903.

Schmidt, Oswald Gottlob. *Luther's Bekanntschaft mit den alten Classikern.* Leipzig, 1883.

Schömer, Rosa. "Über die Quellen zu Vondels *Maeghden.*" *Festschrift der Nationalbibliothek in Wien,* 1926, pp. 737-44.

Schöne, Albrecht. *Emblematik und Drama im Zeitalter des Barock.* 1964; 2nd ed. Munich: Beck, 1968.

Schöne, Albrecht. "Ermordete Majestät. Oder Carolus Stuardus." In *Die Dramen des Andreas Gryphius.* Ed. Gerhard Kaiser. Stuttgart: Metzler, 1968, pp. 117-69.

Schönle, Gustav. *Deutsch-niederländische Beziehungen in der Literatur des 17. Jahrhunderts.* Leidse Germanistische en Anglistische Reeks, 7. Leiden: Universitaire Pers, 1968.

Schwartz, Rudolf. *Esther im deutschen und neulateinischen Schuldrama des Reformationszeitalters.* Leipzig, 1898.

Senger, Matthias. *Leonhard Culmann. A Literary Biography and an Edition of Five Plays.* Bibliotheca Humanistica et Reformatorica, 35. Nieuwkoop: B. de Graaf, 1982.

Serrarens, A. "Vondel's Gysbrecht en Maeghden in 't licht der Contra-Reformatie." *TNTL,* 25 (1937), 225-56.

Sieveke, F. G. "Der Dialogführung im *Acolastus* des Gnapheus." *ACNL.* Eds. J. IJsewijn and E. Kessler. Louvain: Louvain University Press, 1973, pp. 595-602.

Skopnik, Günter. *Das Straßburger Schultheater.* Frankfurt a. Main: Selbstverlag des Elsaß-Lothringen Instituts, 1935.

Skrine, Peter. "New Light on Jesuit Drama in Germany." *GLL,* 34 (1981), 306-14.

Smit, W. A. P. "Vondel en zijn bekering." *NTg,* 29 (1935), 254-67.

Smit, W. A. P. "Judas en Ruben in Vondels *Joseph in Dothan.*" *NTg,* 41 (1948), 97-107.

Smit, W. A. P. *Van Pascha tot Noah. Een verkenning van Vondels drama's naar continuiteit en ontwikkeling in hun grondmotief en structuur.* 3 vols. Zwolle: W. E. J. Tjeenk Willink, 1956 (I), 1959 (II), 1962 (III).

Smit, W. A. P. "État des recherches sur Sénèque et les dramaturges hollandais." In *Les Tragédies de Sénèque et le théâtre de la Renaissance.* Ed. J. Jacquot. Paris: Éditions du centre national de la recherche scientifique, 1964, pp. 221-30.

Smit, W. A. P. "The Dutch Theater of the Renaissance-A Problem and a Task for the Literary Historian." *Dutch Studies,* 1 (1974), 44-69.

Solomon, Janis Little. "Die Parabel vom verlorenen Sohn. Zur Arbeitsethik des 16. Jahrhunderts." In *Arbeit als Thema in der deutschen Literatur vom Mittelalter bis zur Gegenwart.* Eds. Reinhold Grimm and Jost Hermand. Königstein: Athenäum, 1979, pp. 29-50.

Sommerfeld, Martin, ed. *Judithdramen des 16./17. Jahrhunderts nebst Luthers Vorrede zum Buch Judith.* Berlin: Junker and Dünnhaupt, 1933.

Sonnino, Lee. *Handbook of Sixteenth-Century Rhetoric.* London: Routledge, Kegan, Paul, 1966.

South, M. S. "Leo Armenius oder die Häresie des Andreas Gryphius: Überlegungen zur figuralen Parallelstruktur." *ZDP,* 94 (1975), 161-83.

Spengler, Franz. *Der verlorene Sohn im Drama des 16. Jahrhunderts.* Innsbruck, 1888.

Spengler, Franz. "Kilian Reuther von Mellerstadt." In *Forschungen zur neueren Litteraturgeschichte. Festgabe für Richard Heinzel*. Weimar, 1898, pp. 123-9.

Spingarn, Joel. *A History of Literary Criticism in the Renaissance*. New York, 1899.

Stachel, Paul. *Seneca und das deutsche Renaissancedrama*. Berlin: Mayer and Müller, 1907.

Staiger, Emil. "Die christliche Tragödie. Andreas Gryphius und der Geist des Barocks." *Eckart*, 12 (1936), 145-9.

Stammler, Wolfgang. *Von der Mystik zum Barock*. Stuttgart: Metzler, 1927.

Steen, J. van der. "Vondels Jempsar en de slang." *NTg*, 53 (1959), 326-32.

Steinhagen, Harold. *Wirklichkeit und Handeln im barocken Drama. Historisch-ästhetische Studien zum Trauerspiel des Andreas Gryphius*. Tübingen: Max Niemayer, 1977.

Sterck, J. F. M. *Het leven van Joost van den Vondel*. Haarlem: F. Bohn, 1926.

Sterck, J. F. M. *Onder Amsterdamsche humanisten*. Hilversum and Amsterdam: Paul Brand, 1934.

Sterck, J. F. M. ed. *Vondel-brieven uit de XVIIe eeuw aan en over den Dichter*. Amsterdam-Sloterdijk: Wereldbibliotheek, 1935.

Sterck, J. F. M. "Vondels epos *Constantijn*." In his *Rondom Vondel*. Amsterdam: Wereldbibliotheek, 1927, pp. 26-40.

Stone, Donald, Jr. *French Humanist Tragedy*. Totowa: Rowman and Littlefield, 1974.

Strauss, Gerald. *Luther's House of Learning*. Baltimore and London: Johns Hopkins, 1978.

Street, J. S. *French Sacred Drama from Bèze to Corneille*. Cambridge: Cambridge University, 1983.

Susini, Eugène. "Claude Malingre, Sieur de Saint-Lazare, et son Histoire de Catherine de Georgie." *EG*, 23 (1968), 37-53.

Szarota, E. M. "Die Ursulagestalt in Vondels *Maeghden*." *NTg*, 59 (1966), 73-89.

Szarota, E. M. *Künstler, Grübler und Rebellen. Studien zum europäischen Märtyrerdrama des 17. Jahrhunderts*. Munich and Bern: Francke, 1967.

Szarota, E. M. "Versuch einer neuen Periodisierung des Jesuitendramas." *Daphnis*, 3 (1974), 158-77.

Szarota, E. M. "Das Jesuitendrama als Vorläufer der modernen Massenmedien." *Daphnis*, 4 (1975), 129-43.

Szarota, E. M. *Geschichte, Politik und Gesellschaft im Drama des 17. Jahrhunderts*. Bern and Munich: Francke, 1976.

Szarota, E. M. "Jesuitendrama und die Bibel." In *Aspekte des religiösen Dramas*. Ed. Heimo Reinitzer. Hamburg: Wittig, 1979, pp. 37-58.

Szarota, E. M., ed. *Das Jesuitendrama im deutschen Sprachgebiet. Eine Periochen-Edition*. 3 vols. Munich: Fink. 1979; 1980; 1983.

Szyrocki, Marian. *Der junge Gryphius*. Berlin: Rütten and Loening, 1959.

Tarot, Rolf. "Literatur zum deutschen Drama und Theater des 16. und 17. Jahrhunderts. Ein Forschungsbericht (1945-1962)." *Euphorion*, 57 (1963), 411-53.

Tarot, Rolf. "Schuldrama und Jesuitentheater." In *Handbuch des deutschen Dramas*. Ed. Walter Hinck. Düsseldorf: Bagel, 1980, pp. 35-47.

Taylor, Archer. *Problems in German Literary History of the Fifteenth and Sixteenth Centuries*. New York and London: Modern Languages Association and Oxford, 1939.

Tetzlaff, Otto W. "Neulateinische Dramen der Niederlande in ihrer Einwirkung auf die deutsche Literatur des sechzehnten Jahrhunderts." *Amsterdamer Beiträge zur älteren Germanistik*, 1 (1972), 111-92.

Theiss, Winfried. *Exemplarische Allegorik. Untersuchungen zu einem literaturhistorischen Phänomen bei Hans Sachs*. Munich: Fink, 1968.

Thulin, Oskar. *Johannes der Täufer im geistlichen Schauspiel des Mittelalters und der Reformationszeit*. Leipzig: Dieterich, 1930.

Tracy, James D. "Against the 'Barbarians': The Young Erasmus and His Humanist Contemporaries." *SCJ*, 11 (1980), 1-22.

Triebel, L. A. "The *Delectare* Motif and the Sixteenth-Century German Stage." *GLL*, 7 (1954), 249-65.

Trillitzsch, Winfried. "Erasmus und Seneca." *Philologus: Zeitschrift für das klassische Altertum*, 108 (1965), 270-93.

Valentin, Jean-Marie. "Hieronymus Ziegler et son *Abel Justus*." *EG*, 23 (1968), 381-8.

Valentin, Jean-Marie. "Aux origines du théâtre néo-latin de la réforme catholique: l'*Euripus* (1549) de Livinus Brechtus." *HumLov,* 21 (1972), 83-188.

Valentin, Jean-Marie. *Le théâtre des Jésuites dans les pays de langue allemande (1554-1680). Salut des âmes et ordre des cités.* 3 vols. Europäische Hochschulschriften, series 1. Deutsche Sprache und Literatur, 255/1-3. Bern, Frankfurt, Las Vegas: Peter Lang, 1978.

Valentin, Jean-Marie. "Hercules Moriens, Christus Patiens: Balde's *Jephtias* und das Problem des christlichen Stoicismus im deutschen Theater des 17. Jahrhunderts." *Argenis,* 2 (1978), 37-72.

Vandervelden, Jos. *Staat en recht bij Vondel.* Haarlem: H. D. Tjeenk Willink, 1939.

Vandervelden, Jos. *Vondels weerldbeeld.* Utrecht: Het Spectrum, 1948.

Vandervelden, Jos. *Vondel's schoonheid.* Amsterdam: Lieverlee, 1952.

Vanherpe, Gab. *Het Grieks-christelijk dualisme in Vondels "Lucifer."* Menen: Geo. Verraes Pattyn, 1951.

Verhofstadt, Edward. "Vondel und Gryphius: Versuch einer literarischen Topographie." *Neophilologus,* 53 (1969), 290-99.

Vermaseren, B. A. "Humanistische drama's over de moord op de vader des vaderlands." *TNTL,* 68 (1951), 31-67.

Verstraeten, A. M. *Studiën over Vondel en zijn Josef in Dothan.* Ghent, 1886.

Voogd, G. J. de. *Erasmus en Grotius.* Leiden: Ned. Uitgeversmaatschappij, 1946.

Vornbaum, Reinhold. *Die evangelischen Schulordnungen des sechzehnten Jahrhunderts.* Vol. 1. Gütersloh, 1860.

Vosskamp, Wilhelm. *Zeit- und Geschichtsauffassung im 17. Jahrhunderts bei Gryphius und Lohenstein.* Bonn: Bouvier, 1967.

Way, Sister Agnes Clare. "S. Gregorius Nazianzenus." In *Catalogus translationum et commentariorum: Medieval and Renaissance Latin Translations and Commentaries.* Vol. 2. Ed. Paul Oskar Kristeller. Washington: Catholic University, 1971, pp. 43-192.

Weevers, Theodore. "Vondel's Influence on German Literature." *MLR,* 32 (1937), 1-23.

Wehrli, Max. "Andreas Gryphius und die Dichtung der Jesuiten." *Stimmen der Zeit,* 175 (1964-5), 25-39.

Wehrli, Max. "Bidermann-*Cenodoxus.*" In *Das deutsche Drama,* Vol. 1. Ed. Benno von Wiese. Düsseldorf: August Bagel, 1958, pp. 13-34.

Weilen, Alexander von. *Das ägyptische Joseph im Drama- des XVI. Jahrhunderts. Ein Beitrag zur vergleichenden Literaturgeschichte.* Vienna, 1887.

Weinberg, Bernard. "The Poetic Theories of Minturno." In *Studies in Honor of Frederick W. Shipley.* Washington University Studies, New Series Language and Literature, 14. St. Louis: Lancaster Press, 1942.

Weinberg, Bernard. *A History of Literary Criticism in the Italian Renaissance.* 2 vols. Chicago: University of Chicago, 1961; 1963.

Wellek, René. "The Concept of the Baroque in Literary Scholarship." In his *Concepts of Criticism.* Ed. Stephen G. Nichols, Jr. New Haven and London: Yale University, 1963, pp. 69-127.

Wick, A. "Tobias in der dramatischen Literatur Deutschlands." Diss. Heidelberg 1899.

Wijnmann, H. F. "Jan Tonnis, de schrijver van *Josephs droef en bly-eind spel.*" *Vondel-Kroniek,* 11 (1940), 172-81.

Wimmer, Ruprecht. *Jesuitentheater, Didaktik und Fest. Das Exemplum des ägyptischen Joseph auf den deutschen Bühnen der Gesellschaft Jesu.* Das Abendland-Neue Folge, 13. Frankfurt a. M.: Klostermann, 1982.

Worp, J. A. *De invloed van Seneca's treurspelen op ons tooneel.* Amsterdam, 1892.

Worp, J. A. *Geschiedenis van het drama en van het tooneel in Nederland.* 2 vols. Groningen: J. B. Wolters, 1904.

Wybrands, Christiaan N. *Het Amsterdamsche tooneel van 1617-1772.* Utrecht, 1873.

Young, Karl. *The Drama of the Medieval Church.* Vol. 1. Oxford: Clarendon, 1933.

Youssef, Zobeidah. *Polémique et littérature chez Guez de Balzac.* Paris: Nizet, 1972.

Zeidler, Jacob. *Studien und Beiträge zur Geschichte der Jesuitenkomödie und des Klosterdramas.* Theatergeschichtliche Forschungen, 4. Hamburg, 1891.

# INDEX OF PERSONS

# INDEX OF SUBJECTS